America's Best Low-Tax Retirement Towns

Eve Evans & Elizabeth Niven

VACATION
PUBLICATIONS
HOUSTON

America's Best Low-Tax Retirement Towns

Editor: Mary Lu Abbott

Art Direction and Cover Design: Fred W. Salzmann

Graphics and Layout: Haidy M. Francis, David E. Hart

Senior Tax Research Associates: Emily Coleman, Jaqueline Haugen, Matthew Valdez

Tax Research Associates: Adam Bielamowicz, Katherine Coley, Marie De los Santos, Michele DeAnda, Stephen Logan, Shannon Mitchell

Editorial Research Associates: Justin Boyd, Jennifer Davoren, Maureen L. King, Katie Solan

Contributing Writers: Mary Lu Abbott, Ron Butler, Olin Chism, Jay Clarke, Lynn Grisard Fullman, Mary Ann Hemphill, Dave G. Houser, Carole Jacobs, Kathryn Jones, Jim Kerr, Dale Leatherman, Everett Potter, Candyce H. Stapen, Nina Stewart

Published by Vacation Publications, Inc.
5851 San Felipe Street, Suite 500
Houston, TX 77057

Library of Congress Control Number: 2007939223
ISBN 978-0-9786077-1-5

Printed in the United States of America

America's Best Low-T

CONT

ax **Retirement Towns**

N T S

INTRODUCTION

If you plan to move to another state to retire, have you considered the tax burden you'll face when you arrive? Your retirement dreamland could be a tax heaven — or hell.

Taxes are increasingly important to everyone, but retirees have extra cause for concern since their income may be fixed. In a survey by *Where to Retire* magazine, readers cited a low overall tax rate as one of the five most important factors in choosing a place to retire.

Retirees' interest in the tax scene and the lack of readily available information about tax burdens in specific locations prompted us to undertake a unique — and massive — project: to compare the tax burdens in 203 cities in all 50 states.

That's *total* tax burden — all state and local taxes, fees and assessments — including state and local income tax, property tax, personal property tax, sales tax, auto licensing fees and fees or assessments for things like garbage pickup, street and storm drain maintenance and more.

Nowhere else have we seen information as extensive and specific as what is presented in this book. Rather than base our data on the "average" retired couple, we've calculated the tax liabilities for nine different couples, using three income levels and three home values for each income level. In 30 of our cities, where homes and living costs are generally more expensive, we omitted the lowest income level and home values. In these cities, we calculated the tax liabilities for an additional three higher home values for the highest income level. Most relocating retirees will find that their income and home value fall near those of one of our couples.

For each city, you will find a chart detailing and tallying the taxes due from our couples. Our figures are based on married couples filing jointly who are age 65 or older. We've included tax breaks related to age in our calculations. These additional deductions and exemptions are widespread and frequently quite significant. We suspect that rankings based on tax burdens of residents under the age of 65 could be

dramatically different from those herein. All couples are assumed to be relocating across state lines.

We used three income levels — $30,000, $60,000 and $90,000 in gross

How To Use This Book

Unless you are personally involved in local or state taxation or have an academic interest in the national taxation picture, you probably won't read this book cover to cover. Instead, a good place to start is the table of contents, where you can identify cities of interest and find their location in the book.

For each city covered, we have described both the state and local tax picture as it relates to retirees. At the beginning of this description, we reveal any tax heavens, tax hells and top retirement towns in the state.

In a table with this summary, we estimate tax components and total tax burdens for nine different couples. Find the income and home value that most closely resembles your financial situation, and pay closest attention to the tax estimates for that category. At the far right of the table, you can see how this city ranks against all others in total tax burden placed on retirees. Ranking No. 1 is best (lowest tax burden). The higher the ranking, the higher the tax burden.

If you don't find a city you're interested in, see if we cover a nearby city of similar size. Usually, but not always, same-state cities of similar size will have similar tax burdens.

Perhaps you're undecided as to your ultimate retirement destination and want to get a quick glance at tax-friendly cities for retirees with your income and expected home value. You may wish to turn immediately to our list of tax heavens and hells on pages 184-185. Or, for an idea of how the 203 cities match up for retirees in your income/home value category, turn to the rankings on pages 174-183.

Is your prospective retirement destination a tax heaven or a tax hell? Read on to find out.

income — and extrapolated expenditures for each income level from the Consumer Expenditure Survey of people age 65 and older, issued by the U.S. Department of Labor, Bureau of Labor Statistics (BLS). The BLS survey tracks spending habits of this age group. We've estimated the sales taxes for each income level in each city using the expenditures that we extrapolated from the BLS.

We've determined the amount due in state income tax from the rates provided to us by the individual states, taking into account appropriate exemptions, deductions and credits.

Some cities levy a local income tax, although the type of income subject to the tax differs. We have included local income taxes in our calculations.

For most of our cities, we have calculated property taxes for home values ranging from $125,000 to $525,000. For each income, we cite three home values. Since our detailed breakdowns include home value and income level, you can more closely identify your own tax burden. For instance, if you expect your income to be about $60,000 a year in retirement, you can look up your estimated tax bill according to whether you will live in a home valued at $150,000, $225,000 or $300,000.

Don't plan on moving to a home valued at less than $150,000 in cities such as Los Angeles, San Diego, San Francisco, New York or Honolulu. Few, if any, homes may be available at such a low price. With that in mind, for 30 of the 203 cities, we've included taxes on homes valued at $600,000, $750,000 and $900,000 for the highest income level in order to give a more realistic view of what retirees might expect to pay. Conversely, in some cities home values are lower than average. While we have included home values up to $525,000 in our charts for these cities, retirees likely can find homes at one of the lower values also listed — and have lower tax burdens. Our calculations are meant to be only a guide for retirees looking to relocate.

Personal property taxes are not uncommon, although most cities don't impose a personal property tax on individuals. Items that are taxed vary from city to city. In cities where there are personal property taxes on automobiles, we have calculated these taxes and they appear in the chart.

Finally, registering a vehicle is one cost relocators might overlook. We found that the fees can vary dramatically, so we've broken down automobile registration and renewal fees by gathering the information for two specific cars.

Top Retirement Towns

We recognize that tax considerations are but one of many factors influencing the choice of where to retire. So in this new edition, to help you with your relocation decision, we asked the editors of *Where to Retire* magazine to provide a list of the best retirement towns in America. You can read more about their 102 favorite cities under the appropriate state headings.

It's important to note that you'll find some towns that are tax-friendly and others that are not so friendly in our list of the 102 best. These are not tax heavens, but are the best from an overall quality-of-life standpoint. In the selection process, *Where to Retire* visited hundreds of towns from coast to coast, collecting data on cost of living, health care, recreational and cultural opportunities, climate and more. We feel that these college towns, scenic havens, waterfront retreats, historic communities, mountain escapes and city settings offer the country's best retirement lifestyles.

Fact-Finding

All of the tax rates, assessment rates, deductions, exemptions, rebates, credits and related facts and data included in this book were taken from the official Web sites of, or supplied directly by the local and/or state tax authorities. The same authorities were asked in writing to review our calculations and verify them as correct, or make corrections and return them to us.

The great majority of these public officials were informed and willing to help. In a few cases, however, tax authorities refused to take or return our calls or respond to letters, e-mails or faxes. Rather than drop these cities from the study, we have included the unverified rates and prepared our best estimate of the total tax burden.

It's important to note here that the data-gathering part of this study began in May of 2007 and continued to the end of the same year. In fact, it took nine researchers more than seven months to collect and verify the information contained in this report. We based our work on the tax year 2006, the latest year for which states and municipalities could supply complete information. When rates changed during tax year 2006, we used the rate in effect for the majority of the year. When the rate changed exactly halfway through the year, we used the rate for the latter half of the year. In the very few cases where 2006 rates were not yet available, we used the prior year or latest rates available. Tax rates and qualifiers change frequently, and some of the data herein may already have changed. Nonetheless, this is our fifth study of tax burdens over the last 16 years, and while there is fluctuation and a general tendency for rates to increase over time, rankings have remained remarkably consistent. Still, you should use our calculations as a rough guide only, and be sure to inquire about changes in tax rates or planned tax hikes before you relocate.

Many of the cities featured are locations favored for retirement, while others are urban areas from which large numbers of retirees migrate. Geographically, we cover at least one city from each state, plus Washington, DC.

Book Layout

Our book begins with a brief synopsis of the kinds of taxes you can expect to pay. Next, we've alphabetized our report by state and then by city within the state. The applicable taxes for each city are described in detail. Our comprehensive charts tally it all up and tell you where each city stands in our rankings.

At the end, you'll find our exclusive list of tax heavens and tax hells, plus nine separate rankings of all cities. A rank of No. 1 means that city has the lowest total tax burden in the category. The average total tax burden for each category is also shown.

As in earlier studies, we found that a city's tax climate may not be uniformly favorable or unfavorable across all income levels. Omaha, NE, for example, has higher-than-average total tax burdens for higher incomes and lower-than-average total tax burdens for lower incomes. Also, note that in some cities only the low-priced homes in each income category earn favorable rankings; in other cities, it may be mid-priced homes that net better rankings.

Some places widely known for a high cost of living do not have high tax burdens. For example, in Hawaii, Honolulu and Wailuku have much lower than average tax burdens. We recommend that retirees carefully investigate the cost of homes in any city of interest. Homes at the lower values may be difficult or impossible to find in the highest priced cities, while the higher tax burdens associated with higher priced homes can be avoided in cities with lower median home values.

State Income Tax

Many retirees use the presence or absence of a state income tax as a litmus test for a retirement destination. This is a serious miscalculation, as higher sales and property taxes can offset the lack of a state income tax, particularly for retirees with little or no earned income. The lack of a state income tax doesn't necessarily ensure a low total tax burden.

Only a handful of states don't tax personal income. The others levy some sort of income tax, although the taxable income varies. One state may tax only interest and dividends, while another bases its income tax on adjusted gross income calculated for the federal tax return. Most states allow exemptions to reduce gross income. For instance, some states tax Social Security benefits subject to federal taxation, while other states allow your full monthly check to escape taxation.

Some states allow residents to exempt all or part of federal, state or private pensions, while others don't exclude any pension income from taxation.

Of course, tax rates vary from state to state. Some states have graduated rates; for instance, the first $20,000 in taxable income might be taxed at a rate of 5% while the next $5,000 would be taxed at a rate of 6%. Other states tax all income at the same flat rate.

Most states have standard deductions, although these deductions vary. Some are similar to deductions offered on the federal return, while other states offer additional deductions that may be based on age or income.

Most states offer income tax credits or rebates as well. The most common is credit for income taxes paid to other states. We've assumed our couples do not owe income taxes to any other states. Other credits are often based on low income, for which our couples may not be eligible. In many states, there are a number of credits available that might apply to your situation. We do not attempt to list all of them.

If you're considering several states for retirement, contact state tax offices and request a tax form to determine the full tax bite in each state. Many state Web sites have general tax information, as well as forms, available online. In addition, the Web sites often contain links to city and county sites for additional information.

In order to calculate state and local income tax, it is necessary to make a large number of assumptions about our couples and the nature and source of their income. We will not list these assumptions here, due to space considerations, except for the following:

1) Our couples are age 65, file jointly and take standard deductions rather than itemizing. In some states and under certain circumstances, retirees might reduce their state income tax by filing separately or itemizing deductions.

2) We use three representative gross annual household income levels in our study — $30,000, $60,000 and $90,000. The components of these income totals are extrapolated from the BLS survey. In the survey, income consists of: wages and salaries; self-employment income; Social Security, private and government retirement income; interest, dividends, rental income and other property income; and other income. It should be noted that the BLS survey income components used are average figures for U.S. residents age 65 and older. These averages are not necessarily typical for all such residents and may differ significantly from your personal circumstances.

3) We do not include the effect of the alternative minimum tax calculation in our analysis of income taxes due.

4) We assume that our couples are full-time residents of the state for which income tax is due.

Local Income Tax

Retirees who relocate to certain U.S. cities may be surprised to learn that they owe income taxes not only to the state but also to the local government. Cities call local income taxes by different names, such as wage taxes or occupational license fees. Just as their names are different, local income taxes are assessed in varying ways.

Some cities tax only earned income. Other cities impose taxes based on a percentage of the amount of state income tax due. Still others tax all income, offering exemptions and deductions like those at the state level.

When inquiring about the presence of a local income tax, word your question to include any local tax, assessment or fee applied to any of your income. Some municipalities go to extremes to avoid calling their tax an income tax.

We have used the same local income tax assumptions as were used in calculating state income tax.

Sales Tax

In all but a handful of states, residents pay some form of sales tax on their purchases. In a few states, a sales tax is replaced by a general excise tax or gross receipts tax on businesses. Since these taxes are also passed on to the consumer, we treat them herein as sales taxes.

Usually, a base sales tax rate is determined by the state. Often, local governments add to that base rate, sometimes significantly.

Our sales tax calculations are based on data extrapolated from the BLS survey, which estimates how much people age 65 and over spend each year on certain items at various income levels.

We estimate the sales tax burden in each city by applying local and state sales taxes to each of the following categories named in the BLS survey: food at home (groceries); food away from home; household operations and housekeeping supplies; household furnishings and equipment; apparel and services; transportation; medical services; drugs; medical supplies; entertainment; personal care products and services; and miscellaneous. The BLS survey does not list sales tax as a separate expenditure and, therefore, we have applied sales tax to each category if applicable. This has the effect of inflating sales taxes for all cities, but the methodology has been consistently applied and does not unfairly skew the rankings.

We assume that certain categories — shelter, health insurance, cash contributions and personal insurance and pensions — are universally exempt from sales tax.

We exclude sales tax on utilities from our calculations altogether because it is often difficult to distinguish the basic rate from fees and taxes. Frequently, there are markups in utility bills that we believe are hidden taxes. We recommend that retirees inquire about the typical utility bill for the typical home before relocating.

Generally, residents of a city pay the same sales tax rate on most purchases. However, it is common to find certain items taxed at a different rate. For instance, groceries or drugs may be taxed at a lower rate than clothing, or exempt altogether. Or, there may be an additional tax on food away from

The costs of registering a vehicle and annually renewing license plates are often overlooked by relocators, but these fees can add up (and do, in several states).

home. We've incorporated the applicable varying tax rates in our calculations if the items were included in the BLS survey as a separate category.

In most cases, if any items within a category are taxed, we assume that the whole category is taxed. For example, some cities exempt services from tax but do tax apparel. We assume the entire category of "apparel and services" is taxable. Therefore, we may overstate sales tax burdens in some cities, but this method is consistently applied to all cities.

The most common items exempt from sales tax are drugs, groceries and medical services.

Use Tax

Use tax is due when an item is purchased out of state, either tax-free or at a lower sales tax rate. It is usually calculated as the difference between the actual tax paid and the rate in effect in the state of residence. It has become increasingly important over the last few years as more goods are purchased directly from other states, especially over the Internet. Several state income tax forms have an additional section to declare and pay for use taxes. We have assumed that no use taxes are due for our couples.

Property Tax And Other Fees

Property taxes differ widely from state to state and between cities within the same state. Sometimes property taxes vary from neighborhood to neighborhood or even street to street within the same city. Where multiple tax rates exist in a city, we attempted to select an area where retirees were likely to live. Where this was not possible, we attempted to select an area with representative tax rates for the city in question.

Property taxes may consist of components from several different taxing entities, including the city, county, school district, fire district and others. Property tax rates change annually in many communities. Increases in property tax may be limited due to state or local legislation.

In most states the property tax is

determined by multiplying a property tax rate by an assessed value. Assessment rates are decided either by the state or by local governments. Homes are assessed at such widely varying rates as 1% to 100% of market value, but a low assessment percentage does not translate into lower taxes, as the tax rate may be adjusted to make up the difference.

Some cities appraise property annually, but once every two, three or four years is more common. We assume that the appraised value equals the market value of the home.

In a few cases, municipalities tax homes and the land on which they are built at different rates. We have assumed that the home (or improvement) value is 80% and the land value is 20% of the total market value. Actual allocations will vary significantly depending on the location in question.

Many cities offer tax-saving breaks from the amount of property taxes due, often exempting a certain dollar amount from the home's assessed value. Other exemptions or deductions may be statewide and may be based on age or income. In cities where our couples qualified for these tax breaks, we have included them in our property tax calculations. Some homestead exemptions or credits require one or more years of residency. We assume our couples meet these residency requirements, because we believe it is more useful to reflect ongoing, long-term tax burdens than those of year one.

In some cities, services such as garbage pickup, street maintenance and storm drain utility fees are included in your property tax bill. In other locations, residents pay these fees separately. To make our numbers comparable, where garbage pickup fees are not included in property taxes, we added $180 to the property tax burden as an estimate of the additional annual charge. This estimate was derived from a review of actual costs in a sample of cities. We also added stormwater fees and other additional charges if applicable. Homeowner association fees can be significant and we have included them only if all resi-

dents of a city or town would be subject to such fees. We do not include fees to register or own pets.

Many cities have property tax deferral programs for seniors and some cities have implemented caps on allowable annual increases in appraised property values for residents. We have not included the effect of either of these programs in our calculations, but both warrant research for potential retirement destinations.

There are often property tax exemptions and deductions available to veterans, widows or people with disabilities that should also be investigated, if applicable.

It is necessary to make many assumptions about our couples and their age and income in order to complete property tax calculations. We will not list these assumptions here, except for the following:

1) We selected three home values for each of the income categories used in the income tax analysis. For income of $30,000, we looked at property tax burdens for homes valued at $125,000, $150,000 and $175,000. For income of $60,000, the home values we used were $150,000, $225,000 and $300,000. For income of $90,000, we figured property tax bills for home values of $225,000, $375,000 and $525,000.

2) In 30 of our cities where home values are generally recognized as being higher than average, we omitted the lowest income level and added additional home values of $600,000, $750,000 and $900,000 for the highest income level.

3) We assumed a free-standing, site-built home and lot.

The national median sales price of new homes in July 2007 was $246,200, according to census data. We selected a range of homes we believe reflect home-buying capabilities as determined by incomes shown above.

Auto Licensing Fees

The costs of registering a vehicle and annually renewing license plates

For an idea of how 203 cities match up for retirees in your income/home value category, turn to the rankings on pages 174-183.

are often overlooked by relocators, but these fees can add up (and do, in several states). So we contacted every state's or city's department of motor vehicles and asked for all fees related to registration or renewal of an automobile.

In order to show the wide range of vehicle registration costs in different cities, we've given our couples two cars — a 2005 Ford Explorer and a 2005 Toyota Camry. Their current market values — $14,400 for the Explorer and $16,600 for the Camry — were provided online from nadaguides.com and were taken from the April 2007 edition of the N.A.D.A. Official Used Car Guide.

At the time of registration, relocators can expect to pay for a state title, which generally ranges from $5 to $50. Other common expenses are plate and lien fees.

In many states, registration fees are based on the value of the car, but the method for determining value varies from state to state. Some states base their fees on the automobile's weight or model. You should know this specific information about your car before calling to find out registration fees in a particular city.

New residents may also face a tax on automobiles brought into the state. For instance, the Kentucky sales tax rate is 6%. Relocators to that state who paid a sales tax of 6% or greater on their vehicle in another state at the time of purchase are not subject to additional tax. However, people who paid a sales tax of less than 6% to another state are required to pay the difference on the current market value of the car to Kentucky, in the form of a usage tax. We've universally assumed that our couples do not owe additional tax, but we recommend a call to states being considered as potential retirement destinations to determine the impact of this tax, if any.

A number of years ago, Florida abolished one very unpopular surprise for newcomers — a $295 impact fee per automobile brought into the state. However, there's still a one-time $100 fee paid by everyone registering a car in Florida. In Texas, a new resident is now assessed a $90 fee upon initial registration of a car in the state.

Annual license plate renewal fees also vary. In many states, the costs decrease as the car depreciates. Other states have a flat renewal fee, regardless of the type or year of the vehicle.

It's important to note here that even though we discuss initial registration fees in our text, our charts reflect the ongoing annual or annualized fees for the first year after registration.

In many cities, auto licensing fees resemble personal property taxes in size and method of calculation. In most cases, if the tax is verified and assessed by the department of motor vehicles, we discuss it with other auto registration-related taxes. Otherwise, you'll find it noted in the paragraph devoted to personal property taxes.

Finally, auto emissions inspections are common requirements in many states. Although these tests are often required to initially register a vehicle

and to renew the registration, most of the inspections are carried out by, and fees paid to, a third party. Where this was the case, we did not include testing fees in our calculations. Fees were only included if paid directly to the Department of Motor Vehicles or to another governmental agency.

Personal Property Tax

In addition to a property tax, many local governments tax the personal property of individuals. Items that are taxed vary, even among cities within the same state. Items that are most often taxed are vehicles, including automobiles, boats, motorcycles and motor homes. Usually, but not always, the personal property tax rate in a city or area is the same as the property tax rate there, and items subject to the tax are usually assessed at the same rate as homes.

Many cities levy personal property tax only on mobile homes or mobile home attachments (carports, etc.). Mobile homes may be taxed as real property in some cities and taxed as personal property in other cities. We assume our couples do not own these items.

Intangibles Tax

An intangibles tax is a tax imposed on the value of investments that many retirees depend on for income. Because this tax was not well-known outside the handful of states that levied it, relocating retirees were often shocked to discover its existence after moving, when the first payment was due. That's particularly frustrating because some careful portfolio management might have reduced the tax, had they known about it in advance.

Over the past few years, intangibles taxes have been challenged and overturned by courts in some states and simply phased out in others. For example Florida repealed its intangibles tax on most items as of January 1, 2007. Readers should contact the relevant state tax (or revenue) department for detailed information on taxes on intangibles. We did not include the effect of any intangibles taxes.

ALABAMA

Alabama has a state income tax and a state sales tax.

The state income tax rate is graduated from 2% to 5% depending upon income bracket. For married couples filing jointly, the rates are 2% on the first $1,000 of taxable income; 4% on the next $5,000 of taxable income; and 5% on taxable income above $6,000.

In calculating the tax, there is a deduction from adjusted gross income for federal income tax paid. Federal and state pensions are exempt. Private pensions that qualify as a "defined benefit plan" are exempt. Social Security benefits are exempt. There is a $3,000 exemption from adjusted gross income for married couples filing jointly and a standard deduction of 20% of total adjusted gross income, not to exceed $4,000, for married cou-

ALABAMA TAX TABLE

Instructions

1. Find the Income in the far left column closest to your anticipated retirement income.
2. Find the Home Value closest to the value of the home where you will live in retirement.
3. Follow that row to your estimated Total Tax Burden at age 65 and beyond.

Income	Home Value	Property Tax & Other Fees	Personal Property Tax & Auto Fees	Sales Tax	Local Income Tax	State Income Tax	Total Tax Burden	Rank*
DOTHAN								
$30,000	$125,000	$486	$240	$1,210	-	$380	$2,316	52 of 173
	150,000	548	240	1,210	-	380	2,378	40 of 173
	175,000	609	240	1,210	-	380	2,439	32 of 173
$60,000	$150,000	$548	$240	$2,055	-	$1,332	$4,175	97 of 203
	225,000	731	240	2,055	-	1,332	4,358	51 of 203
	300,000	915	240	2,055	-	1,332	4,542	30 of 203
$90,000	$225,000	$731	$240	$2,522	-	$2,441	$5,934	60 of 203
	375,000	1,099	240	2,522	-	2,441	6,302	25 of 203
	525,000	1,466	240	2,522	-	2,441	6,669	15 of 203
EUFAULA								
$30,000	$125,000	$605	$245	$1,210	-	$380	$2,440	66 of 173
	150,000	692	245	1,210	-	380	2,527	54 of 173
	175,000	780	245	1,210	-	380	2,615	42 of 173
$60,000	$150,000	$692	$245	$2,055	-	$1,332	$4,324	114 of 203
	225,000	955	245	2,055	-	1,332	4,587	63 of 203
	300,000	1,217	245	2,055	-	1,332	4,849	41 of 203
$90,000	$225,000	$955	$245	$2,522	-	$2,441	$6,163	79 of 203
	375,000	1,480	245	2,522	-	2,441	6,688	31 of 203
	525,000	2,005	245	2,522	-	2,441	7,213	23 of 203
FAIRHOPE								
$30,000	$125,000	$606	$268	$908	-	$380	$2,162	38 of 173
	150,000	695	268	908	-	380	2,251	31 of 173
	175,000	783	268	908	-	380	2,339	25 of 173
$60,000	$150,000	$695	$268	$1,541	-	$1,332	$3,836	64 of 203
	225,000	961	268	1,541	-	1,332	4,102	37 of 203
	300,000	1,227	268	1,541	-	1,332	4,368	23 of 203
$90,000	$225,000	$961	$268	$1,892	-	$2,441	$5,562	39 of 203
	375,000	1,493	268	1,892	-	2,441	6,094	20 of 203
	525,000	2,026	268	1,892	-	2,441	6,627	14 of 203

*There are 203 cities in this book, 30 of which have higher than average home prices. We have estimated taxes for a tier of higher home values (and omitted the lowest tier) for these 30 cities. The city with the lowest tax burden for an income/home value combination is given the #1 rating; the higher the rating, the higher the total tax burden.

ples filing jointly.

Major tax credits or rebates include: credit for income taxes paid to other states, employer-sponsored basic skills education credit, rural physician credit, coal credit and capital credit. Our couples do not qualify for these programs.

The state sales tax rate is 4%, but local governments can add to this amount.

Since car registration and renewal fees differ within the state, see city information for details.

Dothan

Dothan has no local income tax but does levy a sales tax.

Most purchases are taxed at a rate of 8%. Major consumer categories taxed at a different rate include: none. Major consumer categories that are exempt from sales tax include: drugs and medical services.

Within the city limits of Dothan, the property tax rate is .031. Homes are assessed at 10% of market value. There are four categories of homestead exemptions available. Property tax does not cover garbage pickup.

Dothan has no personal property tax for individuals.

Our couples relocating to Dothan must pay an ad valorem tax based on the city's valuation of each automobile. The tax is $92 for the Explorer and $100 for the Camry. Our couples also pay a tag fee of $24 to register each automobile and a title fee of $18 per automobile at the time of registration. Thereafter, on an annual basis, our couples will pay an ad valorem tax and a tag fee, per automobile.

Eufaula

Eufaula has no local income tax but does levy a sales tax.

Most purchases are taxed at a rate of 8%. Major consumer categories taxed at a different rate: none. Major consumer categories that are exempt from sales tax include: drugs and medical services.

Within the city limits of Eufaula, the property tax rate is .0415. Homes are assessed at 10% of market value. There are four categories of homestead exemptions available. Property tax does not cover garbage pickup. There is also a transaction fee of $3 per year.

Eufaula has no personal property tax for individuals.

Our couples relocating to Eufaula must pay an ad valorem tax based on the city's valuation of each automobile. The tax is $108 for the Explorer and $89 for the Camry. Our couples also pay a tag fee of $24 to register each automo-

bile and a title fee of $18 per automobile at the time of registration. Thereafter, on an annual basis, our couples will pay an ad valorem tax and a tag fee, per automobile.

Fairhope

Fairhope has no local income tax but does levy a sales tax.

Most purchases are taxed at a rate of 6%. Major consumer categories taxed at a different rate: none. Major consumer categories that are exempt from sales tax include: drugs and medical services.

Within the city limits of Fairhope, the property tax rate is .042. Homes are assessed at 10% of market value. There are four categories of homestead exemptions available. Property tax does not cover garbage pickup.

Fairhope has no personal property tax for individuals.

Our couples relocating to Fairhope must pay an ad valorem tax based on the city's valuation of each automobile. The tax is $119 for the Explorer and $101 for the Camry. Our couples also pay a tag fee of $24 to register each automobile and a title fee of $18 per automobile at the time of registration. Thereafter, on an annual basis, our couples will pay an ad valorem tax and a tag fee, per automobile.

• Alabama's Top Retirement Towns •

Dothan

A low cost of living, a mild climate and traditional Southern hospitality help draw retirees to Dothan. The city is in the rolling, wooded country of southeastern Alabama, 15 miles from the Florida Panhandle and about an hour and a half from the Gulf Coast beaches of Panama City, FL.

Many people discover the area while in the military and often return for retirement. Fort Rucker, 20 miles to the northwest, supports a community of about 14,500 retirees. The headquarters of the Army Aviation Center, Fort Rucker is well-known to thousands of Army aviators and to Air Force pilots and students from more than 60 foreign countries who have received their helicopter training here. The base contributes more than $1 billion annually

to the area's economy.

Its extensive facilities for retirees include Lyster Army Health Clinic, which is supplemented in Dothan by a major regional medical facility, the Southeast Alabama Medical Center, and the smaller Flowers Hospital. In fact, Southeast Alabama Medical Center, which has 370 beds and 2,400 employees, is Houston County's largest employer. Flowers Hospital comes in third.

Houston County is also farming country, with peanuts its biggest crop. It regularly produces more than 100 million pounds per year.

Four-year Troy University-Dothan and two-year Wallace Community College cater to retirees. Artistic opportunities include theater, dance and music, and recreation is afforded by 20 city parks, six swimming pools, four

recreation centers and opportunities for golf, tennis, softball, bike riding, running and walking. The area's lakes and streams and, of course, the Gulf of Mexico make it a paradise for those who like to fish.

Population: 64,053

Climate: High Low

	High	Low
January	61	40
July	91	71

Cost of living: Below average

Housing cost: The median price of homes during the first half of 2007 was $137,358, according to the Alabama Real Estate Research and Education Center.

Information: Dothan Area Chamber of Commerce, (800) 221-1027 or www.dothan.com.

Eufaula

In southeastern Alabama, in an area

known as Wiregrass Country, Eufaula sits on a bluff overlooking beautiful 45,000-acre Lake Eufaula. Early home to the Creek Indians and later a Southern agricultural powerhouse of cotton baled and shipped downriver on the Chattahoochee, the town now has a diversified economy, including tourism, industry and agriculture.

Near the Alabama-Georgia border, and 85 miles southeast of Montgomery, Eufaula is a small town that blends an Old South heritage with a modern-day lifestyle. Antebellum and Victorian houses grace many of the tree-lined streets. More than 700 of Eufaula's homes and other buildings are listed on the National Register of Historic Places, and several open to the public for tours at Christmas and for spring pilgrimages when gardens are in bloom.

Fishing enthusiasts brag about the bass catches on Lake Eufaula, which hosts numerous tournaments and also attracts recreational boaters. A hike through the nearby national wildlife refuge will net sightings of an extensive variety of birds. Three 18-hole golf courses also beckon.

With its small-town charm and lake access, Eufaula has attracted retirees, who find it's also an economical place to live. The cost of living in this region is below the national average, and housing is available at moderate prices. Among other amenities, the Eufaula campus of Wallace Community College offers academic, technical and health-care classes, and the 74-bed Medical Center Barbour is an accredited hospital with emergency, surgical and acute-care services.

Population: 13,350

Climate:

	High	Low
January	57	35
July	91	70

Cost of living: Below average

Housing cost: The median sales price of homes in Barbour County was $128,000 during the first half of 2007, according to The Eufaula Agency, a local real estate firm.

Information: Eufaula-Barbour County Chamber of Commerce, (800) 524-7529 or www.eufaulachamber.com.

Fairhope

Fairhope is a walkable small town on Mobile Bay with an appealing, manicured downtown. Because it was founded as a single-tax community, it now has a substantial amount of public land on the waterfront. The Fairhope Single Tax Corp. owns about 4,500 acres of the city, including most of downtown as well as parkland and residential areas, and gives 99-year leases to homebuyers, who own their homes but not the land.

Among landmarks is a municipal pier, a good vantage point for enjoying spectacular sunsets over the bay. Across the water, Mobile offers big-city amenities.

Fairhope is particularly proud of its thousands of trees. The Beach Park Tree Trail boasts almost 500 trees, and many others line parks and streets. Among outdoor activities, bird-watching is a big attraction. The city has a coastal birding trail and hosts an annual BirdFest in October.

There also are ample opportunities for boating, fishing and other water sports. Several golf courses are nearby, including one in Point Clear that is on Alabama's highly regarded Robert Trent Jones Golf Trail.

"My wife Pat wanted to move south, out of the cold. I have military benefits, so I wanted to be near a military base," says Ted Dwyer, 67, who retired in 2004 from Rocky Hill, CT. "We looked in the panhandle of Florida and then were headed to Mississippi. On the way we stopped in Fairhope, and it's just what we wanted. There are a lot of activities, and the people are so pleasant, so friendly. We really enjoyed meeting new people. We didn't experience that in New England." Mobile has limited military facilities, but Pensacola, about an hour east, offers major military services.

Population: 16,164

Climate:

	High	Low
January	60	40
July	90	73

Cost of living: Below average

Housing cost: The median sales price of a single-family home during the first seven months of 2007 was $194,404, according to the Eastern Shore Chamber of Commerce.

Information: Eastern Shore Chamber of Commerce, (251) 928-6387 or www.eschamber.com.

ALASKA

Alaska has no state income tax and no state sales tax.

Anchorage

Anchorage has no local income tax and no sales tax.

In tax district 3 of Anchorage, the property tax rate is .01528. Homes are assessed at 100% of market value. Homeowners age 65 and older are exempt from property taxes on up to $150,000 of home value. There is also an owner-occupied residential property tax exemption of 10% off the assessed value, up to a maximum of $20,000.

Property tax does not cover garbage pickup.

Anchorage has a personal property tax rate of .01528. Items subject to the tax include mobile homes. The senior property tax exemption applies to mobile homes. We've assumed our couples do not own any of the items subject to personal property tax.

Our couples relocating to Anchorage pay a title fee of $15 per automobile,

a $15 lien recording fee per automobile and a $2 administrative fee per automobile at the time of registration. Persons over 65 are exempt from other registration fees and taxes; in order for both automobiles to qualify for the exemption, one must be titled to the wife and the other to the husband, and the couple must prove Alaska residence. Thereafter, as long as the senior exemption applies to both automobiles, our couples will pay a $2 administrative fee per automobile every two years.

ALASKA TAX TABLE

Instructions

1. Find the Income in the far left column closest to your anticipated retirement income.
2. Find the Home Value closest to the value of the home where you will live in retirement.
3. Follow that row to your estimated Total Tax Burden at age 65 and beyond.

Income	Home Value	Property Tax & Other Fees	Personal Property Tax & Auto Fees	Sales Tax	Local Income Tax	State Income Tax	Total Tax Burden	Rank*
ANCHORAGE								
$30,000	$125,000	$180	$2	-	-	-	$182	2 of 173 ○
	150,000	180	2	-	-	-	182	2 of 173 ○
	175,000	295	2	-	-	-	297	2 of 173 ○
$60,000	$150,000	$180	$2	-	-	-	$182	1 of 203 ○
	225,000	1,020	2	-	-	-	1,022	1 of 203 ○
	300,000	2,166	2	-	-	-	2,168	2 of 203 ○
$90,000	$225,000	$1,020	$2	-	-	-	$1,022	1 of 203 ○
	375,000	3,312	2	-	-	-	3,314	1 of 203 ○
	525,000	5,604	2	-	-	-	5,606	3 of 203 ○

*There are 203 cities in this book, 30 of which have higher than average home prices. We have estimated taxes for a tier of higher home values (and omitted the lowest tier) for these 30 cities. The city with the lowest tax burden for an income/home value combination is given the #1 rating; the higher the rating, the higher the total tax burden.

ARIZONA

Arizona has a state income tax and a state sales tax.

The state income tax rate is graduated from 2.73% to 4.79% depending upon income bracket. For married couples filing jointly, the rates are 2.73% on the first $20,000 of taxable income; 3.04% on the next $30,000 of taxable income; 3.55% on the next $50,000 of taxable income; 4.48% on the next $200,000 of taxable income; and 4.79% on taxable income above $300,000.

In calculating the tax, there is no deduction for federal income tax paid. Federal, state and local pensions are exempt up to $2,500 per person. Private pensions are not exempt. Social Security benefits are exempt. There is a $8,494 standard deduction from Arizona adjusted gross income for married couples filing jointly. There is a $2,100 exemption from Arizona adjusted gross income for each person age 65 or older.

Major tax credits or rebates include: credit for income taxes paid to other states, family income tax credit, property tax credit, which our couples do not qualify for; increased excise tax credit, which one of our couples qualifies for; and clean elections fund, which our couples do qualify for.

The state sales tax rate is 5.6%, but local governments can add to this rate.

Our couples relocating to the cities listed below must pay a vehicle license tax based on year and MSRP of each automobile at the time of registration. The tax is $389 for the Explorer and $290 for the Camry. Our couples also pay a tag fee of $8 per automobile, a title fee of $4 per automobile and an air quality fee of $2 per automobile. Thereafter, on an annual basis, our couples will pay a vehicle license tax and a tag fee, per automobile.

Casa Grande

Casa Grande has no local income tax but does levy a sales tax.

Most purchases are taxed at a rate of 8.6%. Major consumer categories taxed at a different rate include: food away from home, which is taxed at a rate of 8.4%. Major consumer categories that are exempt from sales tax include: groceries, drugs and medical services.

In tax area 0481 of Casa Grande, the property tax rate is .139425 including the state aid to education deduction for all homeowners. There is a $520 cap on the amount of state aid given. Homes are assessed at 10% of market value. Property tax does not cover garbage pickup.

Casa Grande has a personal property tax rate of .139425. Personal property is assessed at 10% of MSRP. Items subject to the tax include mobile homes. We've assumed our couples do not own any of the items subject to personal property tax.

Flagstaff

Flagstaff has no local income tax but does levy a sales tax.

Most purchases are taxed at a rate of 8.126%. On January 1, 2007, the rate increases to 8.326%. Major consumer categories taxed at a different rate include: food away from home, which is taxed at a rate of 10.126%. On January 1, 2007, the rate increases to 10.326%. Major consumer categories that are exempt from sales tax include: groceries, drugs and medical services.

Within the city limits of Flagstaff, the property tax rate is .072731 including the state aid to education deduction for all homeowners. There is a $520 cap on the amount of state aid given. Homes are assessed at 10% of market value. Property tax does not cover garbage pickup.

Flagstaff has a personal property tax rate of .072731. Personal property is assessed at 10% of MSRP. Items subject to the tax include mobile homes. We've assumed our couples do not own any of the items subject to personal property tax.

Green Valley

Green Valley has no local income tax but does levy a sales tax.

Most purchases are taxed at a rate of 6.1%. Major consumer categories taxed at a different rate: none. Major consumer categories that are exempt from sales tax include: groceries, drugs and medical services.

In tax area 3901 of Green Valley, the property tax rate is .096537 including the state aid to education deduction for all homeowners. There is a $520 cap on the amount of state aid given. Homes are valued at approximately 80% of market value and then assessed at 10% of that value. Property tax does not cover garbage pickup.

In tax area 3901 of Green Valley, there is a personal property tax rate of .096537. Personal property is assessed at 10% of MSRP. Items subject to the tax include mobile homes. We've assumed our couples do not own any of the items subject to personal property tax.

Lake Havasu City

Lake Havasu City has no local income tax but does levy a sales tax.

Most purchases are taxed at a rate of 7.85%. Major consumer categories taxed at a different rate: none. Major consumer categories that are exempt from sales tax include: groceries, drugs and medical services.

In tax area 2571 of Lake Havasu City, the property tax rate is .072968 including the state aid to education deduction for all homeowners. There is a $520 cap on the amount of state aid given. Homes are assessed at 10% of market value. Property tax does not cover garbage pickup. There is also an irrigation and drainage fee of approximately $20 per year.

In tax area 2571 of Lake Havasu City, there is a personal property tax rate of .072968. Personal property is assessed at 10% of MSRP. Items subject to the tax include mobile homes. We've assumed our couples do not own any of the items subject to personal property tax.

Phoenix

Phoenix has no local income tax but does levy a sales tax.

Most purchases are taxed at a rate of 8.1%. Major consumer categories taxed at a different rate: none. Major consumer categories that are exempt from sales tax include: groceries, drugs and medical services.

In the Paradise Valley Unified School

Continued on page 18

ARIZONA TAX TABLE

Instructions

1. Find the Income in the far left column closest to your anticipated retirement income.
2. Find the Home Value closest to the value of the home where you will live in retirement.
3. Follow that row to your estimated Total Tax Burden at age 65 and beyond.

Income	Home Value	Property Tax & Other Fees	Personal Property Tax & Auto Fees	Sales Tax	Local Income Tax	State Income Tax†	Total Tax Burden	Rank*
CASA GRANDE								
$30,000	$125,000	$1,923	$563	$1,080	-	($50)	$3,516	151 of 173
	150,000	2,271	563	1,080	-	(50)	3,864	147 of 173
	175,000	2,620	563	1,080	-	(50)	4,213	141 of 173
$60,000	$150,000	$2,271	$563	$1,897	-	$594	$5,325	169 of 203
	225,000	3,317	563	1,897	-	594	6,371	161 of 203
	300,000	4,363	563	1,897	-	594	7,417	154 of 203
$90,000	$225,000	$3,317	$563	$2,358	-	$1,440	$7,678	149 of 203
	375,000	5,408	563	2,358	-	1,440	9,769	143 of 203
	525,000	7,634	563	2,358	-	1,440	11,995	142 of 203
FLAGSTAFF								
$30,000	$125,000	$1,089	$563	$1,058	-	($50)	$2,660	89 of 173
	150,000	1,271	563	1,058	-	(50)	2,842	78 of 173
	175,000	1,453	563	1,058	-	(50)	3,024	74 of 173
$60,000	$150,000	$1,271	$563	$1,858	-	$594	$4,286	111 of 203
	225,000	1,816	563	1,858	-	594	4,831	82 of 203
	300,000	2,362	563	1,858	-	594	5,377	69 of 203
$90,000	$225,000	$1,816	$563	$2,297	-	$1,440	$6,116	74 of 203
	375,000	2,969	563	2,297	-	1,440	7,269	53 of 203
	525,000	4,292	563	2,297	-	1,440	8,592	52 of 203
GREEN VALLEY								
$30,000	$125,000	$1,171	$563	$768	-	($50)	$2,452	67 of 173
	150,000	1,369	563	768	-	(50)	2,650	63 of 173
	175,000	1,567	563	768	-	(50)	2,848	60 of 173
$60,000	$150,000	$1,369	$563	$1,349	-	$594	$3,875	66 of 203
	225,000	1,963	563	1,349	-	594	4,469	56 of 203
	300,000	2,558	563	1,349	-	594	5,064	55 of 203
$90,000	$225,000	$1,963	$563	$1,677	-	$1,440	$5,643	47 of 203
	375,000	3,152	563	1,677	-	1,440	6,832	35 of 203
	525,000	4,341	563	1,677	-	1,440	8,021	34 of 203
LAKE HAVASU CITY								
$30,000	$125,000	$1,112	$563	$988	-	($50)	$2,613	79 of 173
	150,000	1,295	563	988	-	(50)	2,796	74 of 173
	175,000	1,477	563	988	-	(50)	2,978	72 of 173
$60,000	$150,000	$1,295	$563	$1,736	-	$594	$4,188	100 of 203
	225,000	1,842	563	1,736	-	594	4,735	74 of 203
	300,000	2,389	563	1,736	-	594	5,282	64 of 203
$90,000	$225,000	$1,842	$563	$2,158	-	$1,440	$6,003	68 of 203
	375,000	2,936	563	2,158	-	1,440	7,097	44 of 203
	525,000	4,136	563	2,158	-	1,440	8,297	43 of 203
PHOENIX								
$30,000	$125,000	$1,398	$563	$1,020	-	($50)	$2,931	113 of 173
	150,000	1,641	563	1,020	-	(50)	3,174	100 of 173
	175,000	1,885	563	1,020	-	(50)	3,418	94 of 173

Income	Home Value	Property Tax & Other Fees	Personal Property Tax & Auto Fees	Sales Tax	Local Income Tax	State Income Tax[†]	Total Tax Burden	Rank[*]
PHOENIX continued								
$60,000	$150,000	$1,641	$563	$1,792	-	$594	$4,590	131 of 203
	225,000	2,372	563	1,792	-	594	5,321	115 of 203
	300,000	3,102	563	1,792	-	594	6,051	104 of 203
$90,000	$225,000	$2,372	$563	$2,227	-	$1,440	$6,602	100 of 203
	375,000	3,833	563	2,227	-	1,440	8,063	83 of 203
	525,000	5,470	563	2,227	-	1,440	9,700	79 of 203
PRESCOTT								
$30,000	$125,000	$997	$563	$1,102	-	($50)	$2,612	78 of 173
	150,000	1,160	563	1,102	-	(50)	2,775	72 of 173
	175,000	1,324	563	1,102	-	(50)	2,939	66 of 173
$60,000	$150,000	$1,160	$563	$1,918	-	$594	$4,235	104 of 203
	225,000	1,651	563	1,918	-	594	4,726	73 of 203
	300,000	2,141	563	1,918	-	594	5,216	59 of 203
$90,000	$225,000	$1,651	$563	$2,376	-	$1,440	$6,030	69 of 203
	375,000	2,631	563	2,376	-	1,440	7,010	39 of 203
	525,000	3,692	563	2,376	-	1,440	8,071	37 of 203
SCOTTSDALE								
$60,000	$150,000	$1,275	$563	$1,817	-	$594	$4,249	105 of 203
	225,000	1,823	563	1,817	-	594	4,797	79 of 203
	300,000	2,371	563	1,817	-	594	5,345	66 of 203
$90,000	$225,000	$1,823	$563	$2,252	-	$1,440	$6,078	71 of 203
	375,000	2,918	563	2,252	-	1,440	7,173	48 of 203
	525,000	4,110	563	2,252	-	1,440	8,365	46 of 203
	$600,000	$4,746	$563	$2,252	-	$1,440	$9,001	10 of 30
	750,000	6,017	563	2,252	-	1,440	10,272	10 of 30
	900,000	7,289	563	2,252	-	1,440	11,544	9 of 30
SEDONA								
$60,000	$150,000	$1,324	$563	$2,068	-	$594	$4,549	129 of 203
	225,000	1,896	563	2,068	-	594	5,121	103 of 203
	300,000	2,467	563	2,068	-	594	5,692	85 of 203
$90,000	$225,000	$1,896	$563	$2,570	-	$1,440	$6,469	98 of 203
	375,000	3,039	563	2,570	-	1,440	7,612	66 of 203
	525,000	4,183	563	2,570	-	1,440	8,756	55 of 203
	$600,000	$4,755	$563	$2,570	-	$1,440	$9,328	11 of 30
	750,000	5,898	563	2,570	-	1,440	10,471	11 of 30
	900,000	7,107	563	2,570	-	1,440	11,680	10 of 30
SIERRA VISTA								
$30,000	$125,000	$1,038	$563	$1,045	-	($50)	$2,596	77 of 173
	150,000	1,209	563	1,045	-	(50)	2,767	71 of 173
	175,000	1,381	563	1,045	-	(50)	2,939	66 of 173
$60,000	$150,000	$1,209	$563	$1,820	-	$594	$4,186	98 of 203
	225,000	1,724	563	1,820	-	594	4,701	71 of 203
	300,000	2,238	563	1,820	-	594	5,215	58 of 203
$90,000	$225,000	$1,724	$563	$2,255	-	$1,440	$5,982	65 of 203
	375,000	2,753	563	2,255	-	1,440	7,011	40 of 203
	525,000	3,782	563	2,255	-	1,440	8,040	36 of 203

[†]The increased excise tax credit is issued as a refund by the state.
[*]There are 203 cities in this book, 30 of which have higher than average home prices. We have estimated taxes for a tier of higher home values (and omitted the lowest tier) for these 30 cities. The city with the lowest tax burden for an income/home value combination is given the #1 rating; the higher the rating, the higher the total tax burden.

Income	Home Value	Property Tax & Other Fees	Personal Property Tax & Auto Fees	Sales Tax	Local Income Tax	State Income Tax[†]	Total Tax Burden	Rank[*]
TUCSON								
$30,000	$125,000	$1,498	$563	$1,020	-	($50)	$3,031	122 of 173
	150,000	1,762	563	1,020	-	(50)	3,295	112 of 173
	175,000	2,026	563	1,020	-	(50)	3,559	105 of 173
$60,000	$150,000	$1,762	$563	$1,792	-	$594	$4,711	141 of 203
	225,000	2,553	563	1,792	-	594	5,502	120 of 203
	300,000	3,344	563	1,792	-	594	6,293	116 of 203
$90,000	$225,000	$2,553	$563	$2,227	-	$1,440	$6,783	109 of 203
	375,000	4,257	563	2,227	-	1,440	8,487	98 of 203
	525,000	6,096	563	2,227	-	1,440	10,326	101 of 203

[†]The increased excise tax credit is issued as a refund by the state.
[*]There are 203 cities in this book, 30 of which have higher than average home prices. We have estimated taxes for a tier of higher home values (and omitted the lowest tier) for these 30 cities. The city with the lowest tax burden for an income/home value combination is given the #1 rating; the higher the rating, the higher the total tax burden.

Continued from page 15

District area of Phoenix, the property tax rate is .097414 including the state aid to education deduction for all homeowners. There is a $520 cap on the amount of state aid given. Homes are assessed at 10% of market value. Property tax does not cover garbage pickup.

In the Paradise Valley Unified School District area, there is a personal property tax rate of .097414. Personal property is assessed at 10% of MSRP. Items subject to the tax include mobile homes. We've assumed our couples do not own any of the items subject to personal property tax.

Prescott

Prescott has no local income tax but does levy a sales tax.

Most purchases are taxed at a rate of 8.35%. Major consumer categories taxed at a different rate include: groceries, which are taxed at a rate of 2%. Major consumer categories that are exempt from sales tax include: drugs and medical services.

In tax area 0120 of Prescott, the property tax rate is .065357 including the state aid to education deduction for all homeowners. There is a $520 cap on the amount of state aid given. Homes are assessed at 10% of market value. Property tax does not cover garbage pickup.

In tax area 0120 of Prescott, there is a personal property tax rate of .065357. Personal property is assessed at 10% of MSRP. Items subject to the tax include mobile homes. We've assumed our couples do not own any of the items

subject to personal property tax.

Scottsdale

Scottsdale has no local income tax but does levy a sales tax.

Most purchases are taxed at a rate of 7.95%. Major consumer categories taxed at a different rate include: groceries, which are taxed at a rate of 1.65%. Major consumer categories that are exempt from sales tax include: drugs and medical services.

Within the city limits of Scottsdale in the Scottsdale school district, the property tax rate is .07302 including the state aid to education deduction for all homeowners. There is a $520 cap on the amount of state aid given. Homes are assessed at 10% of market value. Property tax does not cover garbage pickup.

Within Scottsdale city limits in the Scottsdale school district, there is a personal property tax rate of .07302. Personal property is assessed at 10% of MSRP. Items subject to the tax include mobile homes. We've assumed our couples do not own any of the items subject to personal property tax.

Sedona

Sedona has no local income tax but does levy a sales tax.

Most purchases are taxed at a rate of 9.35% in Sedona in Yavapai County. Some parts of Sedona are in Coconino County and have a tax rate of 9.725%. Most of Sedona is located in Yavapai County. Major consumer categories taxed at a different rate include: none. Major consumer cate-

gories that are exempt from sales tax include: groceries, drugs and medical services.

Within the city limits of Sedona, the property tax rate is .076245 including the state aid to education deduction for all homeowners. There is a $520 cap on the amount of state aid given. Homes are assessed at 10% of market value. Property tax does not cover garbage pickup.

Within the city limits of Sedona, there is a personal property tax rate of .076245. Personal property is assessed at 10% of MSRP. Items subject to the tax include mobile homes. We've assumed our couples do not own any of the items subject to personal property tax.

Sierra Vista

Sierra Vista has no local income tax but does levy a sales tax.

Most purchases are taxed at a rate of 7.85%. Major consumer categories taxed at a different rate include: groceries, drugs and medical services, which are taxed at a rate of 1.5%, and food away from home, which is taxed at a rate of 8.7%. Major consumer categories that are exempt from sales tax include: none.

In tax area 6830 of Sierra Vista, the property tax rate is .08577 including the state aid to education deduction for all homeowners. There is a $520 cap on the amount of state aid given. Homes are valued at approximately 80% of market value and then assessed at 10% of that value. Property tax does not cover garbage pickup.

In tax area 6830 of Sierra Vista, there

18 *America's Best Low-Tax Retirement Towns*

is a personal property tax rate of .08577. Personal property is assessed at 10% of MSRP. Items subject to the tax include mobile homes. We've assumed our couples do not own any of the items subject to personal property tax.

Tucson

Tucson has no local income tax but does levy a sales tax.

Most purchases are taxed at a rate of 8.1%. Major consumer categories taxed at a different rate: none. Major consumer categories that are exempt from sales tax include: groceries, drugs and medical services.

In tax area 0150 of Tucson, the property tax rate is .131827 including the state aid to education deduction for all homeowners. There is a $520 cap on the amount of state aid given. Homes are valued at approximately 80% of market value and then assessed at 10% of that value. Property tax does not cover garbage pickup.

In tax area 0150 of Tucson, there is a personal property tax rate of .131827. Personal property is assessed at 10% of MSRP. Items subject to the tax include mobile homes. We've assumed our couples do not own any of the items subject to personal property tax.

• Arizona's Top Retirement Towns •

Casa Grande

Old West meets New West in this high desert community 45 minutes southeast of Phoenix and an hour northwest of Tucson. Marked by a casual living style and geared toward those interested in all types of outdoor activities, Casa Grande is blessed by almost year-round sunshine. It takes its name from the Casa Grande Ruins National Monument, an ancient Hohokam Indian site about 20 miles to the north. It has a historic downtown and is home to Central Arizona College.

Casa Grande appeals to retirees who desire a hot, dry climate combined with all the attributes of the perfect haven — small-town feeling, access to higher education and friendly, diverse neighbors. The sunsets are dazzling, and interstate highways provide easy access to the amenities of Phoenix and Tucson.

Arizona's multicultural history enriches everything from attractions to food and architecture. Festivals draw great turnouts. Among the celebrations: the annual Fiddler's Bluegrass Jamboree, the state chili cook-off, the December Electric Light Parade and the O'Odham Tash Festival in February. There's outlet shopping, and golfing and tennis can be enjoyed year-round.

Neal Buckner retired from the real estate market and moved here from northern Colorado in 1999. "My wife and I took a vacation in our motor home and liked it (here) so well that we stayed for one and a half months. This seemed the perfect place for us," he says. After buying a few homes to renovate and sell, he decided to work full time again in real estate while also

playing in a softball league. "There's so much to do — volunteer activities, the college, hiking in the desert, playing tennis, golf or softball, you name it," he says.

Population: 34,554

Climate: High Low
January 67 37
July 105 76

Cost of living: Below average

Housing cost: The median sales price of single-family homes during the first half of 2007 was $192,990, according to data from the Yost Realty Group RE/MAX Casa Grande.

Information: Greater Casa Grande Chamber of Commerce, (800) 916-1515 or www.casagrandechamber.org.

Flagstaff

Anyone who has been to the Grand Canyon or listened to the lyrics of "Route 66" likely has heard about Flagstaff. As one of the towns on the old Route 66 (now Interstate 40) cross-country "Mother Road" and the nearest major city to the canyon's South Rim, Flagstaff for years has been a popular destination for tourists heading west. Retirees also are discovering Flag, as residents call it.

Flagstaff began as a railroad town on the main line between Albuquerque and the West Coast. It gets its name from a tall Ponderosa pine that was made into a flagpole in 1876 to celebrate the nation's centennial. One of the world's largest pine forests still encompasses the city, and awe-inspiring views of the San Francisco Peaks give Flagstaff spectacular year-round beauty. That's especially true in the fall when aspen groves turn the mountains a brilliant gold.

Northern Arizona University, which enrolls about 18,000 students, contributes to the town's decidedly laid-back lifestyle. The revitalized downtown is an active scene, with shops, restaurants and bars.

At an elevation of about 7,000 feet, Flagstaff may not appeal to retirees who can't tolerate high altitudes. But the clean air, four distinct seasons and proximity to the great outdoors continue to draw new residents. Summers are delightful, and winters are cold and often snowy, affording skiing and other sports. The climate encourages year-round activities such as hiking, camping, mountain biking, hunting and fishing.

As the cultural hub of northern Arizona, Flagstaff also boasts a symphony orchestra and the Museum of Northern Arizona, which hosts an annual exhibition of Zuni, Hopi, Navajo and Hispanic artists. The Lowell Observatory, whose telescopes discovered the planet Pluto, takes advantage of Flagstaff's clear night skies.

Flagstaff's biggest drawback is comparatively expensive housing, driven up in part by the pricey second homes of Phoenix residents.

Population: 58,213

Climate: High Low
January 43 16
July 82 50

Cost of living: Above average

Housing cost: The median sales price of homes in Flagstaff during the first half of 2007 was $378,950, according to the Northern Arizona Association of Realtors.

Information: Flagstaff Chamber of Commerce, (928) 774-4505 or www.flagstaffchamber.com.

Green Valley

For many, Green Valley fulfills the dream of paradise in retirement — sunny weather year-round, lots of activities, lower costs. At about 2,900 feet altitude, it enjoys a somewhat cooler climate than the bigger cities of Tucson and Phoenix.

Though part of the Spanish land grant, Green Valley is a comparatively new settlement — and mainly a retirement community, with dozens of neighborhoods that are age-restricted, though there are some that allow families with young children. For those who would like to be able to get around their community by walking or using a golf cart to shopping, recreation and cultural events, Green Valley definitely is an option.

With a population of about 26,500, Green Valley has a phenomenal array of activities — more than 200 active clubs, 23 heated pools, nine golf courses, historic attractions and excellent hiking and bird-watching.

The nearby historic Spanish settlement of Tubac has become an artist's colony, and the much-photographed 1700s San Xavier del Bac Mission is close. Mexico is minutes to the south and Tucson, with its many city amenities, a half-hour to the north. Winter weather is great — warm days, chilly nights — and summer is, well, hot, but not as hot as other parts of Arizona.

Population: 26,500, dropping to 17,000 in summer.

Climate:

	High	Low
January	65	32
July	96	66

Cost of living: Below average

Housing cost: The median sales price of a single-family home during the first half of 2007 was $182,000, according to the Green Valley Association of Realtors.

Information: Green Valley Chamber of Commerce, (800) 858-5872 or www.greenvalleyazchamber.com.

Lake Havasu City

Someone said, "Build a bridge and they will come," or words to that effect, inspiring the late Robert P. McCulloch, chainsaw, oil and building tycoon, to buy the London Bridge (price tag: $2.46 million) and have it shipped stone by stone to the desert, where it was reconstructed.

The final stone was put into place in October 1971. The British put the bridge up for sale because it could no longer handle London's mounting traffic, but it does quite well at Lake Havasu, thank you, quickly becoming Arizona's second-most-visited tourist attraction after the Grand Canyon.

If the idea of altering riverbeds and moving historical landmarks seems somewhat distasteful in this age of ecological concern, rest assured it was done with impressive decorum. Lake Havasu City itself has developed into a model community with expansive home sites, an airport, schools, campgrounds, riding trails, golf courses and marinas, all set under the dramatic backdrop of the Chemehuevi and Mohave mountains.

Because of the bridge, and British touches throughout the town, visitors are quickly caught up in the flavor of merry old England. A hearty dose of the Old American West is also thrown in: beans, chili and barbecue sauce, along with nearby ghost towns and American Indian reservations.

Lake Havasu City is 200 miles northwest of Phoenix and is named after a 45-mile-long lake on the Colorado River. Driving there, you'll pass picturesque towns that unfold like storybook pop-ups — a cowboy here, a pickup truck there, towering saguaros silhouetted against the sky's purple glow. Arizona's desert landscape is one of stark, compelling beauty.

Population: 56,355

Climate:

	High	Low
January	65	40
July	105	80

Cost of living: Above average

Housing cost: The median sales price for a single-family home in the first half of 2007 was $285,000, according to data from Advanced Real Estate in Lake Havasu City.

Information: Lake Havasu City Convention and Visitors Bureau, (800) 242-8278 or www.golakehavasu.com.

Phoenix

If your passion is sports, Phoenix is your town. This sprawling desert metropolis, now the fifth-largest city in the United States, is home to the Phoenix Suns (basketball), the Arizona Cardinals (football), the Phoenix Coyotes (hockey), the Arizona Diamondbacks (baseball), the Arizona Rattlers (arena football) and the Phoenix Mercury (women's basketball). It has spring training, the FBR Open (golf) and the Phoenix International Raceway, plus numerous sports activities at Arizona State University.

Those who like an active urban scene — and not just sporting events — thrive here. Phoenix has the Arizona Opera, the Phoenix Symphony, the Herberger Theater Center, the Arizona Theatre Company, Ballet Arizona, the Phoenix Theatre and the famous Heard Museum, devoted to American Indian art and artifacts.

Along with its glass and silvery glitz and a futuristic skyline, Phoenix has restaurants so trendy that they're kept on speed dials and more golf than you can shake a 9-iron at. And, you can shop until you drop in the area's fashionable malls.

Want to escape the roar of the crowd? Head to Scottsdale's Camelback Mountain, the valley's best-known landmark, where several challenging trails await the hiker's boots.

Douglas N. Cook, retired Penn State professor of theater arts and former artistic director of the Utah Shakespearean Festival, and his actress wife, Joan, have enjoyed their retirement in Phoenix. "We've survived the hot summers and have enjoyed the falls, winters and springs but find the care of an acre of citrus and other fruit trees a complication in retirement benefits," Douglas says.

Population: 1,512,986

Climate:

	High	Low
January	65	43
July	104	81

Cost of living: Average

Housing cost: For the third quarter of 2007, the median sales price was $219,595 for existing homes and $303,340 for new homes, according to the Arizona Real Estate Center at Arizona State University.

Information: Greater Phoenix Convention and Visitors Bureau, (877) 225-5749 or www.visitphoenix.com. Greater Phoenix Chamber of Commerce, (602) 254-

Prescott

Prescott has long been a magnet for retirees, and the reasons are obvious: a mile-high climate that offers respite from Arizona's fierce summer heat, wonderful scenery, great golf courses and exceptional opportunities for outdoor recreation.

Add to all that the Yavapai Regional Medical Center, which has been listed on the tally of 100 top hospitals by Solucient, an information-products company serving the health-care industry. Solucient has the nation's largest health-care database and does an annual rating of hospitals. Yavapai Regional opened a second hospital in 2006 and also has an outpatient center in the area. The extensive medical services include cardiac care and wellness programs.

Prescott's historical and cultural heritage and its many amenities have made it a favorite of list-makers. It has been named one of the top 10 Western towns, one of the 100 best art towns and one of the National Trust for Historic Preservation's Dozen Distinctive Destinations in America.

The town, which has more than 700 buildings on the National Register of Historic Places, is virtually an architectural museum. The Old West is represented by Whiskey Row on the west side of Courthouse Square. The Palace Saloon there once served legends of the West such as Doc Holliday and Wyatt Earp. Prescott also has beautifully restored Victorian homes.

Numerous galleries and several performance venues highlight the art scene, and three museums are devoted to local history, Indian culture and Western art. A half-dozen or so golf courses in the area and hundreds of miles of trails through the Prescott National Forest offer plenty of outdoor recreation. For gambling fans, there's casino action.

Prescott is about equidistant from Phoenix and Flagstaff and is not far from the resort community of Sedona.

Population: 41,528

Climate:

	High	Low
January	52	25
July	90	61

Cost of living: Above average

Housing cost: The median sales price of single-family homes during the third quarter of 2007 was $245,000, according to the Prescott Area Association of Realtors.

Information: Prescott Chamber of Commerce, (800) 266-7534 or www.prescott.org.

Tucson

The city definitely has shed its dusty bravado to emerge as one of the Southwest's leading art centers, with galleries spreading like wildfire. That's no surprise, as Tucson also supports its own professional theater, dance company, opera and symphony. Its 27 major museums include the spectacular Center for Creative Photography, home of the permanent collections of Richard Avedon, Ansel Adams, Edward Weston and Philippe Halsman.

Tucson always has something going on — rodeos, gem shows, mariachi festivals, charity benefits, art walks, sports and nightlife. Students at the University of Arizona add youthfulness to the mix. Residents can enjoy an exhilarating hike in the desert and still make the opening reception at Medicine Man Gallery, the chic art spot in town.

Tucson has several pockets of pure desert landscape. Tohono Chul Park is an oasis of desert plants and trees, and the Tucson Botanical Gardens, virtually in the middle of town, has a fascinating butterfly exhibit each year. At DeGrazia Gallery in the Sun, the desert landscape is as stunning as the paintings on the wall.

"We didn't discover Tucson. It more or less discovered us," says Liz Davies, who moved to Tucson in 1999 from Washington, DC, with her husband, Bob, a retired naval officer. It was love at first sight for both, who are in their mid-60s. "How can you not like this weather?" asks Liz, who describes Tucson as a large city with a small-town flavor.

Population: 518,956

Climate:

	High	Low
January	64	38
July	99	74

Cost of living: Average

Housing cost: The median sales price of single-family homes during the first nine months of 2007 was $220,290, according to the Tucson Association of Realtors.

Information: Metropolitan Tucson Convention and Visitors Bureau, (800) 638-8350 or www.visittucson.org. Tucson Metropolitan Chamber of Commerce, (520) 792-1212 or www.tucsonchamber.org.

ARKANSAS

Arkansas has a state income tax and a state sales tax.

The state income tax rate is graduated from 1% to 7% depending upon income bracket. For married couples filing jointly, the rates are 1% on the first $3,599 of taxable income; 2.5% on the next $3,600 of taxable income; 3.5% on the next $3,600 of taxable income; 4.5% on the next $7,200 of taxable income; 6% on the next $12,100 of taxable income; and 7% on taxable income above $30,099.

In calculating the tax, there is no deduction for federal income tax paid. Federal, state and private pensions are not exempt. However, up to $6,000 of pension income is exempt per person. Social Security benefits are exempt. There is a standard deduction of $4,000 from Arkansas adjusted gross income for married couples filing jointly. There is a $44 credit against tax for married couples filing jointly and a $22 credit against tax per person age 65 or older.

Major tax credits or rebates include: credit for income taxes paid to other states and a special credit of $22 per person for those age 65 or older who don't claim the $6,000 per year pension exemption. Our couples qualify for the special $22 credit.

The state sales tax rate is 6%, but local governments can add to this amount.

Our couples relocating to the cities listed below must pay a registration fee of $25 per automobile, a title fee of $5 per automobile and miscellaneous fees of $3 per automobile at the time of registration. Thereafter, on an annual basis, our couples will pay a registration fee and miscellaneous fees, per automobile.

Fayetteville

Fayetteville has no local income tax but does levy a sales tax.

Most purchases are taxed at a rate of 9%. Major consumer categories taxed at a different rate include: food away from home, which is taxed at a rate of 11%. Major consumer categories that are exempt from sales tax include: drugs and medical services.

Within the city limits of Fayetteville, the property tax rate is .0527. Homes are assessed at 20% of market value. There is a homestead property tax credit of $300 for homeowners. In 2007, the property tax credit increased from $300 to $350. Property tax does not cover garbage pickup.

Within the city limits of Fayetteville, the personal property tax rate is .0527. Personal property is assessed at 20% of market value. Items subject to the tax include automobiles, trucks, recreational vehicles, boats and motors, motorcycles, all-terrain vehicles and livestock.

Hot Springs

Hot Springs has no local income tax but does levy a sales tax.

Most purchases are taxed at a rate of 8.5%. Major consumer categories taxed at a different rate include: food away from home, which is taxed at a rate of 11.5%. Major consumer categories that are exempt from sales tax include: drugs and medical services.

In the Hot Springs School District, the property tax rate is .0414. Homes are assessed at 20% of market value. There is a homestead property tax credit of $300 for homeowners. In 2007, the property tax credit increased from $300 to $350. Property tax does not cover garbage pickup.

In the Hot Springs School District, the personal property tax rate is .0414. Personal property is assessed at 20% of market value. Items subject to the tax include automobiles, trucks, recreational vehicles, boats and motors, motorcycles, all-terrain vehicles and livestock.

Little Rock

Little Rock has no local income tax but does levy a sales tax.

Most purchases are taxed at a rate of 7.5%. Major consumer categories taxed at a different rate include: food away from home, which is taxed at a rate of 9.5%. Major consumer categories that are exempt from sales tax include: drugs and medical services.

In the northern area of the Little Rock School District, the property tax rate is .069. Homes are assessed at 20% of market value. There is a homestead property tax credit of $300 for homeowners. In 2007, the property tax credit increased from $300 to $350. Property tax does not cover garbage pickup.

In the northern area of the Little Rock School District, the personal property tax rate is .069. Personal property is assessed at 20% of market value. Items subject to the tax include automobiles, trucks, recreational vehicles, boats and motors, motorcycles, all-terrain vehicles and livestock.

Mountain Home

Mountain Home has no local income tax but does levy a sales tax.

Most purchases are taxed at a rate of 8%. Major consumer categories taxed at a different rate include: food away from home, which is taxed at a rate of 9%. Major consumer categories that are exempt from sales tax include: drugs and medical services.

Within the city limits of Mountain Home, the property tax rate is .0377. Homes are assessed at 20% of market value. There is a homestead property tax credit of $300 for homeowners. In 2007, the property tax credit increased from $300 to $350. Property tax does not cover garbage pickup.

Within the city limits of Mountain Home, the personal property tax rate is .0377. Personal property is assessed at 20% of market value. Items subject to the tax include automobiles, trucks, recreational vehicles, boats and motors, motorcycles, all-terrain vehicles and livestock.

ARKANSAS TAX TABLE

Instructions

1. Find the Income in the far left column closest to your anticipated retirement income.
2. Find the Home Value closest to the value of the home where you will live in retirement.
3. Follow that row to your estimated Total Tax Burden at age 65 and beyond.

Income	Home Value	Property Tax & Other Fees	Personal Property Tax & Auto Fees	Sales Tax	Local Income Tax	State Income Tax	Total Tax Burden	Rank*
FAYETTEVILLE								
$30,000	$125,000	$1,198	$383	$1,390	-	-	$2,971	117 of 173
	150,000	1,461	383	1,390	-	-	3,234	105 of 173
	175,000	1,725	383	1,390	-	-	3,498	102 of 173
$60,000	$150,000	$1,461	$383	$2,362	-	$1,129	$5,335	170 of 203
	225,000	2,252	383	2,362	-	1,129	6,126	154 of 203
	300,000	3,042	383	2,362	-	1,129	6,916	137 of 203
$90,000	$225,000	$2,252	$383	$2,900	-	$3,095	$8,630	178 of 203
	375,000	3,833	383	2,900	-	3,095	10,211	156 of 203
	525,000	5,414	383	2,900	-	3,095	11,792	138 of 203
HOT SPRINGS								
$30,000	$125,000	$915	$313	$1,328	-	-	$2,556	73 of 173
	150,000	1,122	313	1,328	-	-	2,763	70 of 173
	175,000	1,329	313	1,328	-	-	2,970	69 of 173
$60,000	$150,000	$1,122	$313	$2,259	-	$1,129	$4,823	149 of 203
	225,000	1,743	313	2,259	-	1,129	5,444	118 of 203
	300,000	2,364	313	2,259	-	1,129	6,065	105 of 203
$90,000	$225,000	$1,743	$313	$2,774	-	$3,095	$7,925	156 of 203
	375,000	2,985	313	2,774	-	3,095	9,167	122 of 203
	525,000	4,227	313	2,774	-	3,095	10,409	104 of 203
LITTLE ROCK								
$30,000	$125,000	$1,605	$484	$1,163	-	-	$3,252	143 of 173
	150,000	1,950	484	1,163	-	-	3,597	132 of 173
	175,000	2,295	484	1,163	-	-	3,942	127 of 173
$60,000	$150,000	$1,950	$484	$1,977	-	$1,129	$5,540	181 of 203
	225,000	2,985	484	1,977	-	1,129	6,575	169 of 203
	300,000	4,020	484	1,977	-	1,129	7,610	159 of 203
$90,000	$225,000	$2,985	$484	$2,428	-	$3,095	$8,992	182 of 203
	375,000	5,055	484	2,428	-	3,095	11,062	172 of 203
	525,000	7,125	484	2,428	-	3,095	13,132	160 of 203
MOUNTAIN HOME								
$30,000	$125,000	$823	$290	$1,210	-	-	$2,323	55 of 173
	150,000	1,011	290	1,210	-	-	2,511	52 of 173
	175,000	1,200	290	1,210	-	-	2,700	50 of 173
$60,000	$150,000	$1,011	$290	$2,055	-	$1,129	$4,485	126 of 203
	225,000	1,577	290	2,055	-	1,129	5,051	97 of 203
	300,000	2,142	290	2,055	-	1,129	5,616	81 of 203
$90,000	$225,000	$1,577	$290	$2,522	-	$3,095	$7,484	142 of 203
	375,000	2,708	290	2,522	-	3,095	8,615	105 of 203
	525,000	3,839	290	2,522	-	3,095	9,746	81 of 203

*There are 203 cities in this book, 30 of which have higher than average home prices. We have estimated taxes for a tier of higher home values (and omitted the lowest tier) for these 30 cities. The city with the lowest tax burden for an income/home value combination is given the #1 rating; the higher the rating, the higher the total tax burden.

Hot Springs

Tucked into rolling mountains and surrounded by lakes and forests, Hot Springs has a national park smack in the middle of town. Hot Springs National Park was established in 1832 to protect the springs that flowed from Hot Springs Mountain. The park now also protects eight turn-of-the-century bathhouses.

The national park's 47 hot springs and their watershed provide 26 miles of hiking trails, a campground, picnic areas and scenic drives. With the Ouachita Mountains in their backyard, Hot Springs' residents have year-round recreational opportunities — tournament-quality bass and trout fishing, horseback riding, camping, boating and water skiing. Lake Hamilton and Lake Catherine border the city, and Lake Ouachita is 30 minutes away.

Some of the area's crystal mines are open to the public, a boon for rock hounds. Several spas and hotels still offer thermal baths, a soothing end to a day filled with outdoor activities.

Many housing areas take advantage of the lakes and mountains. Hot Springs Village is the country's largest gated community, covering 26,000 acres in the woods north of Hot Springs. It has some of the state's top-ranked golf courses, 11 lakes, nine country clubs, additional activity centers and miles of hiking trails.

Boat slips are available at Grand Point Bay, an apartment community on Lake Hamilton. Diamondhead, a 2,350-acre gated community on Lake Catherine, offers golf, tennis, a marina and boat slips.

Population: 38,468

Climate:

	High	Low
January	50	33
July	91	72

Cost of living: Below average

Housing cost: The average cost of a single-family home in Garland County for the first half of 2007 was $164,333, according to the Arkansas Association of Realtors.

Information: Greater Hot Springs Chamber of Commerce, (800) 467-4636 or www.hotspringschamber.com.

CALIFORNIA

California has a state income tax and a state sales tax.

The state income tax is graduated from 1% to 9.3% depending upon income bracket. For married couples filing jointly, the rates are 1% on the first $13,244 of taxable income; 2% on the next $18,152 of taxable income; 4% on the next $18,156 of taxable income; 6% on the next $19,236 of taxable income; 8% on the next $18,146 of taxable income; and 9.3% on taxable income above $86,934.

In calculating the tax, there is no deduction for federal income tax paid. Federal, state and private pensions are not exempt. Social Security benefits are exempt. There is a $6,820 standard deduction from California adjusted gross income for married couples filing jointly. There is a $182 credit against tax for married couples filing jointly and a $91 credit per person age 65 or older.

Major tax credits or rebates include: homeowner property tax assistance. Our couples do not qualify for this program.

The state sales tax rate is 7.25%, but local governments can add to this rate.

In calculating property tax, some homes in California are subject to a Mello-Roos Community Facilities District tax. These taxes are levied to finance public improvements and services when no other source of money is available and can substantially increase the property taxes due. We have assumed that our couples do not reside in such a district.

Our couples relocating to the cities listed below must pay a vehicle license fee based on the depreciated value of each automobile. The license fee is $156 for the Explorer and $116 for the Camry. Our couples must also pay a registration fee of $31 per automobile, a non-resident fee of $17 per automobile, a California Highway Patrol fee of $9 per automobile, county fees ranging from $3 to $8 per automobile, and miscellaneous fees of $4 per automobile at the time of registration. Thereafter, on an annual basis, our couples will pay a vehicle license fee, a registration fee, a California Highway Patrol fee, county fees, miscellaneous fees and a $12 smog abatement fee, per automobile.

○ **Tax Heavens:** None
Ψ **Tax Hells:** None
Top Retirement Towns: Carlsbad, Palm Desert, San Diego

Carlsbad

Carlsbad has no local income tax but does levy a sales tax.

Most purchases are taxed at a rate of 7.75%. Major consumer categories taxed at a different rate: none. Major consumer categories that are exempt from sales tax include: groceries, drugs and medical services.

Within tax rate area 09000 of Carlsbad, the property tax rate is .0101846. Homes are assessed at either 100% of market value or purchase price plus 2% per year, whichever is lower. There is a homeowner's exemption of $7,000 off assessed value of the home available to all homeowners meeting residency requirements. Additional fees and special assessments are approximately $65 per year. There are also assistance and tax postponement programs available based on age and income eligibility. Property tax does not cover garbage pickup.

Carlsbad has a personal property tax rate of .0102067 within tax rate area 09000. Personal property is assessed at 100% of market value. Items subject to the tax include mobile homes, boats and aircraft. We've assumed our couples do not own any of the items subject to these taxes.

Los Angeles

Los Angeles has no local income tax but does levy a sales tax.

Most purchases are taxed at a rate of 8.25%. Major consumer categories taxed at a different rate: none. Major consumer categories that are exempt from sales tax include: groceries, drugs and medical services.

Within the city limits of Los Angeles, the property tax rate is .0125. Homes are assessed at either 100% of market value or purchase price plus 2% per year, whichever is lower. There is a homeowner's exemption of $7,000 off assessed value of the home available to all homeowners meeting residency

requirements. There are also assistance and tax postponement programs available based on age and income eligibility. There is a stormwater pollution abatement charge of approximately $24 per year. Property tax includes garbage pickup.

Los Angeles has a personal property tax rate of .0125 within the city limits. Personal property is assessed at 100% of market or appraised value. Items subject to the tax include mobile homes, boats and aircraft. We've assumed our couples do not own any of the items subject to these taxes.

Ojai

Ojai has no local income tax and does not levy an additional sales tax.

Most purchases are taxed at the state rate of 7.25%. Major consumer categories taxed at a different rate: none. Major consumer categories that are exempt from sales tax include: groceries, drugs and medical services.

Within the city limits of Ojai, the property tax rate is .01054329. Homes are assessed at either 100% of market value or purchase price plus 2% per year, whichever is lower. There is a homeowner's exemption of $7,000 off assessed value of the home available to all homeowners meeting residency requirements. There are also assistance and tax postponement programs available based on age and income eligibility. Additional fees and special assessments are approximately $612 per year. Property tax does not cover garbage pickup.

Ojai has a personal property tax rate of .01. Personal property is assessed at 100% of market value. Items subject to the tax include mobile homes, boats and aircraft. We've assumed our couples do not own any of the items subject to these taxes.

Palm Desert

Palm Desert has no local income tax but does levy a sales tax.

Most purchases are taxed at a rate of 7.75%. Major consumer categories taxed at a different rate: none. Major consumer categories that are exempt from sales tax include: groceries, drugs
Continued on page 28

CALIFORNIA TAX TABLE

Instructions

1. Find the Income in the far left column closest to your anticipated retirement income.
2. Find the Home Value closest to the value of the home where you will live in retirement.
3. Follow that row to your estimated Total Tax Burden at age 65 and beyond.

Income	Home Value	Property Tax & Other Fees	Personal Property Tax & Auto Fees	Sales Tax	Local Income Tax	State Income Tax	Total Tax Burden	Rank*
CARLSBAD								
$60,000	$150,000	$1,701	$360	$1,714	-	$155	$3,930	74 of 203
	225,000	2,465	360	1,714	-	155	4,694	69 of 203
	300,000	3,229	360	1,714	-	155	5,458	73 of 203
$90,000	$225,000	$2,465	$360	$2,131	-	$1,474	$6,430	94 of 203
	375,000	3,993	360	2,131	-	1,474	7,958	78 of 203
	525,000	5,521	360	2,131	-	1,474	9,486	74 of 203
	$600,000	$6,284	$360	$2,131	-	$1,474	$10,249	16 of 30
	750,000	7,812	360	2,131	-	1,474	11,777	15 of 30
	900,000	9,340	360	2,131	-	1,474	13,305	15 of 30
LOS ANGELES								
$60,000	$150,000	$1,812	$368	$1,825	-	$155	$4,160	95 of 203
	225,000	2,749	368	1,825	-	155	5,097	99 of 203
	300,000	3,687	368	1,825	-	155	6,035	103 of 203
$90,000	$225,000	$2,749	$368	$2,268	-	$1,474	$6,859	115 of 203
	375,000	4,624	368	2,268	-	1,474	8,734	109 of 203
	525,000	6,499	368	2,268	-	1,474	10,609	111 of 203
	$600,000	$7,437	$368	$2,268	-	$1,474	$11,547	27 of 30
	750,000	9,312	368	2,268	-	1,474	13,422	26 of 30
	900,000	11,187	368	2,268	-	1,474	15,297	26 of 30
OJAI								
$60,000	$150,000	$2,300	$366	$1,604	-	$155	$4,425	121 of 203
	225,000	3,090	366	1,604	-	155	5,215	111 of 203
	300,000	3,881	366	1,604	-	155	6,006	99 of 203
$90,000	$225,000	$3,090	$366	$1,993	-	$1,474	$6,923	123 of 203
	375,000	4,672	366	1,993	-	1,474	8,505	99 of 203
	525,000	6,253	366	1,993	-	1,474	10,086	92 of 203
	$600,000	$7,044	$366	$1,993	-	$1,474	$10,877	21 of 30
	750,000	8,626	366	1,993	-	1,474	12,459	22 of 30
	900,000	10,207	366	1,993	-	1,474	14,040	20 of 30
PALM DESERT								
$60,000	$150,000	$2,112	$370	$1,714	-	$155	$4,351	116 of 203
	225,000	2,950	370	1,714	-	155	5,189	106 of 203
	300,000	3,787	370	1,714	-	155	6,026	102 of 203
$90,000	$225,000	$2,950	$370	$2,131	-	$1,474	$6,925	124 of 203
	375,000	4,625	370	2,131	-	1,474	8,600	103 of 203
	525,000	6,300	370	2,131	-	1,474	10,275	100 of 203
	$600,000	$7,138	$370	$2,131	-	$1,474	$11,113	25 of 30
	750,000	8,813	370	2,131	-	1,474	12,788	23 of 30
	900,000	10,489	370	2,131	-	1,474	14,464	22 of 30
PASO ROBLES								
$60,000	$150,000	$1,956	$366	$1,604	-	$155	$4,081	88 of 203
	225,000	2,779	366	1,604	-	155	4,904	89 of 203
	300,000	3,602	366	1,604	-	155	5,727	87 of 203

Income	Home Value	Property Tax & Other Fees	Personal Property Tax & Auto Fees	Sales Tax	Local Income Tax	State Income Tax	Total Tax Burden	Rank*
PASO ROBLES continued								
$90,000	$225,000	$2,779	$366	$1,993	-	$1,474	$6,612	101 of 203
	375,000	4,425	366	1,993	-	1,474	8,258	90 of 203
	525,000	6,072	366	1,993	-	1,474	9,905	85 of 203
	$600,000	$6,895	$366	$1,993	-	$1,474	$10,728	19 of 30
	750,000	8,541	366	1,993	-	1,474	12,374	18 of 30
	900,000	10,187	366	1,993	-	1,474	14,020	19 of 30
SAN DIEGO								
$60,000	$150,000	$1,656	$360	$1,714	-	$155	$3,885	68 of 203
	225,000	2,407	360	1,714	-	155	4,636	64 of 203
	300,000	3,159	360	1,714	-	155	5,388	71 of 203
$90,000	$225,000	$2,407	$360	$2,131	-	$1,474	$6,372	92 of 203
	375,000	3,911	360	2,131	-	1,474	7,876	77 of 203
	525,000	5,415	360	2,131	-	1,474	9,380	68 of 203
	$600,000	$6,167	$360	$2,131	-	$1,474	$10,132	15 of 30
	750,000	7,671	360	2,131	-	1,474	11,636	14 of 30
	900,000	9,174	360	2,131	-	1,474	13,139	14 of 30
SAN FRANCISCO								
$60,000	$150,000	$1,803	$368	$1,880	-	$155	$4,206	103 of 203
	225,000	2,654	368	1,880	-	155	5,057	98 of 203
	300,000	3,506	368	1,880	-	155	5,909	94 of 203
$90,000	$225,000	$2,654	$368	$2,337	-	$1,474	$6,833	114 of 203
	375,000	4,357	368	2,337	-	1,474	8,536	101 of 203
	525,000	6,059	368	2,337	-	1,474	10,238	98 of 203
	$600,000	$6,911	$368	$2,337	-	$1,474	$11,090	24 of 30
	750,000	8,613	368	2,337	-	1,474	12,792	24 of 30
	900,000	10,316	368	2,337	-	1,474	14,495	23 of 30
SAN JUAN CAPISTRANO								
$60,000	$150,000	$1,691	$370	$1,714	-	$155	$3,930	74 of 203
	225,000	2,475	370	1,714	-	155	4,714	72 of 203
	300,000	3,258	370	1,714	-	155	5,497	75 of 203
$90,000	$225,000	$2,475	$370	$2,131	-	$1,474	$6,450	97 of 203
	375,000	4,042	370	2,131	-	1,474	8,017	82 of 203
	525,000	5,609	370	2,131	-	1,474	9,584	77 of 203
	$600,000	$6,393	$370	$2,131	-	$1,474	$10,368	18 of 30
	750,000	7,960	370	2,131	-	1,474	11,935	16 of 30
	900,000	9,527	370	2,131	-	1,474	13,502	16 of 30
TEMECULA								
$60,000	$150,000	$1,885	$370	$1,714	-	$155	$4,124	91 of 203
	225,000	2,708	370	1,714	-	155	4,947	93 of 203
	300,000	3,530	370	1,714	-	155	5,769	91 of 203
$90,000	$225,000	$2,708	$370	$2,131	-	$1,474	$6,683	105 of 203
	375,000	4,352	370	2,131	-	1,474	8,327	91 of 203
	525,000	5,997	370	2,131	-	1,474	9,972	89 of 203
	$600,000	$6,819	$370	$2,131	-	$1,474	$10,794	20 of 30
	750,000	8,464	370	2,131	-	1,474	12,439	20 of 30
	900,000	10,109	370	2,131	-	1,474	14,084	21 of 30

*There are 203 cities in this book, 30 of which have higher than average home prices. We have estimated taxes for a tier of higher home values (and omitted the lowest tier) for these 30 cities. The city with the lowest tax burden for an income/home value combination is given the #1 rating; the higher the rating, the higher the total tax burden.

Continued from page 25
and medical services.

In Palm Desert, property taxes can vary by parcel, but one property tax rate is .0111688. Homes are assessed at either 100% of market value or purchase price plus 2% per year, whichever is lower. There is a homeowner's exemption of $7,000 off assessed value of the home available to all homeowners meeting residency requirements. There are also assistance and tax postponement programs available based on age and income eligibility. Additional fees and special assessments are approximately $335 per year. Property tax does not cover garbage pickup

Palm Desert has a personal property tax rate of approximately .0125 with the exact rate depending upon location. Personal property is assessed at 100% of market value. Items subject to the tax include mobile homes, boats and aircraft. We've assumed our couples do not own any of the items subject to these taxes.

Paso Robles

Paso Robles has no local income tax and does not levy an additional sales tax.

Most purchases are taxed at the state rate of 7.25%. Major consumer categories taxed at a different rate: none. Major consumer categories that are exempt from sales tax include: groceries, drugs and medical services.

Within the city limits of Paso Robles, the property tax rate is .0109741. Homes are assessed at 100% of market value or purchase price plus 2% per year, whichever is lower. There is a homeowner's exemption of $7,000 off assessed value of the home available to all homeowners meeting residency requirements. There are also assistance and tax postponement programs available based on age and income eligibility. Additional fees and special assessments are approximately $207 per year. Property tax does not cover garbage pickup.

Paso Robles has a personal property tax rate of .0111042. Personal property is assessed at 100% of market value. Items subject to the tax include mobile homes, boats and aircraft. We've assumed our couples do not own any of the items subject to these taxes.

San Diego

San Diego has no local income tax but does levy a sales tax.

Most purchases are taxed at a rate of 7.75%. Major consumer categories taxed at a different rate: none. Major consumer categories that are exempt from sales tax include: groceries, drugs and medical services.

Within tax rate area 08001 of San Diego, the property tax rate is .010025. Homes are assessed at either 100% of market value or purchase price plus 2% per year, whichever is lower. There is a homeowner's exemption of $7,000 off assessed value of the home available to all homeowners meeting residency requirements. There are also assistance and tax postponement programs available based on age and income eligibility. Additional fees and special assessments are approximately $31 per year. There is a storm drain fee of approximately $11 per year. Property tax does not cover garbage pickup.

San Diego has a personal property tax rate of .011125 within tax rate area 08001. Personal property is assessed at 100% of market value. Items subject to the tax include mobile homes, boats and aircraft. We've assumed our couples do not own any of the items subject to these taxes.

San Francisco

San Francisco has no local income tax but does levy a sales tax.

Most purchases are taxed at a rate of 8.5%. Major consumer categories taxed at a different rate: none. Major consumer categories that are exempt from sales tax include: groceries, drugs and medical services.

Within the city limits of San Francisco, the property tax rate is .01135. Homes are assessed at either 100% of market value or purchase price plus 2% per year, whichever is lower. There is a homeowner's exemption of $7,000 off assessed value of the home available to all homeowners meeting residency requirements. There are also assistance and tax postponement programs available based on age and income eligibility. There is an additional San Francisco School District Facilities fee, but seniors can apply to become exempt from it. Property tax does not cover garbage pickup.

San Francisco has a personal proper-

ty tax rate of .01140. Personal property is assessed at 100% of market value. Items subject to the tax include mobile homes, boats and aircraft. We've assumed our couples do not own any of the items subject to these taxes.

San Juan Capistrano

San Juan Capistrano has no local income tax but does levy a sales tax.

Most purchases are taxed at a rate of 7.75%. Major consumer categories taxed at a different rate: none. Major consumer categories that are exempt from sales tax include: groceries, drugs and medical services.

The most common property tax rate in San Juan Capistrano is .0104474. Homes are assessed at either 100% of market value or purchase price plus 2% per year, whichever is lower. There is a homeowner's exemption of $7,000 off assessed value of the home available to all homeowners meeting residency requirements. There are also assistance and tax postponement programs available based on age and income eligibility. Additional fees and special assessments are approximately $17 per year. Some residents may also pay a homeowner's association fee, but not all homes are located in a homeowner's association area so we did not include these fees in our calculations. Property tax does not cover garbage pickup.

The most common personal property tax rate in San Juan Capistrano is .0104738. Personal property is assessed at 100% of market value. Items subject to the tax include mobile homes, boats and aircraft if valued at over $1,350. We've assumed our couples do not own any of the items subject to these taxes.

Temecula

Temecula has no local income tax but does levy a sales tax.

Most purchases are taxed at a rate of 7.75%. Major consumer categories taxed at a different rate: none. Major consumer categories that are exempt from sales tax include: groceries, drugs and medical services.

A common property tax rate in Temecula is .0103649. Homes are assessed at either 100% of market value or purchase price plus 2% per year, whichever is lower. There is a homeowner's exemption of $7,000 off assessed value of the home available to all homeowners meeting residency requirements. There are also assistance and tax postponement programs available based on age and income eligibility. There is a Rancho California water debt fee of $.30 per $100 of assessed land value. Additional assessments and fees total approximately $313 per year. Property tax includes garbage pickup.

Temecula has a personal property tax rate of approximately .0125, with the exact rate depending upon location. Personal property is assessed at 100% of market value. Items subject to the tax include mobile homes, boats and aircraft. We've assumed our couples do not own any of the items subject to these taxes.

• California's Top Retirement Towns •

Carlsbad

If Southern Californians are married to their cars, it's because practically every city here is so spread out that it could take a week to walk from the grocery store to the post office. Carlsbad, with its European-style architecture, historic downtown, small-town friendliness and beautiful beaches, is a happy exception.

Carlsbad started when the railroad came through in the 1880s. Natural springs were discovered that had nearly the same mineral properties as the spa waters in the popular resort town of Karlsbad, Bohemia (now in the Czech Republic). During the early 1900s, Carlsbad, named after the Bohemian town, capitalized on the curative waters and drew many health-minded visitors. A grand spa palace prospered until the 1930s.

Despite its growth, Carlsbad still can call itself "a village by the sea." You can walk to everything in the compact downtown and to the beach, only a couple of blocks away. The historic area is lined with Victorian, Dutch and Bohemian architecture. The visitor center occupies the 1887 Santa Fe railroad depot, among several national historic landmarks.

Carlsbad's seven miles of beaches, backed by high bluffs, are idyllic for walking and shelling, and adjacent to the beaches are several miles of paved paths.

In spring, Carlsbad bursts into a rainbow of colors. From March into May, at The Flower Fields at Carlsbad Ranch, you can roam acres of blooms planted in wide stripes of contrasting colors.

Carlsbad's latest attraction, Legoland, has become a favorite for all ages. Paved pathways wind past replicas of historic cities, mountain ranges, sculpted gardens and historical monuments, all made of little plastic bricks. There's even an area where you can build your own dream retirement home — in miniature, of course.

Population: 92,928

Climate: High Low
January 64 45
July 72 63

Cost of living: Above average

Housing cost: During the first nine months of 2007, the median sales price for detached single-family homes was $773,800 and the median for attached single-family homes was $450,125, according to the North San Diego County Association of Realtors.

Information: Carlsbad Chamber of Commerce, (760) 931-8400 or www.carlsbad.org. Carlsbad Convention and Visitors Bureau, (800) 227-5722 or www.visitcarlsbad.com.

Palm Desert

Palm Desert bills itself as the golf capital of America and, indeed, is the site of numerous nationally known golf and tennis tournaments. Golf carts are permitted to traverse all of the city streets.

Palm Desert seems to have almost as many country clubs as it has residents, and the surrounding Coachella Valley is star-studded. President Dwight D. Eisenhower called Palm Desert home in his later years. On short notice, he was known to pop into a limousine, preceded by another one filled with Secret Service agents, to go visit Palm Springs neighbors. He called on "My Fair Lady" composer Frederick Loewe because he heard Loewe had a fabulous home and wanted to come by for a look.

Even if you don't play golf, you won't be bored in Palm Desert. It offers an active cultural arts scene and enough upscale shopping to rival Rodeo Drive in Beverly Hills. That's not bad for an area once known as Old MacDonald Ranch and used by Gen. George S. Patton to train troops and tank battalions. The restaurants are impressive too, having spawned what's known as "Cal-French" cuisine. The city also is brimming with eye-catching outdoor sculptures, part of an extensive public art program. Free guided tours are given regularly.

Suzy Harvey, 60, moved to Palm Desert with her husband, Wayne, 68, from Whittier, CA. "It was the absolute gorgeous weather 10 months a year that first drew us here, plus the open friendliness of the people," she says. "The city is young enough so that everyone here is here by choice. They're open to new friendships. And, there's a lot of fun things to do."

Population: 47,047

Climate: High Low
January 71 42
July 107 78

Cost of living: Above average

Housing cost: The median sales price of single-family homes during the first half of 2007 was $440,000, according to DataQuick Information Systems based in San Diego.

Information: Palm Desert Chamber of Commerce, (760) 346-6111 or www.pdcc.org.

San Diego

With 70 miles of sandy beaches and a laid-back atmosphere combined with urban amenities, San Diego has something to offer almost any retiree.

The setting, of course, is glorious — on one side the Pacific, on the other the mountains and the desert beyond. Life in San Diego tends to be a bit slower than in other Southern California cities. Though it's California's second-largest city, it's a beach culture and a year-round resort.

Spanish explorers noted San Diego's natural harbor in 1542, and it was finally colonized in the mid 1700s, making it the oldest port on the West Coast. The climate is arguably the best in the United States — very dry with less than 12 inches of rain per year.

The renowned San Diego Zoo and SeaWorld are added attractions for both residents and tourists. The city's cultural centerpiece is Balboa Park, one of the country's best urban parks with more than 10 museums. Highlights include the San Diego Museum of Art, the San Diego Model Railroad Museum and the San Diego Air and Space Museum. The city, however, may be most famous for its splendid sunsets over the Pacific.

Hospitals, educational opportunities and entertainment all rank with the best that a major American city has to offer. San Diego has a broad mix of people but long been known for its conservative bent, in part because of the strong U.S. Navy presence here. And, it's only 16 miles from Mexico, lending an international, multicultural flair.

With dozens of neighborhoods, there's a wide choice in places to live. That said, real estate prices have escalated sharply. Home prices may be lower in San Diego itself than in the metro area, which includes some towns with pricier homes.

Population: 1.3 million

Climate:

	High	Low
January	65	46
July	78	65

Cost of living: Above average

Housing cost: The median sales price during the first half of 2007 was $603,988, according to the California Association of Realtors.

Information: San Diego Convention and Visitors Bureau, (619) 236-1212 or www.sandiego.org.

COLORADO

Colorado has a state income tax and a state sales tax.

The state income tax rate is 4.63% of taxable income.

In calculating the tax, there is no deduction for federal income tax paid. Federal, state and private pensions and Social Security benefits subject to federal tax are not exempt. However, there is an exclusion of up to $24,000 in taxable pension and Social Security benefits for each taxpayer age 65 or older. There is a standard deduction of $12,300 for married couples filing jointly, both age 65 or older. There is also an exemption of $3,300 per person from adjusted gross income.

Major tax credits or rebates include: credit for income taxes paid to other states, which our couples do not qualify for.

The state sales tax rate is 2.9%, but local governments can add to this amount.

Our couples relocating to the cities listed below must pay a personal property tax (ownership tax) based on the year and MSRP of each automobile, which is assessed and collected through the Motor Vehicle Division. Our couples also pay a license fee per automobile based on the weight of each automobile. They must also pay a title fee of $7 per automobile. Prior to registration VIN verification is required. This is performed by a third party for a small fee. The personal property tax is approximately $341 for the Explorer and approximately $255 for the Camry. The license fee is approximately $32 for the Explorer and approximately $30 for the Camry. Thereafter, on an annual basis, our couples will pay a personal property tax and a license fee, per automobile.

Boulder

Boulder has no local income tax but does levy a sales tax.

Most purchases are taxed at a rate of 8.16%. Major consumer categories taxed at a different rate include: food away from home, which is taxed at a rate of 8.31%, and groceries, which are taxed at a rate of 3.41%. Major consumer categories that are exempt from sales tax include: drugs and medical services.

> ○ **Tax Heavens:** None
> ψ **Tax Hells:** None
> **Top Retirement Towns:**
> Colorado Springs, Denver,
> Fort Collins

In tax area 0010 of Boulder, the property tax rate is .073462. Homes are assessed at 7.96% of market value. There is a senior homestead act for homeowners age 65 or older who have lived in their homes for more than 10 years, and a property tax, rent, or heat credit for low-income seniors. Our couples do not qualify for these programs. Property tax does not cover garbage pickup. There is also a storm drainage fee of approximately $79 per year.

Boulder has a personal property tax on automobiles, as discussed above.

Colorado Springs

Colorado Springs has no local income tax but does levy a sales tax.

Most purchases are taxed at a rate of 7.4%. Major consumer categories taxed at a different rate include: none. Major consumer categories that are exempt from sales tax include: groceries, drugs and medical services.

In School District 11 of Colorado Springs, the property tax rate is .056699. Homes are assessed at 7.96% of market value. There is a senior homestead act for homeowners age 65 or older who have lived in their homes for more than 10 years, and a property tax, rent, or heat credit for low-income seniors. Our couples do not qualify for these programs. Property tax does not cover garbage pickup. There is an additional stormwater service fee of approximately $26 per year.

Colorado Springs has a personal property tax on automobiles, as discussed above.

Denver

Denver has a local income tax and a sales tax.

The local income tax (Occupational Privilege Tax) is $6 per month per person. It applies to each person with earned income of at least $500 per month.

Most purchases are taxed at a rate of

7.6%. Major consumer categories taxed at a different rate include: food away from home, which is taxed at a rate of 8.1%. Major consumer categories that are exempt from sales tax include: groceries, drugs and medical services.

Within the city limits of Denver, the property tax rate is .066948. Homes are assessed at 7.96% of market value. There is a senior homestead act for homeowners age 65 or older who have lived in their homes for more than 10 years, and a property tax, rent, or heat credit for low-income seniors. Our couples do not qualify for these programs. Property tax includes garbage pickup. There is an additional storm drain fee of approximately $68 per year.

Denver has a personal property tax on automobiles, as discussed above.

Fort Collins

Fort Collins has no local income tax but does levy a sales tax.

Most purchases are taxed at a rate of 6.7%. Major consumer categories taxed at a different rate include: groceries, which are taxed at a rate of 2.25%. Major consumer categories that are exempt from sales tax include: drugs and medical services.

In tax area 1106 of Fort Collins, the property tax rate is .089731. Homes are assessed at 7.96% of market value. There is a senior homestead act for homeowners age 65 or older who have lived in their homes for more than 10 years, and a property tax, rent, or heat credit for low-income seniors. Our couples do not qualify for these programs. Property tax does not cover garbage pickup. There is also a stormwater fee of approximately $180 per year.

Fort Collins has a personal property tax on automobiles, as discussed above.

Grand Junction

Grand Junction has no local income tax but does levy a sales tax.

Most purchases are taxed at a rate of 7.65%. Major consumer categories taxed at a different rate include: none. Major consumer categories that are exempt from sales tax include: groceries, drugs and medical services.

Within the city limits of Grand

Junction, the property tax rate is .064348. Some residents may pay special assessments depending on location. Homes are assessed at 7.96% of market value. There is a senior homestead act for homeowners age 65 or older who have lived in their homes for more than 10 years, and a property tax, rent, or heat credit for low-income seniors. Our couples do not qualify for these programs. Property tax does not cover garbage pickup.

Grand Junction has a personal property tax on automobiles, as discussed above.

COLORADO TAX TABLE

Instructions

1. Find the Income in the far left column closest to your anticipated retirement income.
2. Find the Home Value closest to the value of the home where you will live in retirement.
3. Follow that row to your estimated Total Tax Burden at age 65 and beyond.

Income	Home Value	Property Tax & Other Fees	Personal Property Tax & Auto Fees	Sales Tax	Local Income Tax	State Income Tax	Total Tax Burden	Rank*
BOULDER								
$30,000	$125,000	$990	$539	$1,116	-	-	$2,645	83 of 173
	150,000	1,136	539	1,116	-	-	2,791	73 of 173
	175,000	1,282	539	1,116	-	-	2,937	65 of 173
$60,000	$150,000	$1,136	$539	$1,930	-	$437	$4,042	84 of 203
	225,000	1,575	539	1,930	-	437	4,481	58 of 203
	300,000	2,013	539	1,930	-	437	4,919	46 of 203
$90,000	$225,000	$1,575	$539	$2,386	-	$1,695	$6,195	83 of 203
	375,000	2,452	539	2,386	-	1,695	7,072	43 of 203
	525,000	3,329	539	2,386	-	1,695	7,949	31 of 203
COLORADO SPRINGS								
$30,000	$125,000	$770	$539	$931	-	-	$2,240	43 of 173
	150,000	883	539	931	-	-	2,353	36 of 173
	175,000	996	539	931	-	-	2,466	33 of 173
$60,000	$150,000	$883	$539	$1,637	-	$437	$3,496	37 of 203
	225,000	1,221	539	1,637	-	437	3,834	20 of 203
	300,000	1,560	539	1,637	-	437	4,173	14 of 203
$90,000	$225,000	$1,221	$539	$2,034	-	$1,695	$5,489	34 of 203
	375,000	1,898	539	2,034	-	1,695	6,166	22 of 203
	525,000	2,575	539	2,034	-	1,695	6,843	16 of 203
DENVER								
$30,000	$125,000	$734	$539	$964	$138	-	$2,375	59 of 173
	150,000	867	539	964	138	-	2,508	51 of 173
	175,000	1,001	539	964	138	-	2,642	46 of 173
$60,000	$150,000	$867	$539	$1,694	$138	$437	$3,675	54 of 203
	225,000	1,267	539	1,694	138	437	4,075	34 of 203
	300,000	1,667	539	1,694	138	437	4,475	27 of 203
$90,000	$225,000	$1,267	$539	$2,105	$138	$1,695	$5,744	51 of 203
	375,000	2,066	539	2,105	138	1,695	6,543	29 of 203
	525,000	2,866	539	2,105	138	1,695	7,343	25 of 203
FORT COLLINS								
$30,000	$125,000	$1,253	$539	$901	-	-	$2,693	91 of 173
	150,000	1,431	539	901	-	-	2,871	80 of 173
	175,000	1,610	539	901	-	-	3,050	78 of 173
$60,000	$150,000	$1,431	$539	$1,562	-	$437	$3,969	79 of 203
	225,000	1,967	539	1,562	-	437	4,505	60 of 203
	300,000	2,503	539	1,562	-	437	5,041	54 of 203

Income	Home Value	Property Tax & Other Fees	Personal Property Tax & Auto Fees	Sales Tax	Local Income Tax	State Income Tax	Total Tax Burden	Rank *
FORT COLLINS continued								
$90,000	$225,000	$1,967	$539	$1,933	-	$1,695	$6,134	76 of 203
	375,000	3,038	539	1,933	-	1,695	7,205	49 of 203
	525,000	4,110	539	1,933	-	1,695	8,277	41 of 203
GRAND JUNCTION								
$30,000	$125,000	$820	$542	$963	-	-	$2,325	56 of 173
	150,000	948	542	963	-	-	2,453	46 of 173
	175,000	1,076	542	963	-	-	2,581	40 of 173
$60,000	$150,000	$948	$542	$1,692	-	$437	$3,619	48 of 203
	225,000	1,332	542	1,692	-	437	4,003	30 of 203
	300,000	1,717	542	1,692	-	437	4,388	24 of 203
$90,000	$225,000	$1,332	$542	$2,103	-	$1,695	$5,672	49 of 203
	375,000	2,101	542	2,103	-	1,695	6,441	26 of 203
	525,000	2,869	542	2,103	-	1,695	7,209	22 of 203

*There are 203 cities in this book, 30 of which have higher than average home prices. We have estimated taxes for a tier of higher home values (and omitted the lowest tier) for these 30 cities. The city with the lowest tax burden for an income/home value combination is given the #1 rating; the higher the rating, the higher the total tax burden.

• Colorado's Top Retirement Towns •

Colorado Springs

This city was made for walking, beginning with its location in the foothills of Pikes Peak, which encompasses expansive alpine tundra and untouched evergreen forest wilderness that reach within a few miles of downtown. In addition, Colorado Springs has city parks that would pass for national parks anywhere else, plus a quaint historic district. Even the weather seems to cooperate for walking, with the sun shining the majority of days.

"The Springs" maintains a small-town feel despite its burgeoning population — it's the second-largest city in Colorado, behind Denver. Old Colorado City, founded in 1859 in a gold rush and the first real town in the region, is now part of Colorado Springs' west side. For a walk back to the Wild West, you'll enjoy strolling along the district's old wooden sidewalks and past the renovated redbrick Victorian office buildings that now house cafes, boutiques and fascinating museums. Don't leave the Colorado Springs Pioneers Museum without seeing its 1903 courtroom, used for many motion pictures and "Perry Mason" TV shows.

Or take a walk around The Broadmoor, a legendary golf and spa resort that ranked as the finest west of the Mississippi during the 1920s and remains highly rated. Visitors are welcome to roam the extensive grounds. For national park-caliber walking, the world-famous Garden of the Gods Park is a local favorite, with miles of trails through its red-rock formations.

Colorado Springs has several colleges, including a campus of the University of Colorado, and it has a number of hospitals providing extensive medical services, including top-ranked cardiac care.

Population: 372,437
Climate: High   Low
January   42   14
July   84   55
Cost of living: Below average
Housing cost: The average sales price of a single-family home during the first nine months of 2007 was $262,174, according to the Pikes Peak Association of Realtors.
Information: Greater Colorado Springs Chamber of Commerce, (719) 635-1551 or www.coloradospringschamber.org.

Denver

Many retirees find the active lifestyle they want in the city where the Plains end and the Rocky Mountains begin. In a scenic setting with a higher altitude and lower humidity, it combines the vibrancy of a major city with easy access to expanses of the great outdoors.

With championship sports, skiing, cultural and educational opportunities, top medical care and 300 days of sunshine, what's not to like?

It's an energetic city where people get outside to enjoy a variety of activities in all seasons. For those who like spectator sports, Denver has the action, with eight major franchises in football, baseball, basketball, hockey, arena football, soccer and lacrosse.

It also can keep enthusiasts of the cultural arts on the go, with a symphony orchestra, opera, ballet and theater, an acclaimed performing arts complex and numerous museums and galleries. Denver's Red Rocks Amphitheatre is famous for its outdoor concerts amid the beauty of the foothills landscape.

The city boasts the nation's largest public park system and numerous recreational trails for biking and walking. Golfers have a choice of about 70 courses in the area, and skiers have world-class slopes within easy reach.

Denver's nightlife is especially popular among singles, particularly in its lower downtown historic area called LoDo, with a cosmopolitan mix of dining, shopping and entertainment.

It's an educational and medical hub. A number of the dozen colleges in the metro area offer enrichment classes, and the city has numerous nationally recognized medical facilities.

Population: 566,974

Climate:

	High	Low
January	43	15
July	88	59

Cost of living: *Slightly above average*

Housing cost: *The median sales price of a single-family home during the second quarter of 2007 was $252,688, according to the Colorado Association of Realtors.*

Information: *Denver Metro Cham-ber of Commerce, (303) 534-8500 or www.den verchamber.org.*

Fort Collins

Perhaps you want to retire where you can hike the Rockies in the morning, cheer cowboys at a rodeo in the afternoon and attend the opera at night, all without leaving city limits. Fort Collins is that place.

Fort Collins nestles where the prairie merges with rolling foothills at 4,979 feet — and that's about as "tropical" as the Rockies get. With lots of winter sun, any snow falling on Fort Collins tends to melt quickly.

Founded as a military post on the Cache La Poudre River, Fort Collins became a civilian settlement in the 1870s with the opening of Colorado State University, now the second-largest in the state. Today, the Wild West meets the 21st century in Fort Collins' Old Town, where boutiques, trendy restaurants, art galleries, museums and microbreweries occupy turn-of-the-century buildings and students with orange hair and multiple piercings enliven the local scene.

Culture cravers will love MOCA, the Museum of Contemporary Art, as well as Lincoln Center, with a symphony, opera, traveling shows from Broadway and a changing art gallery. On the other end of the spectrum, the Larimer County Fairgrounds hosts rodeos and county fairs.

You don't have to venture far to get a workout, with more than 40 parks within city limits, including 23 miles of recreational trails, three city golf courses, a pool and a year-round ice-skating rink. Also the Fort Collins Senior Center provides exercise and wellness classes, a gym, pool, library and community garden.

Horsetooth Mountain Park, with 2,410 acres of woods and meadows, offers a bounty of recreation. One of the state's most celebrated scenic drives goes to the Cache la Poudre Canyon with majestic cliffs and rugged rock formations in dense stands of pine. The Poudre River creates quiet pools for fishing, kayaking and canoeing and raging rapids for rafting. Colorado State University offers continuing education at half price for seniors 60 and older.

Population: 129,467

Climate:

	High	Low
January	42	14
July	86	57

Cost of living: *Average*

Housing cost: *The median sales price of a single-family home for July 2007 was $240,000, according to the Fort Collins Board of Realtors.*

Information: *Fort Collins Area Chamber of Commerce, (970) 482-3746 or www.fc chamber.org.*

CONNECTICUT

Connecticut has a state income tax and a state sales tax.

The state income tax rate is graduated from 3% to 5% depending upon income bracket. For married couples filing jointly, the rates are 3% on the first $20,000 of taxable income and 5% on taxable income above $20,000.

In calculating the tax, there is no deduction for federal income tax paid. Federal, state and private pensions are not exempt. Some Social Security benefits subject to federal tax are not exempt. There is a personal exemption of up to $24,000 from adjusted gross income for married couples filing jointly.

Major tax credits or rebates include: credit for income taxes paid to other states, which our couples do not

> **O Tax Heavens:** None
> **Ψ Tax Hells:** Hartford, New Haven

qualify for; property tax credit of up to $500 of Connecticut income tax liability, which some of our couples qualify for; and personal tax credit against income tax due of up to 75% depending on filing status and income bracket, which our couples do qualify for.

The state sales tax rate is 6%.

Our couples relocating to the cities listed below must pay a registration fee of $75 for two years per automobile, a federal clean air fee of $10 per automobile, a title fee of $25 per automobile, a plate fee of $5 per automobile, a lien fee of $10 per automobile and a $10

administration fee per automobile at the time of registration. Thereafter, every two years, our couples will pay a registration fee and a clean air fee per automobile.

Hartford

Hartford has no local income tax and does not levy an additional sales tax.

Most purchases are taxed at the state rate of 6%. Major consumer categories taxed at a different rate: none. Major consumer categories that are exempt from sales tax include: groceries, drugs and medical services. Clothing costing less than $50 is also exempt.

Within the city limits of Hartford, the property tax rate is .0423. Homes are assessed at 70% of market value. There is a $500 credit against tax for

---

CONNECTICUT TAX TABLE

Instructions

1. Find the Income in the far left column closest to your anticipated retirement income.
2. Find the Home Value closest to the value of the home where you will live in retirement.
3. Follow that row to your estimated Total Tax Burden at age 65 and beyond.

Income	Home Value	Property Tax & Other Fees	Personal Property Tax & Auto Fees	Sales Tax	Local Income Tax	State Income Tax	Total Tax Burden	Rank*	
HARTFORD									
$30,000	$125,000	$2,951	$1,493	$755	-	-	$5,199	171 of 173	Ψ
	150,000	3,692	1,493	755	-	-	5,940	171 of 173	Ψ
	175,000	4,432	1,493	755	-	-	6,680	171 of 173	Ψ
$60,000	$150,000	$4,442	$1,493	$1,327	-	-	$7,262	199 of 203	Ψ
	225,000	6,662	1,493	1,327	-	-	9,482	199 of 203	Ψ
	300,000	8,883	1,493	1,327	-	-	11,703	199 of 203	Ψ
$90,000	$225,000	$6,662	$1,493	$1,649	-	$2,394	$12,198	202 of 203	Ψ
	375,000	11,104	1,493	1,649	-	2,394	16,640	200 of 203	Ψ
	525,000	15,545	1,493	1,649	-	2,394	21,081	200 of 203	Ψ
NEW HAVEN									
$30,000	$125,000	$3,443	$1,002	$755	-	-	$5,200	172 of 173	Ψ
	150,000	4,182	1,002	755	-	-	5,939	170 of 173	Ψ
	175,000	4,921	1,002	755	-	-	6,678	170 of 173	Ψ
$60,000	$150,000	$4,432	$1,002	$1,327	-	-	$6,761	196 of 203	Ψ
	225,000	6,648	1,002	1,327	-	-	8,977	197 of 203	Ψ
	300,000	8,864	1,002	1,327	-	-	11,193	197 of 203	Ψ
$90,000	$225,000	$6,648	$1,002	$1,649	-	$2,394	$11,693	199 of 203	Ψ
	375,000	11,080	1,002	1,649	-	2,394	16,125	199 of 203	Ψ
	525,000	15,512	1,002	1,649	-	2,394	20,557	198 of 203	Ψ

*There are 203 cities in this book, 30 of which have higher than average home prices. We have estimated taxes for a tier of higher home values (and omitted the lowest tier) for these 30 cities. The city with the lowest tax burden for an income/home value combination is given the #1 rating; the higher the rating, the higher the total tax burden.

homeowners age 65 or older with gross income of $37,200 or less. There is an additional homeowner's tax credit of 10% off tax bills, from $150 up to $250, for married couples with at least one spouse age 65 or over and gross income of $35,300 or less. Property tax includes garbage pickup.

The personal property tax rate in Hartford is .06482. Personal property is assessed at 70% of market value. Items subject to the tax include motor vehicles.

New Haven

New Haven has no local income tax and does not levy an additional sales tax.

Most purchases are taxed at the state rate of 6%. Major consumer categories taxed at a different rate: none. Major consumer categories that are exempt from sales tax include: groceries, drugs and medical services. Clothing costing less than $50 is also exempt.

Within the city limits of New Haven, the property tax rate is .04221. Homes are assessed at 70% of market value. There is a homeowner's tax credit of 10% off tax bills, from $150 up to $250, for married couples with at least one spouse age 65 or over and with gross income of $35,300 or less. Property tax includes garbage pickup.

The personal property tax rate in New Haven is .04221. Personal property is assessed at 70% of market value. Items subject to the tax include motor vehicles.

DELAWARE

Delaware has a state income tax but no state sales tax.

The state income tax rate is graduated from zero to 5.95% depending upon income bracket. For married couples filing jointly, no tax is paid on the first $2,000 of taxable income; after that, the rates are 2.2% on the next $3,000 of taxable income; 3.9% on the next $5,000 of taxable income; 4.8% on the next $10,000 of taxable income; 5.2% on the next $5,000 of taxable income; 5.5% on the next $35,000 of taxable income; and 5.95% on taxable income above $60,000.

In calculating the tax, there is no deduction for federal income tax paid. Federal, state and private pensions are not exempt, but there is an exclusion of up to $12,500 from pension income per person age 60 or over and up to $2,000 per person under age 60. Social Security benefits are exempt. There is a $6,500 standard deduction from Delaware

adjusted gross income for married couples filing jointly and an additional exemption of $2,500 from adjusted gross income per person age 65 or older.

Major tax credits or rebates include: credit for income taxes paid to other states, which our couples do not qualify for, as well as personal credit of $110 per person against tax and an additional $110 credit against tax per person age 60 or older, both of which our couples do qualify for.

Wilmington

Wilmington has a local income tax but does not levy a sales tax.

The local income tax rate is 1.25% of wages, salaries and self-employ-ment income.

In the Red Clay School District, the property tax rate is .030537. Homes are assessed at 100% of 1983 market value. We estimated the taxable value for our various home values based on the taxable values of actual homes with similar market values. There are various exemptions off the different components of the property tax. Property tax includes garbage pickup.

Wilmington has no personal property tax for individuals.

Our couples relocating to Wilmington must pay a vehicle document fee per automobile based on the NADA trade-in value of the automobile. The document fee is $737 for the Explorer and $550 for the Camry. Our couples must also pay a $25 title fee per automobile and a $20 registration fee per automobile at the time of registration. Thereafter, on an annual basis, our couples will pay a registration fee per automobile.

DELAWARE TAX TABLE

Instructions

1. Find the Income in the far left column closest to your anticipated retirement income.
2. Find the Home Value closest to the value of the home where you will live in retirement.
3. Follow that row to your estimated Total Tax Burden at age 65 and beyond.

Income	Home Value	Property Tax & Other Fees	Personal Property Tax & Auto Fees	Sales Tax	Local Income Tax	State Income Tax	Total Tax Burden	Rank*
WILMINGTON								
$30,000	$125,000	-	$40	-	$71	-	$111	1 of 173 ○
	150,000	5	40	-	71	-	116	1 of 173 ○
	175,000	61	40	-	71	-	172	1 of 173 ○
$60,000	$150,000	$718	$40	-	$298	$149	$1,205	2 of 203 ○
	225,000	973	40	-	298	149	1,460	2 of 203 ○
	300,000	1,137	40	-	298	149	1,624	1 of 203 ○
$90,000	$225,000	$1,056	$40	-	$581	$1,603	$3,280	2 of 203 ○
	375,000	1,958	40	-	581	1,603	4,182	2 of 203 ○
	525,000	2,416	40	-	581	1,603	4,640	1 of 203 ○

*There are 203 cities in this book, 30 of which have higher than average home prices. We have estimated taxes for a tier of higher home values (and omitted the lowest tier) for these 30 cities. The city with the lowest tax burden for an income/home value combination is given the #1 rating; the higher the rating, the higher the total tax burden.

Wilmington

Centrally located on Interstate 95 about midway between Washington, DC, and New York City, Wilmington boasts its own riches of cultural opportunities along with easy access to urban centers in the Northeast and a variety of recreation. It's convenient to the beaches of Delaware, Maryland and New Jersey and to hiking and skiing in the Poconos in Pennsylvania.

It's a comparatively small city, with about 73,000 residents, but has world-class museums along with opera, theater, championship golf, Thoroughbred racing, plentiful tennis courts and a great restaurant scene. World-renowned Winterthur Museum & Country Estate is located outside the city, in a beautiful pastoral setting. The former home of Henry Francis du Pont has what's considered the premier collection of antiques and Americana displayed in its period rooms and galleries.

A port city, Wilmington has a revitalized riverfront boasting a landscaped river walk with shops. Its restored Amtrak station is busy with trains headed north and south. Wilmington has advanced medical care, and there are several colleges in the area. It's only about 30 miles from Philadelphia, with its multiple amenities and international air service. History buffs have fertile ground to plow. This community was established in 1638 by Scandinavian settlers.

Although the cost of living is slightly above the national average, Delaware has tax-free shopping, dining and entertainment.

Population: 72,862

Climate:

	High	Low
January	38	22
July	85	66

Cost of living: Above average

Housing cost: The median sales price of single-family homes during the first 10 months of 2007 in New Castle County was $235,000, according to the New Castle County Board of Realtors.

Information: Greater Wilmington Convention and Visitors Bureau, (800) 489-6664 or www.wilmcvb.org.

FLORIDA

Florida has no state income tax but does have a state sales tax.

The state sales tax rate is 6%, but local governments can add to this amount.

Our couples relocating to the cities below must pay a registration fee of $191 for the Explorer and $181 for the Camry. This includes an initial registration fee of $100 per automobile, a new license plate fee of $10 per automobile, a title fee for an out-of-state vehicle of $33 per automobile, a fee for recording a lien of $2 per automobile and a registration fee of $46 for the Explorer and $36 for the Camry. Thereafter, on an annual basis, our couples will pay a registration fee per automobile.

Boca Raton

Boca Raton has no local income tax but does levy a sales tax.

Most purchases are taxed at a rate of 6.5%. Major consumer categories taxed at a different rate: none. Major consumer categories that are exempt from sales tax include: drugs, groceries and medical services.

Within the city limits of Boca Raton, the property tax rate is .0194062. Homes are assessed at 100% of market value. There is a homestead exemption of $25,000 off assessed value available to all homeowners who own and reside on the property on January 1 of the tax year. There is an additional senior citizen exemption of $20,000 off assessed value for the county component of property tax if federal adjusted gross income is $23,463 or less in the prior calendar year. Property tax does not cover garbage pickup. There is also a fire assessment fee of $20 per year.

The personal property tax rate is the same as the real property tax rate. Personal property is assessed at 100% of market value. Items subject to the tax include mobile homes on rented land that are not registered as real property and mobile home attachments. We've assumed our couples do not own any items subject to the tax.

Bradenton

Bradenton has no local income tax but does levy a sales tax.

Most purchases are taxed at a rate of

○ Tax Heavens: Key West, Naples
Ψ Tax Hells: None
Top Retirement Towns: DeLand, Gainesville, Jacksonville, Mount Dora, Ocala, Ormond Beach Pensacola, St. Augustine, Sarasota Venice

---

6.5%. Major consumer categories taxed at a different rate: none. Major consumer categories that are exempt from sales tax include: drugs, groceries and medical services.

Within the city limits of Bradenton, the property tax rate is .0206071. Homes are assessed at 100% of market value. There is a homestead exemption of $25,000 off assessed value available to all homeowners who own and reside on the property on January 1 of the tax year. There is an additional senior citizen exemption of $20,000 off assessed value for the county component of property tax if federal adjusted gross income is $23,463 or less in the prior calendar year. Property tax does not cover garbage pickup.

The personal property tax rate is the same as the real property tax rate. Personal property is assessed at 100% of market value. Items subject to the tax include mobile homes on rented land that are not registered as real property and mobile home attachments. We've assumed our couples do not own any items subject to the tax.

Celebration

Celebration has no local income tax but does levy a sales tax.

Most purchases are taxed at a rate of 7%. Major consumer categories taxed at a different rate: none. Major consumer categories that are exempt from sales tax include: drugs, groceries and medical services.

For residents living in Celebration, the property tax rate is .0158777. Homes are assessed at 100% of market value. There is a homestead exemption of $25,000 off assessed value available to all homeowners who own and reside on the property on January 1 of the tax year. There is an additional senior citizen exemption of $25,000

---

off assessed value for the county component of property tax if federal adjusted gross income is $23,463 or less in the prior calendar year. There is a maintenance fee of approximately $439 per year, which includes garbage disposal, and a debt fee that varies by location of approximately $613 per year. In addition, all homeowners in Celebration are subject to a homeowners association fee of approximately $790 per year.

The personal property tax rate is the same as the real property tax rate. Personal property is assessed at 100% of market value. Items subject to the tax include mobile homes on rented land that are not registered as real property and mobile home attachments. We've assumed our couples do not own any items subject to the tax.

Dade City

Dade City has no local income tax but does levy a sales tax.

Most purchases are taxed at a rate of 7%. Major consumer categories taxed at a different rate: none. Major consumer categories that are exempt from sales tax include: drugs, groceries and medical services.

In District 10DC of Dade City, the property tax rate is .0231839. Homes are assessed at 100% of market value. There is a homestead exemption of $25,000 off assessed value available to all homeowners who own and reside on the property on January 1 of the tax year. Property tax does not cover garbage pickup.

The personal property tax rate is the same as the real property tax rate. Personal property is assessed at 100% of market value. Items subject to the tax include mobile homes on rented land that are not registered as real property and mobile home attachments. We've assumed our couples do not own any items subject to the tax.

DeLand

DeLand has no local income tax but does levy a sales tax.

Most purchases are taxed at a rate of 6.5%. Major consumer categories taxed at a different rate: none. Major con-

Continued on page 46

FLORIDA TAX TABLE

Instructions

1. Find the Income in the far left column closest to your anticipated retirement income.
2. Find the Home Value closest to the value of the home where you will live in retirement.
3. Follow that row to your estimated Total Tax Burden at age 65 and beyond.

Income	Home Value	Property Tax & Other Fees	Personal Property Tax & Auto Fees	Sales Tax	Local Income Tax	State Income Tax	Total Tax Burden	Rank*
BOCA RATON								
$60,000	$150,000	$2,626	$81	$1,438	-	-	$4,145	93 of 203
	225,000	4,081	81	1,438	-	-	5,600	128 of 203
	300,000	5,537	81	1,438	-	-	7,056	143 of 203
$90,000	$225,000	$4,081	$81	$1,787	-	-	$5,949	61 of 203
	375,000	6,992	81	1,787	-	-	8,860	113 of 203
	525,000	9,903	81	1,787	-	-	11,771	135 of 203
	$600,000	$11,359	$81	$1,787	-	-	$13,227	29 of 30
	750,000	14,270	81	1,787	-	-	16,138	29 of 30
	900,000	17,180	81	1,787	-	-	19,048	29 of 30
BRADENTON								
$30,000	$125,000	$2,091	$81	$818	-	-	$2,990	118 of 173
	150,000	2,606	81	818	-	-	3,505	126 of 173
	175,000	3,121	81	818	-	-	4,020	131 of 173
$60,000	$150,000	$2,756	$81	$1,438	-	-	$4,275	108 of 203
	225,000	4,301	81	1,438	-	-	5,820	139 of 203
	300,000	5,847	81	1,438	-	-	7,366	152 of 203
$90,000	$225,000	$4,301	$81	$1,787	-	-	$6,169	80 of 203
	375,000	7,392	81	1,787	-	-	9,260	127 of 203
	525,000	10,484	81	1,787	-	-	12,352	146 of 203
CELEBRATION								
$60,000	$150,000	$3,827	$81	$1,548	-	-	$5,456	175 of 203
	225,000	5,018	81	1,548	-	-	6,647	171 of 203
	300,000	6,208	81	1,548	-	-	7,837	162 of 203
$90,000	$225,000	$5,018	$81	$1,924	-	-	$7,023	127 of 203
	375,000	7,399	81	1,924	-	-	9,404	134 of 203
	525,000	9,781	81	1,924	-	-	11,786	136 of 203
	$600,000	$10,972	$81	$1,924	-	-	$12,977	28 of 30
	750,000	13,353	81	1,924	-	-	15,358	28 of 30
	900,000	15,735	81	1,924	-	-	17,740	28 of 30
DADE CITY								
$30,000	$125,000	$2,498	$81	$881	-	-	$3,460	149 of 173
	150,000	3,078	81	881	-	-	4,040	153 of 173
	175,000	3,658	81	881	-	-	4,620	154 of 173
$60,000	$150,000	$3,078	$81	$1,548	-	-	$4,707	140 of 203
	225,000	4,817	81	1,548	-	-	6,446	163 of 203
	300,000	6,556	81	1,548	-	-	8,185	167 of 203
$90,000	$225,000	$4,817	$81	$1,924	-	-	$6,822	112 of 203
	375,000	8,294	81	1,924	-	-	10,299	160 of 203
	525,000	11,772	81	1,924	-	-	13,777	167 of 203
DELAND								
$30,000	$125,000	$1,968	$81	$818	-	-	$2,867	103 of 173
	150,000	2,477	81	818	-	-	3,376	116 of 173
	175,000	2,986	81	818	-	-	3,885	122 of 173
$60,000	$150,000	$2,750	$81	$1,438	-	-	$4,269	107 of 203
	225,000	4,278	81	1,438	-	-	5,797	137 of 203
	300,000	5,805	81	1,438	-	-	7,324	150 of 203

Income	Home Value	Property Tax & Other Fees	Personal Property Tax & Auto Fees	Sales Tax	Local Income Tax	State Income Tax	Total Tax Burden	Rank*
DELAND continued								
$90,000	$225,000	$4,278	$81	$1,787	-	-	$6,146	77 of 203
	375,000	7,333	81	1,787	-	-	9,201	124 of 203
	525,000	10,388	81	1,787	-	-	12,256	144 of 203
FORT LAUDERDALE								
$30,000	$125,000	$2,229	$81	$755	-	-	$3,065	125 of 173
	150,000	2,779	81	755	-	-	3,615	133 of 173
	175,000	3,329	81	755	-	-	4,165	135 of 173
$60,000	$150,000	$3,058	$81	$1,327	-	-	$4,466	125 of 203
	225,000	4,707	81	1,327	-	-	6,115	152 of 203
	300,000	6,357	81	1,327	-	-	7,765	160 of 203
$90,000	$225,000	$4,707	$81	$1,649	-	-	$6,437	95 of 203
	375,000	8,006	81	1,649	-	-	9,736	142 of 203
	525,000	11,305	81	1,649	-	-	13,035	158 of 203
GAINESVILLE								
$30,000	$125,000	$2,289	$81	$787	-	-	$3,157	133 of 173
	150,000	2,903	81	787	-	-	3,771	143 of 173
	175,000	3,518	81	787	-	-	4,386	147 of 173
$60,000	$150,000	$3,253	$81	$1,382	-	-	$4,716	142 of 203
	225,000	5,097	81	1,382	-	-	6,560	167 of 203
	300,000	6,941	81	1,382	-	-	8,404	175 of 203
$90,000	$225,000	$5,097	$81	$1,718	-	-	$6,896	120 of 203
	375,000	8,784	81	1,718	-	-	10,583	167 of 203
	525,000	12,472	81	1,718	-	-	14,271	176 of 203
JACKSONVILLE								
$30,000	$125,000	$1,577	$81	$881	-	-	$2,539	72 of 173
	150,000	2,032	81	881	-	-	2,994	88 of 173
	175,000	2,486	81	881	-	-	3,448	96 of 173
$60,000	$150,000	$2,273	$81	$1,548	-	-	$3,902	69 of 203
	225,000	3,637	81	1,548	-	-	5,266	114 of 203
	300,000	5,000	81	1,548	-	-	6,629	128 of 203
$90,000	$225,000	$3,637	$81	$1,924	-	-	$5,642	46 of 203
	375,000	6,364	81	1,924	-	-	8,369	93 of 203
	525,000	9,091	81	1,924	-	-	11,096	124 of 203
JUPITER								
$30,000	$125,000	$2,070	$81	$818	-	-	$2,969	115 of 173
	150,000	2,558	81	818	-	-	3,457	122 of 173
	175,000	3,046	81	818	-	-	3,945	128 of 173
$60,000	$150,000	$2,670	$81	$1,438	-	-	$4,189	101 of 203
	225,000	4,134	81	1,438	-	-	5,653	129 of 203
	300,000	5,598	81	1,438	-	-	7,117	146 of 203
$90,000	$225,000	$4,134	$81	$1,787	-	-	$6,002	67 of 203
	375,000	7,063	81	1,787	-	-	8,931	117 of 203
	525,000	9,992	81	1,787	-	-	11,860	139 of 203
KEY WEST								
$60,000	$150,000	$1,327	$81	$1,659	-	-	$3,067	15 of 203
	225,000	2,015	81	1,659	-	-	3,755	18 of 203
	300,000	2,703	81	1,659	-	-	4,443	26 of 203

*There are 203 cities in this book, 30 of which have higher than average home prices. We have estimated taxes for a tier of higher home values (and omitted the lowest tier) for these 30 cities. The city with the lowest tax burden for an income/home value combination is given the #1 rating; the higher the rating, the higher the total tax burden.

Income	Home Value	Property Tax & Other Fees	Personal Property Tax & Auto Fees	Sales Tax	Local Income Tax	State Income Tax	Total Tax Burden	Rank*
KEY WEST continued								
$90,000	$225,000	$2,015	$81	$2,062	-	-	$4,158	8 of 203 O
	375,000	3,390	81	2,062	-	-	5,533	11 of 203
	525,000	4,766	81	2,062	-	-	6,909	17 of 203
	$600,000	$5,454	$81	$2,062	-	-	$7,597	7 of 30
	750,000	6,830	81	2,062	-	-	8,973	7 of 30
	900,000	8,206	81	2,062	-	-	10,349	7 of 30
LAKELAND								
$30,000	$125,000	$1,982	$81	$881	-	-	$2,944	114 of 173
	150,000	2,501	81	881	-	-	3,463	124 of 173
	175,000	3,020	81	881	-	-	3,982	130 of 173
$60,000	$150,000	$2,798	$81	$1,548	-	-	$4,427	122 of 203
	225,000	4,355	81	1,548	-	-	5,984	147 of 203
	300,000	5,911	81	1,548	-	-	7,540	157 of 203
$90,000	$225,000	$4,355	$81	$1,924	-	-	$6,360	91 of 203
	375,000	7,468	81	1,924	-	-	9,473	136 of 203
	525,000	10,581	81	1,924	-	-	12,586	151 of 203
LEESBURG								
$30,000	$125,000	$2,070	$81	$881	-	-	$3,032	123 of 173
	150,000	2,579	81	881	-	-	3,541	127 of 173
	175,000	3,087	81	881	-	-	4,049	132 of 173
$60,000	$150,000	$2,722	$81	$1,548	-	-	$4,351	116 of 203
	225,000	4,248	81	1,548	-	-	5,877	143 of 203
	300,000	5,773	81	1,548	-	-	7,402	153 of 203
$90,000	$225,000	$4,248	$81	$1,924	-	-	$6,253	86 of 203
	375,000	7,299	81	1,924	-	-	9,304	129 of 203
	525,000	10,349	81	1,924	-	-	12,354	147 of 203
LONGBOAT KEY								
$60,000	$150,000	$1,949	$81	$1,548	-	-	$3,578	44 of 203
	225,000	3,011	81	1,548	-	-	4,640	66 of 203
	300,000	4,072	81	1,548	-	-	5,701	86 of 203
$90,000	$225,000	$3,011	$81	$1,924	-	-	$5,016	22 of 203
	375,000	5,134	81	1,924	-	-	7,139	45 of 203
	525,000	7,257	81	1,924	-	-	9,262	66 of 203
	$600,000	$8,318	$81	$1,924	-	-	$10,323	17 of 30
	750,000	10,441	81	1,924	-	-	12,446	21 of 30
	900,000	12,564	81	1,924	-	-	14,569	24 of 30
MIAMI								
$30,000	$125,000	$2,260	$81	$881	-	-	$3,222	140 of 173
	150,000	2,876	81	881	-	-	3,838	145 of 173
	175,000	3,492	81	881	-	-	4,454	151 of 173
$60,000	$150,000	$3,261	$81	$1,548	-	-	$4,890	152 of 203
	225,000	5,109	81	1,548	-	-	6,738	173 of 203
	300,000	6,957	81	1,548	-	-	8,586	179 of 203
$90,000	$225,000	$5,109	$81	$1,924	-	-	$7,114	128 of 203
	375,000	8,806	81	1,924	-	-	10,811	171 of 203
	525,000	12,502	81	1,924	-	-	14,507	178 of 203
MOUNT DORA								
$30,000	$125,000	$2,135	$81	$881	-	-	$3,097	127 of 173
	150,000	2,681	81	881	-	-	3,643	135 of 173
	175,000	3,226	81	881	-	-	4,188	138 of 173
$60,000	$150,000	$2,974	$81	$1,548	-	-	$4,603	133 of 203
	225,000	4,610	81	1,548	-	-	6,239	155 of 203
	300,000	6,246	81	1,548	-	-	7,875	163 of 203

Income	Home Value	Property Tax & Other Fees	Personal Property Tax & Auto Fees	Sales Tax	Local Income Tax	State Income Tax	Total Tax Burden	Rank*
MOUNT DORA continued								
$90,000	$225,000	$4,610	$81	$1,924	-	-	$6,615	102 of 203
	375,000	7,882	81	1,924	-	-	9,887	148 of 203
	525,000	11,154	81	1,924	-	-	13,159	161 of 203
NAPLES								
$60,000	$150,000	$1,654	$81	$1,327	-	-	$3,062	14 of 203
	225,000	2,510	81	1,327	-	-	3,918	23 of 203
	300,000	3,366	81	1,327	-	-	4,774	38 of 203
$90,000	$225,000	$2,510	$81	$1,649	-	-	$4,240	10 of 203 ○
	375,000	4,222	81	1,649	-	-	5,952	17 of 203
	525,000	5,934	81	1,649	-	-	7,664	28 of 203
	$600,000	$6,790	$81	$1,649	-	-	$8,520	8 of 30
	750,000	8,502	81	1,649	-	-	10,232	9 of 30
	900,000	10,213	81	1,649	-	-	11,943	11 of 30
NORTH FORT MYERS								
$30,000	$125,000	$1,819	$81	$755	-	-	$2,655	88 of 173
	150,000	2,229	81	755	-	-	3,065	96 of 173
	175,000	2,639	81	755	-	-	3,475	101 of 173
$60,000	$150,000	$2,229	$81	$1,327	-	-	$3,637	51 of 203
	225,000	3,459	81	1,327	-	-	4,867	85 of 203
	300,000	4,688	81	1,327	-	-	6,096	108 of 203
$90,000	$225,000	$3,459	$81	$1,649	-	-	$5,189	26 of 203
	375,000	5,918	81	1,649	-	-	7,648	69 of 203
	525,000	8,377	81	1,649	-	-	10,107	94 of 203
OCALA								
$30,000	$125,000	$2,098	$81	$818	-	-	$2,997	119 of 173
	150,000	2,562	81	818	-	-	3,461	123 of 173
	175,000	3,027	81	818	-	-	3,926	125 of 173
$60,000	$150,000	$2,562	$81	$1,438	-	-	$4,081	88 of 203
	225,000	3,955	81	1,438	-	-	5,474	119 of 203
	300,000	5,349	81	1,438	-	-	6,868	136 of 203
$90,000	$225,000	$3,955	$81	$1,787	-	-	$5,823	54 of 203
	375,000	6,742	81	1,787	-	-	8,610	104 of 203
	525,000	9,529	81	1,787	-	-	11,397	129 of 203
ORLANDO								
$30,000	$125,000	$1,900	$81	$818	-	-	$2,799	100 of 173
	150,000	2,372	81	818	-	-	3,271	108 of 173
	175,000	2,845	81	818	-	-	3,744	115 of 173
$60,000	$150,000	$2,644	$81	$1,438	-	-	$4,163	96 of 203
	225,000	4,063	81	1,438	-	-	5,582	126 of 203
	300,000	5,482	81	1,438	-	-	7,001	140 of 203
$90,000	$225,000	$4,063	$81	$1,787	-	-	$5,931	59 of 203
	375,000	6,901	81	1,787	-	-	8,769	110 of 203
	525,000	9,739	81	1,787	-	-	11,607	130 of 203
ORMOND BEACH								
$30,000	$125,000	$2,071	$81	$818	-	-	$2,970	116 of 173
	150,000	2,577	81	818	-	-	3,476	125 of 173
	175,000	3,082	81	818	-	-	3,981	129 of 173

*There are 203 cities in this book, 30 of which have higher than average home prices. We have estimated taxes for a tier of higher home values (and omitted the lowest tier) for these 30 cities. The city with the lowest tax burden for an income/home value combination is given the #1 rating; the higher the rating, the higher the total tax burden.

Income	Home Value	Property Tax & Other Fees	Personal Property Tax & Auto Fees	Sales Tax	Local Income Tax	State Income Tax	Total Tax Burden	Rank*
ORMOND BEACH continued								
$60,000	$150,000	$2,809	$81	$1,438	-	-	$4,328	115 of 203
	225,000	4,325	81	1,438	-	-	5,844	140 of 203
	300,000	5,841	81	1,438	-	-	7,360	151 of 203
$90,000	$225,000	$4,325	$81	$1,787	-	-	$6,193	82 of 203
	375,000	7,357	81	1,787	-	-	9,225	126 of 203
	525,000	10,389	81	1,787	-	-	12,257	145 of 203
PALM COAST								
$30,000	$125,000	$1,692	$81	$881	-	-	$2,654	87 of 173
	150,000	2,102	81	881	-	-	3,064	95 of 173
	175,000	2,512	81	881	-	-	3,474	100 of 173
$60,000	$150,000	$2,302	$81	$1,548	-	-	$3,931	76 of 203
	225,000	3,532	81	1,548	-	-	5,161	105 of 203
	300,000	4,762	81	1,548	-	-	6,391	120 of 203
$90,000	$225,000	$3,532	$81	$1,924	-	-	$5,537	37 of 203
	375,000	5,992	81	1,924	-	-	7,997	81 of 203
	525,000	8,453	81	1,924	-	-	10,458	107 of 203
PENSACOLA								
$30,000	$125,000	$2,077	$81	$944	-	-	$3,102	129 of 173
	150,000	2,619	81	944	-	-	3,644	136 of 173
	175,000	3,160	81	944	-	-	4,185	137 of 173
$60,000	$150,000	$2,961	$81	$1,659	-	-	$4,701	139 of 203
	225,000	4,585	81	1,659	-	-	6,325	160 of 203
	300,000	6,209	81	1,659	-	-	7,949	166 of 203
$90,000	$225,000	$4,585	$81	$2,062	-	-	$6,728	107 of 203
	375,000	7,833	81	2,062	-	-	9,976	151 of 203
	525,000	11,080	81	2,062	-	-	13,223	162 of 203
PUNTA GORDA								
$30,000	$125,000	$1,963	$81	$881	-	-	$2,925	112 of 173
	150,000	2,309	81	881	-	-	3,271	108 of 173
	175,000	2,654	81	881	-	-	3,616	109 of 173
$60,000	$150,000	$2,309	$81	$1,548	-	-	$3,938	77 of 203
	225,000	3,346	81	1,548	-	-	4,975	96 of 203
	300,000	4,383	81	1,548	-	-	6,012	100 of 203
$90,000	$225,000	$3,346	$81	$1,924	-	-	$5,351	32 of 203
	375,000	5,420	81	1,924	-	-	7,425	60 of 203
	525,000	7,495	81	1,924	-	-	9,500	75 of 203
ST. AUGUSTINE								
$30,000	$125,000	$2,069	$81	$755	-	-	$2,905	108 of 173
	150,000	2,599	81	755	-	-	3,435	118 of 173
	175,000	2,947	81	755	-	-	3,783	117 of 173
$60,000	$150,000	$2,910	$81	$1,327	-	-	$4,318	113 of 203
	225,000	4,500	81	1,327	-	-	5,908	144 of 203
	300,000	6,090	81	1,327	-	-	7,498	156 of 203
$90,000	$225,000	$4,500	$81	$1,649	-	-	$6,230	85 of 203
	375,000	7,680	81	1,649	-	-	9,410	135 of 203
	525,000	10,860	81	1,649	-	-	12,590	152 of 203
ST. PETERSBURG								
$30,000	$125,000	$2,471	$81	$881	-	-	$3,433	148 of 173
	150,000	3,049	81	881	-	-	4,011	152 of 173
	175,000	3,628	81	881	-	-	4,590	153 of 173

Income	Home Value	Property Tax & Other Fees	Personal Property Tax & Auto Fees	Sales Tax	Local Income Tax	State Income Tax	Total Tax Burden	Rank*
ST. PETERSBURG continued								
$60,000	$150,000	$3,148	$81	$1,548	-	-	$4,777	145 of 203
	225,000	4,885	81	1,548	-	-	6,514	166 of 203
	300,000	6,622	81	1,548	-	-	8,251	169 of 203
$90,000	$225,000	$4,885	$81	$1,924	-	-	$6,890	119 of 203
	375,000	8,268	81	1,924	-	-	10,273	157 of 203
	525,000	11,832	81	1,924	-	-	13,837	168 of 203
SANIBEL ISLAND								
$60,000	$150,000	$2,250	$81	$1,327	-	-	$3,658	52 of 203
	225,000	3,492	81	1,327	-	-	4,900	88 of 203
	300,000	4,734	81	1,327	-	-	6,142	110 of 203
$90,000	$225,000	$3,492	$81	$1,649	-	-	$5,222	27 of 203
	375,000	5,976	81	1,649	-	-	7,706	71 of 203
	525,000	8,460	81	1,649	-	-	10,190	96 of 203
	$600,000	$9,702	$81	$1,649	-	-	$11,432	26 of 30
	750,000	12,186	81	1,649	-	-	13,916	27 of 30
	900,000	14,670	81	1,649	-	-	16,400	27 of 30
SARASOTA								
$30,000	$125,000	$1,915	$81	$881	-	-	$2,877	104 of 173
	150,000	2,319	81	881	-	-	3,281	111 of 173
	175,000	2,724	81	881	-	-	3,686	114 of 173
$60,000	$150,000	$2,416	$81	$1,548	-	-	$4,045	86 of 203
	225,000	3,630	81	1,548	-	-	5,259	113 of 203
	300,000	4,844	81	1,548	-	-	6,473	123 of 203
$90,000	$225,000	$3,630	$81	$1,924	-	-	$5,635	43 of 203
	375,000	6,058	81	1,924	-	-	8,063	83 of 203
	525,000	8,486	81	1,924	-	-	10,491	109 of 203
SIESTA KEY								
$60,000	$150,000	$2,042	$81	$1,548	-	-	$3,671	53 of 203
	225,000	3,032	81	1,548	-	-	4,661	68 of 203
	300,000	4,022	81	1,548	-	-	5,651	83 of 203
$90,000	$225,000	$3,032	$81	$1,924	-	-	$5,037	24 of 203
	375,000	5,011	81	1,924	-	-	7,016	41 of 203
	525,000	6,990	81	1,924	-	-	8,995	61 of 203
	$600,000	$7,980	$81	$1,924	-	-	$9,985	14 of 30
	750,000	9,959	81	1,924	-	-	11,964	17 of 30
	900,000	11,938	81	1,924	-	-	13,943	18 of 30
TAMPA								
$30,000	$125,000	$2,201	$81	$881	-	-	$3,163	135 of 173
	150,000	2,786	81	881	-	-	3,748	142 of 173
	175,000	3,372	81	881	-	-	4,334	145 of 173
$60,000	$150,000	$3,110	$81	$1,548	-	-	$4,739	143 of 203
	225,000	4,867	81	1,548	-	-	6,496	165 of 203
	300,000	6,625	81	1,548	-	-	8,254	170 of 203
$90,000	$225,000	$4,867	$81	$1,924	-	-	$6,872	116 of 203
	375,000	8,383	81	1,924	-	-	10,388	162 of 203
	525,000	11,899	81	1,924	-	-	13,904	169 of 203

*There are 203 cities in this book, 30 of which have higher than average home prices. We have estimated taxes for a tier of higher home values (and omitted the lowest tier) for these 30 cities. The city with the lowest tax burden for an income/home value combination is given the #1 rating; the higher the rating, the higher the total tax burden.

Income	Home Value	Property Tax & Other Fees	Personal Property Tax & Auto Fees	Sales Tax	Local Income Tax	State Income Tax	Total Tax Burden	Rank*
VENICE								
$30,000	$125,000	$1,811	$81	$881	-	-	$2,773	98 of 173
	150,000	2,224	81	881	-	-	3,186	101 of 173
	175,000	2,638	81	881	-	-	3,600	106 of 173
$60,000	$150,000	$2,247	$81	$1,548	-	-	$3,876	67 of 203
	225,000	3,486	81	1,548	-	-	5,115	101 of 203
	300,000	4,726	81	1,548	-	-	6,355	119 of 203
$90,000	$225,000	$3,486	$81	$1,924	-	-	$5,491	35 of 203
	375,000	5,965	81	1,924	-	-	7,970	79 of 203
	525,000	8,445	81	1,924	-	-	10,450	106 of 203
VERO BEACH								
$30,000	$125,000	$1,633	$81	$881	-	-	$2,595	76 of 173
	150,000	2,014	81	881	-	-	2,976	84 of 173
	175,000	2,396	81	881	-	-	3,358	92 of 173
$60,000	$150,000	$2,177	$81	$1,548	-	-	$3,806	62 of 203
	225,000	3,322	81	1,548	-	-	4,951	94 of 203
	300,000	4,466	81	1,548	-	-	6,095	107 of 203
$90,000	$225,000	$3,322	$81	$1,924	-	-	$5,327	31 of 203
	375,000	5,611	81	1,924	-	-	7,616	67 of 203
	525,000	7,900	81	1,924	-	-	9,905	85 of 203
WINTER HAVEN								
$30,000	$125,000	$2,193	$81	$881	-	-	$3,155	132 of 173
	150,000	2,784	81	881	-	-	3,746	141 of 173
	175,000	3,374	81	881	-	-	4,336	146 of 173
$60,000	$150,000	$3,165	$81	$1,548	-	-	$4,794	148 of 203
	225,000	4,936	81	1,548	-	-	6,565	168 of 203
	300,000	6,708	81	1,548	-	-	8,337	173 of 203
$90,000	$225,000	$4,936	$81	$1,924	-	-	$6,941	125 of 203
	375,000	8,479	81	1,924	-	-	10,484	163 of 203
	525,000	12,022	81	1,924	-	-	14,027	173 of 203

*There are 203 cities in this book, 30 of which have higher than average home prices. We have estimated taxes for a tier of higher home values (and omitted the lowest tier) for these 30 cities. The city with the lowest tax burden for an income/home value combination is given the #1 rating; the higher the rating, the higher the total tax burden.

Continued from page 39
sumer categories that are exempt from sales tax include: drugs, groceries and medical services.

Within the city limits of DeLand, the property tax rate is .02036840. Homes are assessed at 100% of market value. There is a homestead exemption of $25,000 off assessed value available to all homeowners who own and reside on the property on January 1 of the tax year. There is an additional senior citizen exemption of $25,000 off assessed value for the county and city components of property tax if federal adjusted gross income is $23,463 or less in the prior calendar year. Property tax does not cover garbage pickup. There is also a stormwater fee of approximately $24 per year.

The personal property tax rate is the same as the real property tax rate. Personal property is assessed at 100% of market value. Items subject to the tax include mobile homes on rented land that are not registered as real property and mobile home attachments. We've assumed our couples do not own any items subject to the tax.

Fort Lauderdale

Fort Lauderdale has no local income tax and does not levy an additional sales tax.

Most purchases are taxed at the state rate of 6%. Major consumer categories taxed at a different rate: none. Major consumer categories that are exempt from sales tax include: drugs, groceries and medical services.

In District 0312 of Fort Lauderdale, the property tax rate is .0219919. Homes are assessed at 100% of market value. There is a homestead exemption of $25,000 off assessed value available to all homeowners who own and reside on the property on January 1 of the tax year. There is an additional senior citizen exemption of $25,000 off assessed value for the county and city components of property tax if federal adjusted gross income is $23,463 or less in the prior calendar year. Property tax does not cover garbage pickup. There is a stormwater fee of $35 per year and a fire rescue fee of $94 per year.

The personal property tax rate is the same as the real property tax rate. Personal property is assessed at 100% of market value. Items subject to the tax include mobile homes on rented land that are not registered as real property and mobile home attachments. We've assumed our couples do not own any items subject to the tax.

Gainesville

Gainesville has no local income tax but does levy a sales tax.

Most purchases are taxed at a rate of 6.25%. Major consumer categories taxed at a different rate: none. Major consumer categories that are exempt from sales tax include: drugs, groceries and medical services.

In the St. John's Water District 36 of Gainesville, the property tax rate is .0245841. Homes are assessed at 100% of market value. There is a homestead exemption of $25,000 off assessed value available to all homeowners who own and reside on the property on January 1 of the tax year. There is an additional senior citizen exemption of $25,000 off assessed value for the county and city components of property tax if federal adjusted gross income is $23,463 or less in the prior calendar year. Property tax does not cover garbage pickup.

The personal property tax rate is the same as the real property tax rate. Personal property is assessed at 100% of market value. Items subject to the tax include mobile homes on rented land that are not registered as real property and mobile home attachments. We've assumed our couples do not own any items subject to the tax.

Jacksonville

Jacksonville has no local income tax but does levy a sales tax.

Most purchases are taxed at a rate of 7%. Major consumer categories taxed at a different rate: none. Major consumer categories that are exempt from sales tax include: drugs, groceries and medical services.

Within the city limits of Jacksonville, the property tax rate is .0181825. Homes are assessed at 100% of market value. There is a homestead exemption of $25,000 off assessed value available to all homeowners who own and reside on the property on January 1 of the tax year. There is an additional senior citizen exemption of $25,000 off assessed value for the county and city components of property tax if federal adjusted

gross income is $23,463 or less in the prior calendar year. Property tax includes garbage pickup.

The personal property tax rate is the same as the real property tax rate. Personal property is assessed at 100% of market value. Items subject to the tax include mobile homes on rented land that are not registered as real property and mobile home attachments. We've assumed our couples do not own any items subject to the tax.

Jupiter

Jupiter has no local income tax but does levy a sales tax.

Most purchases are taxed at a rate of 6.5%. Major consumer categories taxed at a different rate: none. Major consumer categories that are exempt from sales tax include: drugs, groceries and medical services.

Within the city limits of Jupiter, the property tax rate is .0195253. Homes are assessed at 100% of market value. There is a homestead exemption of $25,000 off assessed value available to all homeowners who own and reside on the property on January 1 of the tax year. There is an additional senior citizen exemption of $25,000 off assessed value for the county component of property tax if federal adjusted gross income is $23,463 or less in the prior calendar year. Property tax does not cover garbage pickup. There is also a stormwater fee of $49 per year.

The personal property tax rate is the same as the real property tax rate. Personal property is assessed at 100% of market value. Items subject to the tax include mobile homes on rented land that are not registered as real property and mobile home attachments. We've assumed our couples do not own any items subject to the tax.

Key West

Key West has no local income tax but does levy a sales tax.

Most purchases are taxed at a rate of 7.5%. Major consumer categories taxed at a different rate: none. Major consumer categories that are exempt from sales tax include: drugs, groceries and medical services.

Within the city limits of Key West, the property tax rate is .0091728. Homes are assessed at 100% of market value after deductions. There is a homestead

exemption of $25,000 off assessed value available to all homeowners who own and reside on the property on January 1 of the tax year. There is an additional senior citizen exemption of $25,000 off assessed value for the county and city components of property tax if federal adjusted gross income is $23,463 or less in the prior calendar year. Property tax does not cover garbage pickup.

The personal property tax rate is the same as the real property tax rate. Personal property is assessed at 100% of market value. Items subject to the tax include mobile homes on rented land that are not registered as real property and mobile home attachments. We've assumed our couples do not own any items subject to the tax.

Lakeland

Lakeland has no local income tax but does levy a sales tax.

Most purchases are taxed at a rate of 7%. Major consumer categories taxed at a different rate: none. Major consumer categories that are exempt from sales tax include: drugs, groceries and medical services.

In District 11510 of Lakeland, the property tax rate is .020753. Homes are assessed at 100% of market value. There is a homestead exemption of $25,000 off assessed value available to all homeowners who own and reside on the property on January 1 of the tax year. There is an additional senior citizen exemption of $25,000 off assessed value for the county and city components of property tax if federal adjusted gross income is $23,463 or less in the prior calendar year. Property tax does not cover garbage pickup. There is also a stormwater fee of approximately $24 per year.

The personal property tax rate is the same as the real property tax rate. Personal property is assessed at 100% of market value. Items subject to the tax include mobile homes on rented land that are not registered as real property and mobile home attachments. We've assumed our couples do not own any items subject to the tax.

Leesburg

Leesburg has no local income tax but does levy a sales tax.

Most purchases are taxed at a rate of

7%. Major consumer categories taxed at a different rate: none. Major consumer categories that are exempt from sales tax include: drugs, groceries and medical services.

Within the city limits of Leesburg, the property tax rate is .0203389. Homes are assessed at 100% of market value. There is a homestead exemption of $25,000 off assessed value available to all homeowners who own and reside on the property on January 1 of the tax year. There is an additional senior citizen exemption of $25,000 off assessed value for the county operational component of property tax if federal adjusted gross income is $23,463 or less in the prior calendar year. Property tax does not cover garbage pickup.

The personal property tax rate is the same as the real property tax rate. Personal property is assessed at 100% of market value. Items subject to the tax include mobile homes on rented land that are not registered as real property and mobile home attachments. We've assumed our couples do not own any items subject to the tax.

Longboat Key

Longboat Key has no local income tax but does levy a sales tax.

Most purchases are taxed at a rate of 7%. Major consumer categories taxed at a different rate: none. Major consumer categories that are exempt from sales tax include: drugs, groceries and medical services.

For most residents living in the town of Longboat Key, the property tax rate is .0141531. Homes are assessed at 100% of market value. There is a homestead exemption of $25,000 off assessed value available to all homeowners who own and reside on the property on January 1 of the tax year. There is an additional senior citizen exemption of $5,000 off assessed value for the county component and $25,000 off assessed value for the town component of property tax if federal adjusted gross income is $23,463 or less in the prior calendar year. Property tax does not cover garbage pickup.

The personal property tax rate is the same as the real property tax rate. Personal property is assessed at 100% of market value. Items subject to the tax include mobile homes on rented land

that are not registered as real property and mobile home attachments. We've assumed our couples do not own any items subject to the tax.

Miami

Miami has no local income tax but does levy a sales tax.

Most purchases are taxed at a rate of 7%. Major consumer categories taxed at a different rate: none. Major consumer categories that are exempt from sales tax include: drugs, groceries and medical services.

In District 0100 of Miami, the property tax rate is .0246443. Homes are assessed at 100% of market value. There is a homestead exemption of $25,000 off assessed value available to all homeowners who own and reside on the property on January 1 of the tax year. There is an additional senior citizen exemption of $25,000 off assessed value for the county and city components of property tax if federal adjusted gross income is $23,463 or less in the prior calendar year. Property tax does not cover garbage pickup.

The personal property tax rate is the same as the real property tax rate. Personal property is assessed at 100% of market value. Items subject to the tax include mobile homes on rented land that are not registered as real property and mobile home attachments. We've assumed our couples do not own any items subject to the tax.

Mount Dora

Mount Dora has no local income tax but does levy a sales tax.

Most purchases are taxed at a rate of 7%. Major consumer categories taxed at a different rate: none. Major consumer categories that are exempt from sales tax include: drugs, groceries and medical services.

Within the city limits of Mount Dora, the property tax rate is .0218139. Homes are assessed at 100% of market value. There is a homestead exemption of $25,000 off assessed value available to all homeowners who own and reside on the property on January 1 of the tax year. There is an additional senior citizen exemption of $25,000 off assessed value for the county operational and city components of property tax if federal adjusted gross income is $23,463 or less in the prior calendar year. Property tax does

not cover garbage pickup. There is also a stormwater fee of approximately $42 per year and a recycling fee of $25 per year.

The personal property tax rate is the same as the real property tax rate. Personal property is assessed at 100% of market value. Items subject to the tax include mobile homes on rented land that are not registered as real property and mobile home attachments. We've assumed our couples do not own any items subject to the tax.

Naples

Naples has no local income tax and does not levy an additional sales tax.

Most purchases are taxed at the state rate of 6%. Major consumer categories taxed at a different rate: none. Major consumer categories that are exempt from sales tax include: drugs, groceries and medical services.

In District 4 of Naples, the property tax rate is .0114119. Homes are assessed at 100% of market value. There is a homestead exemption of $25,000 off assessed value available to all homeowners who own and reside on the property on January 1 of the tax year. There is an additional senior citizen exemption of $25,000 off assessed value for the county general fund, water pollution, conservation Collier, Caribbean Gardens and city general and debt components of property tax if federal adjusted gross income is $23,463 or less in the prior calendar year. Property tax does not cover garbage pickup. There is also a stormwater fee of $48 per year.

The personal property tax rate is the same as the real property tax rate. Personal property is assessed at 100% of market value. Items subject to the tax include mobile homes on rented land that are not registered as real property and mobile home attachments. We've assumed our couples do not own any items subject to the tax.

North Fort Myers

North Fort Myers has no local income tax and does not levy an additional sales tax.

Most purchases are taxed at the state rate of 6%. Major consumer categories taxed at a different rate: none. Major consumer categories that are exempt from sales tax include: drugs, groceries and medical services.

For residents living within the North Fort Myers Light/Fire District 001, the property tax rate is .0163937. Homes are assessed at 100% of market value. There is a homestead exemption of $25,000 off assessed value available to all homeowners who own and reside on the property on January 1 of the tax year. Property tax does not cover garbage pickup.

The personal property tax rate is the same as the real property tax rate. Personal property is assessed at 100% of market value. Items subject to the tax include mobile homes on rented land that are not registered as real property and mobile home attachments. We've assumed our couples do not own any items subject to the tax.

Ocala

Ocala has no local income tax but does levy a sales tax.

Most purchases are taxed at a rate of 6.5%. Major consumer categories taxed at a different rate: none. Major consumer categories that are exempt from sales tax include: drugs, groceries and medical services.

In District 1001 of Ocala, the property tax rate is .018577. Homes are assessed at 100% of market value. There is a homestead exemption of $25,000 off assessed value available to all homeowners who own and reside on the property on January 1 of the tax year. Property tax does not cover garbage pickup. There is also a stormwater fee of $60 per year.

The personal property tax rate is the same as the real property tax rate. Personal property is assessed at 100% of market value. Items subject to the tax include mobile homes on rented land that are not registered as real property and mobile home attachments. We've assumed our couples do not own any items subject to the tax.

Orlando

Orlando has no local income tax but does levy a sales tax.

Most purchases are taxed at a rate of 6.5%. Major consumer categories taxed at a different rate: none. Major consumer categories that are exempt from sales tax include: drugs, groceries and medical services.

In District 08 of Orlando, the proper-

ty tax rate is .0189190. Homes are assessed at 100% of market value. There is a homestead exemption of $25,000 off assessed value available to all homeowners who own and reside on the property on January 1 of the tax year. There is an additional senior citizen exemption of $25,000 off assessed value for the county and city components of property tax if federal adjusted gross income is $23,463 or less in the prior calendar year.. Property tax does not cover garbage pickup. There is also a stormwater fee of approximately $99 per year.

The personal property tax rate is the same as the real property tax rate. Personal property is assessed at 100% of market value. Items subject to the tax include mobile homes on rented land that are not registered as real property and mobile home attachments. We've assumed our couples do not own any items subject to the tax.

Ormond Beach

Ormond Beach has no local income tax but does levy a sales tax.

Most purchases are taxed at a rate of 6.5%. Major consumer categories taxed at a different rate: none. Major consumer categories that are exempt from sales tax include: drugs, groceries and medical services.

Within the city limits of Ormond Beach, the property tax rate is .02021314. Homes are assessed at 100% of market value. There is a homestead exemption of $25,000 off assessed value available to all homeowners who own and reside on the property on January 1 of the tax year. There is an additional senior citizen exemption of $25,000 off assessed value for the county, mosquito control, city and inlet and port authority components of property tax if federal adjusted gross income is $23,463 or less in the prior calendar year. Property tax does not cover garbage pickup. There is also a stormwater fee of $72 per year and a recycling fee of $30 per year.

The personal property tax rate is the same as the real property tax rate. Personal property is assessed at 100% of market value. Items subject to the tax include mobile homes on rented land that are not registered as real property and mobile home attachments. We've

assumed our couples do not own any items subject to the tax.

Palm Coast

Palm Coast has no local income tax but does levy a sales tax.

Most purchases are taxed at a rate of 7%. Major consumer categories taxed at a different rate: none. Major consumer categories that are exempt from sales tax include: drugs, groceries and medical services.

In District 61 of Palm Coast, the property tax rate is .0164011. Homes are assessed at 100% of market value. There is a homestead exemption of $25,000 off assessed value available to all homeowners who own and reside on the property on January 1 of the tax year. There is an additional senior citizen exemption of $25,000 off assessed value for the county and city components of property tax if federal adjusted gross income is $23,463 or less in the prior calendar year. Property tax does not cover garbage pickup. There is also a stormwater fee of $72 per year.

The personal property tax rate is the same as the real property tax rate. Personal property is assessed at 100% of market value. Items subject to the tax include mobile homes on rented land that are not registered as real property and mobile home attachments. We've assumed our couples do not own any items subject to the tax.

Pensacola

Pensacola has no local income tax but does levy a sales tax.

Most purchases are taxed at a rate of 7.5%. Major consumer categories taxed at a different rate: none. Major consumer categories that are exempt from sales tax include: drugs, groceries and medical services.

Within the city limits of Pensacola, the property tax rate is .021650. Homes are assessed at 100% of market value. There is a homestead exemption of $25,000 off assessed value available to all homeowners who own and reside on the property on January 1 of the tax year. There is an additional senior citizen exemption of $25,000 off assessed value for the county and city components of property tax if federal adjusted gross income is $23,463 or less in the prior calendar year. Property tax does not cover garbage pickup. There is also a stormwater fee of $75 per year.

The personal property tax rate is the same as the real property tax rate. Personal property is assessed at 100% of market value. Items subject to the tax include mobile homes on rented land that are not registered as real property and mobile home attachments. We've assumed our couples do not own any items subject to the tax.

Punta Gorda

Punta Gorda has no local income tax but does levy a sales tax.

Most purchases are taxed at a rate of 7%. Major consumer categories taxed at a different rate: none. Major consumer categories that are exempt from sales tax include: drugs, groceries and medical services.

Within the city limits of Punta Gorda, the property tax rate is .0138291. Homes are assessed at 100% of market value. There is a homestead exemption of $25,000 off assessed value available to all homeowners who own and reside on the property on January 1 of the tax year. Property tax does not cover garbage pickup. There is also a canal maintenance fee of $400 per year.

The personal property tax rate is the same as the real property tax rate. Personal property is assessed at 100% of market value. Items subject to the tax include mobile homes on rented land that are not registered as real property and mobile home attachments. We've assumed our couples do not own any items subject to the tax.

St. Augustine

St. Augustine has no local income tax and does not levy an additional sales tax.

Most purchases are taxed at the state rate of 6%. Major consumer categories taxed at a different rate: none. Major consumer categories that are exempt from sales tax include: drugs, groceries and medical services.

In District 452 of St. Augustine, the property tax rate is .0211998. Homes are assessed at 100% of market value. There is a homestead exemption of $25,000 off assessed value available to all homeowners who own and reside on the property on January 1 of the tax year. There is an additional senior citizen exemption of $25,000 off assessed

value for the county and city components of property tax if federal adjusted gross income is $23,463 or less in the prior calendar year. Property tax does not cover garbage pickup. There is also a fire assessment fee of approximately $80 per year.

The personal property tax rate is the same as the real property tax rate. Personal property is assessed at 100% of market value. Items subject to the tax include mobile homes on rented land that are not registered as real property and mobile home attachments. We've assumed our couples do not own any items subject to the tax.

St. Petersburg

St. Petersburg has no local income tax but does levy a sales tax.

Most purchases are taxed at a rate of 7%. Major consumer categories taxed at a different rate: none. Major consumer categories that are exempt from sales tax include: drugs, groceries and medical services.

Within the city limits of St. Petersburg, the property tax rate is .0231552. Homes are assessed at 100% of market value. There is a homestead exemption of $25,000 off assessed value available to all homeowners who own and reside on the property on January 1 of the tax year. There is an additional senior citizen exemption of $15,000 off assessed value for the city component of property tax if federal adjusted gross income is $23,463 or less in the prior calendar year. Property tax does not cover garbage pickup. There is also a stormwater management fee of approximately $74 per year.

The personal property tax rate is .0219178. Personal property is assessed at 100% of market value. Items subject to the tax include mobile homes on rented land that are not registered as real property and mobile home attachments. We've assumed our couples do not own any items subject to the tax.

Sanibel Island

Sanibel Island has no local income tax and does not levy an additional sales tax.

Most purchases are taxed at the state rate of 6%. Major consumer categories taxed at a different rate: none. Major

consumer categories that are exempt from sales tax include: drugs, groceries and medical services.

For residents living on Sanibel Island, the property tax rate is .0165601. Homes are assessed at 100% of market value. There is a homestead exemption of $25,000 off assessed value available to all homeowners who own and reside on the property on January 1 of the tax year. There is an additional senior citizen exemption of $25,000 off assessed value for the city and debt service components of property tax if federal adjusted gross income is $23,463 or less in the prior calendar year. Property tax does not cover garbage pickup.

The personal property tax rate is the same as the real property tax rate. Personal property is assessed at 100% of market value. Items subject to the tax include mobile homes on rented land that are not registered as real property and mobile home attachments. We've assumed our couples do not own any items subject to the tax.

Sarasota

Sarasota has no local income tax but does levy a sales tax.

Most purchases are taxed at a rate of 7%. Major consumer categories taxed at a different rate: none. Major consumer categories that are exempt from sales tax include: drugs, groceries and medical services.

In District 0200 of Sarasota, the property tax rate is .0161855. Homes are assessed at 100% of market value. There is a homestead exemption of $25,000 off assessed value available to all homeowners who own and reside on the property on January 1 of the tax year. There is an additional senior citizen exemption of $5,000 off assessed value for the county component and $25,000 off assessed value for the city component of property tax if federal adjusted gross income is $23,463 or less in the prior calendar year. Property tax does not cover garbage pickup. There is also a stormwater fee of approximately $79 per year and a fire/rescue fee based on the square footage of the home.

The personal property tax rate is the same as the real property tax rate. Personal property is assessed at 100% of market value. Items subject to the tax include mobile homes on rented land that are not registered as real property and mobile home attachments. We've assumed our couples do not own any items subject to the tax.

Siesta Key

Siesta Key has no local income tax but does levy a sales tax.

Most purchases are taxed at a rate of 7%. Major consumer categories taxed at a different rate: none. Major consumer categories that are exempt from sales tax include: drugs, groceries and medical services.

In District 5800 of Siesta Key, the property tax rate is .0131947. Homes are assessed at 100% of market value. There is a homestead exemption of $25,000 off assessed value available to all homeowners who own and reside on the property on January 1 of the tax year. There is an additional senior citizen exemption of $5,000 off assessed value for the county component of property tax if federal adjusted gross income is $23,463 or less in the prior calendar year. Property tax does not cover garbage pickup. There is also a stormwater fee of approximately $79 per year and a fire assessment fee based on the square footage of the home.

The personal property tax rate is the same as the real property tax rate. Personal property is assessed at 100% of market value. Items subject to the tax include mobile homes on rented land that are not registered as real property and mobile home attachments. We've assumed our couples do not own any items subject to the tax.

Tampa

Tampa has no local income tax but does levy a sales tax.

Most purchases are taxed at a rate of 7%. Major consumer categories taxed at a different rate: none. Major consumer categories that are exempt from sales tax include: drugs, groceries and medical services.

In District TBH of Tampa, the property tax rate is .023437. Homes are assessed at 100% of market value. There is a homestead exemption of $25,000 off assessed value available to all homeowners who own and reside on the property on January 1 of the tax year. There is an additional senior citizen exemption of $25,000 off assessed

value for the county general and city components of property tax if federal adjusted gross income is $23,463 or less in the prior calendar year. Property tax does not cover garbage pickup.

The personal property tax rate is the same as the real property tax rate. Personal property is assessed at 100% of market value. Items subject to the tax include mobile homes on rented land that are not registered as real property and mobile home attachments. We've assumed our couples do not own any items subject to the tax.

Venice

Venice has no local income tax but does levy a sales tax.

Most purchases are taxed at a rate of 7%. Major consumer categories taxed at a different rate: none. Major consumer categories that are exempt from sales tax include: drugs, groceries and medical services.

In District 0300 of Venice, the property tax rate is .0165299. Homes are assessed at 100% of market value. There is a homestead exemption of $25,000 off assessed value available to all homeowners who own and reside on the property on January 1 of the tax year. There is an additional senior citizen exemption of $5,000 off assessed value for the county component of property tax if federal adjusted gross income is $23,463 or less in the prior calendar year. Property tax does not cover garbage pickup.

The personal property tax rate is the same as the real property tax rate. Personal property is assessed at 100% of market value. Items subject to the tax include mobile homes on rented land that are not registered as real property and mobile home attachments. We've assumed our couples do not own any items subject to the tax.

Vero Beach

Vero Beach has no local income tax but does levy a sales tax.

Most purchases are taxed at a rate of 7%. Major consumer categories taxed at a different rate: none. Major consumer categories that are exempt from sales tax include: drugs, groceries and medical services.

In the Tax Code 7 area of Vero Beach, the property tax rate is

.01526269. Homes are assessed at 100% of market value. There is a homestead exemption of $25,000 off assessed value available to all homeowners who own and reside on the property on January 1 of the tax year. There is an additional senior citizen exemption of $25,000 off assessed value for the county and land acquisition bond components of property tax if federal adjusted gross income is $23,463 or less in the prior calendar year. Property tax does not cover garbage pickup. There is also a county landfill fee of approximately $75 per year and a drainage fee of $15 per year.

The personal property tax rate is the same as the real property tax rate. Personal property is assessed at 100% of market value. Items subject to the tax include mobile homes on rented land that are not registered as real property and mobile home attachments. We've assumed our couples do not own any items subject to the tax.

Winter Haven

Winter Haven has no local income tax but does levy a sales tax.

Most purchases are taxed at a rate of 7%. Major consumer categories taxed at a different rate: none. Major consumer categories that are exempt from sales tax include: drugs, groceries and medical services.

In district 10410 of Winter Haven, the property tax rate is .023620. Homes are assessed at 100% of market value. There is a homestead exemption of $25,000 off assessed value available to all homeowners who own and reside on the property on January 1 of the tax year. There is an additional senior citizen exemption of $25,000 off assessed value for the county and city components of property tax if federal adjusted gross income is $23,463 or less in the prior calendar year. Property tax does not cover garbage pickup. There is also a stormwater fee of approximately $32 per year.

The personal property tax rate is the same as the real property tax rate. Personal property is assessed at 100% of market value. Items subject to the tax include mobile homes on rented land that are not registered as real property and mobile home attachments. We've assumed our couples do not own any items subject to the tax.

DeLand

DeLand's oak-lined streets of Greek Revival, Victorian and Tudor homes are the epitome of Main Street USA. A former outpost on the St. Johns River, a byway to the Atlantic Ocean, DeLand was Florida's first designated Main Street town.

Towns don't get any friendlier, with seniors and college students mingling at Internet cafes along Woodland Boulevard, a historic district with quaint shops, restaurants and bookstores. Some of the renovated brick buildings date to the late 1800s.

DeLand is home to Stetson University, adjoining downtown. Its renowned music college puts on year-round performances. Seniors can take advantage of discounted nondegree classes at the college and also participate in educational programs through Elderhostel. The DeLand Museum of Art, located across the street from the university, houses excellent exhibits by prominent artists. The DeLand Fall Festival of the Arts showcases area talent, as does the annual Volusia County Fair and Youth Show, where everything from pigs to key lime pies compete for blue ribbons.

Northwest of town is Ocala National Forest, with crystal-blue lakes and stunning temperate-to-subtropical wooded areas. With its springs and junglelike shores, the sprawling St. Johns River draws anglers, boaters, swimmers and wildlife enthusiasts.

Rent a houseboat and float past colorful birds, manatees, alligators and a colony of wild monkeys. Or check out the original fountain of youth at DeLeon Springs State Park, where you can swim in refreshing natural pools and splash your face with water that's rumored to be the next best thing to Botox. If you crave waves and surf, it's just a 30-minute drive to Daytona Beach.

Population: 25,873

Climate: High Low
January 70 44
July 91 71

Cost of living: Below average

Housing cost: The median sales price for a single-family home during the first 10 months of 2007 was $194,900, according to the Orlando Regional Realtor Association.

Information: DeLand Area Chamber of Commerce, (386) 734-4331 or www.delandchamber.org.

Gainesville

As the home of Florida's oldest and largest university, the University of Florida and its more than 46,000 students, Gainesville pulses with a youthful vibe. But it also feels like a traditional, old Southern town with the preservation of late 19th- and early 20th-century buildings. More than 30 structures are listed on the National Register of Historic Places.

One attraction for retirees is an innovative community called Oak Hammock at the university. The resort-style development offers a variety of housing: villas, apartments, club homes near the golf course and assisted living. It's affiliated with the university, and many of the residents are alumni who graduated, moved away and return to experience Gainesville at a different stage in their lives. Oak Hammock helped create an Institute for Learning in Retirement, offering courses in subjects ranging from history to music appreciation and philosophy.

Proximity to a major university with a renowned system of teaching hospitals offers residents access to top-notch health care and to the school's first-class art museums and galleries. The city also has a lively music scene.

Gainesville dates to 1853 when it was created as a new community on the proposed Florida Railroad. It's located about halfway between Atlanta and Miami and within a two-hour drive of major Florida attractions like Walt Disney World, Universal Studios and Busch Gardens.

There's plenty to do in Gainesville, too. Residents can enjoy the outdoors almost year-round on championship-caliber golf courses, on biking trails or in nature parks, preserves and botanical gardens. An urban forest surrounds the town.

Housing options range from historic homes to planned communities and rural properties. Locals complain about increasing traffic congestion, but they brag about the variety of restaurants and a progressive mindset regarding preservation of the town's historic and natural environment.

Population: 108,655

Climate: High Low
January 66 42
July 91 71

Cost of living: Below average to average

Housing cost: The median price of an existing single-family in the first half of 2007 was $216,300, according to the National Association of Realtors.

Information: City of Gainesville, (352) 334-5000 or www.cityofgainesville.org. Gainesville Area Chamber of Commerce, (352) 334-7100 or www. gainesvillechamber.com.

Jacksonville

With the Atlantic on one side and the St. Johns River and its tributaries, as well as the Intracoastal Waterway, running through the area, you're never far from water sports in Jacksonville. Indeed, there are sports of all types, including the NFL's Jacksonville Jaguars, the Jacksonville Suns minor league baseball team, arena football with the Jacksonville Tomcats and PGA golf.

If it's culture you crave, catch the numerous performances at the historic Florida Theatre or the Times-Union Center for the Performing Arts, a complex with three halls, one of them home to the Jacksonville Symphony Orchestra. A riverfront park is the setting for open-air concerts and festivals.

Tucked beneath the Georgia border, Jacksonville has a Florida retirement lifestyle within striking distance of relatives and friends in the Northeast. The climate offers a slight change in seasons while allowing outdoor recreation year-round. The Timucuan Preserve coastal trail for hiking, biking and horseback riding eventually will link several local, state and national parks.

Numerous military installations are located around the city, and many of the retirees here once had careers in the armed forces. Jacksonville also is a major medical hub, with advanced care and cutting-edge technology in most fields. Among medical centers are Baptist Health with several hospitals, the famed Mayo Clinic, Memorial Hospital and Shands Jacksonville, which is affiliated with the University of Florida Health Science Center Jacksonville.

As well, it's an educational center with 16 colleges and universities in the area, among them the University of North Florida and Jacksonville University.

Population: 794,555
Climate: High   Low
January   64   42
July   91   72
Cost of living: Below average to average
Housing cost: The median price during the first half of 2007 was $198,150, according to the National Association of Realtors.
Information: Jacksonville Regional Chamber of Commerce, (904) 366-6600 or www.myjaxchamber.com.

Mount Dora

Only 25 miles northwest of Orlando, Mount Dora is the real version of America's hometown that Walt Disney World works so hard to re-create. Tall oak trees draped with Spanish moss line the streets, some of which showcase classic Floridian houses from the 1930s. Church bells chime twice daily, antiques shops abound, and theater and music flourish. Lake Dora offers prime fishing and boating plus Florida's only inland operational lighthouse. For razzle-dazzle, rides and shows, residents head the short distance to Mickey's homeland.

Mount Dora is ideal for retirees who yearn for a classic small town and want to get away from traffic and winter. It has a relaxed pace, but still has a beat, one that strums to the rhythms of concerts, plays and other performances. On weekend evenings, kick back on the porch of the Lakeside Inn and listen to music under the stars. Or browse the stalls of thousands of antiques dealers who come for the Renninger's Antiques Extravaganzas three times a year.

"We found Mount Dora while celebrating an anniversary at the Lakeside Inn. I spent 50 years in the music business, and I could feel the creative vibe Mount Dora brings," says Mickey

Carroll, 66, former composer, concert promoter, musician and entertainer. "With the famous IceHouse Theatre, the well-known Mount Dora Arts Festival, plus all the other wonderful concerts and events that Mount Dora has to offer, I brought my wife, Patty; daughter, Jessica; and son, Michael, to Mount Dora. My family and I have found a synergy with this small city in regard to creativity, friendship and a love for the arts."

Population: 11,564
Climate: High   Low
January   68   45
July   91   71
Cost of living: Below average
Housing cost: The median sales price of single-family homes during the first half of 2007 was $230,000, according to data from Atkins Realty.
Information: Mount Dora Area Chamber of Commerce, (352) 383-2165 or www.mountdora.com.

Ocala

This growing town in north-central Florida is the state's equestrian capital, surrounded by rolling hills, verdant pastures and hundreds of horse farms. It also neighbors the 380,000-acre Ocala National Forest, a pristine wilderness with boundless recreational opportunities, and Interstate 75, with quick access to Orlando's theme parks and Gainesville's University of Florida.

Amenities abound in town, too, as it's a medical, educational, cultural and shopping hub. Ocala boasts three hospitals, 350 physicians and the Centers, a nonprofit medical campus with a range of mental-health care. Continuing education is available at Webster University and Central Florida Community College, with the latter offering senior-specific classes through its Pathways program.

Besides its notable permanent collection, the Appleton Museum of Art hosts visiting exhibits and numerous events. Live theater, music and dance add to the cultural scene.

The seat of Marion County, Ocala boasts historic areas crowned by colorful Victorian homes. Retirees are helping fuel the growth in the area, choosing from a variety of housing, including condos, townhomes and a number of

master-planned communities with resort-style living targeted toward those 55-plus.

Reasonable housing costs, the scenic countryside and a pleasant climate that's cooler than south Florida are attracting out-of-state retirees like Jerry and Nancy Brown, who moved from Dayton, OH.

Jerry, who says he started thinking about possible retirement sites "when I was about 22," finds that the area "offers all of the activities I like — lakes and rivers to fish in, wonderful golf courses — and great value in housing." He also is enthusiastic about the climate. "It's amazing to me, the conditions in the summertime. I keep waiting for it to get bad. It never has," he says.

"We have over 200 days a year when we need neither heat nor air conditioning," Nancy says. "We call them the comfort days."

Population: 52,488
Climate: High   Low
January   70   45
July   92   71
Cost of living: Below average
Housing cost: The median price of homes sold in Ocala during the first half of 2007 was $166,750, according to the Florida Association of Realtors.
Information: Ocala-Marion County Chamber of Commerce, (352) 629-8051 or www.ocalacc.com.

Ormond Beach

Ormond Beach is not as well-known nationally as its next-door neighbor, Daytona Beach. That's fine with many Ormond Beach residents. Their community also has its Atlantic beach for sun-worshippers and seashell-gatherers, plus lots of seabirds. But it does quite nicely without all the development and spring-break frolicking.

An early visitor was John D. Rockefeller, who with other tycoons helped develop the town's reputation as a haven from colder climes. Rockefeller's winter home, The Casements, is on the National Register of Historic Places. Open to the public, it now serves as a cultural center for Ormond Beach.

The town has a significant senior population: about 28 percent of residents are 65 or older. As might be expected, there are numerous services catering to those 50 and beyond. Joanne Magley, marketing and public relations manager for Florida Hospital Memorial System, cites Premier Health, a health and wellness program with free membership to those 50 and up. She says its aim is to "make the most of an active lifestyle" through a variety of programs and screenings. In addition to health activities, the program offers merchant and cafe discounts.

FHMS operates three hospitals in the area: Florida Hospital Ormond Memorial and Florida Hospital Oceanside, both in Ormond Beach, and nearby Florida Hospital Flagler. Ormond Memorial and Flagler have earned recognition with rankings among the best hospitals nationwide. FHMS is a leader in heart and stroke care.

Ormond Beach has a reputation among East Floridians as a place of peace and quiet. Its light industrial base makes for a clean environment. Its civic facilities offer a low-key lifestyle, with such cultural amenities as live theater at the Ormond Beach Performing Arts Center. And for entertaining the grandkids, Orlando is little more than an hour away.

Population: 38,504

Climate: High   Low
January   70   47
July   91   72

Cost of living: Above average

Housing cost: A two-bedroom, two-bath home in town averages around $250,000, while a larger beachfront property can cost nearly $1 million, according to Ormond Beach brokerage Highet Realty.

Information: Ormond Beach Chamber of Commerce, (386) 677-3454 or www.ormondchamber.com.

Pensacola

Pensacola lies at the western edge of Florida, stretching along Pensacola Bay and the Gulf of Mexico. Retirees love it for its mild temperatures, sugar-sand beaches and terrific fishing. It's a town that long has been popular with springbreakers.

It's also a military town, known as the cradle of Navy aviation and home to the famed Blue Angels, the precision flying team. At its heart is a vast air base

where some of the country's best Navy pilots have trained.

On the waterfront, the Pensacola Beach Gulf Pier is the longest pier on the Gulf of Mexico at 1,471 feet. It affords great views of dolphins, sea turtles and red snapper. The beach at the Gulf Islands National Seashore is a treasure. For water sports, think deep-sea fishing, diving, boating and snorkeling.

This corner of northwest Florida is known for its year-round outdoor festivals, which offer a glimpse of the cultural, ethnic and religious diversity of its residents. The Pensacola Greyhound Track and Five Flags Speedway are both popular action spots, and the Blue Angels practice here from March to November. When it comes to dining, you can get your fill of grits, pecan pie and other Southern fare. Nightlife options include the lively bars and restaurants of Seville Quarter.

On the cultural side are the Pensacola Symphony Orchestra, ballet, opera and several museums, among them the Pensacola Museum of Art. Additionally, the National Museum of Naval Aviation displays more than 150 preserved Navy, Marine Corps and Coast Guard planes, and the T.T. Wentworth Jr. Florida State Museum has a collection of 100,000 items of Americana.

The University of West Florida in Pensacola provides ongoing educational opportunities for residents. But the balmy climate, low cost of living and a plethora of beach activities make Pensacola one of the most desirable places to retire.

Population: 53,248

Climate: High   Low
January   60   42
July   90   74

Cost of living: Below average

Housing cost: The median price during the first half of 2007 was $165,750, according to the Florida Association of Realtors.

Information: Pensacola Bay Area Convention and Visitors Bureau, (800) 874-1234 or www.visitpensacola.com.

St. Augustine

No place in the nation is as old as St. Augustine, which had just completed its first urban renewal plan when the Pilgrims sat down to the first Thanks-

giving dinner in 1620.

From the day of its founding in September 1565, the town on Florida's northeast coast has been inhabited continuously by people of European and African descent. Along with 37 buildings on the National Register of Historic Places, the city is laced with 42 miles of beaches that remain pristine, thanks to building code ordinances.

About 45 minutes from both Jacksonville and Daytona Beach, the town annually hosts major events and festivals, many with historical themes and others celebrating the area's food, including conch chowder, barbecue and fresh seafood.

Adult-education opportunities are available at St. Johns River Community College and through county and state programs. Retirees often serve as guides at the St. Augustine Lighthouse, learn to fire a Spanish cannon as reenactors at one of the town's forts or serve as docents at the World Golf Hall of Fame, which salutes the game and its greatest players.

Flagler Hospital provides state-of-the-art cardiac and general health care, and there is a Mayo Clinic in Jacksonville. Great shoreline and offshore fishing, kayak excursions into backwater bays and quiet beachcombing appeal to nature enthusiasts.

The area's climate makes play possible year-round at more than a dozen area golf courses. January and February can have chilly nights. Frost, however, is extremely rare. Even in the depths of winter the sun warms enough that only a sweater might be required.

The city has little room for new construction without destroying existing buildings, and approvals for demolition are rare. Condos and some individual homes are available in the city, while new housing is springing up outside town and at the beaches.

Population: 12,064

Climate: High   Low
January   65   46
July   89   73

Cost of living: Average to above average

Housing cost: The average sales price for a single-family, three-bedroom home was $304,933 for the first eight months of 2007, according to the St. Augustine and St. Johns County Board of Realtors.

Information: St. Johns County Chamber of Commerce, (904) 829-5681 or www.staugustinechamber.com. St. Augustine, Ponte Vedra and The Beaches Visitors and Convention Bureau, (800) 653-2489 or www.getaway4florida.com.

Sarasota

Sarasota is a picture-postcard example of the sort of place that attracts retirees. A mild winter climate, fabulous beaches, a casual lifestyle and a civic atmosphere that's favorable to older residents place it among Florida's favored destinations.

It remains distinctive among the state's cities, with more cultural amenities than many larger places. The Van Wezel Performing Arts Hall is an active venue. Symphonic, operatic, chamber music and ballet performances are frequent. Artist communities, galleries, theaters and museums add flavor. The Sarasota Senior Theater, which features the talents of people over 55, is an indicator of the important role that older residents play in the city's life. The seniors also work with youngsters to help them learn about the theater.

The city has a noted circus heritage. The Sarasota circus connections date from the early 20th century, when the town became the winter home of the Ringling Bros. and Barnum & Bailey Circus. Later the Ringling family played a prominent role in the community, and today an art museum and circus museum are continuing evidence of their influence and generosity.

Another of the city's distinctions is Sarasota Memorial Hospital, which has earned numerous accolades and been ranked among the best hospitals in the country. The second-largest acute-care public hospital in Florida, with 806 beds, Sarasota Memorial has been cited as outstanding in a number of fields, including cardiology and cancer. It's also noted for geriatric care, including assessments and a memory disorder clinic, and its primary stroke center is outstanding. It also offers a number of community-wellness programs.

Education is another area in which Sarasota retirees are actively involved. The Sarasota Institute of Lifelong Learning has a program of lectures on music and current events and seminars to complement some of the topics. The University of South Florida Sarasota-Manatee also has an Academy for Lifelong Learning with short courses.

Population: 52,942

Climate:

	High	Low
January	72	51
July	91	73

Cost of living: Above average

Housing cost: The median sales price of homes during the first half of 2007 was $316,905, according to the Sarasota Association of Realtors.

Information: Greater Sarasota Chamber of Commerce, (941) 955-8187 or www.sarasotachamber.com.

Venice

It doesn't have canals like its namesake in Italy, but Venice is one of the most livable cities in Florida. When it was created in the 1920s, Venice was one of the first cities to adopt the concept of zoning, so residential and business districts are kept separate. Gracious Mediterranean-style homes built in the 1920s blend with more modern structures both in residential and business areas.

Beach lovers are drawn to Venice for its three white-sand beaches, including one where dogs are allowed. Beachcombing is a major pursuit, and the sands are loaded with prehistoric shark teeth, which the city has adopted as its symbol.

Water-oriented activities, including boating and fishing, are available year-round. Venice has nine golf courses, and the county has a few dozen more.

Cultural opportunities far exceed what newcomers expect in a small town. Venice itself has a symphony orchestra, a theater group and art center, and it's only about 20 miles from Sarasota, the artistic hub of Florida's Gulf Coast. So residents enjoy a cultural scene usually found only in much larger cities.

"We wanted to get out of snow," says Terry Redman, 62, who moved to Venice with wife Sandy from Niles, MI. "And we fell in love of being close to the water." The Redmans built a home on a waterfront lot and frequently go boating.

Population: 20,952

Climate:

	High	Low
January	73	52
July	91	73

Cost of living: Above average

Housing cost: The median sales price for single-family homes during the first half of 2007 was $299,900, according to the Venice Area Board of Realtors.

Information: Venice Area Chamber of Commerce, (941) 488-2236 or www.venicechamber.com.

GEORGIA

Georgia has a state income tax and a state sales tax.

The state income tax rate is graduated from 1% to 6% depending upon income bracket. For married couples filing jointly, the rates are 1% on the first $1,000 of taxable income; 2% on the next $2,000 of taxable income; 3% on the next $2,000 of taxable income; 4% on the next $2,000 of taxable income; 5% on the next $3,000 of taxable income; and 6% on taxable income above $10,000.

In calculating the tax, there is no deduction for federal income tax paid. There is a retirement income exclusion of up to $25,000 per person age 62 or older. The exclusion increases to $30,000 in 2007 and $35,000 in 2008. Retirement income includes all unearned income and the first $4,000 of earned income for each person age 62 or older. Social Security benefits are exempt. There is a standard deduction of $3,000 from adjusted gross income for married couples filing jointly. There is a personal exemption of $2,700 per person and an additional age deduction of $1,300 per person age 65 or older.

Major tax credits or rebates include: credit for taxes paid to other states, which our couples do not qualify for; and low income credit, which one of our couples qualifies for.

The state sales tax rate is 4%, but local governments can add to this amount.

Since automobile ad valorem taxes paid with registration and renewal fees differ within the state, see city information for details.

Athens

Athens has no local income tax but does levy a sales tax.

Most purchases are taxed at a rate of 7%. Major consumer categories taxed at a different rate include: groceries, which are taxed at a rate of 3%. Major consumer categories that are exempt from sales tax include: drugs and medical services.

Within the city limits of Athens, the property tax rate is .03305. Homes are assessed at 40% of market value. There are various exemptions off the differ-

ent components of the property tax. Property tax does not cover garbage pickup. There is also a stormwater fee of $42 per year.

Athens has a personal property tax rate of .03305. Boats, motors and aircraft are subject to the tax and assessed at 40% of fair market value.

Our couples relocating to Athens must pay an ad valorem tax (personal property tax) based on the local tax rate and the age, make and model of each vehicle. The tax due upon initial registration is $186 for the Explorer and $227 for the Camry. Our couples also pay a registration fee of $20 per automobile and a title fee of $18 per automobile. Thereafter, on an annual basis, our couples will pay an ad valorem tax and a registration fee, per automobile.

Atlanta

Atlanta has no local income tax but does levy a sales tax.

Most purchases are taxed at a rate of 8%. Major consumer categories taxed at a different rate include: groceries, which are taxed at a rate of 4%. Major consumer categories that are exempt from sales tax include: drugs and medical services.

Within the city limits of Atlanta, the property tax rate is .043863. Homes are assessed at 40% of market value. There are various exemptions off the different components of the property tax. Property tax includes garbage pickup.

Atlanta has a personal property tax rate of .043863. Boats, motors and aircraft are subject to the tax and assessed at 40% of fair market value.

Our couples relocating to Atlanta must pay an ad valorem tax (personal property tax) based on the local tax rate and the age, make and model of each vehicle. The tax due upon initial registration is $237 for the Explorer and $288 for the Camry. Our couples

also pay a registration fee of $20 per automobile and a title fee of $18 per automobile. Thereafter, on an annual basis, our couples will pay an ad valorem tax and a registration fee, per automobile.

Dahlonega

Dahlonega has no local income tax but does levy a sales tax.

Most purchases are taxed at a rate of 7%. Major consumer categories taxed at a different rate include: groceries, which are taxed at a rate of 3%. Major consumer categories that are exempt from sales tax include: drugs and medical services.

Within the city limits of Dahlonega, the property tax rate is .028195. Homes are assessed at 40% of market value. There are various exemptions off the different components of the property tax. Property tax does not cover garbage pickup.

Dahlonega has a personal property tax rate of .028195. Boats, motors and aircraft are subject to the tax and assessed at 40% of fair market value.

Our couples relocating to Dahlonega must pay an ad valorem tax (personal property tax) based on the local tax rate and the age, make and model of each vehicle. The tax due upon initial registration is $153 for the Explorer and $186 for the Camry. Our couples also pay a registration fee of $20 per automobile and a title fee of $18 per automobile. Thereafter, on an annual basis, our couples will pay an ad valorem tax and a registration fee, per automobile.

Gainesville

Gainesville has no local income tax but does levy a sales tax.

Most purchases are taxed at a rate of 7%. Major consumer categories taxed at a different rate include: groceries, which are taxed at a rate of 3%. Major consumer categories that are exempt from sales tax include: drugs and medical services.

Within the city limits of Gainesville, the local property tax rate is .01072 and the county property tax rate is .00723. Homes are assessed at 100% of market value by the city of Gainesville and 40%

GEORGIA TAX TABLE

Instructions

1. Find the Income in the far left column closest to your anticipated retirement income.
2. Find the Home Value closest to the value of the home where you will live in retirement.
3. Follow that row to your estimated Total Tax Burden at age 65 and beyond.

Income	Home Value	Property Tax & Other Fees	Personal Property Tax & Auto Fees	Sales Tax	Local Income Tax	State Income Tax[†]	Total Tax Burden	Rank[*]
ATHENS								
$30,000	$125,000	$1,281	$406	$957	-	($20)	$2,624	80 of 173
	150,000	1,612	406	957	-	(20)	2,955	83 of 173
	175,000	1,942	406	957	-	(20)	3,285	86 of 173
$60,000	$150,000	$1,612	$406	$1,655	-	$98	$3,771	60 of 203
	225,000	2,604	406	1,655	-	98	4,763	76 of 203
	300,000	3,595	406	1,655	-	98	5,754	90 of 203
$90,000	$225,000	$2,604	$406	$2,046	-	$1,348	$6,404	93 of 203
	375,000	4,587	406	2,046	-	1,348	8,387	94 of 203
	525,000	6,570	406	2,046	-	1,348	10,370	102 of 203
ATLANTA								
$30,000	$125,000	$112	$526	$1,109	-	($20)	$1,727	13 of 173
	150,000	324	526	1,109	-	(20)	1,939	17 of 173
	175,000	649	526	1,109	-	(20)	2,264	21 of 173
$60,000	$150,000	$438	$526	$1,912	-	$98	$2,974	13 of 203
	225,000	1,073	526	1,912	-	98	3,609	13 of 203
	300,000	1,708	526	1,912	-	98	4,244	18 of 203
$90,000	$225,000	$2,977	$526	$2,361	-	$1,348	$7,212	130 of 203
	375,000	5,609	526	2,361	-	1,348	9,844	147 of 203
	525,000	8,241	526	2,361	-	1,348	12,476	149 of 203
DAHLONEGA								
$30,000	$125,000	$881	$352	$957	-	($20)	$2,170	39 of 173
	150,000	1,163	352	957	-	(20)	2,452	45 of 173
	175,000	1,445	352	957	-	(20)	2,734	52 of 173
$60,000	$150,000	$1,504	$352	$1,655	-	$98	$3,609	47 of 203
	225,000	2,350	352	1,655	-	98	4,455	55 of 203
	300,000	3,196	352	1,655	-	98	5,301	65 of 203
$90,000	$225,000	$2,350	$352	$2,046	-	$1,348	$6,096	73 of 203
	375,000	4,042	352	2,046	-	1,348	7,788	74 of 203
	525,000	5,733	352	2,046	-	1,348	9,479	73 of 203
GAINESVILLE								
$30,000	$125,000	$1,399	$417	$957	-	($20)	$2,753	95 of 173
	150,000	1,739	417	957	-	(20)	3,093	99 of 173
	175,000	2,079	417	957	-	(20)	3,433	95 of 173
$60,000	$150,000	$1,754	$417	$1,655	-	$98	$3,924	72 of 203
	225,000	2,774	417	1,655	-	98	4,944	92 of 203
	300,000	3,795	417	1,655	-	98	5,965	96 of 203
$90,000	$225,000	$3,088	$417	$2,046	-	$1,348	$6,899	121 of 203
	375,000	5,129	417	2,046	-	1,348	8,940	118 of 203
	525,000	7,171	417	2,046	-	1,348	10,982	123 of 203

[†]The low income tax credit is issued as a reduction of income tax due or as a refund if the credit is greater than the tax liability.
[*]There are 203 cities in this book, 30 of which have higher than average home prices. We have estimated taxes for a tier of higher home values (and omitted the lowest tier) for these 30 cities. The city with the lowest tax burden for an income/home value combination is given the #1 rating; the higher the rating, the higher the total tax burden.

Income	Home Value	Property Tax & Other Fees	Personal Property Tax & Auto Fees	Sales Tax	Local Income Tax	State Income Tax[†]	Total Tax Burden	Rank[*]
ST. SIMONS ISLAND								
$30,000	$125,000	$1,134	$306	$806	-	($20)	$2,226	41 of 173
	150,000	1,426	306	806	-	(20)	2,518	53 of 173
	175,000	1,718	306	806	-	(20)	2,810	58 of 173
$60,000	$150,000	$1,620	$306	$1,398	-	$98	$3,422	32 of 203
	225,000	2,496	306	1,398	-	98	4,298	48 of 203
	300,000	3,372	306	1,398	-	98	5,174	57 of 203
$90,000	$225,000	$2,496	$306	$1,730	-	$1,348	$5,880	55 of 203
	375,000	4,248	306	1,730	-	1,348	7,632	68 of 203
	525,000	6,000	306	1,730	-	1,348	9,384	69 of 203
SAVANNAH								
$30,000	$125,000	$713	$488	$806	-	($20)	$1,987	27 of 173
	150,000	1,117	488	806	-	(20)	2,391	42 of 173
	175,000	1,522	488	806	-	(20)	2,796	56 of 173
$60,000	$150,000	$1,721	$488	$1,398	-	$98	$3,705	58 of 203
	225,000	2,943	488	1,398	-	98	4,927	90 of 203
	300,000	4,119	488	1,398	-	98	6,103	109 of 203
$90,000	$225,000	$3,352	$488	$1,730	-	$1,348	$6,918	122 of 203
	375,000	5,778	488	1,730	-	1,348	9,344	131 of 203
	525,000	8,203	488	1,730	-	1,348	11,769	134 of 203
THOMASVILLE								
$30,000	$125,000	$1,270	$381	$806	-	($20)	$2,437	64 of 173
	150,000	1,578	381	806	-	(20)	2,745	69 of 173
	175,000	1,886	381	806	-	(20)	3,053	79 of 173
$60,000	$150,000	$1,743	$381	$1,398	-	$98	$3,620	49 of 203
	225,000	2,667	381	1,398	-	98	4,544	62 of 203
	300,000	3,591	381	1,398	-	98	5,468	74 of 203
$90,000	$225,000	$2,667	$381	$1,730	-	$1,348	$6,126	75 of 203
	375,000	4,515	381	1,730	-	1,348	7,974	80 of 203
	525,000	6,362	381	1,730	-	1,348	9,821	83 of 203

[†]The low income tax credit is issued as a reduction of income tax due or as a refund if the credit is greater than the tax liability.
[*]There are 203 cities in this book, 30 of which have higher than average home prices. We have estimated taxes for a tier of higher home values (and omitted the lowest tier) for these 30 cities. The city with the lowest tax burden for an income/home value combination is given the #1 rating; the higher the rating, the higher the total tax burden.

of market value by Hall County. There are various exemptions off the different components of property tax. Property tax does not cover garbage pickup.

Gainesville has a personal property tax rate of .01072, and Hall County has a personal property tax rate of .00723. Boats, motors and aircraft are subject to the tax and assessed at 100% of market value for the city of Gainesville and 40% market value for Hall County.

Our couples relocating to Gainesville must pay an ad valorem tax (personal property tax) based on the local tax rate and the age, make and model of each vehicle. The tax due upon initial registration is $187 for the Explorer and $227 for the Camry. Our couples also pay a registration fee of $20 per

automobile and a title fee of $18 per automobile. Thereafter, on an annual basis, our couples will pay an ad valorem tax and a registration fee, per automobile.

St. Simons Island

St. Simons Island has no local income tax but does levy a sales tax.

Most purchases are taxed at a rate of 6%. As of July 1, 2007, most purchases are taxed at a rate of 7%. Major consumer categories taxed at a different rate include: groceries, which are taxed at a rate of 2%. As of July 1, 2007, groceries are taxed at a rate of 3%. Major consumer categories that are exempt from sales tax include: drugs and medical services.

Within the city limits of St. Simons Island, the property tax rate is .024031. Homes are assessed at 40% of market value. There are various exemptions off the different components of property tax. Property tax does not cover garbage pickup.

St. Simons Island has a personal property rate of .024031. Boats, motors and aircraft are subject to the tax and assessed at 40% of fair market value.

Our couples relocating to St. Simons Island must pay an ad valorem tax (personal property tax) based on the local tax rate and the age, make and model of each vehicle. The tax due upon initial registration is $141 for the Explorer and $171 for the Camry. Our couples also pay a registration fee of

$20 per automobile and a title fee of $18 per automobile. Thereafter, on an annual basis, our couples will pay an ad valorem tax and a registration fee, per automobile.

Savannah

Savannah has no local income tax but does levy a sales tax.

Most purchases are taxed at a rate of 6%. As of January 1, 2007, most purchases are taxed at a rate of 7%. Major consumer categories taxed at a different rate include: groceries, which are taxed at a rate of 2%. As of January 1, 2007, groceries are taxed at a rate of 3%. Major consumer categories that are exempt from sales tax include: drugs and medical services.

Within the city limits of Savannah, the property tax rate is .040424. Homes are assessed at 40% of market value. There are various exemptions off the different components of property tax. Property

tax does not cover garbage pickup.

Savannah has a personal property tax rate of .040424. Boats, motors and aircraft are subject to the tax and assessed at 40% of fair market value

Our couples relocating to Savannah must pay an ad valorem tax (personal property tax) based on the local tax rate and the age, make and model of each vehicle. The tax due upon initial registration is $238 for the Explorer and $290 for the Camry. Our couples also pay a registration fee of $20 per automobile and a title fee of $18 per automobile. Thereafter, on an annual basis, our couples will pay an ad valorem tax and a registration fee, per automobile.

Thomasville

Thomasville has no local income tax but does levy a sales tax.

Most purchases are taxed at a rate of 6%. As of January 1, 2007, most purchases are taxed at a rate of 7%. Major

consumer categories taxed at a different rate include: groceries, which are taxed at a rate of 2%. As of January 1, 2007, groceries are taxed at a rate of 3%. Major consumer categories that are exempt from sales tax include: drugs and medical services.

Within the city limits of Thomasville, the property tax rate is .030792. Homes are assessed at 40% of market value. There are various exemptions off the different components of property tax. Property tax does not cover garbage pickup.

Thomasville has a personal property rate of .030792. Boats, motors and aircraft are subject to the tax and assessed at 40% of fair market value.

Our couples relocating to Thomasville must pay a title transfer fee of $18 per automobile and a tag fee of $20 per automobile at the time of registration. Thereafter, on an annual basis, our couples will pay a tag fee per automobile.

• Georgia's Top Retirement Towns •

Athens

When college founders were looking for a site for the University of Georgia, they chose a remote location where students would be removed from temptations. They picked Athens, naming it after the Greek center of learning.

Today, Athens is home to a great university offering every imaginable course of study for students of all ages, including seniors. But it couldn't be any closer to those unnamed temptations if it tried. Considered one of the country's hottest college towns, Athens is also known for its hip and bustling nightlife and is renowned for its rocking music scene.

Athens-area retirees can hit the books in the Georgia Center for Continuing Education, the university's lifelong learning program. The university offers group classes, online courses and independent study programs for seniors looking to update a previous certification or delve into some new subject.

If you're too cool for school (but like the idea of living near one), you won't have any problem staying busy. Just head downtown, where jazz, classical, blues, country and rock performances go 24/7 in famous venues like the 40

Watt Club and the Georgia Theatre. In late June, AthFest attracts more than 120 bands that play on indoor and outdoor stages throughout the weekend.

Athens also has received kudos for its thriving arts district and has a historic downtown lined with galleries and art studios. The Georgia Museum of Art, the state's official venue, houses a significant collection on the university campus.

The Athens Welcome Center, in an 1820 Federal-style building, doubles as a museum and a one-stop information clearinghouse for all local attractions. You'll find the restored downtown and other historic districts brimming with sophisticated restaurants, shops and galleries, live theater companies and a symphony orchestra. There's also a year-round slate of performances and exhibitions at the University of Georgia's Performing and Visual Arts Complex — just in case you're looking for ways to cut class without actually leaving campus.

Population: About 65,000, plus about 36,500 students

Climate:

	High	Low
January	51	33
July	90	69

Cost of living: Below average

Housing cost: The average sales price of homes in Clarke County during the first half of 2007 was $185,000, according to the Athens Area Association of Realtors.

Information: Athens Convention and Visitors Bureau, (800) 653-0603 or www.visitathensga.com. Athens Area Chamber of Commerce, (706) 549-6800 or www.athenschamber.net.

Dahlonega

When gold was discovered in Dahlonega accidentally in the early 1800s by a deer hunter who tripped over a rock loaded with the ore, it started a rush into this beautiful Appalachian area. Today, Dahlonega is witnessing a resurgence in interest from those seeking a balanced community. Spas and resorts dot the landscape, where 30 waterfalls, lakes, mountains and rivers provide the visual serenity retirees want. The handsomely restored downtown is a hub of activity. The moderate, four-season climate draws many "halfbacks" — those who first moved from colder climates in the Northeast to warm but seasonless Florida and then relocated partway back up the East Coast.

Dahlonega is a haven for artists, wine lovers, health advocates and outdoor enthusiasts. About 65 miles from Atlanta, it has evolved into a center for the performing and visual arts and is a gateway to vineyards.

The historic Holly Theatre hosts live productions, and Music in the Park showcases local musicians. North Georgia College & State University adds to the cultural mix. Hikers take off for the surrounding Chattahoochee National Forest and nearby Springer Mountain, the southern terminus of the Appalachian Trail.

Besides golfing, fishing, hiking or biking, try some less traditional sports such as ice-skating in Hancock Park in the winter or ballroom dancing. And, along with galleries to explore, the downtown square boasts several ice cream and gelato shops.

"We drove around the picturesque town square in 1994 and were hooked," admits retiree Charlie Davis. "We bought almost immediately and then moved here permanently from West Palm Beach, FL, in 1999. We've never regretted a moment." Dahlonega's residents have a neighborly attitude he finds uncommonly pleasant. Moreover, the college setting, scenery, history and plethora of community activities keep him completely satisfied.

Population: 4,757

Climate:

	High	Low
January	49	26
July	86	62

Cost of living: Below average

Housing cost: The median sales price of single-family homes during the first half of 2007 was $185,000, according to data from RE/MAX Mountain Properties.

Information: Dahlonega-Lumpkin County Chamber of Commerce/Convention and Visitors Bureau, (800) 231-5543 or www.dahlonega.org.

The Golden Isles And Brunswick

Known as the Golden Isles, St. Simons, Little St. Simons (a private resort), Sea Island and Jekyll Island are a cluster of barrier islands off the lower coast of Georgia. Brunswick is the mainland port town.

For a look at how these islands appeared before development, visit the nearby Cumberland Island National Seashore, so pristine that you need to bring your own food and water. Rent a bike and explore the dune fields, maritime forests and salt marshes.

The Golden Isles add myriad recreational opportunities to this beauty. Golfers can aim at more than 200 holes, and the Intracoastal Waterway provides access to great fishing in the rivers and marshes. Horseback ride or bike along the shore, relax on the beaches or go sailing, swimming, kayaking or canoeing. Birding is great as the area is on the Southern flyway.

Housing options are plentiful, including quaint cottages, stylish condos, waterfront estates and historic residences. Prices are highest on the islands, with Sea Island at the top. St. Simons is the most developed island and has the most varied housing options — small cottages, condos and pricey homes — as well as the most new developments.

The state of Georgia now owns Jekyll Island, formerly a late 19th-century private resort for wealthy barons. Development is limited to 35 percent of the island's area. Many of the retirees here are extremely generous with their time and money, volunteering in Jekyll's National Historic Landmark District and working on behalf of the island's preservation.

For less-expensive housing, consider the Brunswick area, where there are historic homes and new-home subdivisions starting from about $200,000.

Population: 17,300 in Brunswick, 14,600 on St. Simons Island, 700 on Sea Island and 600 on Jekyll Island, with 73,554 in Glynn County.

Climate:

	High	Low
January	65	50
July	95	72

Cost of living: Above average

Housing cost: The average sales price of a single-family home in the first quarter of 2007 was $155,000 in Brunswick ($236,700 including mainland Glynn County), $611,000 on Jekyll Island and $750,000 on St. Simons Island, according to data from Sea Palms Realty. Home prices on Sea Island are $1 million-plus.

Information: Brunswick-Golden Isles Chamber of Commerce, (912) 265-0620 or www.bgicoc.com.

Savannah

Located on the mouth of the Savannah River that forms the border between Georgia and South Carolina, Savannah is a pretty Southern belle, both sophisticated and fun-loving. Spanish moss hangs off giant live oak trees, and fountains grace many of the parklike squares, which date to the original city plan from 1733. The city's expansive historic district has everything from warehouses to churches and elegant mansions fronting old brick streets.

Food lovers treasure the city for its good eats, ranging from fine restaurants with noted chefs to Southern family-style feasts and rustic shacks where you can chow down on mounds of freshly caught crabs.

"People move here for the aesthetic beauty, the weather and the hospitality, as well as the stellar health care," says Erica Backus of the city's chamber of commerce.

Winters are mild enough to allow outdoor recreation most of the year, and there are plenty of options. Savannah sits along the coast in a network of rivers and creeks with access to the Atlantic Ocean. Retirees can enjoy fishing, boating, golfing, tennis, birding, hiking and biking. Beaches are nearby.

The city has a strong cultural arts scene with plays, concerts and museums. It is home to the renowned Telfair Museum of Art with three sites showcasing American art, decorative arts and period rooms. Several colleges are in the area, including the acclaimed Savannah College of Art and Design, and leisure-leaning classes are available.

Among the extensive health-care facilities are two major medical centers with three hospitals providing state-of-the-art care that includes teaching and research facilities.

Retirees are valued in Savannah, and the area has seen the growth of new-home developments catering to baby boomers.

Population: 127,889

Climate:

	High	Low
January	60	38
July	92	72

Cost of living: Below average

Housing cost: The average sales price of single-family homes during the first nine months of 2007 was $283,019, according to the Savannah MLXchange, an internet database used by realty agents in Savannah.

Information: Savannah Area Chamber of Commerce, (877) 728-2662 or www.savannahchamber.com.

Thomasville

A former winter retreat for wealthy Northerners in the late 19th century, this little town of about 19,000 may be one of the best-kept retirement secrets.

During the Victorian era, well-heeled visitors came to stay in the town's upscale hotels. Many visitors went on to build grand Victorian cottages or buy acreage for exclusive winter plantations. Harper's magazine called it "the best winter resort on three continents." Within a 35-mile radius of town are 71 plantations, including some from the antebellum period and some that were hunting retreats.

Today, Thomasville offers culture and class on a budget, with a below-average cost of living and generous state income tax exemptions on retirement income for residents 62 and older.

An award-winning revitalization program restored Thomasville to a bustling and picture-perfect Main Street town that reflects the Old South in charming Victorian storefronts and tree-shaded streets. During the program, locals stripped away decades of paint and "modern" facades, restoring more than 100 buildings that today house 150-plus commercial establishments — from banks to an 1880s drugstore. While locals once drove a half-hour into Tallahassee to shop, now city slickers visit Thomasville for its boutiques.

Over the years, Thomasville's vacationing elite established a cultural center for theater, dance and the arts as well as a state-of-the-art health-care system. The town is a medical hub, with more than 130 doctors and a growing hospital that opened a cardiovascular center in 2006 and also has cancer care among extensive services. Thomas University, a four-year liberal arts institution, has special programs for seniors.

Thomasville's comfortable climate means you can golf, hike and cycle year-round. It doesn't hurt that dogwoods, azaleas, fuchsia and roses put on colorful shows in the spring.

Population: 18,988

Climate:

	High	Low
January	63	40
July	92	71

Cost of living: Below average

Housing cost: The median price from April through September 2007 was $153,000, according to data from First Thomasville Realty.

Information: Thomasville-Thomas County Chamber of Commerce, (229) 226-9600 or www.thomasvillechamber.com. Thomasville Visitors Center, (866) 577-3600 or www.thomasvillega.com.

HAWAII

Hawaii has a state income tax and a state excise tax (sales tax).

The state income tax is graduated from 1.4% to 8.25% depending upon income bracket. For married couples filing jointly, the rates are 1.4% on the first $4,000 of taxable income; 3.2% on the next $4,000 of taxable income; 5.5% on the next $8,000 of taxable income; 6.4% on the next $8,000 of taxable income; 6.8% on the next $8,000 of taxable income; 7.2% on the next $8,000 of taxable income; 7.6% on the next $20,000 of taxable income; 7.9% on the next $20,000 of taxable income; and 8.25% on taxable income above $80,000.

In calculating the tax, there is no deduction for federal income tax paid. Federal and state pensions are exempt. Private pensions are exempt if they do

not include employee contributions. Social Security benefits are exempt. There is a $1,900 standard deduction from Hawaii adjusted gross income for married couples filing jointly. There is a $1,040 personal exemption from Hawaii adjusted gross income per person and an additional $1,040 personal exemption per person age 65 and over.

Major tax credits or rebates include: credit for income taxes paid to other states, low-income housing tax credit and low-income refundable tax credit. Our couples do not qualify for these credits.

The state excise tax rate is 4%. Although this tax is imposed on the seller (unlike sales tax, which is imposed on the buyer), businesses customarily pass the tax on to the buyer.

Since car registration and renewal fees differ within the state, see city information for details.

Honolulu (Oahu)

Honolulu has no local income tax and does not levy an additional excise tax.

Most purchases include the 4% state excise tax. Major consumer categories taxed at a different rate: none. Major consumer categories that are exempt from excise tax include: drugs.

Within the city limits of Honolulu, the property tax rate is .00359. Homes are assessed at 100% of market value. All

---

HAWAII TAX TABLE

Instructions

1. Find the Income in the far left column closest to your anticipated retirement income.
2. Find the Home Value closest to the value of the home where you will live in retirement.
3. Follow that row to your estimated Total Tax Burden at age 65 and beyond.

Income	Home Value	Property Tax & Other Fees	Personal Property Tax & Auto Fees	Sales Tax	Local Income Tax	State Income Tax	Total Tax Burden	Rank *
HONOLULU								
$60,000	$150,000	$180	$392	$1,066	-	$1,736	$3,374	29 of 203
	225,000	449	392	1,066	-	1,736	3,643	15 of 203
	300,000	718	392	1,066	-	1,736	3,912	10 of 203 O
$90,000	$225,000	$449	$392	$1,314	-	$3,821	$5,976	63 of 203
	375,000	987	392	1,314	-	3,821	6,514	28 of 203
	525,000	1,526	392	1,314	-	3,821	7,053	19 of 203
	$600,000	$1,795	$392	$1,314	-	$3,821	$7,322	6 of 30
	750,000	2,334	392	1,314	-	3,821	7,861	4 of 30
	900,000	2,872	392	1,314	-	3,821	8,399	3 of 30
WAILUKU								
$60,000	$150,000	$240	$263	$1,066	-	$1,736	$3,305	25 of 203
	225,000	240	263	1,066	-	1,736	3,305	7 of 203 O
	300,000	240	263	1,066	-	1,736	3,305	3 of 203 O
$90,000	$225,000	$240	$263	$1,314	-	$3,821	$5,638	45 of 203
	375,000	368	263	1,314	-	3,821	5,766	14 of 203
	525,000	743	263	1,314	-	3,821	6,141	7 of 203 O
	$600,000	$930	$263	$1,314	-	$3,821	$6,328	3 of 30
	750,000	1,305	263	1,314	-	3,821	6,703	2 of 30
	900,000	1,680	263	1,314	-	3,821	7,078	1 of 30

*There are 203 cities in this book, 30 of which have higher than average home prices. We have estimated taxes for a tier of higher home values (and omitted the lowest tier) for these 30 cities. The city with the lowest tax burden for an income/home value combination is given the #1 rating; the higher the rating, the higher the total tax burden.

properties are subject to a minimum tax of $100 per year. There is a homeowner's exemption that increases by age. For homeowners age 65-69, the exemption is $100,000. In 2007, this exemption increases to $120,000 for homeowners age 65 and older. There is also a Circuit Breaker tax relief, which limits property tax liability to 4% of gross income. Property tax includes garbage pickup.

Honolulu has no personal property tax for individuals.

Our couples relocating to Honolulu must pay state and city registration fees per automobile plus state and city weight taxes based on the weight of the automobile. They also must pay a license plate fee, an emblem fee, a Hawaii beautification fee and a title fee per automobile at the time of registration. Total fee is approximately $238 for the Explorer and $184 for the Camry. Thereafter, on an annual basis, our couples will pay registration fees, weight fees, an emblem fee and a Hawaii beautification fee, per automobile.

Wailuku (Maui)

Wailuku has no local income tax and does not levy an additional excise tax.

Most purchases include the 4% state excise tax. Major consumer categories taxed at a different rate: none. Major consumer categories that are exempt from excise tax include: drugs.

Within the city limits of Wailuku, the property tax rate is .0025. Homes are assessed at 100% of market value. All properties are subject to a minimum tax of $60 per year. There is a homeowner's exemption of $300,000 for all residents who own and occupy their homes as their primary residence. There is also a Circuit Breaker tax relief, which limits property tax liability to 3% of federal adjusted gross income. Property tax does not cover garbage pickup.

Wailuku has no personal property tax for individuals.

Our couples relocating to Wailuku must pay state and county registration fees per automobile plus state and county weight taxes based on the weight of the automobile. They must also pay a beautification fee, a plate and emblem fee and a title transfer fee per automobile at the time of registration. Total fee is approximately $158 for the Explorer and $125 for the Camry. Thereafter, on an annual basis, our couples will pay registration fees, weight fees, a beautification fee and a plate and emblem fee, per automobile.

• Hawaii's Top Retirement Town •

Honolulu

Some long for the ultimate destination in island living, and for them, no better place to retire exists than Honolulu on the island of Oahu. In the central Pacific Ocean about 2,400 miles southwest of San Francisco, this state capital blends multiple cultures and combines a spectacular beach setting with urban amenities.

There is much to attract retirees. Scenic beauty, unique Hawaiian culture, ocean sports, clean water, near-perfect year-round weather, good educational opportunities and generally long life expectancies are some of the benefits.

Honolulu bursts with cultural activities and attractions, offering concerts and plays to augment the beach scene and golf. The renowned Bishop Museum chronicles the natural and cultural history of the Pacific region, and the unique 1880s Iolani Palace, a National Historic Landmark, was the official residence of Hawaii's last two monarchs. The University of Hawaii has several campuses with performance venues and offers an Osher Lifelong Learning Institute with programs for people age 50 and beyond. Add to all this fine dining in multiple cuisines and shopping.

Within a short drive, it's also possible to escape the city life to go hiking and explore lush, more rural areas of the island.

The city is a medical, military and air-transportation hub and a major tourist destination, as well as the gateway for many visitors to all the islands. Oahu itself received 4.6 million visitors in 2006.

While Honolulu traditionally has been a low-tax destination for retirees, it is one of the most expensive cities in living costs, with housing in particular being considerably above the average price. Flying to and from the mainland also raises transportation expenditures. It's a place where taking an extended-stay vacation is particularly wise to test whether you want to relocate here permanently. But it easily can be a second-home option, offering many condos — and certainly a destination that family and friends will come to visit you.

Population: 377,357

Climate: High Low
January 80 66
July 88 74

Cost of living: Far above average

Housing cost: For the third quarter of 2007, the median sales price was $649,900 for single-family homes and $330,000 for condos, according to the Honolulu Board of Realtors.

Information: Chamber of Commerce of Hawaii, (808) 545-4300 or www.cocha waii.com.

IDAHO

Idaho has a state income tax and a state sales tax.

The state income tax rate is graduated from 1.6% to 7.8% depending upon income bracket. For married couples filing jointly, the rates are 1.6% on the first $2,396 of taxable income; 3.6% on the next $2,396 of taxable income; 4.1% on the next $2,396 of taxable income; 5.1% on the next $2,398 of taxable income; 6.1% on the next $2,396 of taxable income; 7.1% on the next $5,990 of taxable income; 7.4% on the next $29,954 of taxable income; and 7.8% on taxable income above $47,926.

In calculating the tax, there is no deduction for federal income tax paid. Federal pensions are not exempt; however, married couples filing jointly with

> **O Tax Heavens:** Coeur d'Alene
> **Ψ Tax Hells:** None
> **Top Retirement Towns:** Boise, Coeur d'Alene

both spouses age 65 or older qualify for up to a $36,954 deduction, minus any Social Security or railroad retirement benefits received, from their federal pension income. State and private pensions are not exempt. Social Security benefits are exempt. There is a standard deduction of $12,300 from adjusted gross income for married couples filing jointly with both spouses age 65 or older and a $3,300 exemption per person from adjusted gross income.

There is a $10 permanent building

fund tax for each Idaho income tax return filed.

Major tax credits or rebates include: credit for income taxes paid to other states, which our couples do not qualify for; and grocery credit of $20 per person, plus $15 per person age 65 or older, which our couples do qualify for.

The state sales tax rate is 5%. On October 1, 2006, the state sales tax rate increases to 6%.

Since car registration and renewal fees differ within the state, see city information for details.

Boise

Boise has no local income tax and does not levy an additional sales tax.

Most purchases are taxed at the state

IDAHO TAX TABLE

Instructions

1. Find the Income in the far left column closest to your anticipated retirement income.
2. Find the Home Value closest to the value of the home where you will live in retirement.
3. Follow that row to your estimated Total Tax Burden at age 65 and beyond.

Income	Home Value	Property Tax & Other Fees	Personal Property Tax & Auto Fees	Sales Tax	Local Income Tax	State Income Tax[†]	Total Tax Burden	Rank[*]
BOISE								
$30,000	$125,000	$1,046	$159	$757	-	($70)	$1,892	20 of 173
	150,000	1,219	159	757	-	(70)	2,065	22 of 173
	175,000	1,566	159	757	-	(70)	2,412	28 of 173
$60,000	$150,000	$1,219	$159	$1,284	-	$784	$3,446	34 of 203
	225,000	2,259	159	1,284	-	784	4,486	59 of 203
	300,000	3,298	159	1,284	-	784	5,525	76 of 203
$90,000	$225,000	$2,259	$159	$1,576	-	$2,829	$6,823	113 of 203
	375,000	4,337	159	1,576	-	2,829	8,901	116 of 203
	525,000	6,416	159	1,576	-	2,829	10,980	122 of 203
COEUR D'ALENE								
$30,000	$125,000	$683	$112	$757	-	($70)	$1,482	8 of 173 O
	150,000	786	112	757	-	(70)	1,585	6 of 173 O
	175,000	992	112	757	-	(70)	1,791	7 of 173 O
$60,000	$150,000	$786	$112	$1,284	-	$784	$2,966	12 of 203
	225,000	1,404	112	1,284	-	784	3,584	12 of 203
	300,000	2,023	112	1,284	-	784	4,203	16 of 203
$90,000	$225,000	$1,404	$112	$1,576	-	$2,829	$5,921	58 of 203
	375,000	2,642	112	1,576	-	2,829	7,159	47 of 203
	525,000	3,879	112	1,576	-	2,829	8,396	48 of 203

[†]Grocery tax credit is issued as a reduction of income tax due or as a refund if the credit is greater than the tax liability.
[*]There are 203 cities in this book, 30 of which have higher than average home prices. We have estimated taxes for a tier of higher home values (and omitted the lowest tier) for these 30 cities. The city with the lowest tax burden for an income/home value combination is given the #1 rating; the higher the rating, the higher the total tax burden.

rate of 5%. On October 1, 2006, the state sales tax rate increases to 6%. Major consumer categories taxed at a different rate: none. Major consumer categories that are exempt from sales tax include: drugs and medical services.

In Tax Code Area 01 of Boise, the property tax rate is .013856945. Homes are assessed at 100% of market value. There is a homeowner's exemption of 50% up to $75,000 off assessed value of the home. There is a sliding-scale exemption of up to $1,320 for persons age 65 and over with modified income up to $28,000. Property tax does not cover garbage pickup.

In Tax Code Area 01 of Boise, there is a personal property tax rate of .013856945. Personal property is assessed at 100% of market value. Items subject to the tax include mobile homes. The homeowner's exemptions also apply to mobile homes. We've assumed our couples do not own any of the items subject to the personal property tax.

Our couples relocating to Boise must pay a registration fee of $52 per automobile, a county highway fee of $22 per automobile, a plate fee of $6 per automobile, a title fee of $8 per automobile and miscellaneous fees of $9 per automobile. Thereafter, on an annual basis, our couples will pay a registration fee, a county highway fee and miscellaneous fees, per automobile.

Coeur d'Alene

Coeur d'Alene has no local income tax and does not levy an additional sales tax.

Most purchases are taxed at the state rate of 5%. On October 1, 2006, the state sales tax rate increases to 6%. Major consumer categories taxed at a different rate: none. Major consumer categories that are exempt from sales tax include: drugs and medical services.

One of the property tax rates in Coeur d'Alene is .008248874. Homes are assessed at 100% of market value. There is a homeowner's exemption of

50% up to $75,000 off assessed value of the home. There is a sliding-scale exemption of up to $1,320 for persons age 65 and over with modified income up to $28,000. Property tax includes garbage pickup. There is also a street-light service fee of approximately $31 per year and a stormwater utility fee of $48 per year.

One of the personal property tax rates in Coeur d'Alene is .008248874. Personal property is assessed at 100% of market value. Items subject to the tax include mobile homes. The homeowner's exemptions also apply to mobile homes. We've assumed our couples do not own any of the items subject to the personal property tax.

Our couples relocating to Coeur d'Alene must pay a registration fee of $52 per automobile, a plate fee of $6 per automobile, a title fee of $8 per automobile and miscellaneous fees of $10 per automobile. Thereafter, on an annual basis, our couples will pay a registration fee per automobile.

• Idaho's Top Retirement Towns •

Boise

If the dry climate of a high Western desert is your dream environment, head out to Boise, the lively capital of the Gem State of Idaho. Set in Treasure Valley against the canyons and foothills of the western edge of the Rocky Mountains with the Boise River running through it, the city offers outdoor enthusiasts a wide range of activities, including nearby alpine skiing, river touring, hiking and backpacking.

Whether you enjoy the monarch butterflies or mountain bluebirds or cast for cutthroat trout, nature abounds. More than 20 miles of greenbelt grace the city, and golfers can practice their swing on about 20 courses in the area.

The downtown area attracts residents to many cultural events and festivals, such as the annual Art in the Park and Alive After Five outdoor concert series. The annual Idaho Shakespeare Festival draws large crowds to an amphitheater near downtown, in a park setting with native plants and wildlife.

Retirees are among those who have

fueled growth in Boise over the last decade. The area has a variety of housing options, including walkable neighborhoods near restaurants and stores and a resort-style 55-plus community, Touchmark at Meadow Lake Village in Meridian. Boise has a number of hospitals, including St. Luke's and St. Alphonsus regional medical centers, and the four-year, 20,000-student Boise State University offers continuing-education opportunities.

"People who haven't been here don't understand how good the climate is," says Shirl Boyce, 64. "The elevation is only 2,800 feet. You can ski in the morning and go golfing in the afternoon. I don't even use snow tires in the winter."

Population: 198,638
Climate: High Low
January   37   24
July   89   60
Cost of living: Below average to average
Housing cost: The median price of homes during the first half of 2007 was $208,450, according to the National Association of Realtors.

Information: Boise Metro Chamber of Commerce, (208) 472-5200 or www.boisechamber.org. Boise Convention and Visitors Bureau, (800) 635-5240 or www.boise.org.

Coeur d'Alene

The call of the wild meets an appetite for academics in Idaho's colorful and rugged northern panhandle. Gorgeous scenery, clear streams, mountain lakes and 87 parks and campgrounds mix with seven nearby community colleges and universities to offer retirees both outdoor and educational opportunities galore.

Forty-seven major hiking trails and 18 area golf courses, along with fishing, swimming, horseback riding and winter sports, give residents plenty of exercise options. Silverwood Theme Park/ Boulder Beach Water Park entices grandchildren with "Tremors," a 65-mph wooden roller coaster, and a crashing wave pool with a huge waterslide. Adults try their luck at the Coeur d'Alene Casino and the Coeur d'Alene Resort Golf Course.

Coeur d'Alene is only about 35 miles east of Spokane, WA, which adds amenities of a bigger city, including several colleges. Within a 60-mile radius of Coeur d'Alene, educational institutions include North Idaho College, Lewis-Clark State College Coeur d'Alene, University of Idaho Coeur d'Alene, Gonzaga University, Eastern Washington University, Washington State University Spokane and Whitworth University.

"All four seasons are here and the winters aren't too cold," says Bert Morgan, explaining why he and his wife, Judie, moved here from California. "But another good reason we moved here was that I was still working at age 76 to make my mortgage payment in California." In Coeur d'Alene, the couple paid cash for their home and now can live on their Social Security income. Besides, Bert is a fisherman, and the trout here are a lot bigger than in California.

Population: 41,328

Climate:

	High	Low
January	35	22
July	83	55

Cost of living: Average

Housing cost: Between May and October 2007, the median sales price of homes in the Coeur d'Alene area was $203,500 and the average price was $233,518, according to data from the Coeur d'Alene Association of Realtors. Waterfront property runs higher.

Information: Coeur d'Alene Area Chamber of Commerce, (877) 782-9232 or www.cdachamber.com.

ILLINOIS

Illinois has a state income tax and a state sales tax.

The state income tax rate is 3%. In calculating the tax, there is no deduction for federal income tax paid. Federal, state and private pensions are exempt. Social Security benefits are exempt. There is a $2,000 personal exemption from adjusted gross income per person and an additional $1,000 exemption from adjusted gross income per person age 65 or older.

Major tax credits or rebates include: credit for income taxes paid to other states, which our couples do not qualify for; education expense credit, which our couples do not qualify for; and property tax credit, which our couples do qualify for.

The state sales tax rate is 6.25%, but local governments can add to this amount.

O Tax Heavens: None
Ψ Tax Hells: Chicago

Chicago

Chicago has no local income tax but does levy an additional sales tax.

Most purchases are taxed at a rate of 9%. Major consumer categories taxed at a different rate include: groceries and drugs, which are taxed at a rate of 2%. Major consumer categories that are exempt from sales tax: none.

The general city tax rate in Chicago is .05981. Homes are assessed at 16% of market value then multiplied by an equalization factor of 2.732. There is a homestead exemption of $5,000 to $20,000 off assessed value of the home available to all resident homeowners and a senior citizen exemption of an additional $3,000 off the assessed value of the home available to all resident homeowners age 65 or older. There is a circuit breaker rebate program based on gross income and the amount of the property tax bill. There is also a senior citizen assessment freeze if federal adjusted gross income is $45,000 or less. Property tax includes garbage pickup.

Chicago has no personal property tax for individuals.

Our couples relocating to Chicago must pay a registration fee of $78 per automobile, a title fee of $65 per automobile and a reduced senior citizen wheel tax of $30 per automobile. Thereafter, on an annual basis, our couples will pay a registration fee and a reduced senior citizen wheel tax, per automobile.

ILLINOIS TAX TABLE

Instructions

1. Find the Income in the far left column closest to your anticipated retirement income.
2. Find the Home Value closest to the value of the home where you will live in retirement.
3. Follow that row to your estimated Total Tax Burden at age 65 and beyond.

Income	Home Value	Property Tax & Other Fees	Personal Property Tax & Auto Fees	Sales Tax	Local Income Tax	State Income Tax[†]	Total Tax Burden	Rank[*]
CHICAGO								
$30,000	$125,000	$2,790	$216	$1,270	-	-	$4,276	168 of 173 Ψ
	150,000	3,443	216	1,270	-	-	4,929	168 of 173 Ψ
	175,000	4,097	216	1,270	-	-	5,583	166 of 173 Ψ
$60,000	$150,000	$3,443	$216	$2,172	-	$498	$6,329	194 of 203 Ψ
	225,000	5,404	216	2,172	-	400	8,192	196 of 203 Ψ
	300,000	7,365	216	2,172	-	302	10,055	194 of 203 Ψ
$90,000	$225,000	$5,404	$216	$2,700	-	$1,208	$9,528	185 of 203
	375,000	9,326	216	2,700	-	1,012	13,254	193 of 203
	525,000	13,247	216	2,700	-	816	16,979	192 of 203

[†]Credit for property tax paid is issued as a reduction of income tax due.
[*]There are 203 cities in this book, 30 of which have higher than average home prices. We have estimated taxes for a tier of higher home values (and omitted the lowest tier) for these 30 cities. The city with the lowest tax burden for an income/home value combination is given the #1 rating; the higher the rating, the higher the total tax burden.

INDIANA

Indiana has a state income tax and a state sales tax.

The state income tax rate is 3.4%. In calculating the tax, there is no deduction for federal income tax paid. Federal pensions are exempt up to $2,000. State and private pensions are not exempt. Social Security benefits are exempt. There is a $1,000 exemption per person and an additional $1,000 exemption per person age 65 or older. There is an additional exemption of $500 per person age 65 or older with federal adjusted gross income less than $40,000. There is a homeowner's residential property tax deduction of up to $2,500 for property tax paid on principal residence and a renter's deduction of up to $2,500 for rent paid on principal residence.

Major tax credits or rebates include: credit for income taxes paid to other states, credit for local taxes paid outside the state and unified tax credit for the elderly. Our couples do not qualify for

O Tax Heavens: None
Ψ Tax Hells: None

these programs.

The state sales tax rate is 6%.

Bloomington

Bloomington has a local income tax but does not levy an additional sales tax.

The local income tax rate is 1% of Indiana taxable income calculated on the state income tax return.

Most purchases are taxed at the state rate of 6%. Major consumer categories taxed at a different rate: none. Major consumer categories that are exempt from sales tax include: drugs, groceries and medical services.

For residents within the area of Perry Township, the property tax rate is .022828. Homes are assessed at 100% of market value. There are several exemptions available for homeowners, some of which have age, income and resi-

dency requirements. Property tax does not cover garbage pickup.

Bloomington has a personal property tax rate of .022828. Personal property is assessed at trade-in value. Items subject to the tax include boats, boat trailers over 3,000 pounds, trucks over 11,000 pounds, truck campers, travel trailers, RVs, campers, ATVs, snowmobiles and motor homes. We've assumed our couples do not own any of the items subject to the personal property tax.

Our couples relocating to Bloomington must pay an annual excise tax based on the class and age of each vehicle. The tax due upon initial registration is $260 for the Explorer and $207 for the Camry. Our couples also pay a $15 title fee per automobile, a $21 registration fee per automobile and a $25 surtax per automobile. Thereafter, on an annual basis, our couples will pay an excise tax and a surtax, per automobile.

INDIANA TAX TABLE

Instructions

1. Find the Income in the far left column closest to your anticipated retirement income.
2. Find the Home Value closest to the value of the home where you will live in retirement.
3. Follow that row to your estimated Total Tax Burden at age 65 and beyond.

Income	Home Value	Property Tax & Other Fees	Personal Property Tax & Auto Fees	Sales Tax	Local Income Tax	State Income Tax	Total Tax Burden	Rank*
BLOOMINGTON								
$30,000	$125,000	$1,161	$454	$755	$92	$314	$2,776	99 of 173
	150,000	1,705	454	755	87	295	3,296	113 of 173
	175,000	2,068	454	755	83	283	3,643	112 of 173
$60,000	$150,000	$1,705	$454	$1,327	$333	$1,132	$4,951	153 of 203
	225,000	2,794	454	1,327	323	1,099	5,997	150 of 203
	300,000	3,884	454	1,327	323	1,099	7,087	145 of 203
$90,000	$225,000	$2,794	$454	$1,649	$601	$2,045	$7,543	145 of 203
	375,000	4,973	454	1,649	601	2,045	9,722	140 of 203
	525,000	7,152	454	1,649	601	2,045	11,901	140 of 203

*There are 203 cities in this book, 30 of which have higher than average home prices. We have estimated taxes for a tier of higher home values (and omitted the lowest tier) for these 30 cities. The city with the lowest tax burden for an income/home value combination is given the #1 rating; the higher the rating, the higher the total tax burden.

IOWA

Iowa has a state income tax and a state sales tax.

The state income tax rate is graduated from .36% to 8.98% depending upon income bracket. For married couples filing jointly, the rates are .36% on the first $1,300 of taxable income; .72% on the next $1,300 of taxable income; 2.43% on the next $2,600 of taxable income; 4.5% on the next $6,500 of taxable income; 6.12% on the next $7,800 of taxable income; 6.48% on the next $6,500 of taxable income; 6.8% on the next $13,000 of taxable income; 7.92% on the next $19,500 of taxable income; and 8.98% on taxable income above $58,500.

In calculating the tax, there is a deduction for federal income tax paid. Federal, state and private pensions are not exempt; however, there is a pension/retirement income exclusion of up to $12,000 for married couples age 55 or older filing jointly or separately. Some Social Security benefits subject to federal tax are not exempt. There is a $4,060 standard deduction from adjusted gross income for married couples filing jointly. There is a deduction for health insurance premiums paid if the

> **○ Tax Heavens:** None
> **Ψ Tax Hells:** None

payments are not made on a pretax basis and if not included in itemized deductions. There is a $40 credit against tax per person and an additional $20 credit against tax per person age 65 and older.

There is also an alternate method for income tax calculation that may yield a lower tax due for some taxpayers, particularly lower-income taxpayers. This method does not reduce tax liability for our couples.

Major tax credits or rebates include: credit for income taxes paid to other states and earned income credit. Our couples do not qualify for these programs.

The state sales tax rate is 5%, but local governments can add to this amount.

Des Moines

Des Moines has no local income tax but does levy a sales tax.

Most purchases are taxed at a rate of 6%. Major consumer categories taxed at

a different rate: none. Major consumer categories that are exempt from sales tax include: drugs, groceries and medical services.

Within the Des Moines School District, the property tax rate is .04589578. Homes are assessed at 45.5596% of market value. There is a homestead exemption of $3,541 off assessed value for all homeowners. Property tax on new homes (not including land values) is abated for five years. We assumed that our couples qualify for tax abatement. Property tax does not cover garbage pickup. There is also a stormwater maintenance fee of approximately $74 per year.

Des Moines has no personal property tax for individuals.

Our couples relocating to Des Moines must pay a registration fee based on year, make and model of each automobile. The registration fee is $311 for the Explorer and $251 for the Camry. Our couples also pay a $15 title fee per automobile and a $10 lien fee per automobile at the time of registration. Thereafter, on an annual basis, our couples will pay a registration fee per automobile.

IOWA TAX TABLE

Instructions

1. Find the Income in the far left column closest to your anticipated retirement income.
2. Find the Home Value closest to the value of the home where you will live in retirement.
3. Follow that row to your estimated Total Tax Burden at age 65 and beyond.

Income	Home Value	Property Tax & Other Fees	Personal Property Tax & Auto Fees	Sales Tax	Local Income Tax	State Income Tax	Total Tax Burden	Rank*
DES MOINES								
$30,000	$125,000	$2,710	$562	$755	-	-	$4,027	161 of 173
	150,000	3,233	562	755	-	-	4,550	160 of 173
	175,000	3,755	562	755	-	-	5,072	160 of 173
$60,000	$150,000	$3,233	$562	$1,327	-	$1,159	$6,281	193 of 203
	225,000	4,801	562	1,327	-	1,159	7,849	191 of 203
	300,000	6,369	562	1,327	-	1,159	9,417	189 of 203
$90,000	$225,000	$4,801	$562	$1,649	-	$2,871	$9,883	190 of 203
	375,000	7,937	562	1,649	-	2,871	13,019	191 of 203
	525,000	11,074	562	1,649	-	2,871	16,156	186 of 203

*There are 203 cities in this book, 30 of which have higher than average home prices. We have estimated taxes for a tier of higher home values (and omitted the lowest tier) for these 30 cities. The city with the lowest tax burden for an income/home value combination is given the #1 rating; the higher the rating, the higher the total tax burden.

KANSAS

Kansas has a state income tax and a state sales tax.

The state income tax rate is graduated from 3.5% to 6.45% depending upon income bracket. For married couples filing jointly, the rates are 3.5% on the first $30,000 of taxable income; 6.25% on the next $30,000 of taxable income; and 6.45% on taxable income above $60,000.

In calculating the tax, there is no deduction for federal income tax paid. Federal and state pensions are exempt from tax. Private pensions are not exempt. Social Security benefits subject to federal tax are not exempt. There is a $2,250 personal exemption per person from adjusted gross income. There is also a $7,400 standard deduction from adjusted gross income for married couples filing jointly when both are age 65 or older.

Major tax credits or rebates include:

O Tax Heavens: None
Ψ Tax Hells: None

---

credit for income taxes paid to other states and earned income credit, which our couples do not qualify for; and food sales tax refund, which one of our couples qualifies for.

The state sales tax rate is 5.3%, but local governments can add to this amount.

Our couples relocating to the city listed below must pay a registration fee of $36 per automobile, a title fee of $10 per automobile and an inspection fee of $10 per automobile at the time of registration. Thereafter, on an annual basis, our couples will pay a registration fee per automobile.

Wichita

Wichita has no local income tax but

does levy a sales tax.

Most purchases are taxed at a rate of 7.3%. Major consumer categories taxed at a different rate: none. Major consumer categories that are exempt from sales tax include: drugs.

In the Wichita School District, the property tax rate is .116064. Homes are assessed at 11.5% of market value. There is a homestead exemption that is determined on a sliding scale for homeowners age 55 or older with an income less than $28,000. Property tax does not cover garbage pickup. There is also a solid waste fee of $3 per year.

Wichita has a personal property tax rate of .116064 within the Wichita School District. Mobile homes are assessed at 11.5% of market value, boats and trailers are assessed at 30% of market value, and vehicles are assessed based on year, make and model of the vehicle.

KANSAS TAX TABLE

Instructions

1. Find the Income in the far left column closest to your anticipated retirement income.
2. Find the Home Value closest to the value of the home where you will live in retirement.
3. Follow that row to your estimated Total Tax Burden at age 65 and beyond.

Income	Home Value	Property Tax & Other Fees	Personal Property Tax & Auto Fees	Sales Tax	Local Income Tax	State Income Tax	Total Tax Burden	Rank*
WICHITA								
$30,000	$125,000	$1,851	$600	$1,157	-	$42	$3,650	153 of 173
	150,000	2,185	600	1,157	-	42	3,984	149 of 173
	175,000	2,519	600	1,157	-	42	4,318	144 of 173
$60,000	$150,000	$2,185	$600	$1,945	-	$1,513	$6,243	192 of 203
	225,000	3,186	600	1,945	-	1,513	7,244	181 of 203
	300,000	4,187	600	1,945	-	1,513	8,245	168 of 203
$90,000	$225,000	$3,186	$600	$2,399	-	$3,831	$10,016	191 of 203
	375,000	5,188	600	2,399	-	3,831	12,018	181 of 203
	525,000	7,190	600	2,399	-	3,831	14,020	172 of 203

*There are 203 cities in this book, 30 of which have higher than average home prices. We have estimated taxes for a tier of higher home values (and omitted the lowest tier) for these 30 cities. The city with the lowest tax burden for an income/home value combination is given the #1 rating; the higher the rating, the higher the total tax burden.

KENTUCKY

Kentucky has a state income tax and a state sales tax.

The state income tax rate is graduated from 2% to 6% depending upon income bracket. For married couples filing jointly, the rate is 2% on the first $3,000 of taxable income; 3% on the next $1,000 of taxable income; 4% on the next $1,000 of taxable income; 5% on the next $3,000 of taxable income; 5.8% on the next $67,000 of taxable income; and 6% on taxable income above $75,000.

In calculating the tax, there is no deduction for federal income tax paid. Federal, state and private pension income is exempt from tax up to $41,110 each. Federal, state and local government pensions are exempt for pension attributed to service performed prior to January 1, 1998. Social Security benefits are exempt. There is a $1,970 standard deduction for married couples filing jointly, both age 65 or older. There is a deduction for health insurance expense.

Major tax credits or rebates include: credit for income taxes paid to other states, which our couples do not qualify for; personal exemption credit, which our couples do qualify for; and a family-size tax credit, which our couples do not qualify for.

The state sales tax rate is 6% and most purchases are taxed at this rate. There are no local sales taxes. Major consumer categories taxed at a different rate include: none. Major consumer categories that are exempt from sales tax include: groceries, drugs and medical services.

Since car registration and renewal fees differ within the state, see city information for details.

Danville

Danville has a local income tax but does not levy an additional sales tax.

The local income tax is composed of an occupational license tax of 1.75% of self-employment income and 1.95% of wages and salaries.

In calculating the tax, federal, state and private pensions are exempt. Social Security benefits are exempt.

Within the city limits of Danville, the property tax rate is .01044. Homes are

assessed at 100% of market value. There is a homestead exemption of $29,400 off assessed value for homeowners age 65 or older. Property tax does not include garbage pickup.

Danville has a personal property tax rate of .01259 for motor vehicles. Additional items subject to the tax are boats, motor homes, travel trailers and airplanes, which are taxed at varying rates. Personal property is assessed at 100% of the NADA or appropriate guide trade-in value.

Our couples relocating to Danville must pay a usage tax on automobiles, which is 6% of the current trade-in value and is paid when the automobile is initially registered in the state. If a vehicle owner paid a usage or sales tax in another state when the automobile was purchased that was equal to or greater than the Kentucky usage tax, there is no additional charge. If a vehicle owner paid a usage or sales tax to another state that was less than the Kentucky usage tax, the owner is required to pay the difference. We've assumed our couples have paid tax equal to or greater than the Kentucky usage tax. Our couples will pay a title fee of $9 per automobile, $22 per automobile for recording a lien and a maximum of $26 per automobile for registration and miscellaneous fees at the time of registration. Thereafter, on an annual basis, our couples will pay a registration fee per automobile.

Lexington

Lexington has a local income tax but does not levy an additional sales tax.

The local income tax is composed of an occupational license fee of 2.75%, which is applied to wages, salaries and self-employment income.

In calculating the tax, federal, state and private pensions are exempt. Social Security benefits are exempt.

In calculating the occupational license fee, the first $3,000 of earned income per person is exempt from the city/county component of the fee for

taxpayers age 65 or older. In addition the first $3,000 of net profits from a business conducted in Lexington is exempt from the city/county component of the fee for taxpayers age 65 or older.

Within the city limits of Lexington in District 1, the property tax rate is .010309. Homes are assessed at 100% of market value. There is a homestead exemption of $29,400 off assessed value for homeowners age 65 or older. Property tax includes garbage pickup.

Lexington has a personal property tax of .01221 for automobiles. Additional items subject to the tax are aircraft, watercraft, motorcycles, RVs and motor homes (when not primary residence), which are taxed at varying rates. Personal property is assessed at 100% of the NADA or appropriate guide trade-in value.

Our couples relocating to Lexington must pay a usage tax on automobiles, which is 6% of the current trade-in value and is paid when the automobile is initially registered in the state. If a vehicle owner paid a usage or sales tax in another state when the automobile was purchased that was equal to or greater than the Kentucky usage tax, there is no additional charge. If a vehicle owner paid a usage or sales tax to another state that was less than the Kentucky usage tax, the owner is required to pay the difference. We've assumed our couples have paid tax equal to or greater than the Kentucky usage tax. Our couples will pay a title fee of $9 per automobile, $22 per automobile for recording a lien and a maximum of $26 per automobile for registration and miscellaneous fees at the time of registration Thereafter, on an annual basis, our couples will pay a registration fee per automobile.

Louisville

Louisville has a local income tax but does not levy an additional sales tax.

The local income tax is composed of an occupational license tax of 2.2%, which is applied to wages, salaries and self-employment income.

In calculating the tax, federal, state and private pensions are exempt. Social Security benefits are exempt.

KENTUCKY TAX TABLE

Instructions

1. Find the Income in the far left column closest to your anticipated retirement income.
2. Find the Home Value closest to the value of the home where you will live in retirement.
3. Follow that row to your estimated Total Tax Burden at age 65 and beyond.

Income	Home Value	Property Tax & Other Fees	Personal Property Tax & Auto Fees	Sales Tax	Local Income Tax	State Income Tax	Total Tax Burden	Rank*
DANVILLE								
$30,000	$125,000	$1,178	$371	$755	$109	-	$2,413	62 of 173
	150,000	1,439	371	755	109	-	2,674	64 of 173
	175,000	1,700	371	755	109	-	2,935	64 of 173
$60,000	$150,000	$1,439	$371	$1,327	$458	$1,054	$4,649	137 of 203
	225,000	2,222	371	1,327	458	1,054	5,432	117 of 203
	300,000	3,005	371	1,327	458	1,054	6,215	114 of 203
$90,000	$225,000	$2,222	$371	$1,649	$887	$2,608	$7,737	150 of 203
	375,000	3,788	371	1,649	887	2,608	9,303	128 of 203
	525,000	5,354	371	1,649	887	2,608	10,869	121 of 203
LEXINGTON								
$30,000	$125,000	$986	$361	$755	$36	-	$2,138	37 of 173
	150,000	1,243	361	755	36	-	2,395	43 of 173
	175,000	1,501	361	755	36	-	2,653	47 of 173
$60,000	$150,000	$1,243	$361	$1,327	$444	$1,054	$4,429	123 of 203
	225,000	2,016	361	1,327	444	1,054	5,202	109 of 203
	300,000	2,790	361	1,327	444	1,054	5,976	97 of 203
$90,000	$225,000	$2,016	$361	$1,649	$1,007	$2,608	$7,641	148 of 203
	375,000	3,563	361	1,649	1,007	2,608	9,188	123 of 203
	525,000	5,109	361	1,649	1,007	2,608	10,734	117 of 203
LOUISVILLE								
$30,000	$125,000	$1,187	$355	$755	$124	-	$2,421	63 of 173
	150,000	1,497	355	755	124	-	2,731	68 of 173
	175,000	1,807	355	755	124	-	3,041	75 of 173
$60,000	$150,000	$1,497	$355	$1,327	$525	$1,054	$4,758	144 of 203
	225,000	2,428	355	1,327	525	1,054	5,689	132 of 203
	300,000	3,359	355	1,327	525	1,054	6,620	127 of 203
$90,000	$225,000	$2,428	$355	$1,649	$1,022	$2,608	$8,062	161 of 203
	375,000	4,290	355	1,649	1,022	2,608	9,924	149 of 203
	525,000	6,152	355	1,649	1,022	2,608	11,786	136 of 203
MURRAY								
$30,000	$125,000	$1,398	$540	$755	-	-	$2,693	91 of 173
	150,000	1,717	540	755	-	-	3,012	90 of 173
	175,000	2,035	540	755	-	-	3,330	91 of 173
$60,000	$150,000	$1,717	$540	$1,327	-	$1,054	$4,638	136 of 203
	225,000	2,673	540	1,327	-	1,054	5,594	127 of 203
	300,000	3,628	540	1,327	-	1,054	6,549	124 of 203
$90,000	$225,000	$2,673	$540	$1,649	-	$2,608	$7,470	140 of 203
	375,000	4,584	540	1,649	-	2,608	9,381	133 of 203
	525,000	6,495	540	1,649	-	2,608	11,292	126 of 203

*There are 203 cities in this book, 30 of which have higher than average home prices. We have estimated taxes for a tier of higher home values (and omitted the lowest tier) for these 30 cities. The city with the lowest tax burden for an income/home value combination is given the #1 rating; the higher the rating, the higher the total tax burden.

Within the city limits of Louisville, the property tax rate is .012413. Homes are assessed at 100% of market value. There is a homestead exemption of $29,400 off assessed value for homeowners age 65 or older. Property tax includes garbage pickup.

Louisville has a personal property tax of .01201 for motor vehicles and .02257 for other tangible property. Additional items subject to the tax are watercraft, airplanes and recreational vehicles. Personal property is assessed at 100% of the NADA or appropriate guide trade-in value.

Our couples relocating to Louisville must pay a usage tax on automobiles, which is 6% of the current trade-in value and is paid when the automobile is initially registered in the state. If a vehicle owner paid a usage or sales tax in another state when the automobile was purchased that was equal to or greater than the Kentucky usage tax, there is no additional charge. If a vehicle owner paid a usage or sales tax to another state that was less than the Kentucky usage tax, the owner is

required to pay the difference. We've assumed our couples have paid tax equal to or greater than the Kentucky usage tax. Our couples will pay a title fee of $9 per automobile, $21 per automobile for registration and miscellaneous fees, a $22 lien filing fee per automobile and $5 for the state inspection fee per automobile at the time of registration. Thereafter, on an annual basis, our couples will pay a registration fee per automobile.

Murray

Murray has no local income tax and does not levy an additional sales tax.

Within the city limits of Murray, the property tax rate is .012743. Homes are assessed at 100% of market value. There is a homestead exemption of $29,400 off assessed value for homeowners age 65 or older. Property tax does not cover garbage pickup.

Murray has a personal property tax rate of .016398 for motor vehicles. Additional items subject to the tax are boats, motor homes, travel trailers and airplanes, which are taxed at varying

rates. Personal property is assessed at 100% of the NADA or appropriate guide trade-in value.

Our couples relocating to Murray must pay a usage tax on automobiles, which is 6% of the current trade-in value and is paid when the automobile is initially registered in the state. If a vehicle owner paid a usage or sales tax in another state when the automobile was purchased that was equal to or greater than the Kentucky usage tax, there is no additional charge. If a vehicle owner paid a usage or sales tax to another state that was less than the Kentucky usage tax, the owner is required to pay the difference. We've assumed our couples have paid tax equal to or greater than the Kentucky usage tax. Our couples will pay a title fee of $9 per automobile, $22 per automobile for recording a lien, $35 per automobile for a City of Murray sticker fee and $26 per automobile for registration and miscellaneous fees at the time of registration. Thereafter, on an annual basis, our couples will pay a registration fee and a City of Murray sticker fee, per automobile.

• Kentucky's Top Retirement Town •

Murray

The quality of life in this western Kentucky town of 15,725, with rolling woods, pristine lakes and rich farmland, is as good as it gets. Not only does your pocketbook get a break with a low cost of living but also a low crime rate translates into a safe environment. The town is located about two hours from Nashville, TN, and an hour from Paducah, KY, but is still within a day's drive of much of the Eastern Seaboard.

"What you most often hear both from residents and visitors alike is about the open, warm and inviting people who make a difference in lives and the cleanliness of our community," says Tab Brockman, executive director

of the Murray-Calloway County Chamber of Commerce.

The town is rated highly by the young as well as by retirees. Murray State University, with an enrollment of more than 10,000, is acclaimed as being a top university with an affordable tuition. It has a large, modern campus with a huge football stadium.

Downtown Murray has undergone revitalization, and the community boasts stately homes. Golfing and tennis enthusiasts find ample opportunity to enjoy their sports, while swimmers, boaters, hikers, bikers and bird-watchers (many on excursions to view bald eagles) have their choice of bodies of water, including Kentucky Lake, Lake Barkley or Land Between the Lakes.

A 378-bed hospital with 65 doctors in 26 specialties makes for excellent health care. There is a wide range of housing available, including upscale homes and new developments, among them the city's first patio-home community.

Population: 15,725

Climate: High Low
January   44   26
July   90   68

Cost of living: Below average

Housing cost: During the first half of 2007, the median sales price of homes was $114,250, according to the Murray Calloway County Board of Realtors.

Information: Murray-Calloway County Chamber of Commerce, (800) 900-5171 or www.mymurray.com.

LOUISIANA

Louisiana has a state income tax and a state sales tax.

The state income tax is graduated from 2% to 6% depending upon income bracket. For married couples filing jointly, the rates are 2% on the first $14,000 of taxable income; 4% on the next $25,000 of taxable income; and 6% on taxable income above $39,000.

In calculating the tax, there is a deduction for federal income tax paid. Federal and state pension incomes are exempt. Social Security benefits are exempt. There is a deduction of up to $6,000 per person of all other pension income. There is a personal exemption of $4,500 per person for married couples filing jointly and an additional exemption of $1,000 per person age 65 or older.

Major tax credits or rebates include: credit for income taxes paid to other states, which our couples do not qualify for.

The state sales tax rate is 4%, but local governments can add to this amount.

Since car registration fees differ within the state, see city information for details.

Baton Rouge

Baton Rouge has no local income tax but does levy a sales tax.

Most purchases are taxed at a rate of 9%. Major consumer categories taxed at a different rate include: drugs and groceries, which are taxed at a rate of 3%. Major consumer categories that are exempt from sales tax include: medical services.

Within the city limits of Baton Rouge, the property tax rate is .101363. Homes are assessed at 10% of market value. There is a homestead exemption of up to $7,500 off assessed value, which is available to all homeowners. The exemption is not available for the city component of property tax. Property tax includes garbage pickup.

Baton Rouge has no personal property tax for individuals.

Our couples relocating to Baton Rouge must pay a use tax based on the NADA current loan value of each auto-

mobile. The tax rate is 9%; however, the state will give credit to new residents of up to 4% based on sales tax previously paid to another state. We've assumed a 4% credit on the use tax since this is the most common credit given. The use tax would be approximately $539 for the Explorer and $638 for the Camry. Our couples also pay a plate fee of $22 for the Explorer and $26 for the Camry, $19 per automobile for a title fee, $8 per automobile for a handling fee and $10 per automobile for a lien filing fee at the time of registration. Thereafter, our couples will pay a plate fee per automobile every two years.

Natchitoches

Natchitoches has no local income tax but does levy a sales tax.

Most purchases are taxed at a rate of 8.5%. The rate increases to 9% on October 1, 2006. Major consumer categories taxed at a different rate: drugs and groceries, which are taxed at a rate of 4.5%. Major consumer categories that are exempt from sales tax include: medical services.

Within the city limits of Natchitoches, the property tax rate is .10652. Homes are assessed at 10% of market value. There is a homestead exemption of up to $7,500 off assessed value, which is available to all homeowners. The exemption is not available for the city component of property tax. Property tax does not cover garbage pickup.

Natchitoches has no personal property tax for individuals.

Our couples relocating to Natchitoches must pay a use tax based on the NADA current loan value of each automobile. The tax rate is 8.5%; however, the state will give credit to new residents of up to 4% based on sales tax previously paid to another state. We've assumed a 4% credit on the use tax since this is the most common

credit given. The use tax would be approximately $485 for the Explorer and $574 for the Camry. Our couples also pay a license fee of $22 for the Explorer and $26 for the Camry, $19 per automobile for a title fee, $8 per automobile for a handling fee and $10 per automobile for a lien filing fee at the time of registration. Thereafter, our couples will pay a license fee per automobile every two years.

New Orleans

New Orleans has no local income tax but does levy a sales tax.

Most purchases are taxed at a rate of 9%. Major consumer categories taxed at a different rate include: drugs and groceries, which are taxed at a rate of 4.5%. Major consumer categories that are exempt from sales tax include: medical services.

Within the city limits of New Orleans, the property tax rate is .18834. Homes are assessed at 10% of market value. There is a homestead exemption of $7,500 off assessed value, which is available to all homeowners. The exemption is not available for the police and fire component of property tax. Property tax does not cover garbage pickup.

New Orleans has no personal property tax for individuals.

Our couples relocating to New Orleans must pay a use tax based on the NADA current loan value of each automobile. The tax rate is 9%; however, the state will give credit to new residents of up to 4% based on sales tax previously paid to another state. We've assumed a 4% credit on the use tax since this is the most common credit given. The use tax would be approximately $539 for the Explorer and $638 for the Camry. Our couples also pay a plate fee of $22 for the Explorer and $26 for the Camry, $19 per automobile for a title fee, $8 per automobile for a handling fee and $10 per automobile for a lien filing fee at the time of registration. Thereafter, our couples will pay a plate fee per automobile every two years.

LOUISIANA TAX TABLE

Instructions

1. Find the Income in the far left column closest to your anticipated retirement income.
2. Find the Home Value closest to the value of the home where you will live in retirement.
3. Follow that row to your estimated Total Tax Burden at age 65 and beyond.

Income	Home Value	Property Tax & Other Fees	Personal Property Tax & Auto Fees	Sales Tax	Local Income Tax	State Income Tax	Total Tax Burden	Rank*
BATON ROUGE								
$30,000	$125,000	$566	$24	$1,241	-	-	$1,831	16 of 173
	150,000	819	24	1,241	-	-	2,084	24 of 173
	175,000	1,072	24	1,241	-	-	2,337	24 of 173
$60,000	$150,000	$819	$24	$2,134	-	$455	$3,432	33 of 203
	225,000	1,579	24	2,134	-	455	4,192	40 of 203
	300,000	2,339	24	2,134	-	455	4,952	48 of 203
$90,000	$225,000	$1,579	$24	$2,633	-	$1,480	$5,716	50 of 203
	375,000	3,100	24	2,633	-	1,480	7,237	51 of 203
	525,000	4,620	24	2,633	-	1,480	8,757	56 of 203
NATCHITOCHES								
$30,000	$125,000	$840	$24	$1,232	-	-	$2,096	33 of 173
	150,000	1,107	24	1,232	-	-	2,363	37 of 173
	175,000	1,373	24	1,232	-	-	2,629	45 of 173
$60,000	$150,000	$1,107	$24	$2,095	-	$455	$3,681	56 of 203
	225,000	1,906	24	2,095	-	455	4,480	57 of 203
	300,000	2,704	24	2,095	-	455	5,278	62 of 203
$90,000	$225,000	$1,906	$24	$2,576	-	$1,480	$5,986	66 of 203
	375,000	3,503	24	2,576	-	1,480	7,583	65 of 203
	525,000	5,101	24	2,576	-	1,480	9,181	63 of 203
NEW ORLEANS								
$30,000	$125,000	$1,200	$24	$1,295	-	-	$2,519	71 of 173
	150,000	1,671	24	1,295	-	-	2,990	86 of 173
	175,000	2,142	24	1,295	-	-	3,461	97 of 173
$60,000	$150,000	$1,671	$24	$2,206	-	$455	$4,356	118 of 203
	225,000	3,084	24	2,206	-	455	5,769	136 of 203
	300,000	4,496	24	2,206	-	455	7,181	148 of 203
$90,000	$225,000	$3,084	$24	$2,713	-	$1,480	$7,301	135 of 203
	375,000	5,909	24	2,713	-	1,480	10,126	154 of 203
	525,000	8,734	24	2,713	-	1,480	12,951	155 of 203

*There are 203 cities in this book, 30 of which have higher than average home prices. We have estimated taxes for a tier of higher home values (and omitted the lowest tier) for these 30 cities. The city with the lowest tax burden for an income/home value combination is given the #1 rating; the higher the rating, the higher the total tax burden.

• Louisiana's Top Retirement Town •

Natchitoches

While other parts of the state have been more famous for their European flavor, Louisiana's original French colony was in its northwest quadrant in Natchitoches. Named for an Indian tribe that had a village near the town's original settlement, Natchitoches dates to 1714 and is the oldest permanent settlement in the Louisiana Purchase territory.

It feels like a smaller and much quieter version of old New Orleans. The town's national historic district encompasses a 33-block area overlooking serene Cane River Lake. Brick streets run past historic structures with wrought-iron balconies and an architectural gumbo of Queen Anne and Victorian structures and Creole-style cottages.

The movie "Steel Magnolias" was filmed here in 1988, thrusting quaint and quirky Natchitoches (pronounced

NACK-eh-tish) into the national limelight. Hollywood stardom aside, Natchitoches' other claim to fame is Northwestern State University and the Louisiana Scholars' College, which together enroll about 10,000 students. The university enhances Natchitoches' cultural life by supporting a symphony, ballet, dinner theater, plays, music recitals and other entertainment.

This is a town that invites strolling down streets dripping with history and going boating, tubing and fishing on Cane River Lake and at the nearby Kisatchie National Forest. A 35-mile stretch of land along the Cane River contains one of the South's most impressive strings of historically significant plantations, many of which are prime examples of centuries-old Creole architecture.

Residents enjoy a full slate of events and festivals, including a Mardi Gras parade and a 40-day Christmas Festival when the downtown area is transformed into a fairyland of thousands of colored lights, giving Natchitoches the nickname of City of Lights.

Its roster of attractions, mild climate and relatively low cost of living make Natchitoches one of the South's most inviting retirement havens.

Population: 17,730

Climate:

	High	Low
January	59	37
July	94	72

Cost of living: Below average

Housing cost: Single-family homes average $150,000 to $200,000, but patio homes and local resale properties are closer to $130,000, according to local brokerage Cane Heritage Realty.

Information: Natchitoches Area Chamber of Commerce, (318) 352-6894 or www.natchitocheschamber.com. Natchitoches Area Convention and Visitors Bureau, (800) 259-1714 or www.historic natchitoches.com.

MAINE

Maine has a state income tax and a state sales tax.

The state income tax is graduated from 2% to 8.5% depending upon income bracket. For married couples filing jointly, the rates are 2% on the first $9,149 of taxable income; 4.5% on the next $9,100 of taxable income; 7% on the next $18,300 of taxable income; and 8.5% on taxable income above $36,550.

In calculating the tax, there is no deduction for federal income tax paid. There is a federal, state and private pension income exclusion of up to $6,000 per person age 65 or older if included in federal adjusted gross income. The $6,000 must be reduced by any Social Security benefits received, whether taxable or not. Social Security benefits are exempt. There is a $2,850 personal

exemption per person from adjusted gross income. There is an $8,600 standard deduction from adjusted gross income for married couples filing jointly, plus an additional deduction of $1,000 per person age 65 or older.

Major tax credits or rebates include: credit for income taxes paid to other states, low income credit, elderly and disabled credit, and earned income credit. Our couples do not qualify for these programs.

There is a state sales tax but no local sales tax in Maine. Most purchases are

taxed at the state rate of 5%. Major consumer categories taxed at a different rate include: food away from home, which is taxed at 7%. Major consumer categories that are exempt from sales tax include: drugs, groceries and medical services.

Since car registration and renewal fees differ within the state, see city information for details.

Brunswick

Brunswick has no local income tax and does not levy an additional sales tax.

Within the Brunswick city limits, the property tax rate is .02175. Homes are assessed at 65% of market value. There is a homestead exemption of $8,450 off the assessed value of an owner-occupied home. Property tax includes

---

MAINE TAX TABLE

Instructions

1. Find the Income in the far left column closest to your anticipated retirement income.
2. Find the Home Value closest to the value of the home where you will live in retirement.
3. Follow that row to your estimated Total Tax Burden at age 65 and beyond.

Income	Home Value	Property Tax & Other Fees	Personal Property Tax & Auto Fees	Sales Tax	Local Income Tax	State Income Tax	Total Tax Burden	Rank*
BRUNSWICK								
$30,000	$125,000	$1,583	$681	$658	-	-	$2,922	110 of 173
	150,000	1,937	681	658	-	-	3,276	110 of 173
	175,000	2,290	681	658	-	-	3,629	111 of 173
$60,000	$150,000	$1,937	$681	$1,156	-	$891	$4,665	138 of 203
	225,000	2,997	681	1,156	-	891	5,725	133 of 203
	300,000	4,057	681	1,156	-	891	6,785	133 of 203
$90,000	$225,000	$2,997	$681	$1,437	-	$3,045	$8,160	164 of 203
	375,000	5,118	681	1,437	-	3,045	10,281	159 of 203
	525,000	7,238	681	1,437	-	3,045	12,401	148 of 203
CAMDEN								
$30,000	$125,000	$1,556	$687	$658	-	-	$2,901	106 of 173
	150,000	1,864	687	658	-	-	3,209	103 of 173
	175,000	2,171	687	658	-	-	3,516	103 of 173
$60,000	$150,000	$1,864	$687	$1,156	-	$891	$4,598	132 of 203
	225,000	2,785	687	1,156	-	891	5,519	121 of 203
	300,000	3,707	687	1,156	-	891	6,441	121 of 203
$90,000	$225,000	$2,785	$687	$1,437	-	$3,045	$7,954	158 of 203
	375,000	4,629	687	1,437	-	3,045	9,798	144 of 203
	525,000	6,472	687	1,437	-	3,045	11,641	132 of 203

*There are 203 cities in this book, 30 of which have higher than average home prices. We have estimated taxes for a tier of higher home values (and omitted the lowest tier) for these 30 cities. The city with the lowest tax burden for an income/home value combination is given the #1 rating; the higher the rating, the higher the total tax burden.

garbage pickup.

Brunswick has no personal property tax but does assess an excise tax on motor vehicles, which is based on the age and the MSRP of the vehicle.

In addition to the vehicle excise tax, our couples relocating to Brunswick must pay a plate fee of $25 per automobile and a title fee of $23 per automobile at the time of registration. Thereafter, on an annual basis, they will pay the excise tax and a plate fee, per automobile.

Camden

Camden has no local income tax and does not levy an additional sales tax.

Within the Camden city limits, the property tax rate is .01229. Homes are assessed at 100% of market value. There is a homestead exemption of $13,000 off the assessed value of an owner-occupied home. Property tax does not cover garbage pickup.

Camden has no personal property tax but does assess an excise tax on motor vehicles, which is based on the age and MSRP of the vehicle.

In addition to the vehicle excise tax, our couples relocating to Camden must pay a plate fee of $25 per automobile and a title fee of $23 per automobile at the time of registration. Thereafter, on an annual basis, our couples will pay the excise tax, a plate fee and an agent fee, per automobile.

• Maine's Top Retirement Towns •

Brunswick

Start with four distinct, but relatively mild, seasons and rugged coastal surroundings that capture the fancy of many artists. Add excellent town services, theater and historic Bowdoin College, and Brunswick proves a winner on several fronts.

For outdoor enthusiasts, two rivers and ocean access make boating and canoeing popular pastimes. This south Maine coastline has both rocky and sandy areas to explore, and the nearby bays are perfect for sailing.

The quaint New England town also boasts a variety of cultural offerings, including the Bowdoin College Museum of Art and the Maine State Music Theatre. Concerts on the town mall in summer, ice-skating in winter and several festivals ensure an active scene in Brunswick year-round.

Naval Air Station Brunswick, the last remaining active-duty air station on the East Coast, hosts occasional air shows, which sometimes include appearances by the Blue Angels precision flying team.

"We love the winters here and tend to not leave," says Sally Mull, a longtime resident whose husband, Charles, is a retired Navy captain. "We both come from a long line of Navy officers, and we enjoy the military presence here, as well as the college activities, bluegrass festivals, arts festivals and many, many other events."

Population: 21,915
Climate: High Low
January 31 10
July 80 58
Cost of living: Above average
Housing cost: The average sales price of a single-family home during the first half of 2007 was $257,133, according to Morton Real Estate in Brunswick.
Information: Southern Midcoast Maine Chamber, (877) 725-8797 or www.midcoastmaine.com.

Camden

Even Maine's famously cold winters can't chill the lure of Camden, a historic seaside town at the base of the Camden Hills. With its picturesque harbor, Camden is as beautiful today as it was when the late poet Edna St. Vincent Millay immortalized her town in the poem, "Renascence." She wrote: "All I could see from where I stood / Was three long mountains and a wood; / I turned and looked the other way, / And saw three islands in a bay."

Today you're likely to see a lot more retirees in those celebrated mountains, woods and bays. Whatever the season, Camden offers outdoor fun. In spring, you can hike or pedal winding back roads past lakes and lupine fields, while in summer you can canoe down a quiet river or island-hop by kayak. In fall, the Camden Hills blaze every color in the New England autumn palette, and in winter you can work up a sweat by cross-country skiing.

Downtown boasts Victorian mansions and quaint shops. Camden's jewel-box opera house hosts year-round musical performances, and the Camden Amphitheater could almost double as a backdrop for "A Midsummer Night's Dream" — which has been performed here, along with other plays and concerts. In summer, the harbor is dotted with yachts and Camden's famous windjammer fleet.

Area celebrations showcase the region's riches, such as lobster and wild blueberry festivals. Locals say the best thing about Camden is its Norman Rockwell lifestyle. Imagine a town where traffic halts for the soapbox derby and your neighbor runs the local combined gallery, bakery and hardware store. The Penobscot Bay Medical Center in nearby Rockport serves the area.

Population: 5,316
Climate: High Low
January 29 10
July 76 59
Cost of living: Above average
Housing cost: The median sales price of a single-family home for the first nine months of 2007 was $375,000, according to the Camden Real Estate Co.
Information: Camden-Rockport-Lincolnville Chamber of Commerce, (207) 236-4404 or www.camdenme.org.

MARYLAND

Maryland has a state income tax and a state sales tax.

The state income tax rate is graduated from 3% to 4.75% depending upon income bracket. For married couples filing jointly, the rates are 3% on the first $3,000 of taxable income and 4.75% on taxable income above $3,000.

In calculating the tax, there is no

deduction for federal income tax paid. There is a federal, state and private pension income exclusion of up to $22,600 per person age 65 or older less Social Security benefits received. Social

Security benefits are exempt. There is a $2,400 personal exemption per person from Maryland adjusted gross income and a $1,000 personal exemption per person from adjusted gross income for people age 65 or older. There is a variable standard deduction from Maryland adjusted gross income for married couples filing jointly that is based on

MARYLAND TAX TABLE

Instructions

1. Find the Income in the far left column closest to your anticipated retirement income.
2. Find the Home Value closest to the value of the home where you will live in retirement.
3. Follow that row to your estimated Total Tax Burden at age 65 and beyond.

Income	Home Value	Property Tax & Other Fees	Personal Property Tax & Auto Fees	Sales Tax	Local Income Tax	State Income Tax	Total Tax Burden	Rank*
ANNAPOLIS								
$60,000	$150,000	$1,965	$154	$1,092	$21	$811	$4,043	85 of 203
	225,000	2,858	154	1,092	21	811	4,936	91 of 203
	300,000	3,750	154	1,092	21	811	5,828	93 of 203
$90,000	$225,000	$2,858	$154	$1,361	$56	$2,188	$6,617	103 of 203
	375,000	4,643	154	1,361	56	2,188	8,402	95 of 203
	525,000	6,428	154	1,361	56	2,188	10,187	95 of 203
	$600,000	$7,320	$154	$1,361	$56	$2,188	$11,079	23 of 30
	750,000	9,105	154	1,361	56	2,188	12,864	25 of 30
	900,000	10,890	154	1,361	56	2,188	14,649	25 of 30
BALTIMORE								
$30,000	$125,000	$3,000	$154	$621	-	-	$3,775	155 of 173
	150,000	3,600	154	621	-	-	4,375	157 of 173
	175,000	4,200	154	621	-	-	4,975	158 of 173
$60,000	$150,000	$3,600	$154	$1,092	$25	$811	$5,682	183 of 203
	225,000	5,400	154	1,092	25	811	7,482	186 of 203
	300,000	7,200	154	1,092	25	811	9,282	188 of 203
$90,000	$225,000	$5,400	$154	$1,361	$67	$2,188	$9,170	183 of 203
	375,000	9,000	154	1,361	67	2,188	12,770	189 of 203
	525,000	12,600	154	1,361	67	2,188	16,370	190 of 203
EASTON								
$60,000	$150,000	$1,466	$154	$1,092	$18	$811	$3,541	42 of 203
	225,000	2,198	154	1,092	18	811	4,273	47 of 203
	300,000	2,931	154	1,092	18	811	5,006	49 of 203
$90,000	$225,000	$2,198	$154	$1,361	$49	$2,188	$5,950	62 of 203
	375,000	3,664	154	1,361	49	2,188	7,416	59 of 203
	525,000	5,129	154	1,361	49	2,188	8,881	58 of 203
	$600,000	$5,862	$154	$1,361	$49	$2,188	$9,614	12 of 30
	750,000	7,328	154	1,361	49	2,188	11,080	12 of 30
	900,000	8,793	154	1,361	49	2,188	12,545	12 of 30

*There are 203 cities in this book, 30 of which have higher than average home prices. We have estimated taxes for a tier of higher home values (and omitted the lowest tier) for these 30 cities. The city with the lowest tax burden for an income/home value combination is given the #1 rating; the higher the rating, the higher the total tax burden.

income. There is also a $1,200 two-income deduction for married couples filing jointly.

Major tax credits or rebates include: credit for income taxes paid to other states, earned income credit and poverty income credit. Our couples do not qualify for these programs.

The state sales tax rate is 5%.

Our couples relocating to Maryland may have to pay an excise titling tax per automobile depending on the amount of tax paid in the state in which the automobile was purchased. If a vehicle owner paid a sales tax in another state when the automobile was purchased that was equal to or greater than Maryland's sales tax, the excise tax fee is $100. If a vehicle owner paid less than Maryland's sales tax, the owner is required to pay the difference. Our couples also pay a registration fee of $180 for the Explorer and $128 for the Camry, a title fee of $23 per automobile and a security interest-filing fee of $20 per automobile. Thereafter, our couples will pay a registration fee per automobile every two years.

Annapolis

Annapolis has a local income tax but does not levy an additional sales tax.

The local income tax is 2.56% of Maryland state income tax due.

Most purchases are taxed at the state rate of 5%. Major consumer categories taxed at a different rate: none. Major consumer categories that are exempt from sales tax include: groceries, drugs, medical supplies and medical services.

Within the Annapolis city limits, the property tax rate is .0119. Homes are assessed at 100% of market value. There is a homestead property tax credit available if an appraisal results in an increase of more than 10% on the state and city assessments and 2% on the county assessment. There is also a homeowner's property tax credit subject to certain net worth limitations for taxes that exceed a percentage of a homeowner's gross income; it only applies to the first $300,000 of assessed value. Property tax does not cover garbage pickup.

Annapolis has no personal property tax for individuals.

Baltimore

Baltimore has a local income tax but does not levy an additional sales tax.

The local income tax is 3.05% of Maryland state income tax due.

Most purchases are taxed at the state rate of 5%. Major consumer categories taxed at a different rate: none. Major consumer categories that are exempt from sales tax include: groceries, drugs, medical supplies and medical services.

In the area of Roland Park, the property tax rate is .0240. Homes are assessed at 100% of market value. There is a homestead property tax credit available if an appraisal results in an increase of more than 10% on the state portion or 4% on the city portion of the assessed value per year. There is also a homeowner's property tax credit subject to certain net worth limitations for taxes that exceed a percentage of a homeowner's gross income; it applies to the lesser of $300,000 of assessed value or the total assessed value minus any homestead credit. Property tax includes garbage pickup.

Baltimore has no personal property tax for individuals.

Easton

Easton has a local income tax but does not levy an additional sales tax.

The local income tax is 2.25% of Maryland state income tax due.

Most purchases are taxed at the state rate of 5%. Major consumer categories taxed at a different rate: none. Major consumer categories that are exempt from sales tax include: groceries, drugs, medical supplies and medical services.

Within the Easton city limits, the property tax rate is .00977. Homes are assessed at 100% of market value. There is a homestead property tax credit available if an appraisal results in an increase of more than 10% on the state and city assessments. There is also a homeowner's property tax credit subject to certain net worth limitations for taxes that exceed a percentage of a homeowner's gross income; it only applies to the first $300,000 of assessed value. Property tax includes garbage pickup.

Easton has no personal property tax for individuals.

MASSACHUSETTS

Massachusetts has a state income tax and a state sales tax.

There are two state income tax rates depending upon type of income. For most income, including earned income, interest income from Massachusetts financial institutions and pension income, the rate is 5.3% of taxable income. For other income, including dividend income over $1,500, other interest and long-term capital gains, the rate is 12% of taxable income.

In calculating the tax, there is no deduction for federal income tax paid. Federal, state and local government pension income is exempt. Private pension income is not exempt. Social Security benefits are exempt. There is a $200 exemption for married couples

> **O Tax Heavens:** Cape Cod (Barnstable)
> **Ψ Tax Hells:** None

filing jointly from interest earned from Massachusetts banks. There is a deduction of up to $2,000 per person for payments made to Social Security, Medicare, railroad, federal or Massachusetts retirement systems. There is a personal exemption from 5.3% income of $7,700 total for married couples filing jointly. There is a $700 age deduction from 5.3% income per person for persons age 65 or older.

Major tax credits or rebates include: credit for taxes paid to another state, no-tax status credit and a limited-income credit. Our lowest income

level qualifies for the no-tax status credit.

The state sales tax rate is 5%.

Our couples relocating to the cities below must pay a vehicle excise tax (personal property tax) to the city of residence based on the year and MSRP of each automobile. The vehicle excise tax is $402 for the Explorer and $300 for the Camry at the time of initial registration. Our couples also pay a plate issue fee of $36 for two years per automobile and a title fee of $50 per automobile. Thereafter, our couples will pay a vehicle excise tax on an annual basis and a plate renewal fee every two years, per automobile.

Boston

Boston has no local income tax and

MASSACHUSETTS TAX TABLE

Instructions

1. Find the Income in the far left column closest to your anticipated retirement income.
2. Find the Home Value closest to the value of the home where you will live in retirement.
3. Follow that row to your estimated Total Tax Burden at age 65 and beyond.

Income	Home Value	Property Tax & Other Fees	Personal Property Tax & Auto Fees	Sales Tax	Local Income Tax	State Income Tax	Total Tax Burden	Rank*
BOSTON								
$60,000	$150,000	$165	$508	$1,010	-	$1,466	$3,149	18 of 203
	225,000	948	508	1,010	-	1,466	3,932	24 of 203
	300,000	1,772	508	1,010	-	1,466	4,756	37 of 203
$90,000	$225,000	$948	$508	$1,262	-	$2,892	$5,610	42 of 203
	375,000	2,596	508	1,262	-	2,892	7,258	52 of 203
	525,000	4,245	508	1,262	-	2,892	8,907	59 of 203
	$600,000	$5,069	$508	$1,262	-	$2,892	$9,731	13 of 30
	750,000	6,717	508	1,262	-	2,892	11,379	13 of 30
	900,000	8,366	508	1,262	-	2,892	13,028	13 of 30
CAPE COD (BARNSTABLE)								
$30,000	$125,000	$389	$508	$585	-	-	$1,482	8 of 173 O
	150,000	599	508	585	-	-	1,692	9 of 173 O
	175,000	809	508	585	-	-	1,902	11 of 173
$60,000	$150,000	$599	$508	$1,010	-	$1,466	$3,583	45 of 203
	225,000	1,229	508	1,010	-	1,466	4,213	41 of 203
	300,000	1,859	508	1,010	-	1,466	4,843	40 of 203
$90,000	$225,000	$1,229	$508	$1,262	-	$2,892	$5,891	56 of 203
	375,000	2,489	508	1,262	-	2,892	7,151	46 of 203
	525,000	3,749	508	1,262	-	2,892	8,411	49 of 203

*There are 203 cities in this book, 30 of which have higher than average home prices. We have estimated taxes for a tier of higher home values (and omitted the lowest tier) for these 30 cities. The city with the lowest tax burden for an income/home value combination is given the #1 rating; the higher the rating, the higher the total tax burden.

does not levy an additional sales tax.

Most purchases are taxed at the state rate of 5%. Major consumer categories that are taxed at a different rate: none. Major consumer purchases that are exempt from sales tax include: drugs, groceries, apparel and services, medical supplies and medical services.

Within Boston city limits, the property tax rate is .01099. Homes are assessed at 100% of market value. There is a residential exemption for a property tax bill reduction of up to $1,525. There is an elderly exemption and an elderly tax reduction available to homeowners who meet certain age, income, residency and net worth requirements. Property tax includes garbage pickup.

Boston has no personal property tax for individuals.

Cape Cod (Barnstable)

Cape Cod has no local income tax and does not levy an additional sales tax.

Most purchases are taxed at the state rate of 5%. Major consumer categories that are taxed at a different rate: none. Major consumer purchases that are exempt from sales tax include: drugs, groceries, apparel and services, medical supplies and medical services.

Barnstable has a property tax rate of .00821. Homes are assessed at 100% of market value. There is a residential exemption for a property tax bill reduction of up to $841. There is an elderly exemption available to homeowners age 65 or older who meet certain income, residency and net worth requirements. Residents pay a Land Bank Fund fee of 3% of property taxes owed. Property tax does not cover garbage pickup.

Cape Cod has a personal property contents tax on homes other than the owner's primary residence. We've assumed our couples own a primary residence in Barnstable.

MICHIGAN

Michigan has a state income tax and a state sales tax.

The state income tax rate is 3.9% of taxable income. In calculating the tax, there is no deduction for federal income tax paid. Federal, state, and local government pensions are exempt. Up to $81,840 of private pension income is excluded for married couples

---

○ **Tax Heavens:** None
Ψ **Tax Hells:** Detroit
Top Retirement Towns: Petoskey, Traverse City

---

filing jointly. Social Security benefits are exempt. There is an interest/dividends/capital gains deduction of up to

$18,255 for married couples filing jointly age 65 or older. This deduction must first be reduced by any pension deduction taken. There is a $3,300 personal exemption per person from adjusted gross income plus an exemption for persons age 65 or older of $2,100 per person from adjusted gross income.

Major tax credits or rebates include:

MICHIGAN TAX TABLE

Instructions

1. Find the Income in the far left column closest to your anticipated retirement income.
2. Find the Home Value closest to the value of the home where you will live in retirement.
3. Follow that row to your estimated Total Tax Burden at age 65 and beyond.

Income	Home Value	Property Tax & Other Fees	Personal Property Tax & Auto Fees	Sales Tax	Local Income Tax	State Income Tax†	Total Tax Burden	Rank*
DETROIT								
$30,000	$125,000	$3,134	$203	$755	$137	($1,200)	$3,029	121 of 173
	150,000	3,761	203	755	137	(1,200)	3,656	137 of 173
	175,000	4,388	203	755	137	(1,200)	4,283	143 of 173
$60,000	$150,000	$3,761	$203	$1,327	$655	($556)	$5,390	172 of 203
	225,000	5,641	203	1,327	655	(556)	7,270	183 of 203
	300,000	7,522	203	1,327	655	(556)	9,151	185 of 203
$90,000	$225,000	$5,641	$203	$1,649	$1,338	$1,676	$10,507	195 of 203 Ψ
	375,000	9,402	203	1,649	1,338	1,676	14,268	195 of 203 Ψ
	525,000	13,163	203	1,649	1,338	1,676	18,029	195 of 203 Ψ
PETOSKEY								
$30,000	$125,000	$1,033	$203	$755	-	($68)	$1,923	25 of 173
	150,000	1,240	203	755	-	(275)	1,923	16 of 173
	175,000	1,446	203	755	-	(481)	1,923	12 of 173
$60,000	$150,000	$1,240	$203	$1,327	-	$694	$3,464	35 of 203
	225,000	1,860	203	1,327	-	694	4,084	35 of 203
	300,000	2,480	203	1,327	-	210	4,220	17 of 203
$90,000	$225,000	$1,860	$203	$1,649	-	$1,760	$5,472	33 of 203
	375,000	3,099	203	1,649	-	1,760	6,711	32 of 203
	525,000	4,339	203	1,649	-	1,760	7,951	32 of 203
TRAVERSE CITY								
$30,000	$125,000	$2,436	$203	$755	-	($182)	$3,212	138 of 173
	150,000	2,887	203	755	-	(411)	3,434	117 of 173
	175,000	3,338	203	755	-	(641)	3,655	113 of 173
$60,000	$150,000	$2,887	$203	$1,327	-	$694	$5,111	156 of 203
	225,000	4,241	203	1,327	-	626	6,397	162 of 203
	300,000	5,594	203	1,327	-	(63)	7,061	144 of 203
$90,000	$225,000	$4,241	$203	$1,649	-	$1,760	$7,853	154 of 203
	375,000	6,948	203	1,649	-	1,760	10,560	166 of 203
	525,000	9,655	203	1,649	-	1,760	13,267	163 of 203

†Credit for local income tax is issued as a reduction of state income tax due and credit for property tax paid is issued as a refund if the credit is greater than the tax liability.
*There are 203 cities in this book, 30 of which have higher than average home prices. We have estimated taxes for a tier of higher home values (and omitted the lowest tier) for these 30 cities. The city with the lowest tax burden for an income/home value combination is given the #1 rating; the higher the rating, the higher the total tax burden.

credit for taxes paid to other states, which our couples do not qualify for; city income tax credit, which our couples do qualify for if city income tax was paid; and homestead property tax credit, which our couples do qualify for.

The state sales tax rate is 6%. Most purchases are taxed at the state rate. Major consumer categories taxed at a different rate: none. Major consumer categories that are exempt from sales tax include: groceries, drugs and medical services.

Our couples relocating to the cities listed below must pay a registration fee of $128 for the Explorer and $96 for the Camry and a title fee of $15 per automobile. Thereafter, on an annual basis, our couples will pay a registration fee per automobile.

Detroit

Detroit has a local income tax but does not levy an additional sales tax.

The local income tax rate is 2.5% of taxable income for residents and 1.25% of taxable income for non-residents who work in the city limits. Federal, state, and private pensions are exempt. Social Security benefits are exempt. There is a $600 exemption per person plus an additional $600 exemption per person age 65 or older.

Within the city limits of Detroit, the property tax rate is .0677. Homes are assessed at 50% of market value. There is a principal residence exemption from local school operating tax up to a rate of .018. Property tax includes garbage pickup.

Detroit has no personal property tax for individuals.

Petoskey

Petoskey has no local income tax and does not levy an additional sales tax.

Within the city limits of Petoskey, the property tax rate is .03453. Homes are assessed at 50% of market value. There is a principal residence exemp-tion from local school operating tax up to a rate of .018. Property tax includes garbage pickup.

Petoskey has no personal property tax for individuals.

Traverse City

Traverse City has no local income tax and does not levy an additional sales tax.

Within the city limits of Traverse City, the property tax rate is .0540945. New homes are assessed at 50% of market value. After purchase, taxable value may only increase at the rate of inflation or 5%, whichever is less. There is a principal residence exemption from local school operating tax up to a rate of .018. Property tax does not cover garbage pickup. In addition, special assessments may be levied at the local level for specific infrastructure improvements.

Traverse City has no personal property tax for individuals.

• Michigan's Top Retirement Towns •

Petoskey

Located in the northwest corner of the lower peninsula of Michigan, Petoskey perches on a rolling hillside overlooking Traverse Bay. Early French fur traders and missionaries called the region L'Arbre Croche after a crooked tree hanging over a high bluff used as a landmark for approaching canoes.

Today, the war canoes are gone, but remaining are rambling Victorian cottages, turn-of-the-century inns with gingerbread trim and early 20th-century storefronts that recall the region's storied past as an elite summer destination for wealthy executives from Detroit, Chicago, Indianapolis and points in Ohio.

The historic city is still small enough to feel like Main Street USA, yet big enough to provide a wealth of cultural and recreational options to sophisticated retirees. Add a four-season climate with crimson autumns, snowy winters (120 inches of the white stuff) and breezy, moderate summers where air conditioning is rarely needed, and it's no wonder that Petoskey is one of the fastest-growing regions in Michigan. Today, it's a chic recreational paradise with alpine skiing, groomed cross-country trails, championship golf courses and (something you won't find everywhere) morel-mushroom hunting in the spring.

Downtown, quaint streets are lit by old-fashioned gas lamps and lined with period buildings housing restaurants, boutiques, galleries and a nostalgic general store. Pennsylvania Park is the setting for a summer concert series, and during the holidays, Petoskey is a Dickens Christmas come to life with parades featuring live reindeer and a street fair.

The Crooked Tree Arts Center and the Little Traverse Civic Theatre deliver a full slate of productions. The Little Traverse History Museum, housed in the 1892 waterfront railroad depot, includes exhibits on the late author Ernest Hemingway, who summered at a nearby lake.

At Lake Michigan, a paved recreational path for joggers, cyclists and inline skaters borders the scenic shoreline, and water sports include sailing and fishing for lake trout and Coho salmon. The Petoskey Winter Sports Park is the site of a winter carnival.

Two great places to make new ski and hiking buddies are the Friendship Center, with a plethora of senior services, and the Virginia McCune Community Arts Center, with changing exhibits, theater and crafts. You can expand your intellectual horizons at North Central Michigan College, a half-mile walk from downtown.

Population: 6,112

Climate:
	High	Low
January	26	14
July	75	59

Cost of living: Average

Housing cost: The median sales price of a single-family home for the first eight months of 2007 was $202,500, according to the Emmet Association of Realtors.

Information: Petoskey Regional Chamber of Commerce, (231) 347-4150 or www.petoskey.com. Petoskey-Harbor Springs-Boyne Country Visitors Bureau, (800) 845-2828 or www.boynecountry.com.

Traverse City

In a scenic setting at the base of two bays that merge and open into Lake Michigan, Traverse City is a popular four-season playground. Many who come here as tourists return to stay in retirement.

It's near the northwestern edge of Michigan's lower peninsula, which juts like a boxing glove toward the upper peninsula and Canada. Summers are filled with boating, fishing, hiking and golfing, and winters bring cross-country skiing through quiet snowy woods, downhill skiing and snowmobiling.

The Traverse City area is a major center for growing and processing cherries (you'll find plenty of cherry-based dishes in local restaurants) and for viniculture, producing notable wines. On the artistic side, the newly inaugurated Traverse City Film Festival runs in midsummer, and the Old Town Playhouse and local musical groups provide other entertainment. The internationally known Interloc-hen Center for the Arts is only 13 miles away and has an extremely active concert schedule.

Traverse City has a powerful plus: Munson Medical Center. Five times in seven years, it has been listed on the tally of 100 top hospitals by Solucient, an information-products company serving the health-care industry. Solucient has the nation's largest health-care database and does an annual rating of hospitals. The hospital has strong support in the community. An 18-month campaign raised $10 million for a new emergency room, which opened in early 2007.

At 391 beds, the center is surprisingly large for a community of less than 15,000 but it does serve a 32-county area. The center offers a wide range of medical services, including an award-winning heart-surgery program. Of special interest to retirees are extensive programs devoted to senior health. These include a geriatric assessment clinic; a Fitness Forever program to improve strength, cardiovascular endurance, balance and flexibility; a gentle tai chi exercise class for those with arthritis; and even a grandparenting class that crosses the generational divide.

An active senior center serves the town, in which 15.2 percent of the residents are 65 or older. A fine resource is the Traverse Area District Library's Senior Corner Web site, www.seniors.tcnet.org. A senior academy at the town's Northwestern Michigan College offers noncredit courses.

Population: 14,407

Climate: High Low
January 27 14
July 81 58

Cost of living: Below average

Housing cost: The median sales price of a single-family home during the first nine months of 2007 was $173,250, according to the Traverse Area Association of Realtors.

Information: Traverse City Convention and Visitors Bureau, (800) 940-1120 or www.visittraversecity.com. Traverse City Area Chamber of Commerce, (231) 947-5075 or www.tcchamber.org

MINNESOTA

Minnesota has a state income tax and a state sales tax.

The state income tax rate is graduated from 5.35% to 7.85% depending upon income bracket. For married couples filing jointly, the rates are 5.35% on the first $29,980 of taxable income; 7.05% on the next $89,120 of taxable income; and 7.85% on taxable income above $119,100.

In calculating the tax, there is no deduction for federal income tax paid. Federal, state and private pensions are not exempt. Social Security benefits subject to federal tax are not exempt. There is a $3,300 personal exemption per person from adjusted gross income. There is a $12,300 standard deduction from adjusted gross income for married couples filing jointly when both are age 65 or older. There are age 65 or older/disabled subtractions for singles or couples meeting certain income requirements.

Major tax credits or rebates include: credit for taxes paid to other states, which our couples do not qualify for; and a marriage credit, which one of our couples qualifies for. There is also a property tax refund for homeowners whose total household income is less

> **O Tax Heavens:** None
> **Ψ Tax Hells:** None

than $91,120 and renters whose total household income is less than $49,160. The amount of the refund varies depending on the number of dependents, household income and property taxes paid. For 2006, the maximum refund is $1,700. In addition, there is a special property tax refund for homeowners if net property tax increased more than 12% from the prior year and if the increase is $100 or more. The maximum refund is $1,000.

The state sales tax rate is 6.5%, but local governments can add to this amount.

Our couples relocating to the city listed below must pay to register their automobiles based on the age and base value of the automobile. The registration tax is $189 for the Explorer and $189 for the Camry. Our couples must also pay a transfer fee of $24 per automobile, which includes a title fee, public safety fee, lien filing fee and license plate fee, at the time of registration. Thereafter, on an annual basis, our cou-

ples will pay a registration tax and a service fee, per automobile.

Minneapolis

Minneapolis has no local income tax but does levy a sales tax.

Most purchases are taxed at a rate of 7.15%. Major consumer categories taxed at a different rate include: food away from home, which is taxed at a rate of 10.15%. Major consumer categories that are exempt from sales tax include: drugs, groceries, apparel and services, and medical services.

In the Watershed District 6 of Minneapolis, there are two property tax rates based on different components; the property tax rate based on tax capacity (taxable value) is 1.2798 and the tax rate based on market value is .0014479. To calculate tax capacity (taxable value), homes are assessed at 1% of the first $500,000 of market value of the home plus 1.25% of market value in excess of $500,000. There is a homestead credit of up to $304 available to all residents that is applied to the tax capacity component of tax. Property tax does not cover garbage pickup.

Minneapolis has no personal property tax for individuals.

MINNESOTA TAX TABLE

Instructions

1. Find the Income in the far left column closest to your anticipated retirement income.
2. Find the Home Value closest to the value of the home where you will live in retirement.
3. Follow that row to your estimated Total Tax Burden at age 65 and beyond.

Income	Home Value	Property Tax & Other Fees	Personal Property Tax & Auto Fees	Sales Tax	Local Income Tax	State Income Tax[†]	Total Tax Burden	Rank[*]
MINNEAPOLIS								
$30,000	$125,000	$1,701	$207	$927	-	($518)	$2,317	53 of 173
	150,000	2,079	207	927	-	(743)	2,470	48 of 173
	175,000	2,458	207	927	-	(983)	2,609	41 of 173
$60,000	$150,000	$2,079	$207	$1,609	-	$1,586	$5,481	178 of 203
	225,000	3,215	207	1,609	-	962	5,993	149 of 203
	300,000	4,351	207	1,609	-	617	6,784	132 of 203
$90,000	$225,000	$3,215	$207	$2,011	-	$4,199	$9,632	188 of 203
	375,000	5,487	207	2,011	-	3,739	11,444	177 of 203
	525,000	7,740	207	2,011	-	3,739	13,697	165 of 203

†Property tax refund is paid directly to the homeowner by the state. It is included above as a reduction (or refund) of state income tax.
*There are 203 cities in this book, 30 of which have higher than average home prices. We have estimated taxes for a tier of higher home values (and omitted the lowest tier) for these 30 cities. The city with the lowest tax burden for an income/home value combination is given the #1 rating; the higher the rating, the higher the total tax burden.

MISSISSIPPI

Mississippi has a state income tax and a state sales tax.

The state income tax rate is graduated from 3% to 5% depending upon income bracket. For married couples filing jointly, the rates are 3% on the first $5,000 of taxable income; 4% on the next $5,000 of taxable income; and 5% on taxable income above $10,000.

In calculating the tax, there is no deduction for federal income tax paid. Federal, state and private pensions are exempt. Social Security benefits are exempt. There is a $4,600 standard deduction from adjusted gross income for married couples filing jointly. There is a $12,000 exemption for married couples filing jointly. There is an additional $1,500 exemption for each person age 65 or older.

Major tax credits or rebates include: credit for taxes paid to other states and credit for premiums paid during the taxable year for certain qualified long-term care insurance policies. Our couples do not qualify for these programs.

The state sales tax rate is 7%.

Since car registration and renewal fees differ within the state, see city information for details.

Biloxi

Biloxi has no local income tax and does not levy an additional sales tax.

Most purchases are taxed at the state rate of 7%. Major consumer categories taxed at a different rate include: none. Major consumer categories that are exempt from sales tax include: drugs.

Within Biloxi city limits, the property tax rate is .10462. Owner-occupied homes are assessed at 10% of market value. The regular homestead exemption is a scaled tax credit of up to $300 on the first $7,500 of a home's assessed value and is available to all homeowners. There is also an elderly homestead exemption of $7,500 off the assessed value of a home for residents age 65 or older. Only one of these exemptions can be taken at once; we've assumed our couples take the elderly homestead exemption. Property tax includes garbage pickup.

Biloxi has no personal property tax for individuals.

> ○ **Tax Heavens:** None
> ψ **Tax Hells:** None
> **Top Retirement Towns:**
> Hattiesburg, Oxford, Vicksburg

Our couples relocating to Biloxi must pay an ad valorem tax based on the county's valuation of each car. The estimated tax due upon initial registration is $280 for the Explorer and $200 for the Camry. Our couples also pay a $10 registration fee per automobile, a $5 title fee per automobile and a $15 privilege tax per automobile. Thereafter, on an annual basis, our couples will pay an ad valorem tax, a privilege tax and a registration fee, per automobile.

Hattiesburg

Hattiesburg has no local income tax and does not levy an additional sales tax.

Most purchases are taxed at the state rate of 7%. Major consumer categories taxed at a different rate include: food away from home, which is taxed at a rate of 8%. Major consumer categories that are exempt from sales tax include: drugs.

Within the Hattiesburg city limits, the property tax rate is .17021. Owner-occupied homes are assessed at 10% of market value. The regular homestead exemption is a scaled tax credit of up to $300 on the first $7,500 of a home's assessed value and is available to all homeowners. There is also an elderly homestead exemption of $7,500 off the assessed value of a home for residents age 65 or older. Only one of these exemptions can be taken at once; we've assumed our couples take the elderly homestead exemption. Property tax does not cover garbage pickup.

Hattiesburg has no personal property tax for individuals.

Our couples relocating to Hattiesburg must pay an ad valorem tax based on the county's valuation of each car. The estimated tax due upon initial registration is $618 for the Explorer and $442 for the Camry. Our couples also pay a $10 registration fee per automobile, a $5 title fee per automobile and a $15 privilege tax per automobile. Thereafter, on an annual basis, our couples will pay an

ad valorem tax, a privilege tax and a registration fee, per automobile.

Oxford

Oxford has no local income tax and does not levy an additional sales tax.

Most purchases are taxed at the state rate of 7%. Major consumer categories taxed at a different rate include: food away from home, which is taxed at a rate of 8%. Major consumer categories that are exempt from sales tax include: drugs.

Within the Oxford city limits, the property tax rate is .10992. Owner-occupied homes are assessed at 10% of market value. The regular homestead exemption is a scaled tax credit of up to $300 on the first $7,500 of a home's assessed value and is available to all homeowners. There is also an elderly homestead exemption of $7,500 off the assessed value of a home for residents age 65 or older. Only one of these exemptions can be taken at once; we've assumed our couples take the elderly homestead exemption. Property tax does not cover garbage pickup.

Oxford has no personal property tax for individuals.

Our couples relocating to Oxford must pay an ad valorem tax based on the county's valuation of each car. The estimated tax due upon initial registration is $315 for the Explorer and $225 for the Camry. Our couples also pay a $10 registration fee per automobile, a $5 title fee per automobile and a $15 privilege tax per automobile. Thereafter, on an annual basis, our couples will pay an ad valorem tax, a privilege tax and a registration fee, per automobile.

Vicksburg

Vicksburg has no local income tax and does not levy an additional sales tax.

Most purchases are taxed at the state rate of 7%. Major consumer categories taxed at a different rate include: food away from home, which is taxed at a rate of 8%. Major consumer categories that are exempt from sales tax include: drugs.

Within the Vicksburg city limits, the property tax rate is .11982. Owner-occupied homes are assessed at 10% of market value. The regular homestead exemption is a scaled tax credit of up to $300 on the first $7,500 of a home's assessed value and is available to all homeowners. There is also an elderly homestead exemption of $7,500 off the assessed value of a home for residents age 65 or older. Only one of these exemptions can be taken at once; we've assumed our couples take the elderly homestead exemption. Property

MISSISSIPPI TAX TABLE

Instructions

1. Find the Income in the far left column closest to your anticipated retirement income.
2. Find the Home Value closest to the value of the home where you will live in retirement.
3. Follow that row to your estimated Total Tax Burden at age 65 and beyond.

Income	Home Value	Property Tax & Other Fees	Personal Property Tax & Auto Fees	Sales Tax	Local Income Tax	State Income Tax	Total Tax Burden	Rank*
BILOXI								
$30,000	$125,000	$523	$410	$1,109	-	-	$2,042	32 of 173
	150,000	785	410	1,109	-	-	2,304	34 of 173
	175,000	1,046	410	1,109	-	-	2,565	38 of 173
$60,000	$150,000	$785	$410	$1,865	-	$269	$3,329	27 of 203
	225,000	1,569	410	1,865	-	269	4,113	38 of 203
	300,000	2,354	410	1,865	-	269	4,898	45 of 203
$90,000	$225,000	$1,569	$410	$2,300	-	$1,516	$5,795	53 of 203
	375,000	3,139	410	2,300	-	1,516	7,365	56 of 203
	525,000	4,708	410	2,300	-	1,516	8,934	60 of 203
HATTIESBURG								
$30,000	$125,000	$1,031	$845	$1,138	-	-	$3,014	120 of 173
	150,000	1,457	845	1,138	-	-	3,440	120 of 173
	175,000	1,882	845	1,138	-	-	3,865	121 of 173
$60,000	$150,000	$1,457	$845	$1,915	-	$269	$4,486	127 of 203
	225,000	2,733	845	1,915	-	269	5,762	135 of 203
	300,000	4,010	845	1,915	-	269	7,039	142 of 203
$90,000	$225,000	$2,733	$845	$2,363	-	$1,516	$7,457	139 of 203
	375,000	5,286	845	2,363	-	1,516	10,010	152 of 203
	525,000	7,839	845	2,363	-	1,516	12,563	150 of 203
OXFORD								
$30,000	$125,000	$730	$439	$1,138	-	-	$2,307	51 of 173
	150,000	1,004	439	1,138	-	-	2,581	58 of 173
	175,000	1,279	439	1,138	-	-	2,856	61 of 173
$60,000	$150,000	$1,004	$439	$1,915	-	$269	$3,627	50 of 203
	225,000	1,829	439	1,915	-	269	4,452	53 of 203
	300,000	2,653	439	1,915	-	269	5,276	61 of 203
$90,000	$225,000	$1,829	$439	$2,363	-	$1,516	$6,147	78 of 203
	375,000	3,478	439	2,363	-	1,516	7,796	75 of 203
	525,000	5,126	439	2,363	-	1,516	9,444	70 of 203
VICKSBURG								
$30,000	$125,000	$779	$502	$1,124	-	-	$2,405	61 of 173
	150,000	1,079	502	1,124	-	-	2,705	66 of 173
	175,000	1,378	502	1,124	-	-	3,004	73 of 173
$60,000	$150,000	$1,079	$502	$1,890	-	$269	$3,740	59 of 203
	225,000	1,977	502	1,890	-	269	4,638	65 of 203
	300,000	2,876	502	1,890	-	269	5,537	78 of 203
$90,000	$225,000	$1,977	$502	$2,332	-	$1,516	$6,327	89 of 203
	375,000	3,775	502	2,332	-	1,516	8,125	85 of 203
	525,000	5,572	502	2,332	-	1,516	9,922	87 of 203

*There are 203 cities in this book, 30 of which have higher than average home prices. We have estimated taxes for a tier of higher home values (and omitted the lowest tier) for these 30 cities. The city with the lowest tax burden for an income/home value combination is given the #1 rating; the higher the rating, the higher the total tax burden.

tax does not cover garbage pickup.

Vicksburg has no personal property tax for individuals.

Our couples relocating to Vicksburg must pay an ad valorem tax based on the county's valuation of each car. The estimated tax due upon initial registration is $356 for the Explorer and $254 for the Camry. Our couples also pay a $10 registration fee per automobile, a $5 title fee per automobile and a $15 privilege tax per automobile. Thereafter, on an annual basis, our couples will pay an ad valorem tax, a privilege tax and a registration fee, per automobile.

• Mississippi's Top Retirement Towns •

Hattiesburg

Forget about the land of cotton. Mississippi has become the land to retire to, with a well-established state program called Hometown Mississippi Retirement devoted to luring new retirees. The state offers strong incentives for retirees, exempting most retirement income from the state income tax.

Hattiesburg was the first certified retirement city in the state program. An important part of Hattiesburg's retiree-luring effort is the Retirement Connection, an organization of senior volunteers who contact prospective new residents and give them the scoop on the town.

The historic downtown is lined with architecture ranging from Victorian to Italian Renaissance and is among the most well-preserved historic districts in the state. Even some of the enormous oak trees here are historic.

The University of Southern Mississippi offers a full slate of cultural events and the Osher Lifelong Learning Institute with classes, socials and field trips geared for those 50 and older. Hattiesburg is also a thriving arts community. The Saenger Theater, an elegant Art Deco movie palace listed on the National Register of Historic Places, hosts varied performances, including musicals by the Hattiesburg Civic Light Opera. The fine arts departments at both USM and William Carey College offer productions from Beethoven to Broadway.

The city is a regional health-care hub, with two major medical centers offering extensive services including emergency trauma and cardiac care.

Hattiesburg's mild, subtropical climate makes for year-round outdoor fun and changing seasonal beauty. There are nationally acclaimed golf courses among a number in the area, and the 41-mile Longleaf Trace, a paved rails-to-trails project, is ideal for biking, hiking, horseback riding and birding. Canoeing and kayaking are popular on the Okatoma River and in the Black Creek Wilderness. Hattiesburg is only about 83 miles from the Mississippi coast with its beaches and casinos.

Population: 48,012

Climate: High Low
January 60 36
July 92 71

Cost of living: Below average

Housing cost: The median sales price of homes, including condos, was $142,500 for the first nine months of 2007, according to the Hattiesburg Area Association of Realtors.

Information: Area Development Partnership, (800) 238-4288 or www.theADP.com. Hometown Mississippi Retirement, (800) 370-3323 or www.visitmississippi.org/retire.

Oxford

You don't even have to crack the books to get a classical education in this gracious Southern town snuggled in the forested hillsides of northern Mississippi. The town was immortalized by the late William Faulkner, who peopled his novels with vivid characters based on Oxford's residents.

Soak up history, culture and more during the town's annual Oxford Conference for the Book, which celebrates books and writing each spring. With scores of writers calling Oxford home, from the late Faulkner to modern-day stars like John Grisham, it's an intoxicating place, and the conference lets you rub elbows with some of today's literary greats. To learn more about the town's most famous resident, check out the long-running Faulkner and Yoknapatawpha Conference in late July.

Or pursue your academic dreams at the notable University of Mississippi. Those 65 and older can enjoy classes with free tuition in the university's Lifetime Learner program. Ole Miss, as the school is known, also has a year-round slate of cultural activities, with concerts and theater performances ranging from opera to Shakespeare and dance companies.

The hub of Oxford's historic downtown is a 150-year-old courthouse square with massive columns and centuries-old oaks. Restored buildings house everything from gourmet restaurants and upscale clothing boutiques to home decor shops, the oldest department store in the South and the nationally acclaimed Square Books Store, where renowned authors sign books and read from their latest works. You'll find stacks of autographed books by local authors and a staircase leading to the upstairs veranda and cafe.

Beyond the town square are quiet neighborhoods of antebellum mansions peeking past towering oaks and creeping ivy. Outdoor enthusiasts will find hunting, fishing, hiking and boating at nearby Sardis Lake and Holly Springs National Forest. There are three area golf courses, including one at the college.

Population: 14,051, plus about 12,500-13,000 students

Climate: High Low
January 47 34
July 92 69

Cost of living: Below average

Housing cost: The median sales price of homes in Oxford during the first half of 2007 was $192,250, according to the North Central Mississippi Board of Realtors.

Information: Oxford-Lafayette County Chamber of Commerce, (662) 234-4651 or www.oxfordms.com. Retiree Attraction Program, (800) 880-6967 or www.retire.oxfordms.com.

Vicksburg

Favorable living costs leave more money for recreation, travel and enjoying the good life — and there's plenty of that in this town perched on bluffs above the Mississippi River.

Vicksburg has blocks of beautifully restored antebellum mansions and inns, many of them on the National Register of Historic Places and open for public tours. The historic downtown is alive with boutiques, cafes, art galleries, museums and a variety of retail shops. Among the favorite stops is the Biedenharn Coca-Cola Museum, in a restored 1890 candy store where Coca-Cola was first bottled.

Outdoor enthusiasts head to well-maintained trails around town for running, cycling and walking. In addition, the beautiful Natchez Trace Parkway is nearby, offering hiking trails, historic attractions and scenic drives. This 444-mile-long national park wanders through dense woodlands and bucolic meadows to retrace the footsteps of American Indians, pioneers and soldiers from Nashville to Natchez.

A prime attraction, the beautiful Vicksburg National Military Park and Cemetery spreads across 1,844 acres, with 1,330 monuments to the Civil War battle where the Union Army laid siege to Vicksburg. Golfers can head to Vicksburg Country Club (private) or Clear Creek Golf Course (public). For those interested in gaming, Vicksburg is home to four casinos.

The Vicksburg Senior Center sponsors classes, activities, barbecues and dances, while the Hinds Community College Vicksburg-Warren campus has a Creative Learning in Retirement program with classes, seminars, field trips and socials for seniors. Retirees looking to share their time and talents will find a variety of volunteer opportunities here, and there are options for those who want to work some in retirement.

The River Region Medical Center has state-of-the-art facilities offering extensive services, including cardiovascular care. Vicksburg is 45 miles west of Jackson, the capital.

Population: 25,740

Climate: High Low

	High	Low
January	59	35
July	92	71

Cost of living: Below average

Housing cost: The median sales price of a single-family home for the first half of 2007 was $121,906, according to the Vicksburg-Warren County Board of Realtors.

Information: Vicksburg Convention and Visitors Bureau, (800) 221-3536 or www.visitvicksburg.com. Vicksburg-Warren County Chamber of Commerce, (888) 842-5728 or www.vicksburgchamber.org. Hometown Mississippi Retirement, (800) 370-3323 or www.visitmississippi.org/retire.

MISSOURI

M issouri has a state income tax and a state sales tax.

The state income tax rate is graduated from 1.5% to 6% depending upon income bracket. For all filers, the rates are 1.5% on the first $1,000 of taxable income; 2% on the next $1,000 of taxable income; 2.5% on the next $1,000 of taxable income; 3% on the next $1,000 of taxable income; 3.5% on the next $1,000 of taxable income; 4% on the next $1,000 of taxable income; 4.5% on the next $1,000 of taxable income; 5% on the next $1,000 of taxable income; 5.5% on the next $1,000 of taxable income; and 6% on taxable income above $9,000. Taxable income is calculated individually by spouse, even if filing jointly.

In calculating the tax, there is a

O **Tax Heavens:** None
Ψ **Tax Hells:** Kansas City
Top Retirement Towns: Branson

---

deduction of up to $10,000 for married couples filing jointly for federal income tax liability. Federal, state and private pensions are not exempt. However, there is a pension exemption of up to $6,000 per person. Eligibility is subject to certain income limitations. Social Security benefits subject to federal tax are not exempt. There is a standard deduction of $12,300 from Missouri adjusted gross income for married couples filing jointly, both age 65 or older. There is a $4,200 exemption from Missouri adjusted gross income for married couples filing jointly.

Major tax credits or rebates include: credit for taxes paid to other states and property tax credit. Our couples do not qualify for these credits.

The state sales tax rate is 4.225%, but local governments can add to this amount. In the Branson/Lakes area the state also collects an additional 1% tourism community enhancement district sales tax.

Our couples relocating to the cities listed below must pay to register their automobiles based on horsepower. The registration fee is $33 for the Explorer and $21 for the Camry. Our couples must also pay a $9 title fee per automobile, a $3 title processing fee per automobile and a $4 registration processing fee per automobile at the time of registration. Thereafter, on an annual basis,

MISSOURI TAX TABLE

Instructions

1. Find the Income in the far left column closest to your anticipated retirement income.
2. Find the Home Value closest to the value of the home where you will live in retirement.
3. Follow that row to your estimated Total Tax Burden at age 65 and beyond.

Income	Home Value	Property Tax & Other Fees	Personal Property Tax & Auto Fees	Sales Tax	Local Income Tax	State Income Tax	Total Tax Burden	Rank*
BRANSON								
$30,000	$125,000	$1,178	$496	$1,205	-	-	$2,879	105 of 173
	150,000	1,377	496	1,205	-	-	3,078	98 of 173
	175,000	1,577	496	1,205	-	-	3,278	85 of 173
$60,000	$150,000	$1,377	$496	$2,076	-	$1,301	$5,250	165 of 203
	225,000	1,976	499	2,076	-	1,301	5,852	141 of 203
	300,000	2,575	496	2,076	-	1,301	6,448	122 of 203
$90,000	$225,000	$1,976	$496	$2,562	-	$3,125	$8,159	163 of 203
	375,000	3,173	496	2,562	-	3,125	9,356	132 of 203
	525,000	4,371	496	2,562	-	3,125	10,554	110 of 203
KANSAS CITY								
$30,000	$125,000	$2,059	$904	$1,121	$56	-	$4,140	164 of 173 Ψ
	150,000	2,434	904	1,121	56	-	4,515	158 of 173
	175,000	2,810	904	1,121	56	-	4,891	156 of 173
$60,000	$150,000	$2,434	$904	$1,927	$239	$1,301	$6,805	197 of 203 Ψ
	225,000	3,562	904	1,927	239	1,301	7,933	192 of 203
	300,000	4,689	904	1,927	239	1,301	9,060	184 of 203
$90,000	$225,000	$3,562	$904	$2,377	$464	$3,125	$10,432	193 of 203
	375,000	5,816	904	2,377	464	3,125	12,686	188 of 203
	525,000	8,070	904	2,377	464	3,125	14,940	180 of 203

*There are 203 cities in this book, 30 of which have higher than average home prices. We have estimated taxes for a tier of higher home values (and omitted the lowest tier) for these 30 cities. The city with the lowest tax burden for an income/home value combination is given the #1 rating; the higher the rating, the higher the total tax burden.

our couples will pay a registration fee and registration processing, per automobile.

Branson

Branson has no local income tax but does levy a sales tax.

Most purchases are taxed at a rate of 8.6%. Major consumer categories taxed at a different rate include: food away from home, which is taxed at a rate of 8.975%; and groceries, which are taxed at a rate of 4.6%. Major consumer categories that are exempt from sales tax include: drugs and medical services.

Within the city limits of Branson, the property tax rate is .042013 for homes. Homes are assessed at 19% of market value. There is a senior citizen tax rebate for residents age 65 and older who are married filing jointly with a household income of up to $27,000. In addition, there is a homestead preservation credit for homeowners age 65 and older whose income is less than $72,380. Homeowners may apply for only one of these two credits. Property tax does not cover garbage pickup.

Branson has a personal property tax rate of .042013. Personal property is assessed at 33.3% of current market value. Items subject to the personal property tax include motor vehicles, boats, RVs and airplanes.

Kansas City

Kansas City has a local income tax and levies a sales tax.

The local income tax rate is 1% of earned income, consisting of wages, salaries and self-employment income.

Most purchases are taxed at a rate of 7.725%. Major consumer categories taxed at a different rate include: food away from home, which is taxed at a rate of 9.725%; and groceries, which are taxed at a rate of 4.725%. Major consumer categories that are exempt from sales tax include: drugs and medical services.

In the Country Club district in Jackson County, the property tax rate is .079101 for homes. Homes are assessed at 19% of market value. There is a senior citizen tax credit for residents age 65 and older who are married filing jointly with a household income of up to $27,000. In addition, there is a homestead preservation credit for homeowners age 65 and older whose income is less than $72,380. Homeowners may apply for only one of these two credits. Property tax does not cover garbage pickup.

Kansas City has a personal property tax rate of .070528 within Jackson County. Personal property is assessed at 33.3% of current market value. Items subject to the personal property tax include motor vehicles, boats, RVs and airplanes. In addition, there is a $13 city sticker fee per vehicle.

• Missouri's Top Retirement Town •

Branson

Fans of country music need look no farther than this little Ozark mountain town to satisfy vacation dreams of day-in, day-out live musical entertainment — plus superb camping and recreational opportunities.

In little more than 20 years, Branson has grown from an obscure hillbilly hangout to one of America's hottest tourism and entertainment centers. In 2006, 7.9 million people visited Branson, taking in more than 100 musical performances beneath the neon marquees of 52 theaters that, in total, boast many more seats (60,317) than Broadway. In the process, they've helped make Branson one of the top drive destinations in the country.

The town's musical heritage has roots in a raffish group known as the Baldknobbers formed in the late 1950s. Presley's Mountain Music Jubilee opened in 1967, ushering in a new era. By the time Roy Clark, star of Grand Ole Opry and the TV series "Hee Haw," moved here from Nashville in 1983 to open his own show, Branson was on its way to the big time. Clark was followed by a parade of other country stars — not simply to do an occasional show but to build impressive state-of-the-art music theaters where they perform regularly year-round.

Pop celebrities have grabbed the coattails of success here, as well. Dick Clark's American Bandstand Theater opened its doors to a revolving lineup of rock-n-roll legends from the 1950s and '60s.

There's nearly as much action going on beyond the theater stages of Branson. Silver Dollar City, built to resemble a turn-of-the-century Ozark village, is widely recognized as a top Midwest theme park. Ever popular, too, is Shepherd of the Hills Homestead and Outdoor Theatre. Inspired by Harold Bell Wright's popular 1907 novel "Shepherd of the Hills," set in the Branson area, this theme park houses a historic homestead once belonging to the characters in Wright's novel.

New on the scene are the world's largest Titanic museum, strikingly presented as a half-scale replica of the fateful ship's interior, and the Butterfly Palace and Rainforest Adventure, where you can roam among a swarm of exotic butterflies beneath a giant dome. Shoppers, too, will find new hunting grounds at the $450 million Branson Landing development on the town's Lake Taneycomo waterfront. This dramatic revitalization of the historic downtown features a town square with a $7.5 million water attraction created by the designers of the fountains at the Bellagio resort in Las Vegas.

Population: 7,435

Climate:

	High	Low
January	44	21
July	90	64

Cost of living: Below average

Housing cost: The average sales price for a single-family home was $215,744 for the first half of 2007, according to the Tri-Lakes Association of Realtors.

Information: Branson-Lakes Area Chamber of Commerce/Convention and Visitors Bureau, (800) 214-3661 or www.explore branson.com.

MONTANA

Montana has a state income tax but does not levy a state sales tax.

The state income tax rate is graduated from 1% to 6.9% depending upon income bracket. For married couples filing jointly, the rates are 1% on the first $2,400 of taxable income; 2% on the next $1,900 of taxable income; 3% on the next $2,200 of taxable income; 4% on the next $2,300 of taxable income; 5% on the next $2,500 of taxable income; 6% on the next $3,200 of taxable income; and 6.9% on taxable income above $14,500.

In calculating the tax, there is no deduction for federal income tax paid. Federal, state and private pensions are exempt up to $3,600 per person if fed-

eral adjusted gross income is less than $33,000. Some Social Security benefits are not exempt. There is a 20% standard deduction from Montana adjusted gross income, subject to a minimum deduction of $3,300 and maximum of $7,420 for married couples filing jointly. There is a $1,980 personal exemption per person from adjusted gross income, plus a $1,980 age exemption per person if age 65 or older. There is an exemption of interest income up to $1,600 for a married couple filing jointly if at least one is 65 years or older.

Major tax credits or rebates include: credit for income taxes paid to other states, which our couples do not qualify for; and elderly homeowner/renter credit, which some of our couples qualify for.

Since car registration fees differ within the state, see city information for details.

Billings

Billings has no local income tax and no sales tax.

In the Billings School District 2, property taxes are determined in a complex calculation, which takes into account the reappraisal value of a home. There is an elderly homeowner credit for homeowners 62 years of age and older

---

MONTANA TAX TABLE

Instructions

1. Find the Income in the far left column closest to your anticipated retirement income.
2. Find the Home Value closest to the value of the home where you will live in retirement.
3. Follow that row to your estimated Total Tax Burden at age 65 and beyond.

Income	Home Value	Property Tax & Other Fees	Personal Property Tax & Auto Fees	Sales Tax	Local Income Tax	State Income Tax†	Total Tax Burden	Rank*
BILLINGS								
$30,000	$125,000	$1,327	$658	-	-	($142)	$1,843	17 of 173
	150,000	1,613	658	-	-	(428)	1,843	11 of 173
	175,000	1,898	658	-	-	(713)	1,843	9 of 173 ○
$60,000	$150,000	$1,613	$658	-	-	$1,676	$3,947	78 of 203
	225,000	2,469	658	-	-	1,676	4,803	80 of 203
	300,000	3,326	658	-	-	1,676	5,660	84 of 203
$90,000	$225,000	$2,469	$658	-	-	$4,298	$7,425	138 of 203
	375,000	4,182	658	-	-	4,298	9,138	120 of 203
	525,000	5,895	658	-	-	4,298	10,851	120 of 203
KALISPELL								
$30,000	$125,000	$886	$452	-	-	-	$1,338	4 of 173 ○
	150,000	1,144	452	-	-	-	1,596	7 of 173 ○
	175,000	1,401	452	-	-	(216)	1,637	5 of 173 ○
$60,000	$150,000	$1,144	$452	-	-	$1,676	$3,272	24 of 203
	225,000	1,916	452	-	-	1,676	4,044	33 of 203
	300,000	2,687	452	-	-	1,676	4,815	39 of 203
$90,000	$225,000	$1,916	$452	-	-	$4,298	$6,666	104 of 203
	375,000	3,459	452	-	-	4,298	8,209	89 of 203
	525,000	5,003	452	-	-	4,298	9,753	82 of 203

†The Elderly Homeowner Credit is included as a reduction of income tax due or as a refund if the credit is greater than the tax liability.
*There are 203 cities in this book, 30 of which have higher than average home prices. We have estimated taxes for a tier of higher home values (and omitted the lowest tier) for these 30 cities. The city with the lowest tax burden for an income/home value combination is given the #1 rating; the higher the rating, the higher the total tax burden.

who meet certain residency and income requirements, which is taken as a reduction of state income tax due or a refund. There is also a property tax assistance program for homeowners who meet certain residency and income requirements and a property tax refund for homeowners who have owned and occupied the home as their primary residence for a certain amount of time. Special assessments of approximately $300 per year are added to property tax, including garbage pickup and storm drainage fees.

Billings has no personal property tax for individuals.

Our couples relocating to Billings must pay a county option tax, which is based on the depreciated value of the automobile and is $126 for the Explorer and $80 for the Camry. Our couples

must also pay a registration fee of $217 per automobile, a title fee of $17 per automobile, a highway fee of $5 per automobile and a lien filing fee of $8 per automobile at the time of registration. Thereafter, on an annual basis, our couples will pay a registration fee, a county option tax and a highway fee, per automobile.

Kalispell

Kalispell has no local income tax and no sales tax.

In Kalispell School District 5, property taxes are determined in a complex calculation, which takes into account the reappraisal value of a home. There is an elderly homeowner credit for homeowners 62 years of age and older who meet certain residency and income requirements, which is taken as

a reduction of state income tax due or a refund. There is also a property tax assistance program for homeowners who meet certain residency and income requirements and a property tax refund for homeowners who have owned and occupied the home as their primary residence for a certain amount of time. Property tax includes garbage pickup.

Kalispell has no personal property tax for individuals.

Our couples relocating to Kalispell must pay a registration fee of $217 per automobile, a title fee of $17 per automobile, a highway fee of $5 per automobile and a lien filing fee of $8 per automobile at the time of registration. Thereafter, on an annual basis, our couples will pay a registration fee and a highway fee, per automobile

• Montana's Top Retirement Town •

Kalispell

When Montana-born and -raised Fred Leistiko retired from the military in 1991, he and his wife, Connie, a retired assistant dean of the University of Akron School of Law, returned to his family ranch near Kalispell. From there, they made frequent forays all over the country.

"We were looking for that last great place," Fred says. "Then we realized we were living it right here, so we built a house in Kalispell in 1995."

Kalispell is the hub of the Flathead Valley in northwest Montana, just south of Glacier National Park. Combining the national park with three additional wilderness areas, the wild and scenic Flathead River and Flathead Lake make a total wilderness area equal to the size of Vermont. No wonder Fred declares,

"There's everything you need, all the sports you love."

From bird-watching to skydiving, there's hardly a sport that is not available. This vast natural playground also offers fishing, horseback riding, wildlife viewing in the backcountry, camping, downhill and cross-country skiing, snowmobiling, biking and boating. Glacier National Park alone has more than 700 miles of hiking trails.

Fred describes Kalispell as a growing town that still has a small-town atmosphere. "There are museums, an orchestra. You can get involved in anything you want," adds Fred, part-time manager of the Kalispell City Airport and president of the Hockaday Museum of Art.

The Kalispell Regional Medical Center is rated among the top 100 hos-

pitals in the country and has the nation's first rural air ambulance. Fred notes that nice homes can be bought in the $200,000s, but "there are also multi-million-dollar homes. Kalispell has mountains on all sides, a huge lake, everything you want. It is just a fun place to be," he says.

Population: 19,432

Climate:

	High	Low
January	28	13
July	80	47

Cost of living: Average

Housing cost: The median sales price for a single-family home for the first half of 2007 was $222,000, according to the Northwest Montana Association of Realtors.

Information: Kalispell Area Chamber of Commerce, (888) 888-2308 or www.kalispellchamber.com.

NEBRASKA

Nebraska has a state income tax and a state sales tax.

The state income tax is graduated from 2.56% to 6.84% depending upon income bracket. For married couples filing jointly, the rates are 2.56% on the first $4,000 of taxable income; 3.57% on the next $27,000 of taxable income; 5.12% on the next $19,000 of taxable income; and 6.84% on taxable income above $50,000.

In calculating the tax, there is no deduction for federal income tax paid. Federal, state and private pensions are not exempt. Social Security benefits subject to federal tax are not exempt. There is an $8,580 standard deduction from adjusted gross income for married couples filing jointly plus an additional $1,030 per person age 65 or older.

Major tax credits or rebates include: credit for income taxes paid to other states, which our couples do not qualify for; and personal exemption credit

against tax of $106 per person, which our couples do qualify for.

The state sales tax rate is 5.5%, but local governments can add to this amount.

Omaha

Omaha has no local income tax but does levy a sales tax.

Most purchases are taxed at a rate of 7%. Major consumer categories taxed at a different rate: none. Major consumer categories that are exempt from sales tax include: groceries, drugs, medical services and medical supplies.

In the Omaha School District 100, the property tax rate is .0207512. Homes are assessed at 100% of market value. There is a homestead exemption of up to $132,880 off assessed value for

homeowners age 65 or older, depending on income. Property tax includes garbage pickup.

Omaha has no personal property tax for individuals.

Our couples relocating to Omaha must pay a motor vehicle tax of $378 for the Explorer and $234 for the Camry. The motor vehicle tax is based on the age and MSRP of the automobile. Our couples must also pay a wheel tax of $35 per automobile, a plate fee of $7 per automobile, a registration fee of $15 per automobile, a title fee of $17 per automobile, miscellaneous fees of $5 and a motor vehicle fee of $20 for the first automobile registered and $5 for each additional automobile at the time of registration. Thereafter, on an annual basis, our couples will pay a motor vehicle tax, a wheel tax, a motor vehicle fee, miscellaneous fees and a registration fee, per automobile.

NEBRASKA TAX TABLE

Instructions

1. Find the Income in the far left column closest to your anticipated retirement income.
2. Find the Home Value closest to the value of the home where you will live in retirement.
3. Follow that row to your estimated Total Tax Burden at age 65 and beyond.

Income	Home Value	Property Tax & Other Fees	Personal Property Tax & Auto Fees	Sales Tax	Local Income Tax	State Income Tax	Total Tax Burden	Rank*
OMAHA								
$30,000	$125,000	-	$680	$870	-	-	$1,550	11 of 173
	150,000	355	680	870	-	-	1,905	14 of 173
	175,000	874	680	870	-	-	2,424	29 of 173
$60,000	$150,000	$3,113	$680	$1,529	-	$1,247	$6,569	195 of 203 Ψ
	225,000	4,669	680	1,529	-	1,247	8,125	194 of 203 Ψ
	300,000	6,225	680	1,529	-	1,247	9,681	191 of 203
$90,000	$225,000	$4,669	$680	$1,906	-	$3,558	$10,813	196 of 203 Ψ
	375,000	7,782	680	1,906	-	3,558	13,926	194 of 203 Ψ
	525,000	10,894	680	1,906	-	3,558	17,038	193 of 203

*There are 203 cities in this book, 30 of which have higher than average home prices. We have estimated taxes for a tier of higher home values (and omitted the lowest tier) for these 30 cities. The city with the lowest tax burden for an income/home value combination is given the #1 rating; the higher the rating, the higher the total tax burden.

NEVADA

N evada has no state income tax but does have a state sales tax.

The state sales tax rate is 2%, but local governments add at least 4.5% to this rate, resulting in a minimum sales tax rate of 6.5% in Nevada.

Since car registration and renewal fees differ within the state, see city information for details.

Carson City

Carson City has no local income tax but does levy a sales tax.

Most purchases are taxed at a rate of 7.125%. Major consumer categories taxed at a different rate: none. Major consumer categories that are exempt from sales tax include: drugs, groceries and medical services.

In the Carson City tax district 1.0, the property tax rate is .029287. Homes are assessed at a percentage of replacement cost. Property taxes have been estimated by using taxable values for actual homes with similar market values or by using estimates based on average taxable values where actual values were not available. There is a senior citizen rebate for homeowners age 62 or older with annual household income of $26,714 or less. Property tax does not cover garbage pickup.

Carson City tax district 1.0 has a personal property tax rate of .029287. Personal property is assessed at 35% of taxable value. Items subject to the tax include mobile homes.

Our couples relocating to Carson City must pay a governmental services tax based on the value of each automobile and a registration fee of $33 per automobile. The governmental services tax is $319 for the Explorer and $238 for the Camry. Our couples must also pay a title fee of $29 per automobile, a VIN inspection fee of $1 per automobile and a prison industry fee of $1 per automobile at the time of registration. Thereafter, on an annual basis, our couples will pay a governmental services tax, which is reduced annually until the vehicles are approximately 10 years old, and a registration fee, per automobile.

Henderson

Henderson has no local income tax

but does levy a sales tax.

Most purchases are taxed at a rate of 7.75%. Major consumer categories taxed at a different rate: none. Major consumer categories that are exempt from sales tax include: drugs, groceries and medical services.

In the Henderson tax district 500, the property tax rate is .028941. Homes are assessed at 35% of taxable value. For new homes, the taxable value is roughly equivalent to the market value. There is a senior citizen rebate for homeowners age 62 or older with annual household income of $26,714 or less. Property tax does not cover garbage pickup. There may be additional localized property tax assessments for special improvements.

Henderson has no personal property tax for individuals.

Our couples relocating to Henderson must pay a governmental services tax based on the value of each automobile, a supplemental governmental services tax of one-fourth of the governmental services tax per automobile and a registration fee of $33 per automobile. The governmental services tax is $319 for the Explorer and $238 for the Camry. The supplemental governmental services tax is $80 for the Explorer and $59 for the Camry. Our couples must also pay a title fee of $29 per automobile, a VIN inspection fee of $1 per automobile and a prison industry fee of $1 per automobile at the time of registration. Thereafter, on an annual basis, our couples will pay a governmental services tax and a supplemental governmental services tax, both of which are reduced annually until the vehicles are approximately 10 years old, and a registration fee, per automobile.

Las Vegas

Las Vegas has no local income tax but does levy a sales tax.

Most purchases are taxed at a rate of 7.75%. Major consumer categories taxed at a different rate: none. Major

consumer categories that are exempt from sales tax include: drugs, groceries and medical services.

In the Las Vegas tax district 200, the property tax rate is .032802. Homes are assessed at 35% of taxable value. For new homes, the taxable value is roughly equivalent to the market value. There is a senior citizen rebate for homeowners age 62 or older with annual household income of $26,714 or less. Property tax does not cover garbage pickup. There may be additional localized property tax assessments for special improvements.

Las Vegas has no personal property tax for individuals.

Our couples relocating to Las Vegas must pay a governmental services tax based on the value of each automobile, a supplemental governmental services tax of one-fourth of the governmental services tax per automobile and a registration fee of $33 per automobile. The governmental services tax is $319 for the Explorer and $238 for the Camry. The supplemental governmental services tax is $80 for the Explorer and $59 for the Camry. Our couples must also pay a title fee of $29 per automobile, a VIN inspection fee of $1 per automobile and a prison industry fee of $1 per automobile at the time of registration. Thereafter, on an annual basis, our couples will pay a governmental services tax and a supplemental governmental services tax, both of which are reduced annually until the vehicle is approximately 10 years old, and a registration fee, per automobile.

Reno

Reno has no local income tax but does levy a sales tax.

Most purchases are taxed at a rate of 7.375%. Major consumer categories taxed at a different rate: none. Major consumer categories that are exempt from sales tax include: drugs, groceries, and medical services.

In Reno Tax District 1015, the property tax rate is .036462. Homes are assessed at 35% of appraised value. For new homes, appraised value is roughly equivalent to market value. There is a senior citizen rebate for homeowners age 62 or older with annual household

NEVADA TAX TABLE

Instructions

1. Find the Income in the far left column closest to your anticipated retirement income.
2. Find the Home Value closest to the value of the home where you will live in retirement.
3. Follow that row to your estimated Total Tax Burden at age 65 and beyond.

Income	Home Value	Property Tax & Other Fees	Personal Property Tax & Auto Fees	Sales Tax	Local Income Tax	State Income Tax	Total Tax Burden	Rank*
CARSON CITY								
$30,000	$125,000	$1,016	$557	$897	-	-	$2,470	68 of 173
	150,000	1,183	557	897	-	-	2,637	62 of 173
	175,000	1,350	557	897	-	-	2,804	57 of 173
$60,000	$150,000	$1,183	$557	$1,576	-	-	$3,316	26 of 203
	225,000	1,990	557	1,576	-	-	4,123	39 of 203
	300,000	2,300	557	1,576	-	-	4,433	25 of 203
$90,000	$225,000	$1,990	$557	$1,959	-	-	$4,506	14 of 203
	375,000	2,418	557	1,959	-	-	4,934	5 of 203 O
	525,000	3,158	557	1,959	-	-	5,674	5 of 203 O
HENDERSON								
$30,000	$125,000	$1,446	$680	$975	-	-	$3,101	128 of 173
	150,000	1,699	680	975	-	-	3,354	115 of 173
	175,000	1,953	680	975	-	-	3,608	107 of 173
$60,000	$150,000	$1,699	$680	$1,714	-	-	$4,093	90 of 203
	225,000	2,459	680	1,714	-	-	4,853	84 of 203
	300,000	3,219	680	1,714	-	-	5,613	80 of 203
$90,000	$225,000	$2,459	$680	$2,131	-	-	$5,270	29 of 203
	375,000	3,979	680	2,131	-	-	6,790	34 of 203
	525,000	5,498	680	2,131	-	-	8,309	44 of 203
LAS VEGAS								
$30,000	$125,000	$1,615	$680	$975	-	-	$3,270	145 of 173
	150,000	1,902	680	975	-	-	3,557	129 of 173
	175,000	2,189	680	975	-	-	3,844	120 of 173
$60,000	$150,000	$1,902	$680	$1,714	-	-	$4,296	112 of 203
	225,000	2,763	680	1,714	-	-	5,157	104 of 203
	300,000	3,624	680	1,714	-	-	6,018	101 of 203
$90,000	$225,000	$2,763	$680	$2,131	-	-	$5,574	40 of 203
	375,000	4,485	680	2,131	-	-	7,296	54 of 203
	525,000	6,207	680	2,131	-	-	9,018	62 of 203
RENO								
$30,000	$125,000	$1,775	$557	$928	-	-	$3,260	144 of 173
	150,000	2,094	557	928	-	-	3,579	131 of 173
	175,000	2,413	557	928	-	-	3,898	123 of 173
$60,000	$150,000	$2,094	$557	$1,631	-	-	$4,282	110 of 203
	225,000	3,051	557	1,631	-	-	5,239	112 of 203
	300,000	4,009	557	1,631	-	-	6,197	112 of 203
$90,000	$225,000	$3,051	$557	$2,027	-	-	$5,635	43 of 203
	375,000	4,966	557	2,027	-	-	7,550	64 of 203
	525,000	6,880	557	2,027	-	-	9,464	71 of 203

*There are 203 cities in this book, 30 of which have higher than average home prices. We have estimated taxes for a tier of higher home values (and omitted the lowest tier) for these 30 cities. The city with the lowest tax burden for an income/home value combination is given the #1 rating; the higher the rating, the higher the total tax burden.

income of $26,714 or less. Annual increases in property tax are limited to 3% of the prior year's tax burden. Property tax does not cover garbage pickup.

Reno has no personal property tax for individuals.

Our couples relocating to Reno must pay a governmental services tax based on the value of each automobile and a registration fee of $33 per automobile. The governmental services tax is $319 for the Explorer and $238 for the Camry. Our couples must also pay a title fee of $29 per automobile, a VIN inspection fee of $1 per automobile and a prison industry fee of $1 per automobile at the time of registration. Thereafter, on an annual basis, our couples will pay a governmental services tax, which is reduced annually until the vehicle is approximately 10 years old. and a registration fee, per automobile.

• Nevada's Top Retirement Towns •

Henderson

With a high-desert climate, vast Lake Mead at the back door and Las Vegas as its big-city neighbor, Henderson has diverse indoor and outdoor lures that have made it popular for retirement. Among the nation's fastest-growing cities, it has numerous planned developments attracting retirees, among them Sun City Anthem, a Del Webb active-adult community. It's home to a number of golf courses and upscale resort-residential communities.

Established in the 1930s when the Hoover Dam was built on the Colorado River, Lake Mead offers a glimpse of three of America's four desert ecosystems (Mojave, Great Basin and Sonoran), providing desert flora and fauna unlike anywhere else. The Lake Mead National Recreation Area also provides a bounty of outdoor activities, including hiking, biking, fishing and houseboating.

By contrast, but also within minutes of Henderson, residents can take in the shows, shopping and dining of the Las Vegas Strip — yet live away from the glitz. Retirees who have moved to Henderson say it has its own sense of community, activities and opportunities for involvement. Opened in 2002, Nevada State College is one of several schools in Henderson, and the University of Nevada at Las Vegas is nearby.

Henderson's extensive trail system and excellent parks and recreation programs encourage a healthy, outdoor lifestyle. Two campuses of St. Rose Dominican Hospitals provide acute care in Henderson, with a variety of surgical and other medical services, and Las Vegas adds a number of medical facilities with advanced care.

Beware: It gets hot in this desert climate, with the average daily high temperature in both July and August exceeding 100 degrees.

Population: 240,614
Climate: High Low
January 57 37
July 104 78
Cost of living: Above average
Housing cost: The median sales price of a single-family home during the first half of 2007 was $309,361, according to the Greater Las Vegas Association of Realtors.
Information: City of Henderson Department of Cultural Arts and Tourism, (877) 775-5252 or www.visithenderson.com.

Las Vegas

Las Vegas is the world's head-turner — from the opulence of the Wynn to the Luxor, Paris, Mirage, Caesars Palace, Mandalay Bay, the MGM Grand and dozens of other showbiz and gambling palaces. Wasn't that Debbie Reynolds soaking her toes in the Bellagio fountain?

Restaurants on the Strip are legendary, but there are plenty of memorable off-Strip dining spots as well — Rosemary's, the Lotus of Siam and Chicago Joe's among them. Beyond the city glitz, though, there's a great outdoor playground at your doorstep. You can head to Hoover Dam and Lake Mead (the largest man-made lake in the United States), the Mount Charleston Wilderness Area and Red Rock Canyon National Conservation Area.

Many consider Las Vegas nothing more than an illusion. Even the popular television crime drama "CSI" is filmed in Hollywood except for some general location shots in Las Vegas, its setting. But, beyond the Strip, Las Vegas is a real city. It has 54 public parks (with dog runs at many of them) and more than 500 churches and synagogues that counter its Sin City reputation. It's also home to the University of Nevada, Las Vegas.

"When we visited there three or four times a year, we spent all our time on the Strip," says retired Kansas City accountant Tom Kochis, "but after we moved here we found something different — nice places to live, good local entertainment and great restaurants."

Population: 552,539
Climate: High Low
January 57 37
July 104 78
Cost of living: Above average
Housing cost: The median sales price of single-family homes during the first 11 months of 2007 was about $300,000, according to the Greater Las Vegas Association of Realtors.
Information: Las Vegas Convention and Visitors Authority, (877) 847-4858 or www.visitlasvegas.com. Las Vegas Chamber of Commerce, (702) 735-1616 or www.lvchamber.com.

Reno

A river runs through the downtown of this medium-sized city of about 210,000, which feels much smaller than it is. It has a relaxed, casual atmosphere — you can go fly-fishing in the middle of the city.

Retirees enjoy diverse outdoor activities, the benefits of a university and an exciting nightlife. Low humidity moderates the four seasons.

At an elevation of 4,500 feet, Reno is best suited for active retirees who like a small-town feeling with big-city perks. Golf is served up on 40 area courses, most of them close enough to Lake Tahoe ski resorts to accommodate both sports on the same day.

Residents go rafting, kayaking and strolling along the river, all against a backdrop of scenic beauty. Nighttime brings theater, orchestra and dance performances, world-class entertainment and gaming at major casinos. Museums and the University of Nevada, Reno add to the cultural scene.

Joel Barish, 64, who moved to Sierra Canyon, a Del Webb community five miles from downtown Reno, says the proximity of family and friends, wonderful topography, reasonable home prices and great neighbors motivated him to relocate. But, if he had to name his primary reason for choosing the area, it would be no state income tax.

Population: 210,255

Climate:	High	Low
January	45	21
July	92	51

Cost of living: Above average

Housing cost: The median sales price for a single-family home during the second quarter of 2007 was $334,000, according to the Reno/Sparks Association of Realtors.

Information: Reno-Sparks Convention and Visitors Authority, (800) 367-7366 or www.rscva.com. Reno Sparks Chamber of Commerce, (775) 337-3030 or www. reno-sparkschamber.org.

NEW HAMPSHIRE

New Hampshire has no state income tax but does levy an interest and dividends tax.

The state interest and dividends tax rate is 5%. In calculating the tax, there is no deduction for federal income tax paid. Interest from United States government obligations, New Hampshire state and municipal bonds, individual retirement accounts and dividends representing capital gains or return of capital are exempt from tax. There is a $1,200 personal exemption per person age 65 or older and an exemption of the first $4,800 of taxable income for married couples filing jointly.

Major tax credits or rebates: none.

New Hampshire has no state sales tax but does impose a meals and rentals tax of 8% on the cost of meals,

---

○ **Tax Heavens:** Portsmouth
Ψ **Tax Hells:** None
Top Retirement Towns:
Portsmouth

---

hotel rooms and vehicle rentals.

Portsmouth

Portsmouth has no local income tax and does not levy a sales tax or an additional meals and rentals tax.

Within the city limits of Portsmouth, the property tax rate is .01572. Homes are assessed at 90% of market value. There is an elderly tax exemption of $125,000 to $225,000 off assessed value for persons age 65 or older with federal adjusted gross income of $37,740 or less and assets of less than $102,000, excluding home value.

There is also a low and moderate income homeowners property tax relief available to homeowners with federal adjusted gross income of $40,000 or less. Property tax includes garbage pickup.

Portsmouth has no personal property tax for individuals.

Our couples relocating to Portsmouth must pay a city registration fee based on the year and list price of each automobile, a state registration fee of $43 per automobile, a state title fee of $25 per automobile and a state plate fee of $8 per automobile at the time of registration. The city registration fee is $324 for the Explorer and $240 for the Camry. Thereafter, on an annual basis, our couples will pay a city registration fee and a state registration fee, per automobile.

NEW HAMPSHIRE TAX TABLE

Instructions

1. Find the Income in the far left column closest to your anticipated retirement income.
2. Find the Home Value closest to the value of the home where you will live in retirement.
3. Follow that row to your estimated Total Tax Burden at age 65 and beyond.

Income	Home Value	Property Tax & Other Fees	Personal Property Tax & Auto Fees	Sales Tax	Local Income Tax	State Income Tax	Total Tax Burden	Rank*
PORTSMOUTH								
$30,000	$125,000	$1,552	$590	$113	-	-	$2,255	46 of 173
	150,000	1,905	590	113	-	-	2,608	59 of 173
	175,000	2,259	590	113	-	-	2,962	68 of 173
$60,000	$150,000	$2,122	$590	$201	-	-	$2,913	9 of 203 ○
	225,000	3,183	590	201	-	-	3,974	26 of 203
	300,000	4,244	590	201	-	-	5,035	53 of 203
$90,000	$225,000	$3,183	$590	$251	-	$73	$4,097	6 of 203 ○
	375,000	5,306	590	251	-	73	6,220	23 of 203
	525,000	7,428	590	251	-	73	8,342	45 of 203

*There are 203 cities in this book, 30 of which have higher than average home prices. We have estimated taxes for a tier of higher home values (and omitted the lowest tier) for these 30 cities. The city with the lowest tax burden for an income/home value combination is given the #1 rating; the higher the rating, the higher the total tax burden.

• New Hampshire's Top Retirement Town •

Portsmouth

At the southeastern tip of New Hampshire, Portsmouth is an unexpected gem of New England culture. It was first settled by the English in 1623 and developed into a major shipbuilding and world trade port.

Today, it's a vibrant cosmopolitan center, yet a friendly small town of fewer than 21,000 residents. Its bustling downtown brims with art galleries, museums, theaters and restaurants. A walking tour along the Portsmouth Harbour Trail wanders through the town's treasure trove of history, with numerous structures from the 1800s and some from the 1700s. With several colleges in the region, including the

University of New Hampshire only a short distance away in Durham, students often add to the lively downtown scene.

While it has numerous cultural arts offerings, it's also only 45 minutes from Boston for added urban amenities, and it's close to summer and winter sports. Beaches are minutes away along New Hampshire's 18 miles of Atlantic coastline, and mountains and lakes are 45 minutes or so north. It's adjacent to the Maine border, with Portland less than an hour north.

Portsmouth Regional Hospital is an area leader in several fields, including cardiac care. New Hampshire is one of two states that have neither a general sales tax nor income tax, though it does levy a tax on interest and dividends.

Population: 20,618

Cost of living: Above average

Climate:

	High	Low
January	34	15
July	83	59

Housing cost: The median sales price of a single-family home during the third quarter of 2007 was $309,000, according to Coldwell Banker Residential Brokerage in Portsmouth.

Information: Greater Portsmouth Chamber of Commerce, (603) 436-3988 or www.portcity.org.

NEW JERSEY

New Jersey has a state income tax and a state sales tax.

The state income tax rate is graduated from 1.4% to 8.97% depending upon income bracket. For married couples filing jointly, the rates are 1.4% on the first $20,000 of taxable income; 1.75% on the next $30,000 of taxable income; 2.45% on the next $20,000 of taxable income; 3.5% on the next $10,000 of taxable income;

> ○ **Tax Heavens:** Cape May
> Ψ **Tax Hells:** None
> **Top Retirement Towns:** Cape May

5.525% on the next $70,000 of taxable income; 6.37% on the next $350,000 of taxable income; and 8.97% on taxable income above $500,000.

In calculating the tax, there is no deduction for federal income tax paid. There is an exclusion of up to $20,000 on federal, state and private pensions from adjusted gross income for married couples filing jointly with one or both spouses age 62 or older and gross income of $100,000 or less. There is another retirement income exclusion for married couples filing jointly if one spouse is age 62 or older and the entire pension exclusion was not used. The amount of the exclu-

NEW JERSEY TAX TABLE

Instructions

1. Find the Income in the far left column closest to your anticipated retirement income.
2. Find the Home Value closest to the value of the home where you will live in retirement.
3. Follow that row to your estimated Total Tax Burden at age 65 and beyond.

Income	Home Value	Property Tax & Other Fees	Personal Property Tax & Auto Fees	Sales Tax	Local Income Tax	State Income Tax†	Total Tax Burden	Rank*
CAPE MAY								
$30,000	$125,000	$862	$129	$830	-	($50)	$1,771	14 of 173
	150,000	998	129	830	-	(50)	1,907	15 of 173
	175,000	1,135	129	830	-	(50)	2,044	13 of 173
$60,000	$150,000	$998	$129	$1,433	-	$230	$2,790	7 of 203 ○
	225,000	1,407	129	1,433	-	230	3,199	5 of 203 ○
	300,000	1,817	129	1,433	-	230	3,609	5 of 203 ○
$90,000	$225,000	$1,407	$129	$1,785	-	$708	$4,029	5 of 203 ○
	375,000	2,226	129	1,785	-	708	4,848	4 of 203 ○
	525,000	3,044	129	1,785	-	696	5,654	4 of 203 ○
NEWARK								
$30,000	$125,000	$1,760	$129	$830	-	($50)	$2,669	90 of 173
	150,000	2,112	129	830	-	(50)	3,021	92 of 173
	175,000	2,464	129	830	-	(50)	3,373	93 of 173
$60,000	$150,000	$2,112	$129	$1,433	-	$230	$3,904	70 of 203
	225,000	3,168	129	1,433	-	225	4,955	95 of 203
	300,000	4,224	129	1,433	-	206	5,992	98 of 203
$90,000	$225,000	$3,168	$129	$1,785	-	$689	$5,771	52 of 203
	375,000	5,280	129	1,785	-	643	7,837	76 of 203
	525,000	7,392	129	1,785	-	597	9,903	84 of 203
TOMS RIVER								
$30,000	$125,000	$1,223	$129	$830	-	($50)	$2,132	36 of 173
	150,000	1,467	129	830	-	(50)	2,376	38 of 173
	175,000	1,711	129	830	-	(50)	2,620	43 of 173
$60,000	$150,000	$1,467	$129	$1,433	-	$230	$3,259	22 of 203
	225,000	2,200	129	1,433	-	230	3,992	27 of 203
	300,000	2,934	129	1,433	-	230	4,726	35 of 203
$90,000	$225,000	$2,200	$129	$1,785	-	$708	$4,822	21 of 203
	375,000	3,667	129	1,785	-	678	6,259	24 of 203
	525,000	5,134	129	1,785	-	646	7,694	29 of 203

†Property tax credit or deduction is issued as a reduction of income tax due or added to the homestead credit rebate if an income tax return was not filed.

*There are 203 cities in this book, 30 of which have much higher than average home prices. We have estimated taxes for a tier of higher home values (and omitted the lowest tier) for these 30 cities. The city with the lowest tax burden for an income/home value combination is given the #1 rating; the higher the rating, the higher the total tax burden.

sion varies and is subject to certain limitations. There is an additional exclusion of $6,000 for married couples filing jointly for taxpayers who are unable to receive Social Security benefits. Social Security benefits are exempt. There is a $1,000 personal exemption per person from New Jersey adjusted gross income plus an additional $1,000 exemption per person age 65 or older.

Major tax credits or rebates include: credit for income taxes paid to other states, which our couples do not qualify for, and homestead property tax deduction or credit, which our couples do qualify for.

The state sales tax rate is 7%.

Our couples relocating to the cities listed below must pay a registration fee based on the weight and year of each automobile. The registration fee is $84 for the Explorer and $59 for the Camry. There is a senior deduction of $7 from the registration fee for persons age 65 or older. Our couples also pay a title fee of $40 per automobile at the time of registration. Thereafter, on an annual basis, our couples will pay a registration fee per automobile.

Cape May

Cape May has no local income tax and does not levy an additional sales tax.

Most purchases are taxed at the state rate of 7%. Major consumer cat-
egories taxed at a different rate: none. Major consumer categories that are exempt from sales tax include: drugs, groceries, medical services and apparel and services.

Within the city limits of Cape May, the property tax rate is .0077. Homes are assessed at 88.56% of market value. There is a homestead rebate program based upon income and the amount of property tax paid. There is also an elderly deduction of $250 on property taxes due for homeowners age 65 or older with an income of less than $10,000 (excluding Social Security, governmental pension or local retirement programs). Property tax does not cover garbage pickup.

Cape May has no personal property tax for individuals.

Newark

Newark has no local income tax and does not levy an additional sales tax.

Most purchases are taxed at the state rate of 7%. Major consumer categories taxed at a different rate: none. Major consumer categories that are exempt from sales tax include: drugs, groceries, medical services and apparel and services.

Within the city limits of Newark, the property tax rate is .0249. Homes are assessed at 70.68% of market value. There is a homestead rebate program based upon income and the amount of property tax paid. There is also an elderly deduction of $250 on property taxes due for homeowners age 65 or older with an income of less than $10,000 (excluding Social Security, governmental pension or local retirement programs). Property tax includes garbage pickup.

Newark has no personal property tax for individuals.

Toms River (Ocean County)

Toms River has no local income tax and does not levy an additional sales tax.

Most purchases are taxed at the state rate of 7%. Major consumer categories taxed at a different rate: none. Major consumer categories that are exempt from sales tax include: drugs, groceries, medical services and apparel and services.

In the Toms River Fire District 1 of Toms River Township, the property tax rate is .03158. Homes are assessed at 38.71% of market value. There is a homestead rebate program based upon income and the amount of property tax paid. There is also an elderly deduction of $250 on property taxes due for homeowners age 65 or older with an income of less than $10,000 (excluding Social Security, governmental pension or local retirement programs). Property tax includes garbage pickup.

Toms River has no personal property tax for individuals.

• New Jersey's Top Retirement Town •

Cape May

Imagine living in a historic town of life-size Victorian dollhouses where you can walk to everything from the library to the lighthouse. At the southern tip of New Jersey, Cape May has been a seaside haven since the late 1700s, when Philadelphians came to flee the sweltering summer heat. By the mid-1800s, it became known as the queen of seaside resorts.

Now a National Historic Landmark, Cape May is lined with the country's largest concentration of Victorian homes — some 600 beautiful gems with gingerbread, latticework and scrolls, painted in a rainbow of colors. A quaint pedestrian

mall is lined with cafes, restaurants, boutiques, shops and galleries. For a town its size, Cape May has an astounding number and variety of eateries, many housed in Victorian splendor.

Events and tours in the area abound, including a food and wine festival, a jazz festival, Christmas candlelight tours, garden tours, butterfly and dragonfly walks and hummingbird garden tours.

Cape May's beach is a small gem with sparkling crystallike sands and a homespun boardwalk with pizza joints. For wider, longer beaches for strolling, check out neighboring Cape May Point. Walkers head to Higbee Beach Wildlife

Management Area, a 600-acre preserve of beach, meadows, ponds and holly and scrub oak forests once known as Diamond Beach because of the Cape May "diamonds" (actually pieces of almost pure quartz) that wash up here. Smoothed by surf and sand, they are used in local jewelry.

At Cape May Point State Park, a boardwalk bridges marshes and meanders through mangroves to birding lookouts and a 19th-century lighthouse. In spring and fall, legions of bird-watchers come to spy on migrating birds and Monarch butterflies. The Cape May Bird Observatory, considered one of the top birding spots, hosts a variety of walks and events.

Cape May has an 18-hole golf course. The town of Cape May Court House, 12 miles northeast, has an Atlantic Cape Community College campus offering continuing-education and enrichment classes and the Cape Regional Medical Center with services including cancer and cardiac care.

Population: 3,809 in town, 97,724 in the county

Climate:

	High	Low
January	42	27
July	83	67

Cost of living: Above average

Housing cost: The median sales price of a single-family home during the second quarter of 2007 was $334,000, according to the New Jersey Association of Realtors.

Information: Chamber of Commerce of Greater Cape May, (609) 884-5508 or www.capemaychamber.com. Cape May County Department of Tourism, (800) 227-2297 or www.thejerseycape.net.

NEW MEXICO

New Mexico has a state income tax and a state gross receipts tax (sales tax).

The state income tax is graduated from 1.7% to 5.3% depending upon income bracket. For married couples filing jointly, the rates are 1.7% on the first $8,000 of taxable income; 3.2% on the next $8,000 of taxable income; 4.7% on the next $8,000 of taxable income; and 5.3% on taxable income above $24,000.

In calculating the tax, there is no deduction for federal income tax paid. Federal, state and private pensions are not exempt. Social Security benefits subject to federal tax are not exempt. There is a $12,300 standard deduction from adjusted gross income for married couples filing jointly when both are age 65 or older. There is a personal exemption of $3,300 per person. There is an additional deduction up to $2,500 per person for married couples filing jointly, both age 65 or older, with federal adjusted gross income of $40,667 or less. There is also a medical care expense deduction ranging from 10% to 25% of unreimbursed expenses and an additional medical care expense deduction for persons age 65 or older of $3,000 if medical expenses are $28,000 or more.

Major tax credits or rebates include: credit for taxes paid to other states and low income tax rebate. Our couples do not qualify for these programs.

The state gross receipts tax rate is 5%, but local governments can add to this amount. Although this tax is imposed on the seller (unlike a sales tax which is imposed on the buyer), businesses customarily pass the tax on to the buyer.

Our couples relocating to the cities listed below must pay a registration fee of $62 per automobile and a transfer fee of $6 per automobile at the time of registration. In addition, an excise tax of 3% is due at the time of registration unless at least 3% was paid in another state when the automobile was purchased. Thereafter, on an annual basis, our couples will pay a registration fee per automobile.

Albuquerque

Albuquerque has no local income tax but does levy a gross receipts tax (sales tax).

Most purchases are taxed at a rate of 6.875%. Major consumer categories taxed at a different rate: none. Major consumer categories that are exempt from gross receipts tax: drugs and groceries.

For residents within the MRGCD district of Albuquerque, the property tax rate is .042446. Homes are assessed at 100% of market value. Taxable value is one-third of assessed value. There is a head-of-household exemption of $2,000 off taxable value and a property tax rebate of up to $250 for homeowners age 65 or older with modified gross income of $16,000 or less. Property tax does not cover garbage pickup.

Albuquerque has no personal property tax for individuals.

Las Cruces

Las Cruces has no local income tax but does levy a gross receipts tax (sales tax).

Most purchases are taxed at a rate of 7.125%. Major consumer categories taxed at a different rate: none. Major consumer categories that are exempt from gross receipts tax: drugs and groceries.

Within the city limits of Las Cruces, the property tax rate is .026985. Homes are assessed at 100% of market value. Taxable value is one-third of assessed value. There is a head-of-household exemption of $2,000 off taxable value and a property tax rebate of up to $250 for homeowners age 65 or older with modified gross income of $16,000 or less. Property tax does not cover garbage pickup.

Las Cruces has no personal property tax for individuals.

Ruidoso

Ruidoso has no local income tax but does levy a gross receipts tax (sales tax).

Most purchases are taxed at a rate of 7.8125%. Major consumer categories taxed at a different rate: none. Major consumer categories that are exempt from gross receipts tax: drugs and groceries.

Within the city limits of Ruidoso, the property tax rate is .026125. Homes are assessed at 90% of market value. Taxable value is one-third of assessed value. There is a head-of-household exemption of $2,000 off taxable value and a property tax rebate of up to $250 for homeowners age 65 or older with modified gross income of $16,000 or less. Property tax does not cover garbage pickup.

Ruidoso has no personal property tax for individuals.

Santa Fe

Santa Fe has no local income tax but does levy a gross receipts tax (sales tax).

Most purchases are taxed at a rate of 7.625%. This rate increases to 7.875% on July 1, 2007. Major consumer categories taxed at a different rate: none. Major consumer categories that are exempt from gross receipts tax include: drugs and groceries.

For most residents within the city limits of Santa Fe, the property tax rate is .017690. Homes are assessed at 100% of market value. Taxable value is one-third of assessed value. There is a head-of-household exemption of $2,000 off taxable value and a property tax rebate of up to $250 for homeowners age 65 or older with modified gross income of $16,000 or less. Property tax does not cover garbage pickup.

Santa Fe has no personal property tax for individuals.

Silver City

Silver City has no local income tax but does levy a gross receipts tax (sales tax).

Most purchases are taxed at a rate of 7.125%. This rate increases to 7.25% on January 1, 2007. Major consumer categories taxed at a different rate: none. Major consumer categories that are exempt from gross receipts tax: drugs and groceries.

Within the city limits of Silver City,

the property tax rate is .016373. Homes are assessed at approximately 100% of market value. Taxable value is one-third of assessed value. There is a head-of-household exemption of $2,000 off taxable value and a property tax rebate of up to $250 for homeowners age 65 or older with modified gross income of $16,000 or less. Property tax does not cover garbage pickup.

Silver City has a personal property tax rate of .016373. Personal property is assessed at 100% of market value. Items subject to the tax include mobile homes.

NEW MEXICO TAX TABLE

Instructions

1. Find the Income in the far left column closest to your anticipated retirement income.
2. Find the Home Value closest to the value of the home where you will live in retirement.
3. Follow that row to your estimated Total Tax Burden at age 65 and beyond.

Income	Home Value	Property Tax & Other Fees	Personal Property Tax & Auto Fees	Sales Tax	Local Income Tax	State Income Tax	Total Tax Burden	Rank*
ALBUQUERQUE								
$30,000	$125,000	$1,864	$124	$915	-	-	$2,903	107 of 173
	150,000	2,217	124	915	-	-	3,256	107 of 173
	175,000	2,571	124	915	-	-	3,610	108 of 173
$60,000	$150,000	$2,217	$124	$1,586	-	$956	$4,883	151 of 203
	225,000	3,278	124	1,586	-	956	5,944	145 of 203
	300,000	4,339	124	1,586	-	956	7,005	141 of 203
$90,000	$225,000	$3,278	$124	$1,982	-	$3,018	$8,402	172 of 203
	375,000	5,400	124	1,982	-	3,018	10,524	165 of 203
	525,000	7,522	124	1,982	-	3,018	12,646	153 of 203
LAS CRUCES								
$30,000	$125,000	$1,250	$124	$948	-	-	$2,322	54 of 173
	150,000	1,475	124	948	-	-	2,547	56 of 173
	175,000	1,700	124	948	-	-	2,772	53 of 173
$60,000	$150,000	$1,475	$124	$1,644	-	$956	$4,199	102 of 203
	225,000	2,150	124	1,644	-	956	4,874	86 of 203
	300,000	2,825	124	1,644	-	956	5,549	79 of 203
$90,000	$225,000	$2,150	$124	$2,054	-	$3,018	$7,346	136 of 203
	375,000	3,499	124	2,054	-	3,018	8,695	106 of 203
	525,000	4,848	124	2,054	-	3,018	10,044	91 of 203
RUIDOSO								
$30,000	$125,000	$1,107	$124	$1,039	-	-	$2,270	47 of 173
	150,000	1,303	124	1,039	-	-	2,466	47 of 173
	175,000	1,499	124	1,039	-	-	2,662	48 of 173
$60,000	$150,000	$1,303	$124	$1,803	-	$956	$4,186	98 of 203
	225,000	1,891	124	1,803	-	956	4,774	77 of 203
	300,000	2,479	124	1,803	-	956	5,362	67 of 203
$90,000	$225,000	$1,891	$124	$2,252	-	$3,018	$7,285	134 of 203
	375,000	3,067	124	2,252	-	3,018	8,461	96 of 203
	525,000	4,242	124	2,252	-	3,018	9,636	78 of 203
SANTA FE								
$30,000	$125,000	$882	$124	$1,015	-	-	$2,021	30 of 173
	150,000	1,029	124	1,015	-	-	2,168	27 of 173
	175,000	1,177	124	1,015	-	-	2,316	23 of 173
$60,000	$150,000	$1,029	$124	$1,759	-	$956	$3,868	65 of 203
	225,000	1,471	124	1,759	-	956	4,310	49 of 203
	300,000	1,914	124	1,759	-	956	4,753	36 of 203
$90,000	$225,000	$1,471	$124	$2,198	-	$3,018	$6,811	111 of 203
	375,000	2,356	124	2,198	-	3,018	7,696	70 of 203
	525,000	3,240	124	2,198	-	3,018	8,580	50 of 203

Income	Home Value	Property Tax & Other Fees	Personal Property Tax & Auto Fees	Sales Tax	Local Income Tax	State Income Tax	Total Tax Burden	Rank*
SILVER CITY								
$30,000	$125,000	$829	$124	$948	-	-	$1,901	21 of 173
	150,000	966	124	948	-	-	2,038	20 of 173
	175,000	1,102	124	948	-	-	2,174	19 of 173
$60,000	$150,000	$966	$124	$1,644	-	$956	$3,690	57 of 203
	225,000	1,375	124	1,644	-	956	4,099	36 of 203
	300,000	1,784	124	1,644	-	956	4,508	28 of 203
$90,000	$225,000	$1,375	$124	$2,054	-	$3,018	$6,571	99 of 203
	375,000	2,194	124	2,054	-	3,018	7,390	58 of 203
	525,000	3,013	124	2,054	-	3,018	8,209	40 of 203

*There are 203 cities in this book, 30 of which have higher than average home prices. We have estimated taxes for a tier of higher home values (and omitted the lowest tier) for these 30 cities. The city with the lowest tax burden for an income/home value combination is given the #1 rating; the higher the rating, the higher the total tax burden.

• New Mexico's Top Retirement Towns •

Albuquerque

New Mexico calls itself the Land of Enchantment, and retirees tend to agree. Albuquerque, the state's largest city and a retiree center, is well-placed to take advantage of New Mexico's wonders. It's near the center of the state, with interstates 25 and 40 intersecting adjacent to downtown. It sits on a high desert plain with mountains to the immediate east. Santa Fe is about one hour northeast, and Taos is about one hour beyond that.

The spectacular skies and sunsets have to be experienced to be fully appreciated. Winters tend to be nippy and summers hot, but the unusually low humidity makes it seem cooler in summer than the thermometer shows. In fact, Albuquerque's fine weather has helped to make it the "ballooning capital of the world," home to resident ballooners and an international balloon festival.

Outdoor activities abound, including year-round golf and tennis, fishing and boating within driving distance, and skiing at Sandia Peak just outside the city. The Rio Grande flows close to the city center, drawing hikers and mountain bikers along its wooded banks and attracting the adventurous for whitewater rafting to the north.

The 25,000-student University of New Mexico is here, offering educational, cultural and spectator-sports opportunities. Its medical center, UNM Hospitals, offers varied specialty fields and trauma and emergency care.

Albuquerque's Spanish roots can be found in its Old Town, which dates to 1706 and is comprised of a central plaza and church, surrounded by historic adobe buildings that house shops, galleries and restaurants.

Kirtland Air Force Base abuts Albuquerque, and its numerous base facilities are available to military retirees. These include the base exchange and commissary, a golf course and bowling center, two fitness centers, indoor and outdoor swimming pools and an RV park.

Population: 504,949
Climate: High Low
January 47 22
July 93 65
Cost of living: Average
Housing cost: The median price for the first half of 2007 was $196,650, according to the National Association of Realtors.
Information: Greater Albuquerque Chamber of Commerce, (505) 764-3700 or www.abqchamber.com.

Las Cruces

Las Cruces, 44 miles north of El Paso and the home of New Mexico State University, embraces the state's rich, cultural history — Indian, Spanish, pioneers, cowboys, agriculture, cattle and the legend of Billy the Kid.

Las Cruces (The Crosses) takes its name from the crosses that marked the graves of settlers ambushed and massacred by Apache warriors as they traveled along the Camino Real, the route established by the Spaniards between Mexico City and Santa Fe.

University events contribute to the active scene here, and Dona Ana Community College has Academy for Learning and continuing-education programs for seniors. Among numerous attractions in the area, the White Sands National Monument amazes with its huge wavelike dunes. If you pop into the Gadsden Museum, you'll find an impressive display of paintings by the late Peter Hurd, whose home, studio and gallery in nearby San Patricio is open to the public. Hurd was married to painter Henriette Wyeth Hurd (N.C. Wyeth's eldest daughter), forming a Western branch of one of America's great art dynasties. Peter's son, Michael Hurd, now runs the San Patricio gallery and carries on the family art tradition with brilliant, moving works of his own.

With its history, traditions, scenery, temperate climate at an altitude of 3,908 feet and mouthwatering cuisine, it's small wonder that many seniors are choosing retirement or second homes in Las Cruces. Astronaut Frank Borman is among those who have moved to Las Cruces.

Jim and Marsha Cowen settled in the city from northern New Mexico. "Las Cruces is small, and yet it has everything we needed or wanted — perfect weather, two good hospitals if we ever need them, a great sense of place, and we're close to an airport (El Paso)," Marsha says.

Population: 86,268

Climate: High Low
January   55   28
July   95   67

Cost of living: Slightly above average

Housing cost: The median sales price for a single-family home for the first half of 2007 was $220,875, according to the Las Cruces Association of Realtors.

Information: Las Cruces Convention and Visitors Bureau, (575) 541-2444 or www.lascrucescvb.org. The Greater Las Cruces Chamber of Commerce, (575) 524-1968 or www.lascruces.org.

Ruidoso

Although a small town, Ruidoso draws retirees with its affordability and mountain resort feel. Located in the Sacramento Mountains of south-central New Mexico at about 7,000 feet, Ruidoso is two and a half hours north of El Paso and three hours south of Albuquerque. It's in the Lincoln National Forest, birthplace of Smokey Bear.

This is the home of the Mescalero Apaches, whose ceremonial dances in July at their Inn of the Mountain Gods Resort and Casino bring many tourists. In fact, Ruidoso's population of about 9,000 swells to more than 35,000 in peak months. The pleasant climate and abundant sunshine boost its appeal.

Ski Apache — the nation's southernmost ski area — brings skiers and snowboarders, while the Ruidoso Downs Race Track and several riding paths attract horse enthusiasts. Outdoor sports are extremely popular, including fishing, golfing, hiking, biking and rafting. Shoppers revel in art galleries, quirky clothing shops, boutiques and fine restaurants. Ruidoso also sells itself as Billy the Kid territory and was a major player in the Lincoln County range wars of the 1800s.

The $22 million Spencer Theater for the Performing Arts anchors the town's cultural offerings, hosting dance companies, Broadway musicals, plays and vocal performers throughout the year. Ruidoso also has a community choir and orchestra, and the history of the horse is chronicled at the Smithsonian-affiliated Hubbard Museum of the American West.

Senior-specific classes are offered through the Lifelong Learning Academy at Eastern New Mexico University-Ruidoso. Lincoln County Medical Center, an affiliate of Presbyterian Healthcare Services, is the area's general acute-care hospital.

Population: 9,359 permanent residents and 35,000 seasonally

Climate: High Low
January   45   19
July   82   37

Cost of living: Average

Housing cost: The average price of homes during the first half of 2007 was $223,000, according to data from A+ Realty Services in Ruidoso.

Information: Ruidoso Valley Chamber of Commerce, (877) 784-3676 or www.ruidosonow.com.

Santa Fe

Located at 7,000 feet, where the sweeping desert meets the towering Sangre de Cristo mountains, Santa Fe is the perfect place to retire if you want to put some serious miles on your walking shoes while admiring some of the country's most fascinating history, spectacular architecture and gorgeous scenery.

The entire town is a historic walking tour, beginning with its 400-year-old Plaza. The shady square, now lined with chic boutiques and restaurants, was once the dusty terminus of the Santa Fe Trail. You can walk in any direction past an eyeful of architectural gems, including the 1610 Palace of the Governors, where American Indian artisans now spread out their crafts for sale.

Beyond the Plaza, Santa Fe's crooked, narrow streets are lined with centuries-old churches, museums and pastel adobe houses, many of them tucked behind hand-carved wooden gates. Santa Fe's Canyon Road art colony and San Miguel Mission — the oldest church in the United States — are an easy stroll from downtown.

Culture lovers enjoy a feast at Santa Fe's many art galleries and museums. Georgia O'Keeffe, who first visited in 1929, immortalized the region's clear desert light and vivid colors in her many paintings. Today, Santa Fe has become the cultural capital of the Southwest and is one of the world's largest art markets, with more than 200 galleries and numerous performing arts organizations and museums. The world-famous Georgia O'Keeffe Museum, opened in 1997, houses the largest collection of O'Keeffe works and is the only museum in the country dedicated solely to one woman's work.

Santa Fe is the state capital, and with a host of noted restaurants, it can please many palates. For intellectual stimulation, the College of Santa Fe has enrichment classes and St. John's College offers literary seminars for the community. The city has a regional medical center with noted heart and vascular treatment and cancer care.

Population: 72,056

Climate: High Low
January   47   16
July   85   53

Cost of living: Above average

Housing cost: The median sales price of a single-family home during the third quarter of 2007 was $376,950, according to the Santa Fe Association of Realtors.

Information: Santa Fe Chamber of Commerce, (505) 988-3279 or www.santafechamber.com. Santa Fe Convention and Visitors Bureau, (800) 777-2489 or www.santafe.org.

Silver City

Located on the edge of the Gila National Forest in a high-desert dreamscape of ponderosa pine, plunging gorges and red rock mesas in southwest New Mexico, Silver City is an almost equal distance from El Paso and Tucson via Interstate 10. The town dates back to the silver boom in 1870, and instead of dying when the silver was depleted 23 years later, it continued to thrive.

That was thanks partly to its healthy climate (at an elevation of 5,395 feet), which was particularly beneficial to tuberculosis patients, among them Billy the Kid's mother. Before gaining fame with his six-gun, Billy waited on tables at the Star Hotel. Other personalities of the Old West left their mark, including Geronimo, Judge Roy Bean and Butch Cassidy.

Remnants of the town's colorful past are evidenced in a wealth of Victorian buildings that line downtown streets, haughty and grand among the newer homes and developments being built. Dozens of cafes and bars celebrate the area's history, among them the Buckhorn Saloon and Opera House (in Pinos Altos, seven miles north), Nancy's Silver Cafe, the Buffalo Bar and a restaurant called Spaghetti Western.

Silver City's economy is still based on mining (copper now instead of silver), ranching, agriculture, education and tourism. It's still a healing center with its Gila Regional Medical Center. Silver City's Big Ditch, once the main street but washed away by floods a century ago, is now an enchanting green park for everyone to enjoy.

And there's golf at the 18-hole championship Silver City Golf Course, home of the annual Billy Casper Benefit Golf Tournament. Casper is a former PGA golfer and a popular Silver City resident.

Population: 9,992

Climate:

	High	Low
January	49	24
July	87	59

Cost of living: Below average

Housing cost: The median sales price for a single-family home was $171,250 for the first half of 2007, according to the Silver City Association of Realtors.

Information: Silver City and Grant County Chamber of Commerce, (800) 548-9378 or www.silvercity.org.

NEW YORK

New York has a state income tax and a state sales tax.

The state income tax rate is graduated from 4% to 6.85% depending upon income bracket. For married couples filing jointly, the rates are 4% on the first $16,000 of taxable income; 4.5% on the next $6,000 of taxable income; 5.25% on the next $4,000 of taxable income;

> **O Tax Heavens:** None
> **Ψ Tax Hells:** Buffalo, Syracuse

5.9% on the next $14,000 of taxable income; and 6.85% on taxable income above $40,000.

In calculating the tax, there is no deduction for federal income tax paid. Federal and state pensions are exempt. Private pensions are not exempt, but there is an exclusion of up to $20,000 of private pension income per person. Social Security benefits are exempt. There is a $15,000 standard deduction from adjusted gross income for married couples filing jointly.

NEW YORK TAX TABLE

Instructions

1. Find the Income in the far left column closest to your anticipated retirement income.
2. Find the Home Value closest to the value of the home where you will live in retirement.
3. Follow that row to your estimated Total Tax Burden at age 65 and beyond.

Income	Home Value	Property Tax & Other Fees	Personal Property Tax & Auto Fees	Sales Tax	Local Income Tax	State Income Tax	Total Tax Burden	Rank*
BUFFALO								
$30,000	$125,000	$1,129	$66	$1,087	-	-	$2,282	50 of 173
	150,000	1,477	66	1,087	-	-	2,630	61 of 173
	175,000	1,824	66	1,087	-	-	2,977	71 of 173
$60,000	$150,000	$3,563	$66	$1,911	-	$533	$6,073	189 of 203
	225,000	5,649	66	1,911	-	533	8,159	195 of 203 Ψ
	300,000	7,735	66	1,911	-	533	10,245	196 of 203 Ψ
$90,000	$225,000	$6,022	$66	$2,382	-	$1,965	$10,435	194 of 203 Ψ
	375,000	10,194	66	2,382	-	1,965	14,607	196 of 203 Ψ
	525,000	14,367	66	2,382	-	1,965	18,780	196 of 203 Ψ
NEW YORK CITY								
$60,000	$150,000	$1,076	$81	$1,829	$158	$533	$3,677	55 of 203
	225,000	1,801	81	1,829	158	533	4,402	52 of 203
	300,000	2,526	81	1,829	158	533	5,127	56 of 203
$90,000	$225,000	$1,976	$81	$2,280	$1,058	$1,965	$7,360	137 of 203
	375,000	3,427	81	2,280	1,058	1,965	8,811	111 of 203
	525,000	4,877	81	2,280	1,058	1,965	10,261	99 of 203
	$600,000	$5,602	$81	$2,280	$1,058	$1,965	$10,986	22 of 30
	750,000	7,053	81	2,280	1,058	1,965	12,437	19 of 30
	900,000	8,504	81	2,280	1,058	1,965	13,888	17 of 30
SYRACUSE								
$30,000	$125,000	$2,093	$51	$994	-	-	$3,138	131 of 173
	150,000	2,624	51	994	-	-	3,669	138 of 173
	175,000	3,156	51	994	-	-	4,201	139 of 173
$60,000	$150,000	$4,750	$51	$1,748	-	$533	$7,082	198 of 203 Ψ
	225,000	7,408	51	1,748	-	533	9,740	200 of 203 Ψ
	300,000	10,065	51	1,748	-	533	12,397	201 of 203 Ψ
$90,000	$225,000	$7,810	$51	$2,178	-	$1,965	$12,004	200 of 203 Ψ
	375,000	13,125	51	2,178	-	1,965	17,319	201 of 203 Ψ
	525,000	18,441	51	2,178	-	1,965	22,635	201 of 203 Ψ

*There are 203 cities in this book, 30 of which have higher than average home prices. We have estimated taxes for a tier of higher home values (and omitted the lowest tier) for these 30 cities. The city with the lowest tax burden for an income/home value combination is given the #1 rating; the higher the rating, the higher the total tax burden.

Major tax credits or rebates include: credit for income taxes paid to other states, household income tax credit and real property tax credit. Our couples do not qualify for these programs.

The state sales tax rate is 4%, but local governments can add to this amount.

Our couples relocating to the cities listed below must pay a two-year registration fee of $61 for the Explorer and $42 for the Camry, a plate fee of $15 per automobile, a lien filing fee of $5 per automobile and a title fee of $50 per automobile at the time of registration. Buffalo imposes a vehicle use fee every two years of $20 for the Explorer and $10 for the Camry. New York City imposes a $30 city vehicle use fee per automobile every two years. Thereafter, our couples will pay a renewal fee and, possibly, a city vehicle use fee per automobile, every two years.

Buffalo

Buffalo has no local income tax but does levy a sales tax.

Most purchases are taxed at a rate of 8.75%. Major consumer categories taxed at a different rate: none, although clothing and footwear costing less than $110 per item are exempt from the state portion of sales tax. Major consumer categories that are exempt from sales tax include: drugs, groceries, medical services and medical supplies.

In Buffalo, the property tax rate is .027816858. Homes are assessed at 100% of market value. There is an elderly exemption from 5% to 50% off the assessed value of the home for homeowners age 65 or older with gross income (less unreimbursed medical expenses) of less than $32,400. There is a School Tax Relief program (STAR),

which is available to all residents of Buffalo that exempts $417 from property taxes due. For residents of Buffalo that meet certain income qualifications, there is an enhanced STAR; it exempts $790 from property taxes due. Property tax does not cover garbage pickup.

Buffalo has no personal property tax for individuals.

New York City

New York City has a local income tax and levies a sales tax.

The local income tax rate is 2.907% to 3.648% depending upon income bracket. For married couples filing jointly, the rates are 2.907% on the first $21,600 of taxable income; 3.534% on the next $23,400 of taxable income; 3.591% on the next $45,000 of taxable income; and 3.648% on taxable income above $90,000.

In calculating the tax, the same exemptions and deductions are available as those offered at the state level.

Major tax credits or rebates include: household income credit, which our couples do not qualify for, and school tax credit, which all of our couples qualify for.

Most purchases are taxed at a rate of 8.375%. Major consumer categories taxed at a different rate: none, although clothing and footwear costing less than $110 per item are exempt from the state portion of sales tax. Major consumer categories that are exempt from sales tax include: drugs, groceries, medical services and medical supplies.

In New York City, the property tax rate is .16118. Homes are assessed at 6% of market value for Class I (residential) homes. There is an elderly exemption from 5% to 50% off the assessed value of the home for homeowners age 65 or older with gross

income (less unreimbursed medical expenses) of less than $32,400. There is a School Tax Relief program (STAR), which is available to all residents of New York City that exempts $200 from property taxes due. For residents of New York City that meet certain income qualifications, there is an enhanced STAR; it exempts $375 from property taxes due. Property tax includes garbage pickup.

New York City has no personal property tax for individuals.

Syracuse

Syracuse has no local income tax but does levy a sales tax.

Most purchases are taxed at a rate of 8%. Major consumer categories taxed at a different rate: none, although clothing and footwear costing less than $110 per item are exempt from the state portion of sales tax. Major consumer categories that are exempt from sales tax include: drugs, groceries, medical services and medical supplies.

In Syracuse, the property tax rate is .0379013. Homes are assessed at 93.5% of market value. There is an elderly exemption from 5% to 50% off the assessed value of the home for homeowners age 65 or older with gross income (less unreimbursed medical expenses) of less than $32,400. There is a School Tax Relief program (STAR), which is available to all residents of Syracuse that exempts $465 from property taxes due. For residents of Syracuse that meet certain income qualifications, there is an enhanced STAR; it exempts $867 from property taxes due. Property tax includes garbage pickup and a sewer use fee of $302 per year.

Syracuse has no personal property tax for individuals.

NORTH CAROLINA

N orth Carolina has a state income tax and a state sales tax.

The state income tax rate is graduated from 6% to 8.25% depending upon income bracket. For married couples filing jointly, the rates are 6% on the first $21,250 of taxable income; 7% on the next $78,750 of taxable income; 7.75% on the next $100,000 of taxable income; and 8.25% on taxable income above $200,000.

In calculating the tax, there is no deduction for federal income tax paid. Social Security benefits are exempt. There is an exclusion of up to $4,000 in federal, state and local government pensions per person and an exclusion of up to $2,000 in private pensions per person, but no more than $4,000 in total retirement benefits (not including Social Security) may be deducted per person. There is a $7,200 standard deduction from adjusted gross income for married couples filing jointly when both are age 65 or older. There is also a personal exemption of up to $2,500 per person.

Major tax credits or rebates include: credit for income taxes paid to other states and credit for disabled taxpayers. Our couples do not qualify for these programs.

The state sales tax rate is 4.25%, but local governments can add to this amount.

Since car registration and renewal fees differ within the state, see city information for details.

Asheville

Asheville has no local income tax but does levy a sales tax.

Most purchases are taxed at a rate of 6.75%. Major consumer categories taxed at a different rate include: groceries, which are taxed at a rate of 2%. Major consumer categories that are exempt from sales tax include: drugs and medical services.

Within the city limits of Asheville, the property tax rate is .011038. Homes are assessed at 100% of market value. There is an elderly exemption equal to the greater of $20,000 or 50% off assessed value for persons age 65 or older with gross income of $20,500 or less. Property tax includes garbage

pickup. There is a stormwater fee of $28 per year.

Asheville has a personal property tax rate of .011038. Personal property is assessed at 100% of current market value. Items subject to the tax include motor vehicles, aircraft, mobile homes, boats, Jet Skis and trailers.

Our couples relocating to Asheville must pay a highway use tax of $150 per automobile, a title fee of $40 per automobile and a license registration fee of $28 per automobile. The highway use tax is 3% of the value of the vehicle as set by the state, up to a maximum tax of $150. Thereafter, on an annual basis, our couples will pay a registration fee per automobile.

Brevard

Brevard has no local income tax but does levy a sales tax.

Most purchases are taxed at a rate of 6.75%. Major consumer categories taxed at a different rate: groceries, which are taxed at a rate of 2%. Major consumer categories that are exempt from sales tax include: drugs and medical services.

Within the city limits of Brevard, the property tax rate is .01035. Homes are assessed at 100% of market value. There is an elderly exemption equal to the greater of $20,000 or 50% off assessed value for persons age 65 or older with a gross income of $20,500 or less. Property tax does not cover garbage pickup.

Brevard has a personal property tax rate of .01035. Personal property is assessed at 100% of current market value. Items subject to the tax include motor vehicles, mobile homes, boats and motorcycles.

Our couples relocating to Brevard must pay a highway use tax of $150 per automobile, a title fee of $40 per automobile and a license registration fee of $28 per automobile at the time of regis-

tration. The highway use tax is 3% of the value of the vehicle as set by the state, up to a maximum tax of $150. Thereafter, on an annual basis, our couples will pay a registration fee per automobile.

Chapel Hill

Chapel Hill has no local income tax but does levy a sales tax.

Most purchases are taxed at a rate of 6.75%. Major consumer categories taxed at a different rate: groceries, which are taxed at a rate of 2%. Major consumer categories that are exempt from sales tax include: drugs and medical services.

For residents in the Orange County portion of Chapel Hill, the property tax rate is .016135. Homes are assessed at 100% of market value. There is an elderly exemption equal to the greater of $20,000 or 50% off assessed value for persons age 65 or older with gross income of $20,500 or less. Property tax includes garbage pickup. There is a stormwater fee of $39 per year

Chapel Hill has a personal property tax rate of .016135 within Orange County. Personal property is assessed at 100% of current market value. Items subject to the tax include motor vehicles, mobile homes, boats and motorcycles.

Our couples relocating to Chapel Hill must pay a highway use tax of $150 per automobile, a title fee of $40 per automobile, a registration fee of $28 per automobile and a $5 regional registration tax per automobile at the time of registration. The highway use tax is 3% of the current value of the vehicle as set by the state, up to a maximum tax of $150. Thereafter, on an annual basis, our couples will pay a registration fee and a regional registration tax, per automobile.

Edenton

Edenton has no local income tax but does levy a sales tax.

Most purchases are taxed at a rate of 6.75%. Major consumer categories taxed at a different rate: groceries, which are taxed at a rate of 2%. Major consumer categories that are exempt from sales tax include: drugs and medical services.

Within the city limits of Edenton, the property tax rate is .00835. Homes are assessed at 100% of market value. There is an elderly exemption equal to the greater of $20,000 or 50% off assessed value for persons age 65 or older with gross income of $20,500 or less. Property tax does not cover garbage pickup. There is a landfill fee of $132 per year.

Edenton has a personal property tax rate of .00835. Personal property is assessed at 100% of current market value. Items subject to the tax include motor vehicles, mobile homes, boats and motorcycles.

Our couples relocating to Edenton must pay a highway use tax of $150 per automobile, a title fee of $40 per automobile and a registration fee of $28 per automobile at the time of registration. The highway use tax is 3% of the current value of the vehicle as set by the state, up to a maximum tax of $150. Thereafter, on an annual basis, our couples will pay a registration fee per automobile.

Hendersonville

Hendersonville has no local income tax but does levy a sales tax.

Most purchases are taxed at a rate of 6.75%. Major consumer categories taxed at a different rate: groceries, which are taxed at a rate of 2%. Major consumer categories that are exempt from sales tax include: drugs and medical services.

Within the city limits of Hendersonville, the property tax rate is .00995. Homes are assessed at 100% of market value. There is an elderly exemption equal to the greater of $20,000 or 50% off assessed value for persons age 65 or older with gross income of $20,500 or less. Property tax does not cover garbage pickup.

Hendersonville has a personal property tax rate of .00995. Personal property is assessed at 100% of current market value. Items subject to the tax include motor vehicles, mobile homes, boats and motorcycles.

Our couples relocating to Hendersonville must pay a highway use tax of $150 per automobile, a title fee of $40 per automobile and a registration fee of $28 per automobile at the time of registration. The highway use tax is 3% of the current value of the vehicle as set by the state, up to a maximum tax of $150. Thereafter, on an annual basis, our couples will pay a registration fee per automobile.

New Bern

New Bern has no local income tax but does levy a sales tax.

Most purchases are taxed at a rate of 6.75%. Major consumer categories taxed at a different rate: groceries, which are taxed at a rate of 2%. Major consumer categories that are exempt from sales tax include: drugs and medical services.

Within the city limits of New Bern, the property tax rate is .0108. Homes are assessed at 100% of market value. There is an elderly exemption equal to the greater of $20,000 or 50% off assessed value for persons 65 or older with gross income of $20,500 or less. Property tax does not cover garbage pickup. There is an additional recycling fee of approximately $32 per year.

New Bern has a personal property tax rate of .0108. Personal property is assessed at 100% of current market value. Items subject to the tax include motor vehicles, mobile homes, boats and motorcycles. There is also a motor vehicle tax of $5 per automobile per year.

Our couples relocating to New Bern must pay a highway use tax of $150 per automobile, a title fee of $40 per automobile and a registration fee of $28 per automobile at the time of registration. The highway use tax is 3% of the value of the vehicle as set by the state, up to a maximum tax of $150. Thereafter, on an annual basis, our couples will pay a registration fee per automobile.

Pinehurst

Pinehurst has no local income tax but does levy a sales tax.

Most purchases are taxed at a rate of 6.75%. Major consumer categories taxed at a different rate: groceries, which are taxed at a rate of 2%. Major consumer categories that are exempt from sales tax include: drugs and medical services.

Within the city limits of Pinehurst, the property tax rate is .00805. Homes are

assessed at 100% of market value. There is an elderly exemption equal to the greater of $20,000 or 50% off assessed value for persons age 65 or older with household gross income of $20,500 or less. Property tax includes garbage pickup.

Pinehurst has a personal property tax rate of .00805. Personal property is assessed at 100% of current market value. Items subject to the tax include motor vehicles, aircraft, mobile homes, watercraft and motorcycles.

Our couples relocating to Pinehurst must pay a highway use tax of $150 per automobile, a title fee of $40 per automobile and a registration fee of $28 per automobile at the time of registration. The highway use tax is 3% of the value of the vehicle as set by the state, up to a maximum tax of $150. Thereafter, on an annual basis, our couples will pay a registration fee per automobile.

Waynesville

Waynesville has no local income tax but does levy a sales tax.

Most purchases are taxed at a rate of 6.75%. Major consumer categories taxed at a different rate: groceries, which are taxed at a rate of 2%. Major consumer categories that are exempt from sales tax include: drugs and medical services.

Within the town of Waynesville, the property tax rate is .00897. Homes are assessed at 100% of market value. There is an elderly exemption equal to the greater of $20,000 or 50% off assessed value for persons age 65 or older with gross income of less than $20,500 or less. Property tax does not cover garbage pickup. There is also a landfill fee of $50 per year.

Waynesville has a personal property tax rate of .00897. Personal property is assessed at 100% of current market value. Items subject to the tax include motor vehicles, mobile homes, boats and motorcycles.

Our couples relocating to Waynesville must pay a highway use tax of $150 per automobile, a title fee of $40 per automobile and a registration fee of $28 per automobile at the time of registration. The highway use tax is 3% of the value of the vehicle as set by the state, up to a maximum tax of $150. Thereafter, on an annual basis, our couples will pay a registration fee per automobile.

Wilmington

Wilmington has no local income tax but does levy a sales tax.

Most purchases are taxed at a rate of 6.75%. Major consumer categories taxed at a different rate: groceries, which are taxed at a rate of 2%. Major consumer categories that are exempt from sales tax include: drugs and medical services.

Within the city limits of Wilming-ton, the property tax rate is .01145. Homes are assessed at 100% of market value. There is an elderly exemption equal to the greater of $20,000 or 50% off assessed value for persons age 65 or older with gross income of $20,500 or less. Property tax does not cover garbage pickup. There is also a stormwater fee of $60 per year.

Wilmington has a personal property tax rate of .01145. Personal property is assessed at 100% of current market value. Items subject to the tax include motor vehicles, mobile homes, boats and motorcycles.

Our couples relocating to Wilming-ton must pay a highway use tax of $150 per automobile, a title fee of $40 per automobile and a registration fee of $28 per automobile at the time of registration. The highway use tax is 3% of the value of the vehicle as set by the state, up to a maximum tax of $150. Thereafter, on an annual basis, our couples will pay a registration fee per automobile.

NORTH CAROLINA TAX TABLE

Instructions

1. Find the Income in the far left column closest to your anticipated retirement income.
2. Find the Home Value closest to the value of the home where you will live in retirement.
3. Follow that row to your estimated Total Tax Burden at age 65 and beyond.

Income	Home Value	Property Tax & Other Fees	Personal Property Tax & Auto Fees	Sales Tax	Local Income Tax	State Income Tax	Total Tax Burden	Rank*
ASHEVILLE								
$30,000	$125,000	$1,408	$398	$900	-	$61	$2,767	97 of 173
	150,000	1,684	398	900	-	61	3,043	93 of 173
	175,000	1,960	398	900	-	61	3,319	89 of 173
$60,000	$150,000	$1,684	$398	$1,564	-	$1,510	$5,156	160 of 203
	225,000	2,512	398	1,564	-	1,510	5,984	147 of 203
	300,000	3,339	398	1,564	-	1,510	6,811	134 of 203
$90,000	$225,000	$2,512	$398	$1,936	-	$3,458	$8,304	168 of 203
	375,000	4,167	398	1,936	-	3,458	9,959	150 of 203
	525,000	5,823	398	1,936	-	3,458	11,615	131 of 203
BREVARD								
$30,000	$125,000	$1,474	$377	$900	-	$61	$2,812	101 of 173
	150,000	1,733	377	900	-	61	3,071	97 of 173
	175,000	1,991	377	900	-	61	3,329	90 of 173
$60,000	$150,000	$1,733	$377	$1,564	-	$1,510	$5,184	162 of 203
	225,000	2,509	377	1,564	-	1,510	5,960	146 of 203
	300,000	3,285	377	1,564	-	1,510	6,736	131 of 203
$90,000	$225,000	$2,509	$377	$1,936	-	$3,458	$8,280	167 of 203
	375,000	4,061	377	1,936	-	3,458	9,832	146 of 203
	525,000	5,614	377	1,936	-	3,458	11,385	128 of 203
CHAPEL HILL								
$30,000	$125,000	$2,056	$566	$900	-	$61	$3,583	152 of 173
	150,000	2,459	566	900	-	61	3,986	150 of 173
	175,000	2,863	566	900	-	61	4,390	148 of 173
$60,000	$150,000	$2,459	$566	$1,564	-	$1,510	$6,099	190 of 203
	225,000	3,669	566	1,564	-	1,510	7,309	184 of 203
	300,000	4,880	566	1,564	-	1,510	8,520	177 of 203
$90,000	$225,000	$3,669	$566	$1,936	-	$3,458	$9,629	187 of 203
	375,000	6,090	566	1,936	-	3,458	12,050	182 of 203
	525,000	8,510	566	1,936	-	3,458	14,470	177 of 203

Income	Home Value	Property Tax & Other Fees	Personal Property Tax & Auto Fees	Sales Tax	Local Income Tax	State Income Tax	Total Tax Burden	Rank *
EDENTON								
$30,000	$125,000	$1,356	$315	$900	-	$61	$2,632	82 of 173
	150,000	1,565	315	900	-	61	2,841	77 of 173
	175,000	1,773	315	900	-	61	3,049	76 of 173
$60,000	$150,000	$1,565	$315	$1,564	-	$1,510	$4,954	154 of 203
	225,000	2,191	315	1,564	-	1,510	5,580	125 of 203
	300,000	2,817	315	1,564	-	1,510	6,206	113 of 203
$90,000	$225,000	$2,191	$315	$1,936	-	$3,458	$7,900	155 of 203
	375,000	3,443	315	1,936	-	3,458	9,152	121 of 203
	525,000	4,696	315	1,936	-	3,458	10,405	103 of 203
HENDERSONVILLE								
$30,000	$125,000	$1,424	$364	$900	-	$61	$2,749	94 of 173
	150,000	1,673	364	900	-	61	2,998	89 of 173
	175,000	1,921	364	900	-	61	3,246	82 of 173
$60,000	$150,000	$1,673	$364	$1,564	-	$1,510	$5,111	156 of 203
	225,000	2,419	364	1,564	-	1,510	5,857	142 of 203
	300,000	3,165	364	1,564	-	1,510	6,603	126 of 203
$90,000	$225,000	$2,419	$364	$1,936	-	$3,458	$8,177	166 of 203
	375,000	3,911	364	1,936	-	3,458	9,669	138 of 203
	525,000	5,404	364	1,936	-	3,458	11,162	125 of 203
NEW BERN								
$30,000	$125,000	$1,562	$401	$900	-	$61	$2,924	111 of 173
	150,000	1,832	401	900	-	61	3,194	102 of 173
	175,000	2,102	401	900	-	61	3,464	98 of 173
$60,000	$150,000	$1,832	$401	$1,564	-	$1,510	$5,307	168 of 203
	225,000	2,642	401	1,564	-	1,510	6,117	153 of 203
	300,000	3,452	401	1,564	-	1,510	6,927	138 of 203
$90,000	$225,000	$2,642	$401	$1,936	-	$3,458	$8,437	173 of 203
	375,000	4,262	401	1,936	-	3,458	10,057	153 of 203
	525,000	5,882	401	1,936	-	3,458	11,677	133 of 203
PINEHURST								
$30,000	$125,000	$1,006	$306	$900	-	$61	$2,273	48 of 173
	150,000	1,208	306	900	-	61	2,475	49 of 173
	175,000	1,409	306	900	-	61	2,676	49 of 173
$60,000	$150,000	$1,208	$306	$1,564	-	$1,510	$4,588	130 of 203
	225,000	1,811	306	1,564	-	1,510	5,191	108 of 203
	300,000	2,415	306	1,564	-	1,510	5,795	92 of 203
$90,000	$225,000	$1,811	$306	$1,936	-	$3,458	$7,511	143 of 203
	375,000	3,019	306	1,936	-	3,458	8,719	107 of 203
	525,000	4,226	306	1,936	-	3,458	9,926	88 of 203
WAYNESVILLE								
$30,000	$125,000	$1,351	$334	$900	-	$61	$2,646	84 of 173
	150,000	1,576	334	900	-	61	2,871	80 of 173
	175,000	1,800	334	900	-	61	3,095	81 of 173
$60,000	$150,000	$1,576	$334	$1,564	-	$1,510	$4,984	155 of 203
	225,000	2,248	334	1,564	-	1,510	5,656	130 of 203
	300,000	2,921	334	1,564	-	1,510	6,329	118 of 203
$90,000	$225,000	$2,248	$334	$1,936	-	$3,458	$7,976	159 of 203
	375,000	3,594	334	1,936	-	3,458	9,322	130 of 203
	525,000	4,939	334	1,936	-	3,458	10,667	115 of 203

*There are 203 cities in this book, 30 of which have higher than average home prices. We have estimated taxes for a tier of higher home values (and omitted the lowest tier) for these 30 cities. The city with the lowest tax burden for an income/home value combination is given the #1 rating; the higher the rating, the higher the total tax burden.

Income	Home Value	Property Tax & Other Fees	Personal Property Tax & Auto Fees	Sales Tax	Local Income Tax	State Income Tax	Total Tax Burden	Rank*
WILMINGTON								
$30,000	$125,000	$1,671	$411	$900	-	$61	$3,043	124 of 173
	150,000	1,958	411	900	-	61	3,330	114 of 173
	175,000	2,244	411	900	-	61	3,616	109 of 173
$60,000	$150,000	$1,958	$411	$1,564	-	$1,510	$5,443	174 of 203
	225,000	2,816	411	1,564	-	1,510	6,301	159 of 203
	300,000	3,675	411	1,564	-	1,510	7,160	147 of 203
$90,000	$225,000	$2,816	$411	$1,936	-	$3,458	$8,621	177 of 203
	375,000	4,534	411	1,936	-	3,458	10,339	161 of 203
	525,000	6,251	411	1,936	-	3,458	12,056	143 of 203

*There are 203 cities in this book, 30 of which have higher than average home prices. We have estimated taxes for a tier of higher home values (and omitted the lowest tier) for these 30 cities. The city with the lowest tax burden for an income/home value combination is given the #1 rating; the higher the rating, the higher the total tax burden.

• North Carolina's Top Retirement Towns •

Asheville

About 125 miles northwest of Charlotte, Asheville is the largest city in western North Carolina. Mountain peaks surround the town and it's known for its cool summer climate, which made it a draw for the likes of Henry Ford, Thomas Edison and John D. Rockefeller.

In 1895, George Washington Vanderbilt, grandson of "Commodore" Cornelius Vanderbilt, completed Biltmore Estate, a 250-room French Renaissance chateau that is considered America's largest private residence.

The nation's most popular scenic highway, the Blue Ridge Parkway, runs through here. And Asheville's downtown is filled with Art Deco architecture from the late 1920s and early 1930s. Only Miami can rival it.

"The city has a very welcoming environment," says a spokesperson for the Asheville Convention and Visitors Bureau. "We have the benefit of four seasons, but without the bitter cold Northerners must face and the oppressively hot temperatures Southerners face in other parts of the South."

Asheville is the medical and educational hub of the area, home to the top-rated Mission Hospitals campus and the 3,500-student University of North Carolina at Asheville. The college houses the North Carolina Center for Creative Retirement, a pioneer in community programs and lifelong-learning classes for retirees.

Over the past 15 years, the city's center has undergone a dramatic transformation, creating one of the Southeast's most vibrant downtowns. There's a plethora of hip shops, boutiques and galleries. Outdoors enthusiasts are lured by ample opportunities to kayak, hike or mountain bike, and golfers have numerous courses to play.

Population: 75,948
Climate: High Low
January 48 28
July 85 62
Cost of living: Average to above average
Housing cost: The average price of homes during the first half of 2007 was $288,864, according to the North Carolina Association of Realtors.
Information: Asheville Convention and Visitors Bureau, (888) 247-9811 or www.exploreasheville.com.

Brevard

Nature has been the draw in this Blue Ridge mountain town since it was founded in the 1850s. Spring rains feed more than 250 waterfalls in the area, but the local love affair with the outdoors extends year-round. In warmer months, the mountains south of Asheville ring with opera, jazz, bluegrass and classical works during outdoor concerts at the renowned Brevard Music Center.

The center adds an international flair, attracting as many as 400 young musicians from around the world for tutoring under highly ranked professionals. The musicians perform in the center's summerlong music festival, which draws thousands of visitors and residents to an open-air auditorium in the woods. Other events include the light-hearted White Squirrel Festival, celebrating the town's unusual residents.

Summer is prime time for outdoor activities, from camping and hiking in adjacent national forests to fishing and kayaking on rivers and streams. Visitors double the size of Brevard to join in the activities and enjoy the series of concerts and street fairs. With its many festivals, Brevard has numerous volunteer opportunities.

"People here tend to be active and outdoor-oriented," says Mike Ziegler, 66, who retired here from Charlotte, NC, with his wife, Sue, in 1999. "I like hiking and hills and changes in season. Both Brevard and Connestee Falls, the development we live in, have been the best things that have ever happened to us."

Population: 6,654
Climate: High Low
January 44 28
July 79 64
Cost of living: Average to above average
Housing cost: The median sales price of single-family homes during the first half of 2007 was $272,125, according to the Brevard Board of Realtors.
Information: Brevard-Transylvania Cham-

ber of Commerce, (800) 648-4523 or www.brevardncchamber.org.

Chapel Hill

Chapel Hill fits the model of a gracious Southern town, with its quiet streets shaded by beautiful, majestic trees, its traditional homes and its modest hills that ward off any sense of topographical monotony.

But it's not quite typical. It has a large university that strongly affects Chapel Hill's intellectual character and provides many amenities that a town of only about 50,000 inhabitants would not otherwise have.

That educational institution is the University of North Carolina, the nation's first state university, established in 1795. One of its amenities is the UNC Hospitals, which have been ranked among the best in the country. The academic medical center includes four hospitals and the university's School of Medicine, a renowned research institution. The center excels in a number of fields, including geriatrics, cancer and rheumatology.

Retirees can take advantage of the university's Carolina College for Lifelong Learning, which has classes on the arts, sciences, religion and current events as well as special lectures and study trips.

The university's presence has a strong bearing on the fact that 73.7 percent of the town's residents who are 25 and older hold bachelor's degrees and 40.5 percent hold graduate or professional degrees. UNC's attractive campus is a scenic addition to the town, complementing the 13 city parks. Bookstores, museums, galleries and performing arts venues add to the intellectual and artistic ferment.

Chapel Hill is one corner of a North Carolina area known as the Research Triangle. The other two corners are Raleigh, home of North Carolina State University, and Durham, home of Duke University. The cities are only a short drive from each other, giving retirees an exceptional wealth of amenities and activities.

Population: 49,919
Climate: High Low
January 49 27
July 89 66

Cost of living: Average to above average
Housing cost: The median sales price of single-family homes during the first 10 months of 2007 was $260,000, according to the Greater Chapel Hill Association of Realtors.
Information: Chapel Hill-Carrboro Chamber of Commerce, (919) 967-7075 or www.carolinachamber.org.

Hendersonville

On a plateau about 2,500 feet above sea level, between the Blue Ridge and Great Smoky Mountains of western North Carolina, this town was for years a summer retreat for sweltering coastal lowlanders. In recent years it has become a haven for retirees leaving cities in search of a quieter, safer environment.

Downtown Hendersonville, on the National Register of Historic Places, has more than 120 shops, galleries, restaurants and historic sites. It is lauded for its dedication to historic preservation as well as the arts, with museums for both plane and train enthusiasts and an active city arts council.

Retirees will find a Center for Lifelong Learning and other senior-specific classes at Blue Ridge Community College between Hendersonville and the neighboring village of Flat Rock. The Bullington Center, a public garden with an amphitheater and nature trail, offers horticultural classes and a variety of workshops.

Recreational opportunities abound in nearby forests, mountains and rivers, including the Pisgah National Forest and the DuPont State Forest. And in the nearby communities of Flat Rock, Brevard and Asheville, music, art and theater provide a diverse array of cultural events that attract visitors from across the nation.

Bill and Barbara Johnson moved from Rockville, MD, after vacationing in Hendersonville. "We found out we really liked the place," Barbara says. "We wanted a mild winter, a cool summer and a house in the mountains on a golf course."

Though Hendersonville is growing at a rapid rate, it retains "a small-town atmosphere, with friendly people, beautiful developments, remote scenic surroundings and an unhurried pace —

all of the things we were looking for in retirement," Bill says.

The 222-bed Pardee Hospital serves the community.

Population: 11,808
Climate: High Low
January 47 25
July 84 64

Cost of living: Average to above average
Housing cost: The average sales price of homes in the first half of 2007 was $250,296, according to the North Carolina Association of Realtors.
Information: Henderson County Travel and Tourism, (800) 828-4244 or www.historichendersonville.org. Henderson County Chamber of Commerce, (828) 692-1413 or www.hendersonvillechamber.org.

Waynesville

In the far western part of the state, at 2,713 feet altitude, Waynesville is a small mountain town with lots of charm. The Blue Ridge Parkway is nearby. Summer temperatures seldom exceed the low 80s, dropping into the 50s at night, and winters are relatively mild.

Surrounding the town are peaks rising to 6,000 feet. Great Smoky Mountains National Park and Pisgah National Forest are nearby, and three white-water rivers run through the surrounding Haywood County. The setting offers extraordinary opportunities for outdoor recreation, including rafting, fishing, hiking and horseback riding.

There are four 18-hole public golf courses along with nine-hole layouts and country club courses in the area. In nearby Maggie Valley, the Cataloochee Ski Area has five lifts and trails for skiing, snowboarding and snowshoeing.

The 200-year-old town, with its brick sidewalks and historic buildings, has more than 100 retail stores as well as restaurants, galleries and antique shops. Among many area festivals and cultural events, Folkmoot USA is an international celebration of folk music and dance performed by more than 350 people from a dozen countries. The troupe spends two weeks each summer in western North Carolina.

Haywood County is home to two theaters for the performing arts and the Maggie Valley Opry House, where mountain music is played nightly from May through October. Haywood Community College in Clyde, about seven miles from Waynesville, offers continuing-education programs.

Asheville, with its airport, hospitals and plentiful cultural activities and attractions, is only 30 miles away. It's home to the University of North Carolina at Asheville, which includes the North Carolina Center for Creative Retirement, renowned for its roster of classes.

Population: 9,432

Climate: High Low
January   47   23
July   82   58

Cost of living: Average

Housing cost: In the Waynesville area, the average price was $240,226 during the first half of 2007, according to the North Carolina Association of Realtors.

Information: Haywood County Chamber of Commerce, (828) 456-3021 or www.haywood-nc.com.

Wilmington

The 18th-century port city of Wilmington, with North Carolina's largest collection of historic buildings and homes downtown, is increasingly pop-ular with retirees.

Downtown's national historic district is a bustling collection of restaurants, outdoor cafes, coffee shops, banks, governmental offices and retail stores, all framed against the backdrop of the Cape Fear River. The district is home to an eclectic collection of residents, including old Wilmington families, artists and writers, among others.

Historic homes date to the 1700s, blending with others built some 200 years later. Buyers favor the area's rich history, along with hardwood floors, high ceilings, intriguing architecture, front porches and sidewalks. Housing options are abundant, with a choice of waterfront mansions, custom-designed homes in golf course communities, patio homes with outdoor maintenance provided, beachfront condominiums, family neighborhoods, downtown apartments and townhouses and assist-ed-living centers.

Adding to the allure are 31 miles of beaches (including Wrightsville Beach, five miles from downtown, and Carolina and Kure beaches, 20 minutes from downtown), parks and the University of North Carolina-Wilmington, which offers activities for seniors. With hot summers, cool autumns, mild winters and warm springs that come with the Cape Fear Coast, the weather lends itself to street festivals that take place throughout the year.

Ranked as one of the nation's top 100 best small art towns, Wilmington has scores of annual events, access to more than 20 golf courses (with more planned), and places to sail, bike and play tennis. Health-care needs are eas-ily met at several facilities, including New Hanover Regional Medical Center, which offers cancer and car-diac care.

Population: 95,944

Climate: High Low
January   56   36
July   90   72

Cost of living: Average

Housing cost: The median sales price of a single-family home for the first five months of 2007 was $216,429, accord-ing to the Wilmington Regional Associ-ation of Realtors.

Information: Wilmington-Cape Fear Coast Convention and Visitors Bureau, (800) 222-4757 or www.capefearcoast. com. Greater Wilmington Chamber of Commerce, (910) 762-2611 or www.wil mingtonchamber.org.

NORTH DAKOTA

North Dakota has a state income tax and a state sales tax.

There are two methods that can be used to calculate income tax in North Dakota. The state income tax rate using the short-form method (ND1) is graduated from 2.1% to 5.54% depending upon income bracket. For married couples filing jointly, the rates are 2.1% on the first $51,200 of taxable income; 3.92% on the next $72,500 of taxable income; 4.34% on the next $64,750 of taxable income; 5.04% on the next $148,100 of taxable income; and 5.54% on taxable income above $336,500. In calculating the tax using the short-form method, the standard federal deductions are used.

The state income tax rate using the long-form method (ND2) is graduated from 2.67% to 12% depending upon income bracket. For married couples filing jointly, the rates are 2.67% on the first $3,000 of taxable income; 4% on the next $2,000 of taxable income; 5.33% on the next $3,000 of taxable income; 6.67% on the next $7,000 of taxable income; 8% on the next $10,000 of taxable income; 9.33% on the next $10,000 of taxable income; 10.67% on the next $15,000 of taxable income; and

> ○ Tax Heavens: None
> Ψ Tax Hells: None

12% on taxable income above $50,000.

In calculating the tax using the long-form method, there is a deduction for federal income tax paid. Federal and some state pensions are exempt. Private pension income is not exempt. Social Security benefits subject to federal tax are not exempt. There is a standard deduction of up to $600 for interest income received from financial institutions located in North Dakota for married couples filing jointly. There is an additional exemption of $300 from income for married couples filing jointly.

Major tax credits or rebates include: credit for taxes paid to other states, credit for long-term care insurance and credit for contribution to qualifying North Dakota private high school or college. Our couples do not qualify for these programs.

The state sales tax rate is 5%, but local governments can add to this amount.

Fargo

Fargo has no local income tax but does levy a sales tax.

Most purchases are taxed at a rate of 6%. Major consumer categories taxed at a different rate: none. Major consumer categories that are exempt from sales tax include: groceries, medical services and drugs.

In Fargo School District 1, the property tax rate is .46725. Homes are assessed at 50% of market value. Taxable value is 9% of assessed value. There is a homestead credit for homeowners age 65 or older with gross income less than $17,500 (after medical expenses) and with assets of $50,000 or less, excluding the first $100,000 of market value of the home. Property tax does not cover garbage pickup. Residents also pay approximately $29 per year in forestry fees.

Fargo has no personal property tax for individuals.

Our couples relocating to Fargo must pay a registration fee of $93 for the Explorer and $73 for the Camry, a title fee of $7 per automobile and a service charge fee of $8 per automobile. Thereafter, on an annual basis, our couples will pay a registration fee and a service charge fee, per automobile.

NORTH DAKOTA TAX TABLE

Instructions

1. Find the Income in the far left column closest to your anticipated retirement income.
2. Find the Home Value closest to the value of the home where you will live in retirement.
3. Follow that row to your estimated Total Tax Burden at age 65 and beyond.

Income	Home Value	Property Tax & Other Fees	Personal Property Tax & Auto Fees	Sales Tax	Local Income Tax	State Income Tax	Total Tax Burden	Rank*
FARGO								
$30,000	$125,000	$2,837	$172	$755	-	-	$3,764	154 of 173
	150,000	3,363	172	755	-	-	4,290	155 of 173
	175,000	3,889	172	755	-	-	4,816	155 of 173
$60,000	$150,000	$3,363	$172	$1,327	-	$639	$5,501	179 of 203
	225,000	4,940	172	1,327	-	639	7,078	176 of 203
	300,000	6,517	172	1,327	-	639	8,655	180 of 203
$90,000	$225,000	$4,940	$172	$1,649	-	$1,696	$8,457	174 of 203
	375,000	8,094	172	1,649	-	1,696	11,611	179 of 203
	525,000	11,248	172	1,649	-	1,696	14,765	179 of 203

*There are 203 cities in this book, 30 of which have higher than average home prices. We have estimated taxes for a tier of higher home values (and omitted the lowest tier) for these 30 cities. The city with the lowest tax burden for an income/home value combination is given the #1 rating; the higher the rating, the higher the total tax burden.

OHIO

Ohio has a state income tax and a state sales tax.

The state income tax rate is graduated from .681% to 6.87% depending upon income bracket. For married couples filing jointly, the rates are .681% on the first $5,000 of taxable income; 1.361% on the next $5,000 of taxable income; 2.722% on the next $5,000 of taxable income; 3.403% on the next $5,000 of taxable income; 4.083% on the next $20,000 of taxable income; 4.764% on the next $40,000 of taxable income; 5.444% on the next $20,000 of taxable income; 6.32% on the next $100,000 of taxable income; and 6.87% on taxable income above $200,000.

> **O Tax Heavens:** None
> **Ψ Tax Hells:** None

In calculating the tax, there is no deduction for federal income tax paid. Social Security benefits are exempt. There is a $1,400 personal exemption per person. There is a deduction for unreimbursed medical expenses in excess of 7.5% of federal adjusted gross income.

Major tax credits or rebates include: credit for income taxes paid to other states; retirement income credit from tax due of up to $200 for federal, state and private pensions for married couples filing jointly; senior citizen tax credit of $50 per person age 65 or older; exemption tax credit of $20 per person; and joint filing credit of up to $650 from tax for married couples filing jointly if both spouses have earned income of at least $500 included in Ohio adjusted gross income. Our couples qualify for all these programs except for the credit for income taxes paid to other states.

The state sales tax rate is 5.5%, but local governments can add to this amount.

Our couples relocating to the cities listed below must pay a registration fee of $31 per automobile, a title fee of $17 per automobile, a local (permissive) tax of $20 per automobile and

---

OHIO TAX TABLE

Instructions

1. Find the Income in the far left column closest to your anticipated retirement income.
2. Find the Home Value closest to the value of the home where you will live in retirement.
3. Follow that row to your estimated Total Tax Burden at age 65 and beyond.

Income	Home Value	Property Tax & Other Fees	Personal Property Tax & Auto Fees	Sales Tax	Local Income Tax	State Income Tax	Total Tax Burden	Rank*
CINCINNATI								
$30,000	$125,000	$2,199	$109	$818	$118	-	$3,244	142 of 173
	150,000	2,635	109	818	118	-	3,680	139 of 173
	175,000	3,070	109	818	118	-	4,115	134 of 173
$60,000	$150,000	$2,635	$109	$1,438	$501	$597	$5,280	166 of 203
	225,000	3,942	109	1,438	501	597	6,587	170 of 203
	300,000	5,250	109	1,438	501	597	7,895	164 of 203
$90,000	$225,000	$3,942	$109	$1,787	$975	$1,863	$8,676	179 of 203
	375,000	6,558	109	1,787	975	1,863	11,292	175 of 203
	525,000	9,173	109	1,787	975	1,863	13,907	170 of 203
CLEVELAND								
$30,000	$125,000	$2,224	$109	$944	$113	-	$3,390	147 of 173
	150,000	2,633	109	944	113	-	3,799	144 of 173
	175,000	3,042	109	944	113	-	4,208	140 of 173
$60,000	$150,000	$2,633	$109	$1,659	$477	$597	$5,475	177 of 203
	225,000	3,860	109	1,659	477	597	6,702	172 of 203
	300,000	5,086	109	1,659	477	597	7,928	165 of 203
$90,000	$225,000	$3,860	$109	$2,062	$929	$1,863	$8,823	181 of 203
	375,000	6,313	109	2,062	929	1,863	11,276	173 of 203
	525,000	8,766	109	2,062	929	1,863	13,729	166 of 203
COLUMBUS								
$30,000	$125,000	$2,090	$109	$850	$113	-	$3,162	134 of 173
	150,000	2,472	109	850	113	-	3,544	128 of 173
	175,000	2,854	109	850	113	-	3,926	125 of 173

Income	Home Value	Property Tax & Other Fees	Personal Property Tax & Auto Fees	Sales Tax	Local Income Tax	State Income Tax	Total Tax Burden	Rank*
COLUMBUS continued								
$60,000	$150,000	$2,472	$109	$1,493	$477	$597	$5,148	159 of 203
	225,000	3,618	109	1,493	477	597	6,294	158 of 203
	300,000	4,764	109	1,493	477	597	7,440	155 of 203
$90,000	$225,000	$3,618	$109	$1,856	$929	$1,863	$8,375	170 of 203
	375,000	5,910	109	1,856	929	1,863	10,667	169 of 203
	525,000	8,202	109	1,856	929	1,863	12,959	156 of 203

*There are 203 cities in this book, 30 of which have higher than average home prices. We have estimated taxes for a tier of higher home values (and omitted the lowest tier) for these 30 cities. The city with the lowest tax burden for an income/home value combination is given the #1 rating; the higher the rating, the higher the total tax burden.

miscellaneous fees of $4 per automobile at the time of registration. Thereafter, on an annual basis, our couples will pay a registration fee, a local (permissive) tax and miscellaneous fees, per automobile.

Cincinnati

Cincinnati has a local income tax and a sales tax.

The local income tax rate is 2.1%, which is applied to wages, salaries and self-employment income.

Most purchases are taxed at a rate of 6.5%. Major consumer categories taxed at a different rate: none. Major consumer categories that are exempt from sales tax include: drugs, groceries and medical services.

Within the Cincinnati School District, the effective property tax rate after application of the reduction factor is .05693655. Homes are assessed at 35% of market value. There is a reduction of 10% off property taxes for all homeowners. There is a reduction of 2.5% off property taxes for all owner-occupied homes. There is also a homestead exemption available to homeowners age 65 or older whose combined total gross income is $26,200 or less. Effective July 2, 2007, all homeowners age 65 or older are eligible for the homestead exemption regardless of

income. Property tax includes garbage pickup. There is a stormwater fee of approximately $19 per year.

Cincinnati has no personal property tax for individuals.

Cleveland

Cleveland has a local income tax and a sales tax.

The local income tax rate is 2%, which is applied to wages, salaries and self-employment income.

Most purchases are taxed at a rate of 7.5%. Major consumer categories taxed at a different rate: none. Major consumer categories that are exempt from sales tax include: drugs, groceries and medical services.

Within the Highland Heights area of Cleveland, the property tax rate is .053399873. Homes are assessed at 35% of market value. There is a reduction of 10% of property tax due for all homeowners. There is a reduction of 2.5% of property taxes due for all owner-occupied homes. There is also a homestead exemption available to homeowners age 65 or older whose combined total gross income is $26,200 or less. Effective July 2, 2007, all homeowners age 65 or older are eligible for the homestead exemption regardless of income. Property tax does not cover garbage pickup.

Cleveland has no personal property

tax for individuals.

Columbus

Columbus has a local income tax and a sales tax.

The local income tax rate is 2%, which is applied to wages, salaries, rental income and self-employment income.

Most purchases are taxed at a rate of 6.75%. Major consumer categories taxed at a different rate: none. Major consumer categories that are exempt from sales tax include: drugs, groceries and medical services.

Within the Columbus school district, the effective property tax rate after application of the reduction factor is .049893485. Homes are assessed at 35% of market value. There is a reduction of 10% of property taxes due for all homeowners. There is a reduction of 2.5% of property taxes due for all owner-occupied homes. There is also a homestead exemption available to homeowners age 65 or older whose combined total gross income is $26,200 or less. Effective July 2, 2007, all homeowners age 65 or older are eligible for the homestead exemption regardless of income. Property tax does not cover garbage pickup.

Columbus has no personal property tax for individuals.

OKLAHOMA

Oklahoma has a state income tax and a state sales tax.

The state income tax rate is graduated from .5% to 6.75% depending upon income bracket. For married couples filing jointly with taxable income of up to $2,000, the rate is .5%; up to $5,000, the tax is $10 plus 1% of the amount above $2,000; up to $7,500, the tax is $40 plus 2% of the amount above $5,000; up to $9,800, the tax is $90 plus 3% of the amount above $7,500; up to $12,200, the tax is $159 plus 4% of the amount above $9,800; up to $15,000, the tax is $255 plus 5% of the amount above $12,200; up to $21,000, the tax is $395 plus 6% of the amount above $15,000; $21,000 or above, the tax is $755 plus 6.25%

O **Tax Heavens:** None
Ψ **Tax Hells:** None
Top Retirement Towns: Grove

---

of the amount above $21,000.

In calculating the tax, there is no deduction for federal income tax paid There is an exemption of up to $10,000 for military retirement income per person. Federal and state retirement income is exempt up to $10,000 per person. Private retirement income is exempt up to $10,000 per person if income requirements are met. Social Security benefits are exempt. There is a $3,000 standard deduction from federal adjusted gross income for married couples filing jointly. There is a

$1,000 personal deduction from federal adjusted gross income per person. There is an exemption of up to $200 for interest received from a bank, credit union or savings and loan association located in Oklahoma for married couples filing jointly.

Major tax rebates or credits include: credit for income taxes paid to other states, a low-income property tax credit and sales tax relief credit. One of our couples qualifies for the sales tax relief credit, but none of our couples qualify for the other programs.

The state sales tax rate is 4.5%, but local governments can add to this amount.

Our couples relocating to the cities listed below must pay a registration

---

OKLAHOMA TAX TABLE

Instructions

1. Find the Income in the far left column closest to your anticipated retirement income.
2. Find the Home Value closest to the value of the home where you will live in retirement.
3. Follow that row to your estimated Total Tax Burden at age 65 and beyond.

Income	Home Value	Property Tax & Other Fees	Personal Property Tax & Auto Fees	Sales Tax	Local Income Tax	State Income Tax[†]	Total Tax Burden	Rank[*]
GROVE								
$30,000	$125,000	$1,258	$185	$1,347	-	($160)	$2,630	81 of 173
	150,000	1,490	185	1,347	-	(160)	2,862	79 of 173
	175,000	1,721	185	1,347	-	(160)	3,093	80 of 173
$60,000	$150,000	$1,490	$185	$2,286	-	$918	$4,879	150 of 203
	225,000	2,185	185	2,286	-	918	5,574	124 of 203
	300,000	2,880	185	2,286	-	918	6,269	115 of 203
$90,000	$225,000	$2,185	$185	$2,806	-	$2,657	$7,833	153 of 203
	375,000	3,575	185	2,806	-	2,657	9,223	125 of 203
	525,000	4,966	185	2,806	-	2,657	10,614	112 of 203
OKLAHOMA CITY								
$30,000	$125,000	$1,624	$185	$1,267	-	($160)	$2,916	109 of 173
	150,000	1,926	185	1,267	-	(160)	3,218	104 of 173
	175,000	2,228	185	1,267	-	(160)	3,520	104 of 173
$60,000	$150,000	$1,926	$185	$2,151	-	$918	$5,180	161 of 203
	225,000	2,832	185	2,151	-	918	6,086	151 of 203
	300,000	3,738	185	2,151	-	918	6,992	139 of 203
$90,000	$225,000	$2,832	$185	$2,641	-	$2,657	$8,315	169 of 203
	375,000	4,644	185	2,641	-	2,657	10,127	155 of 203
	525,000	6,456	185	2,641	-	2,657	11,939	141 of 203

[†]Sales tax relief credit is issued as a reduction of income tax due or as a refund if the credit is greater than the tax liability.
[*]There are 203 cities in this book, 30 of which have higher than average home prices. We have estimated taxes for a tier of higher home values (and omitted the lowest tier) for these 30 cities. The city with the lowest tax burden for an income/home value combination is given the #1 rating; the higher the rating, the higher the total tax burden.

fee of $91 per automobile, a title fee of $11 per automobile, a lien fee of $15 per automobile, miscellaneous fees of $7 per automobile and a waste tire fee based on the number of tires and rim size per automobile. The waste tire fee is $5 for the Explorer and $5 for the Camry. Thereafter, on an annual basis, our couples will pay a registration fee and one of the miscellaneous fees, per automobile.

Grove (Grand Lake)

Grove has no local income tax but does levy a sales tax.

Most purchases are taxed at a rate of 8.9%. On April 1, 2007, the rate decreases to 8.8%. Major consumer categories taxed at a different rate: none. Major consumer categories that are exempt from sales tax include: drugs and medical services.

Within the city limits of Grove, the property tax rate is .0806. Homes are assessed at 11.5% of market value. There is a homestead exemption of $1,000 off assessed value and an additional homestead exemption of $1,000 off assessed value available to homeowners with gross income of $20,000 or less. There is also a property tax refund available to homeowners age 65 or older with gross income of $12,000 or less. Homeowners age 65 or older may qualify for a valuation freeze if they meet income requirements. Property tax does not cover garbage pickup.

Grove has a personal property tax rate of .0806. Mobile homes that are located on land not owned by the resident are subject to the tax and assessed at 11.5% of market value. We've assumed our couples do not own any items subject to the tax.

Oklahoma City

Oklahoma City has no local income tax but does levy a sales tax.

Most purchases are taxed at a rate of 8.375%. Major consumer categories taxed at a different rate: none. Major consumer categories that are exempt from sales tax include: drugs and medical services.

In the Oklahoma City School District, the property tax rate is .10981. Homes are assessed at 11% of market value. There is a homestead exemption of $1,000 off assessed value and an additional homestead exemption of $1,000 off assessed value available to homeowners with gross income of $20,000 or less. There is also a property tax refund available to homeowners age 65 or older with gross income of $12,000 or less. Homeowners age 65 or older may qualify for a valuation freeze if they meet income requirements. Property tax does not cover garbage pickup. There is also a drainage fee of $44 per year.

Oklahoma City has a personal property tax rate of .10981. Mobile homes that are located on land not owned by the resident are subject to the tax and assessed at 13.75% of market value. We've assumed our couples do not own any items subject to the tax.

• Oklahoma's Top Retirement Town •

Grove (Grand Lake)

In the foothills of the Ozark Mountains, the bustling town of Grove sits along the shores of Grand Lake O' the Cherokees. It's situated on the route of the Trail of Tears followed by American Indians driven west in the 1830s. Only 53 miles from Joplin, MO, it long has been a retirement find among those in the know from Kansas City, MO; Wichita, KS; and Tulsa, OK. They dub it "living the Grand life."

Retirees from states much farther away now have discovered the area's attractions, contributing to rapid growth around Grove.

The main draw, of course, is the tree-lined lake with 1,300 miles of shoreline. The temperate climate ensures four seasons. In the spring, the area flourishes with the brilliance of dogwood and redbud blooms interspersed among the cedars and pines, and fall foliage takes on many hues. The clean air, low crime rate and below-average cost of living are also retirement pluses. Continuing-education opportunities are available at Northeastern Oklahoma A&M College, with an extension campus in Grove.

In addition, the area boasts a regional medical center, more than 30 restaurants and dozens of boat dealers and marinas. The town of 6,011 seems larger than it is, offering antiques and specialty stores, gardens and even paddleboat excursions and a trolley. A commercial center for the area, Grove has an economy based on tourism and trade. The town swells to a population of 30,000 in the summer with vacationers.

A broad range of housing is available. For example, Monkey Island, about eight miles southwest of Grove, is a community of luxurious single-family homes and condos. The Cowskin area, on the arm of the Elk River to the Missouri border, has lake-front homes, cottages, resorts, camping and marina facilities. In the heart of Grove, homes of $50,000 to $100,000 are available, but the average home value is closer to $140,000. According to the chamber of commerce, fully a third to a half of area residents are 50 or older.

Population: 6,011

Climate:

	High	Low
January	46	26
July	94	73

Cost of living: Below average

Housing cost: The average sales price of homes during the first half of 2007 was $137,425.50, according to the Oklahoma Association of Realtors.

Information: Grove Area Chamber of Commerce, (918) 786-9079 or www.grove ok.org.

OREGON

Oregon has a state income tax but no state sales tax.

The state income tax is graduated from 5% to 9% depending upon income bracket. For married couples filing jointly, the rates are 5% on the first $5,500 of taxable income; 7% on the next $8,200 of taxable income; and 9% on taxable income above $13,700.

In calculating the tax, there is a deduction of up to $5,000 for federal income tax paid. Federal pensions for service after October 1, 1991, and state and private pensions are not exempt. Social Security benefits are exempt. There is a $3,685 standard deduction for married couples filing jointly. There is also an age deduction of $1,000 per person age 65 or older.

Major tax credits or rebates include: credit for income taxes paid to other

---

○ **Tax Heavens:** Ashland, Bend, Grants Pass, Medford
Ψ **Tax Hells:** None
Top Retirement Towns: Bend, Eugene, Lincoln City, Portland

---

states, which our couples do not qualify for; exemption tax credit of $159 per person, which our couples qualify for; and retirement income credit, which some of our couples qualify for.

Our couples relocating to the cities listed below must pay a registration fee of $54 per automobile, a title fee of $55 per automobile, a license plate fee of $5 per automobile and a VIN inspection fee of $7 per automobile at the time of registration. In addition, a vehicle inspection fee must be paid to the Oregon Department of Environmental

Quality if relocating to certain cities such as Medford and Portland. Thereafter, our couples will pay a registration fee and, where applicable, a vehicle inspection fee every two years, per automobile.

Ashland

Ashland has no local income tax and no sales tax, with the exception of a 5% tax on food away from home.

In Tax Code Area 0501 of Ashland, the property tax rate is .0146652. New homes are assessed at 48.7% of market value. There are no exemptions or deductions off the property tax. Property tax does not cover garbage pickup. Additional fees include a $30 storm drain fee and a $78 street user fee.

Ashland has no personal property tax for individuals.

OREGON TAX TABLE

Instructions

1. Find the Income in the far left column closest to your anticipated retirement income.
2. Find the Home Value closest to the value of the home where you will live in retirement.
3. Follow that row to your estimated Total Tax Burden at age 65 and beyond.

Income	Home Value	Property Tax & Other Fees	Personal Property Tax & Auto Fees	Sales Tax	Local Income Tax	State Income Tax	Total Tax Burden	Rank*
ASHLAND								
$30,000	$125,000	$1,181	$54	$71	-	$216	$1,522	10 of 173 ○
	150,000	1,359	54	71	-	216	1,700	10 of 173 ○
	175,000	1,538	54	71	-	216	1,879	10 of 173 ○
$60,000	$150,000	$1,359	$54	$126	-	$1,937	$3,476	36 of 203
	225,000	1,895	54	126	-	1,937	4,012	31 of 203
	300,000	2,431	54	126	-	1,937	4,548	32 of 203
$90,000	$225,000	$1,895	$54	$157	-	$4,333	$6,439	96 of 203
	375,000	2,966	54	157	-	4,333	7,510	61 of 203
	525,000	4,038	54	157	-	4,333	8,582	51 of 203
BEND								
$30,000	$125,000	$1,163	$54	-	-	$216	$1,433	7 of 173 ○
	150,000	1,360	54	-	-	216	1,630	8 of 173 ○
	175,000	1,557	54	-	-	216	1,827	8 of 173 ○
$60,000	$150,000	$1,360	$54	-	-	$1,937	$3,351	28 of 203
	225,000	1,950	54	-	-	1,937	3,941	25 of 203
	300,000	2,540	54	-	-	1,937	4,531	29 of 203
$90,000	$225,000	$1,950	$54	-	-	$4,333	$6,337	90 of 203
	375,000	3,130	54	-	-	4,333	7,517	62 of 203
	525,000	4,310	54	-	-	4,333	8,697	54 of 203

Income	Home Value	Property Tax & Other Fees	Personal Property Tax & Auto Fees	Sales Tax	Local Income Tax	State Income Tax	Total Tax Burden	Rank*
EUGENE								
$30,000	$125,000	$1,728	$54	-	-	$216	$1,998	28 of 173
	150,000	2,016	54	-	-	216	2,286	32 of 173
	175,000	2,305	54	-	-	216	2,575	39 of 173
$60,000	$150,000	$2,016	$54	-	-	$1,937	$4,007	81 of 203
	225,000	2,883	54	-	-	1,937	4,874	86 of 203
	300,000	3,749	54	-	-	1,937	5,740	88 of 203
$90,000	$225,000	$2,883	$54	-	-	$4,333	$7,270	133 of 203
	375,000	4,615	54	-	-	4,333	9,002	119 of 203
	525,000	6,347	54	-	-	4,333	10,734	117 of 203
GRANTS PASS								
$30,000	$125,000	$1,003	$54	-	-	$216	$1,273	3 of 173 O
	150,000	1,167	54	-	-	216	1,437	3 of 173 O
	175,000	1,332	54	-	-	216	1,602	4 of 173 O
$60,000	$150,000	$1,167	$54	-	-	$1,937	$3,158	20 of 203
	225,000	1,661	54	-	-	1,937	3,652	16 of 203
	300,000	2,154	54	-	-	1,937	4,145	13 of 203
$90,000	$225,000	$1,661	$54	-	-	$4,333	$6,048	70 of 203
	375,000	2,648	54	-	-	4,333	7,035	42 of 203
	525,000	3,635	54	-	-	4,333	8,022	35 of 203
LINCOLN CITY								
$30,000	$125,000	$1,371	$54	-	-	$216	$1,641	12 of 173
	150,000	1,610	54	-	-	216	1,880	12 of 173
	175,000	1,848	54	-	-	216	2,118	15 of 173
$60,000	$150,000	$1,610	$54	-	-	$1,937	$3,601	46 of 203
	225,000	2,325	54	-	-	1,937	4,316	50 of 203
	300,000	3,039	54	-	-	1,937	5,030	52 of 203
$90,000	$225,000	$2,325	$54	-	-	$4,333	$6,712	106 of 203
	375,000	3,754	54	-	-	4,333	8,141	86 of 203
	525,000	5,184	54	-	-	4,333	9,571	76 of 203
MEDFORD								
$30,000	$125,000	$1,065	$64	-	-	$216	$1,345	6 of 173 O
	150,000	1,242	64	-	-	216	1,522	5 of 173 O
	175,000	1,419	64	-	-	216	1,699	6 of 173 O
$60,000	$150,000	$1,242	$64	-	-	$1,937	$3,243	21 of 203
	225,000	1,773	64	-	-	1,937	3,774	19 of 203
	300,000	2,304	64	-	-	1,937	4,305	21 of 203
$90,000	$225,000	$1,773	$64	-	-	$4,333	$6,170	81 of 203
	375,000	2,835	64	-	-	4,333	7,232	50 of 203
	525,000	3,896	64	-	-	4,333	8,293	42 of 203
PORTLAND								
$30,000	$125,000	$1,616	$75	-	-	$216	$1,907	23 of 173
	150,000	1,904	75	-	-	216	2,195	29 of 173
	175,000	2,191	75	-	-	216	2,482	34 of 173
$60,000	$150,000	$1,904	$75	-	-	$1,937	$3,916	71 of 203
	225,000	2,765	75	-	-	1,937	4,777	78 of 203
	300,000	3,627	75	-	-	1,937	5,639	82 of 203
$90,000	$225,000	$2,765	$75	-	-	$4,333	$7,173	129 of 203
	375,000	4,489	75	-	-	4,333	8,897	115 of 203
	525,000	6,213	75	-	-	4,333	10,621	113 of 203

*There are 203 cities in this book, 30 of which have higher than average home prices. We have estimated taxes for a tier of higher home values (and omitted the lowest tier) for these 30 cities. The city with the lowest tax burden for an income/home value combination is given the #1 rating; the higher the rating, the higher the total tax burden.

Bend

Bend has no local income tax and no sales tax.

Within the city limits of Bend, the property tax rate is .0149827. New homes are assessed at 52.5% of market value. There are no exemptions or deductions off the property tax. Property tax does not cover garbage pickup.

Bend has no personal property tax for individuals.

Eugene

Eugene has no local income tax and no sales tax.

In Tax Area Code 00400 of Eugene, the property tax rate is .019226. New homes are assessed at 60.07% of market value. There are no exemptions or deductions off the property tax. Property tax does not cover garbage pickup. There is also a stormwater fee of approximately $104 per year.

Eugene has no personal property tax for individuals.

Grants Pass

Grants Pass has no local income tax and no sales tax.

In the Tax Code 1 area of Grants Pass, the property tax rate is .0138244. New homes are assessed at 47.6% of market value. There are no exemptions or deductions off the property tax. Property tax does not cover garbage pickup.

Grants Pass has no personal property tax for individuals.

Lincoln City

Lincoln City has no local income tax and no sales tax.

In the Tax Code 402 area of Lincoln City, the property tax rate is .0161546. New homes are assessed at 59% of market value. There are no exemptions or deductions off the property tax. Property tax does not cover garbage pickup.

Lincoln City has no personal property tax for individuals.

Medford

Medford has no local income tax and no sales tax.

In the Tax Code 4901 area of Medford, the property tax rate is .014536. New homes are assessed at 48.7% of market value. There are no exemptions or deductions off the property tax. Property tax does not cover garbage pickup.

Medford has no personal property tax for individuals.

Portland

Portland has no local income tax and no sales tax.

In the Tax Code Area 201 of Portland, the property tax rate is .0201693. New homes are assessed at 56.97% of market value. There are no exemptions or deductions off the property tax. Property tax does not cover garbage pickup.

Portland has no personal property tax for individuals.

• Oregon's Top Retirement Towns •

Bend

For those who love the West Coast — or the high desert and mountains — here's an option that takes advantage of great scenery and isn't as expensive as some other places in the West.

Bend sits in about the middle of Oregon, east of the Cascades and far inland from the frenzy of Interstate 5. It's a midsized town with amenities, the greatest being its natural beauty and outdoor recreation. Elevation is about 3,628 feet.

Fly-fishing enthusiasts cast for trout and salmon here. Golfers have a choice of 20 or so courses. Though snow rarely stays on the ground in town, you can go skiing at nearby Mount Bachelor. Pacific beaches are within reach for outings.

The city boasts about three dozen parks, including 11 acres of greenbelt along the Deschutes River and Mirror Pond downtown. Drake Park by the river is the setting for outdoor concerts in summer, and there's live theater year-round. Both Bend and the nearby Sunriver mountain resort-residential community host major music festivals.

A community college and a campus of Oregon State University offer educational and cultural activities, and a medical center serves the region. An added bonus for the pocketbook: no sales tax in Oregon.

Population: 71,892

Climate: High Low

January 40 23

July 81 46

Cost of living: Above average

Housing cost: The median sales price of a single-family home during the first half of 2007 was $349,250, according to the Central Oregon Association of Realtors.

Information: Bend Chamber of Commerce, (800) 905-2363 or www.bend chamber.org.

Eugene

With an award-winning network of walking and bike paths and the Willamette River running through it, Eugene looks more like a national park than one of the nation's most gorgeous college retirement towns.

Tree-shaded paths meander along lush green riverbanks where soaring osprey are spotted. Four graceful bike and pedestrian-only bridges connect both sides of the river to a downtown pedestrian mall lined with restaurants, boutiques, specialty shops and antiques stores. Add 105 parks, 14 miles of urban walking trails and many emerald-green golf courses, and it could take a rainy day to pull a senior student away from all this gorgeous scenery.

Fortunately, the University of Oregon, which offers continuing education plus a year-round calendar of cultural events, could practically pass for a national park, too. The 250-acre campus is graced with towering trees, gardens and architecture dating to the 1870s, with buildings that house art and history museums. Retirees also can take continuing-education courses at Lane Community College, often ranked among the top community colleges in the country.

Art and culture lovers will find plenty of both beyond the ivy halls in the town's seven museums. At the Hult Center for the Performing Arts downtown, you can enjoy ballet, opera and music ranging from Bach to rock. The Saturday Market, held throughout the summer, is the place to pick up homegrown produce and local arts and crafts, and don't miss the Oregon

Country Fair. This combination outdoor musical festival and renaissance crafts fair, held in late July, has many '60s overtones. You may find yourself flashing a peace sign.

Population: 146,356, plus 5,000-6,000 students

Climate:

	High	Low
January	46	33
July	81	51

Cost of living: Above average

Housing cost: The median sales price of existing single-family homes was $238,850 in the Eugene-Springfield metropolitan area during the first half of 2007, according to the National Association of Realtors.

Information: Eugene Area Chamber of Commerce, (541) 484-1314 or www.eugenechamber.com.

Lincoln City

Tucked amid evergreen forests of spruce and hemlock on the broad, sandy beaches of Oregon's coastline is the small town of Lincoln City, which calls itself the "Kite Capital of the World." The two main resources of this maritime community are tourism and retirement.

A particularly delightful local eccentricity is a treasure hunt for blown-glass floats that are "salted" in the landscape annually from October to Memorial Day by "float fairies." The tradition honors the original glass floats from fishing nets once found in abundance on the beaches and promotes local artists who now create them. Along with float hunts and kite flying, residents enjoy tide pooling, whale-watching, wave riding, antiquing in area shops and browsing the art glass studios. Siletz River and Siletz Bay are prime spots for crabbing, and clamming on the beach and bay is popular.

According to Beverly Cohen, a second-generation Floridian who moved to Lincoln City a number of years ago, the town's beauty and services stole her heart. "Retirees love it here because there is lots of art, loads of volunteer activities, the health care is good, the taxes are good, and it's gorgeous," she says.

The town has a community college, a hospital and an active arts scene with concerts and theater, along with entertainment at a casino resort. Lincoln City's seven miles of beach draw large summer crowds. While winter is quiet, storm-watching is popular, as fierce winds hurl high waves ashore. The area enjoys an ocean climate, but beware: Rainfall averages about 98 inches a year, most of it in the winter.

Population: 7,944

Climate:

	High	Low
January	47	37
July	70	51

Cost of living: Above average

Housing cost: The average sales price of single-family homes during the third quarter of 2007 was $322,639, according to John L. Scott Real Estate in Lincoln City.

Information: Lincoln City Chamber of Commerce, (541) 994-3070 or www.lcchamber.com.

Portland

Portland has a well-founded reputation for being progressive and diverse, which lends the city a welcoming spirit. Add in a healthy economy and a youthful vibe, and it's a great place to live for those seeking a Pacific Northwest retreat.

The Portland area offers an appealing combination of urban amenities set amid dramatic natural beauty. It's located on the Willamette River with the Cascade Range to the east and the Coast Ranges to the west. Portland has a vibrant, walkable downtown, a thriving arts scene and inspired restaurants. A well-executed public transportation system allows for a car-free lifestyle.

If there's not enough to keep you occupied in the city itself, you won't have to travel far to find more gorgeous scenery and outdoor pursuits. Portland is only 45 minutes from Mount Hood, 45 minutes from the Willamette Valley wine country, 50 minutes from the Columbia Gorge and about 90 minutes from the Oregon coast.

There are more than 4,000 restaurants in the area, with every type of food option imaginable, and inclusive neighborhoods give newcomers a real feeling of home. If you love the outdoors, there are parks, trails and green spaces scattered throughout the city, not to mention waterways for rafting, canoeing, kayaking, and fly-fishing. See world-class art at the Portland Art Museum or catch an NBA Trail Blazers game at the Rose Garden arena.

And while you might think that you'll be contending with rain year-round, Portland actually gets less rain than cities such as Atlanta and Seattle. Portland averages about 37 inches annually, most in the winter months.

Population: 537,081

Climate:

	High	Low
January	46	37
July	79	57

Cost of living: Above average

Housing cost: During the first half of 2007, the median sales price was $300,750 for existing homes and $372,400 for new homes, according to the Portland State University Center for Real Estate.

Information: Portland Oregon Visitors Association, (877) 678-5263 or www.pova.org.

PENNSYLVANIA

Pennsylvania has a state income tax and a state sales tax.

The state income tax rate is 3.07%. In calculating the tax, there is no deduction for federal income tax paid. Federal, state and private pensions are exempt. Social Security benefits are exempt.

Major tax credits or rebates include: credit for income taxes paid to other states, which our couples do not qualify for; and tax forgiveness credit, which one of our couples qualifies for.

The state sales tax rate is 6% but local governments can add to this amount.

Our couples relocating to the cities listed below must pay a registration fee of $36 per automobile, a lien fee of $5 per automobile and a title fee of $23 per automobile at the time of registration. Those who are retired and have total annual income of less than $19,200 qualify for a $10 registration fee, in lieu of the $36 registration fee. Our couples do not qualify for this reduced fee. Thereafter, on an annual basis, our couples will pay a registration fee per automobile.

East Stroudsburg

East Stroudsburg has a local income tax but does not levy an additional sales tax.

The local income city wage tax rate is 1% of wages, salaries and self-employ-

ment income. In addition, there is an emergency and municipal services tax of $52 per wage earner if the individual earnings are $12,000 or more.

Most purchases are taxed at the state rate of 6%. Major consumer categories taxed at a different rate: none. Major consumer categories that are exempt from sales tax include: apparel and services, drugs, groceries, medical services and medical supplies.

Within the East Stroudsburg city limit, the property tax rate is .15996. Homes are assessed at 25% of market value. There is a property tax rebate of up to $650 for homeowners age 65 or older with gross income of less than $35,000 (excluding 50% of their Social Security income). Property tax does not cover garbage pickup.

East Stroudsburg has no personal property tax for individuals.

Lancaster

Lancaster has a local income tax but does not levy an additional sales tax.

The local income city wage tax rate is

1.1% of wages, salaries and self-employment income for residents and 0% of wages, salaries and self-employment income for nonresidents who work inside the Lancaster city limits. In addition, there is an emergency and municipal services tax of $52 per wage earner if the individual earnings are $12,000 or more.

Most purchases are taxed at the state rate of 6%. Major consumer categories taxed at a different rate: none. Major consumer categories that are exempt from sales tax include: apparel and services, drugs, groceries, medical services and medical supplies.

Within the Lancaster city limit, the property tax rate is .031572. Homes are assessed at 100% of market value. There is a property tax rebate of up to $650 for homeowners age 65 or older with gross income of less than $35,000 (excluding 50% of their Social Security income). Property tax does not cover garbage pickup.

Lancaster has no personal property tax for individuals.

Philadelphia

Philadelphia has a local income tax and a sales tax.

The local income tax rate is 4.301% of wages, salaries and self-employment income for residents and 3.7716% of

PENNSYLVANIA TAX TABLE

Instructions

1. Find the Income in the far left column closest to your anticipated retirement income.
2. Find the Home Value closest to the value of the home where you will live in retirement.
3. Follow that row to your estimated Total Tax Burden at age 65 and beyond.

Income	Home Value	Property Tax & Other Fees	Personal Property Tax & Auto Fees	Sales Tax	Local Income Tax	State Income Tax	Total Tax Burden	Rank*
EAST STROUDSBURG								
$30,000	$125,000	$4,929	$72	$702	$56	-	$5,759	173 of 173 Ψ
	150,000	5,929	72	702	56	-	6,759	173 of 173 Ψ
	175,000	6,928	72	702	56	-	7,758	173 of 173 Ψ
$60,000	$150,000	$6,179	$72	$1,212	$291	$877	$8,631	203 of 203 Ψ
	225,000	9,178	72	1,212	291	877	11,630	203 of 203 Ψ
	300,000	12,177	72	1,212	291	877	14,629	203 of 203 Ψ
$90,000	$225,000	$9,178	$72	$1,514	$568	$1,717	$13,049	203 of 203 Ψ
	375,000	15,176	72	1,514	568	1,717	19,047	203 of 203 Ψ
	525,000	21,175	72	1,514	568	1,717	25,046	203 of 203 Ψ

Income	Home Value	Property Tax & Other Fees	Personal Property Tax & Auto Fees	Sales Tax	Local Income Tax	State Income Tax	Total Tax Burden	Rank*
LANCASTER								
$30,000	$125,000	$3,877	$72	$702	$62	-	$4,713	169 of 173 Ψ
	150,000	4,666	72	702	62	-	5,502	169 of 173 Ψ
	175,000	5,455	72	702	62	-	6,291	169 of 173 Ψ
$60,000	$150,000	$4,916	$72	$1,212	$314	$877	$7,391	201 of 203 Ψ
	225,000	7,284	72	1,212	314	877	9,759	201 of 203 Ψ
	300,000	9,652	72	1,212	314	877	12,127	200 of 203 Ψ
$90,000	$225,000	$7,284	$72	$1,514	$615	$1,717	$11,202	197 of 203 Ψ
	375,000	12,020	72	1,514	615	1,717	15,938	198 of 203 Ψ
	525,000	16,755	72	1,514	615	1,717	20,673	199 of 203 Ψ
PHILADELPHIA								
$60,000	$150,000	$3,967	$72	$1,414	$1,050	$877	$7,380	200 of 203 Ψ
	225,000	5,950	72	1,414	1,050	877	9,363	198 of 203 Ψ
	300,000	7,933	72	1,414	1,050	877	11,346	198 of 203 Ψ
$90,000	$225,000	$5,950	$72	$1,767	$2,033	$1,717	$11,539	198 of 203 Ψ
	375,000	9,917	72	1,767	2,033	1,717	15,506	197 of 203 Ψ
	525,000	13,884	72	1,767	2,033	1,717	19,473	197 of 203 Ψ
	$600,000	$15,867	$72	$1,767	$2,033	$1,717	$21,456	30 of 30
	750,000	19,834	72	1,767	2,033	1,717	25,423	30 of 30
	900,000	23,800	72	1,767	2,033	1,717	29,389	30 of 30
PITTSBURGH								
$30,000	$125,000	$4,169	$72	$819	$56	-	$5,116	170 of 173 Ψ
	150,000	5,067	72	819	56	-	6,014	172 of 173 Ψ
	175,000	5,965	72	819	56	-	6,912	172 of 173 Ψ
$60,000	$150,000	$5,317	$72	$1,414	$343	$877	$8,023	202 of 203 Ψ
	225,000	8,011	72	1,414	343	877	10,717	202 of 203 Ψ
	300,000	10,704	72	1,414	343	877	13,410	202 of 203 Ψ
$90,000	$225,000	$8,011	$72	$1,767	$568	$1,717	$12,135	201 of 203 Ψ
	375,000	13,398	72	1,767	568	1,717	17,522	202 of 203 Ψ
	525,000	18,786	72	1,767	568	1,717	22,910	202 of 203 Ψ

*There are 203 cities in this book, 30 of which have higher than average home prices. We have estimated taxes for a tier of higher home values (and omitted the lowest tier) for these 30 cities. The city with the lowest tax burden for an income/home value combination is given the #1 rating; the higher the rating, the higher the total tax burden.

wages, salaries and self-employment income for nonresidents who work inside the Philadelphia city limits. Philadelphia also has a school income tax, which applies to unearned income including certain types of interest and dividends. The rate is 4.301%.

Most purchases are taxed at a rate of 7%. Major consumer categories taxed at a different rate: none. Major consumer categories that are exempt from sales tax include: apparel and services, drugs, groceries, medical services and medical supplies.

Within the Philadelphia city limit, the property tax rate is .08264. Homes are assessed at 32% of market value. There is a property tax rebate of up to $650 for homeowners age 65 or older with a gross income of less than $35,000 (excluding 50% of their Social Security income). Property tax includes garbage pickup.

Pittsburgh

Pittsburgh has a local income tax and a sales tax.

The local income tax rate is 1% of wages, salaries and self-employment income for those who work in the Baldwin Borough area of Greater Pittsburgh. In addition, there is an emergency and municipal services tax of $52 per wage earner if the individual earnings are $5,200 or more.

Most purchases are taxed at a rate of 7%. Major consumer categories taxed at a different rate: none. Major consumer categories that are exempt from sales tax include: apparel and services, drugs, groceries, medical services, and medical supplies.

Within the Baldwin Borough area of Greater Pittsburgh, the property tax rate is .035916. New homes are assessed at 100% of market value. There is a property tax rebate of up to $650 for homeowners age 65 or older with gross income of less than $35,000 (excluding 50% of their Social Security income). There is also a homestead exclusion of $15,000 off the assessed value for the county components of the property tax rate for those who meet residency requirements. There is an additional senior citizen property tax relief for those residents 60 or older who have lived in the county for 10 years or more. Property tax includes garbage pickup.

Pittsburgh has no personal property tax for individuals.

Lancaster

Lancaster was the capital of the United States — for one day. That was in 1777, when the Brits chased the Continental Congress out of Philadelphia and the founders paused for a short session before heading for safer territory. The area saw more action in the lead-up to the Civil War.

All is calm now, with the peaceful clop-clop-clop of Amish horses and buggies replacing the militant rattle of muskets. But people are still fleeing from Philadelphia — as well as from Baltimore and Washington, DC — to Lancaster for the pastoral setting that takes them out of the bustle but keeps them within easy reach of metropolitan amenities.

Lancaster is a pleasant place to live.

It's in rolling farm country about 90 minutes from Baltimore and Philadelphia, two hours from Washington and two and a half hours from New York City. It's in Amish and Mennonite (Pennsylvania Dutch) country, which is about as far from metropolitan life as you can imagine.

There are a number of historical sites and neighborhoods with brick sidewalks and Colonial architecture that reflect the town's heritage. The serene rural area of Lancaster County has several communities popular with retirees. On the cultural side, the area offers live theater, concerts, museums and art shows.

An added attraction is Lancaster General Hospital, which has earned recognition as one of the country's top hospitals. The nonprofit hospital has been cited as a leader in several fields, among them heart care, and is strong in geriatric services. Besides the main facility, it has a women's hospital, a rehabilitation hospital and a number of clinics in the area.

Population: 54,779

Climate:

	High	Low
January	37	21
July	85	64

Cost of living: Above average

Housing cost: The average sales price of single-family homes during the first nine months of 2007 was $194,825, according to the Lancaster County Association of Realtors.

Information: Lancaster Chamber of Commerce and Industry, (717) 397-3531 or www.lcci.com.

RHODE ISLAND

Rhode Island has a state income tax and a state sales tax.

There are two methods that can be used to calculate income tax in Rhode Island. The state income tax rate using the alternative flat rate is 8% of federal adjusted gross income. Filers may use this method of calculating their tax liability if it is advantageous for them to do so.

The state income tax rate using the standard method is graduated from 3.75% to 9.9% depending upon income bracket. For married couples filing jointly, the rates are 3.75% on the first $51,200 of taxable income; 7% on the next $72,500 of taxable income; 7.75% on the next $64,750 of taxable income; 9% on the next $148,100 of taxable income; and 9.9% on taxable income above $336,550.

In calculating the tax using the standard method, there is no deduction for federal income tax paid. Federal, state and private pensions are not exempt. Social Security benefits subject to federal tax are not exempt. There is a standard deduction of $10,600 from adjust-

ed gross income for married couples filing jointly when both are age 65 or older. There is a personal exemption of $3,300 per person from adjusted gross income.

Major tax credits or rebates include: credit for income taxes paid to other states, which our couples do not qualify for; and property tax relief credit, which one of our couples qualifies for.

The state sales tax rate is 7%.

Providence

Providence has no local income tax and does not levy an additional sales tax.

Most purchases are taxed at the state rate of 7%. Major consumer categories taxed at a different rate: food away from home, which is taxed at a rate of 8%. Major consumer categories that are exempt from sales tax include: medical services, drugs, groceries, apparel and services.

Within the Providence city limits, the property tax rate is .03023. Homes are assessed at 100% of market value. There is a homestead deduction of 50% off assessed value available to all homeowners and an elderly exemption of $15,000 off assessed value available to homeowners age 65 or older who collect Social Security and have been residents of the city for at least three years. Property tax includes garbage pickup.

Providence has no personal property tax for individuals; however, it does have an excise tax on vehicles, which is essentially the same as the personal property tax in several other states. The tax rate is .07678 and is assessed on 100% of the NADA current market value less the phase-out value of $6,000.

Our couples relocating to Providence must pay a registration fee of $62 per automobile that covers registration for a two-year period and a title fee of $27 per automobile. Thereafter, every two years, our couples will pay a registration fee per automobile.

RHODE ISLAND TAX TABLE

Instructions

1. Find the Income in the far left column closest to your anticipated retirement income.
2. Find the Home Value closest to the value of the home where you will live in retirement.
3. Follow that row to your estimated Total Tax Burden at age 65 and beyond.

Income	Home Value	Property Tax & Other Fees	Personal Property Tax & Auto Fees	Sales Tax	Local Income Tax	State Income Tax†	Total Tax Burden	Rank*
PROVIDENCE								
$30,000	$125,000	$1,436	$1,521	$821	-	-	$3,778	157 of 173
	150,000	1,814	1,521	821	-	(14)	4,142	154 of 173
	175,000	2,192	1,521	821	-	(300)	4,234	142 of 173
$60,000	$150,000	$1,814	$1,521	$1,489	-	$1,204	$6,028	188 of 203
	225,000	2,947	1,521	1,489	-	1,204	7,161	178 of 203
	300,000	4,081	1,521	1,489	-	1,204	8,295	172 of 203
$90,000	$225,000	$2,947	$1,521	$1,867	-	$3,148	$9,483	184 of 203
	375,000	5,215	1,521	1,867	-	3,148	11,751	180 of 203
	525,000	7,482	1,521	1,867	-	3,148	14,018	171 of 203

†Property tax relief is issued as a reduction of income tax due or as a refund if the credit is greater than the tax liability.
*There are 203 cities in this book, 30 of which have higher than average home prices. We have estimated taxes for a tier of higher home values (and omitted the lowest tier) for these 30 cities. The city with the lowest tax burden for an income/home value combination is given the #1 rating; the higher the rating, the higher the total tax burden.

SOUTH CAROLINA

South Carolina has a state income tax and a state sales tax.

The state income tax rate is graduated from 2.5% to 7% depending upon income bracket. For married couples filing jointly, the rates are 2.5% on the first $2,570 of taxable income; 3% on the next $2,570 of taxable income; 4% on the next $2,570 of taxable income; 5% on the next $2,570 of taxable income; 6% on the next $2,570 of taxable income; and 7% on taxable income above $12,850. In 2007, the 2.5% rate changes to 0%. There is an optional flat rate of 6.5% for trade or business income from a sole proprietorship or partnership.

In calculating the tax, there is no deduction for federal income tax paid. Federal, state and private pension income is not exempt. However, there is a retirement income deduction of up to $10,000 per resident age 65 or older. Social Security benefits are exempt. There is an age deduction of up to $15,000 per resident if age 65 or older; this deduction is reduced by any retirement deduction claimed by each person. Fifty percent of self-employment tax per the federal return is deductible from business income.

Major tax credits or rebates include: credit for income taxes paid to other states, which our couples do not qualify for; and two wage-earner credit when both spouses work, which our couples do qualify for.

The state sales tax rate is 5%, but local governments can add to this amount.

Our couples relocating to the cities listed below must pay a $20 registration fee (which is the senior citizen rate) to register each automobile and a $15 title fee per automobile. Thereafter, every two years, our couples will pay a renewal fee per automobile.

Aiken

Aiken has no local income tax but does levy a sales tax.

Most purchases are taxed at a rate of 6%. However, persons age 85 or older qualify for a reduced rate of 5%. Major consumer categories taxed at a different rate: groceries, which are taxed at a rate of 5%. The rate for groceries decreases to 3% on October 1, 2006, and to 0% on November 1, 2007. Major consumer categories that are exempt from sales tax include: drugs and medical services.

Within the city limits of Aiken, the property tax rate is .2962. Homes are assessed at 4% of market value. There is a homestead deduction of $50,000 off market value for homeowners age 65 or older who have been residents for one year. We've assumed that our couples qualify for this exemption. There is a $100,000 exemption off market value for a portion of the school operations levy after the homestead deduction has been taken, which effectively lowers the total property tax rate in Aiken to .2144 for the first $100,000 of a home's market value. Property tax does not cover garbage pickup.

Aiken has a personal property tax rate of .2962. Personal property is assessed at 6% of market value. Items subject to the tax include vehicles.

Beaufort

Beaufort has no local income tax but does levy an additional sales tax.

Most purchases are taxed at a rate of 6%. However, persons age 85 or older qualify for a reduced rate of 5%. Major consumer categories taxed at a different rate: groceries, which are taxed at a rate of 5%. The rate for groceries decreases to 3% on October 1, 2006, and to 0% on November 1, 2007. Major consumer categories that are exempt from sales tax include: drugs and medical services.

Within the city limits of Beaufort, the property tax rate is .2106. Homes are assessed at 4% of market value. There is a homestead deduction of $50,000 off market value for homeowners age 65 or older who have been residents for one year. We've assumed that our couples qualify for this exemption. There is a $100,000 exemption off market value for a portion of the school operations levy after the homestead deduction has been taken, which effectively lowers the total property tax rate in Beaufort to .1354 for the first $100,000 of a home's market value. Property tax does not cover garbage pickup.

Beaufort has a personal property tax rate of .2106. Most personal property is assessed at 10.5% of market value. Items subject to the tax include vehicles.

Charleston

Charleston has no local income tax but does levy a sales tax.

Most purchases are taxed at a rate of 6%. However, persons age 85 or older qualify for a reduced rate of 5%. Major consumer categories taxed at a different rate: groceries, which are taxed at a rate of 5%. The rate for groceries decreases to 3% on October 1, 2006, and to 0% on November 1, 2007. Major consumer categories that are exempt from sales tax include: drugs and medical services.

Within the city limits of Charleston, the property tax rate is .2366. Homes are assessed at 4% of market value. There is a homestead deduction of $50,000 off market value for homeowners age 65 or older who have been residents for one year. We've assumed that our couples qualify for this exemption. There is a $100,000 exemption off market value for a portion of the school operations levy after the homestead deduction has been taken, which effectively lowers the total property tax rate in Charleston to .1637 for the first $100,000 of a home's market value. There is a local option sales tax (LOST) credit of .094% of the home's market value after homestead deduction against the county component of property tax and a credit of .09% of market value after homestead deduction against the city component of property tax. Property tax includes a garbage pickup fee of $89 per year.

Charleston has a personal property tax rate of .2366. Personal property

○ **Tax Heavens:** Beaufort, Charleston, Clemson, Hilton Head, Myrtle Beach
ᴪ **Tax Hells:** None
Top Retirement Towns: Aiken, Beaufort, Charleston, Greenville, Hilton Head, Myrtle Beach

SOUTH CAROLINA TAX TABLE

Instructions

1. Find the Income in the far left column closest to your anticipated retirement income.
2. Find the Home Value closest to the value of the home where you will live in retirement.
3. Follow that row to your estimated Total Tax Burden at age 65 and beyond.

Income	Home Value	Property Tax & Other Fees	Personal Property Tax & Auto Fees	Sales Tax	Local Income Tax	State Income Tax	Total Tax Burden	Rank*
AIKEN								
$30,000	$125,000	$823	$571	$882	-	-	$2,276	49 of 173
	150,000	1,038	571	882	-	-	2,491	50 of 173
	175,000	1,334	571	882	-	-	2,787	55 of 173
$60,000	$150,000	$1,038	$571	$1,505	-	-	$3,114	17 of 203
	225,000	1,926	571	1,505	-	-	4,002	29 of 203
	300,000	2,815	571	1,505	-	-	4,891	44 of 203
$90,000	$225,000	$1,926	$571	$1,851	-	$767	$5,115	25 of 203
	375,000	3,703	571	1,851	-	767	6,892	38 of 203
	525,000	5,481	571	1,851	-	767	8,670	53 of 203
BEAUFORT								
$30,000	$125,000	$586	$706	$882	-	-	$2,174	40 of 173
	150,000	722	706	882	-	-	2,310	35 of 173
	175,000	932	706	882	-	-	2,520	35 of 173
$60,000	$150,000	$722	$706	$1,505	-	-	$2,933	10 of 203 O
	225,000	1,353	706	1,505	-	-	3,564	11 of 203
	300,000	1,985	706	1,505	-	-	4,196	15 of 203
$90,000	$225,000	$1,353	$706	$1,851	-	$767	$4,677	19 of 203
	375,000	2,617	706	1,851	-	767	5,941	16 of 203
	525,000	3,881	706	1,851	-	767	7,205	21 of 203
CHARLESTON								
$30,000	$125,000	$442	$460	$882	-	-	$1,784	15 of 173
	150,000	560	460	882	-	-	1,902	13 of 173
	175,000	750	460	882	-	-	2,092	14 of 173
$60,000	$150,000	$560	$460	$1,505	-	-	$2,525	3 of 203 O
	225,000	1,132	460	1,505	-	-	3,097	3 of 203 O
	300,000	1,703	460	1,505	-	-	3,668	6 of 203 O
$90,000	$225,000	$1,132	$460	$1,851	-	$767	$4,210	9 of 203 O
	375,000	2,275	460	1,851	-	767	5,353	9 of 203 O
	525,000	3,419	460	1,851	-	767	6,497	12 of 203
CLEMSON								
$30,000	$125,000	$628	$505	$882	-	-	$2,015	29 of 173
	150,000	777	505	882	-	-	2,164	26 of 173
	175,000	996	505	882	-	-	2,383	27 of 173
$60,000	$150,000	$777	$505	$1,505	-	-	$2,787	6 of 203 O
	225,000	1,434	505	1,505	-	-	3,444	9 of 203 O
	300,000	2,091	505	1,505	-	-	4,101	11 of 203
$90,000	$225,000	$1,434	$505	$1,851	-	$767	$4,557	15 of 203
	375,000	2,748	505	1,851	-	767	5,871	15 of 203
	525,000	4,062	505	1,851	-	767	7,185	20 of 203
GREENVILLE								
$30,000	$125,000	$952	$1,036	$757	-	-	$2,745	93 of 173
	150,000	1,198	1,036	757	-	-	2,991	87 of 173
	175,000	1,510	1,036	757	-	-	3,303	87 of 173

*There are 203 cities in this book, 30 of which have higher than average home prices. We have estimated taxes for a tier of higher home values (and omitted the lowest tier) for these 30 cities. The city with the lowest tax burden for an income/home value combination is given the #1 rating; the higher the rating, the higher the total tax burden.

Income	Home Value	Property Tax & Other Fees	Personal Property Tax & Auto Fees	Sales Tax	Local Income Tax	State Income Tax	Total Tax Burden	Rank*
GREENVILLE continued								
$60,000	$150,000	$1,198	$1,036	$1,284	-	-	$3,518	39 of 203
	225,000	2,134	1,036	1,284	-	-	4,454	54 of 203
	300,000	3,071	1,036	1,284	-	-	5,391	72 of 203
$90,000	$225,000	$2,134	$1,036	$1,576	-	$767	$5,513	36 of 203
	375,000	4,008	1,036	1,576	-	767	7,387	57 of 203
	525,000	5,881	1,036	1,576	-	767	9,260	65 of 203
HILTON HEAD								
$60,000	$150,000	$600	$607	$1,531	-	-	$2,738	5 of 203 O
	225,000	1,141	607	1,531	-	-	3,279	6 of 203 O
	300,000	1,682	607	1,531	-	-	3,820	8 of 203 O
$90,000	$225,000	$1,141	$607	$1,883	-	$767	$4,398	11 of 203
	375,000	2,223	607	1,883	-	767	5,480	10 of 203 O
	525,000	3,305	607	1,883	-	767	6,562	13 of 203
	$600,000	$3,846	$607	$1,883	-	$767	$7,103	5 of 30
	750,000	4,928	607	1,883	-	767	8,185	5 of 30
	900,000	6,009	607	1,883	-	767	9,266	5 of 30
MYRTLE BEACH								
$30,000	$125,000	$668	$472	$882	-	-	$2,022	31 of 173
	150,000	830	472	882	-	-	2,184	28 of 173
	175,000	1,073	472	882	-	-	2,427	30 of 173
$60,000	$150,000	$830	$472	$1,505	-	-	$2,807	8 of 203 O
	225,000	1,559	472	1,505	-	-	3,536	10 of 203 O
	300,000	2,288	472	1,505	-	-	4,265	19 of 203
$90,000	$225,000	$1,559	$472	$1,851	-	$767	$4,649	16 of 203
	375,000	3,017	472	1,851	-	767	6,107	21 of 203
	525,000	4,475	472	1,851	-	767	7,565	27 of 203

*There are 203 cities in this book, 30 of which have higher than average home prices. We have estimated taxes for a tier of higher home values (and omitted the lowest tier) for these 30 cities. The city with the lowest tax burden for an income/home value combination is given the #1 rating; the higher the rating, the higher the total tax burden.

such as airplanes, most boats and most RVs is assessed at 10.5% of depreciated value. Personal property such as automobiles is assessed at 6% of depreciated value.

Clemson

Clemson has no local income tax but does levy a sales tax.

Most purchases are taxed at a rate of 6%. However, persons age 85 or older qualify for a reduced rate of 5%. Major consumer categories taxed at a different rate: groceries, which are taxed at a rate of 5%. The rate for groceries decreases to 3% on October 1, 2006, and to 0% on November 1, 2007. Major consumer categories that are exempt from sales tax include: drugs and medical services.

Within the city limits of Clemson, the property tax rate is .275. Homes are assessed at 4% of market value if owner-occupied. There is a homestead deduction of $50,000 off market value for homeowners age 65 or older who have been residents for one year. We've assumed that our couples qualify for this exemption. There is a $100,000 exemption off market value for a portion of the school operations levy after the homestead deduction has been taken, which effectively lowers the total property tax rate in Clemson to .2052 for the first $100,000 of a home's market value. There is a local option sales tax (LOST) credit of .1% of the home's market value after homestead deduction against the county component of property tax and a credit of .1239% of market value after homestead deduction against the city component of property tax. Property tax does not cover garbage pickup.

Clemson has a personal property tax rate of .275. Personal property such as boats and watercraft is assessed at 10.5% of depreciated value. Personal property such as automobiles is assessed at 6% of depreciated value.

Greenville

Greenville has no local income tax and does not levy an additional sales tax.

Most purchases are taxed at the state rate of 5%. However, persons age 85 or older qualify for a reduced rate of 4%. Major consumer categories taxed at a different rate: none. The rate for groceries decreases to 3% on October 1, 2006, and to 0% on November 1, 2007. Major consumer categories that are exempt from sales tax include: drugs and medical services.

Within the city limits of Greenville, the property tax rate is .3122. Homes are assessed at 4% of market value. There is a homestead deduction of

$50,000 off market value for homeowners age 65 or older who have been residents for one year. We've assumed that our couples qualify for this exemption. There is a $100,000 exemption off market value for a portion of the school operations levy after the homestead deduction has been taken, which effectively lowers the total property tax rate in Greenville to .24545 for the first $100,000 of a home's market value. Property tax does not cover garbage pickup. There is also a stormwater fee of approximately $36 per year.

Greenville has a personal property tax rate of .3122. Personal property is assessed at 10.5% of market value. Items subject to the tax include vehicles.

Hilton Head

Hilton Head has no local income tax but does levy a sales tax.

Most purchases are taxed at a rate of 6%. However, persons age 85 or older qualify for a reduced rate of 5%. Major consumer categories taxed at a different rate: groceries, which are taxed at a rate of 5%, and food away from home, which is taxed at a rate of 7%. The rate for groceries decreases to 3% on October 1, 2006, and to 0% on November 1, 2007. Major consumer categories that are exempt from sales tax include: drugs and medical services.

In tax district 510 of Hilton Head, the property tax rate is .1803. Homes are assessed at 4% of market value. There is a homestead deduction of $50,000 off market value for homeowners age 65 or older who have been residents for one year. We've assumed that our couples qualify for this exemption. There is a $100,000 exemption off market value for a portion of the school operations levy after the homestead deduction has been taken, which effectively lowers the total property tax rate in Hilton Head to .1051 for the first $100,000 of a home's market value. Property tax does not cover garbage pickup.

Hilton Head has a personal property tax rate of .1803. Most personal property is assessed at 10.5% of market value. Items subject to the tax include automobiles.

Myrtle Beach

Myrtle Beach has no local income tax but does levy a sales tax.

Most purchases are taxed at a rate of 6%. However, persons age 85 or older qualify for a reduced rate of 5%. Major consumer categories taxed at a different rate: groceries, which are taxed at a rate of 5%. The rate for groceries decreases to 3% on October 1, 2006, and to 0% on November 1, 2007. Major consumer categories that are exempt from sales tax include: drugs and medical services.

Within the city limits of Myrtle Beach, the property tax rate is .243. Homes are assessed at 4% of market value. There is a homestead deduction of $50,000 off market value for homeowners age 65 or older who have been residents for one year. We've assumed that our couples qualify for this exemption. There is a $100,000 exemption off market value for a portion of the school operations levy after the homestead deduction has been taken, which effectively lowers the total property tax rate in Myrtle Beach to .162525 for the first $100,000 of a home's market value. Property tax does not cover garbage pickup.

Myrtle Beach has a personal property tax rate of .243. Personal property is assessed at 6% of market value. Items subject to the tax include automobiles.

• South Carolina's Top Retirement Towns •

Aiken

The adage adopted by Aiken that "you can have it all" may just be true. Certainly its warm climate, rich history and thriving equestrian scene give residents the feeling that they live in a special area. And a below-average cost of living is a nice bonus.

First explored by Hernando de Soto and later a Confederate stronghold, Aiken became a winter colony for wealthy Northerners at the turn of the last century, a place where they could indulge in horse racing, foxhunting and polo.

The horsey community projects the same atmosphere that attracted visitors in previous centuries, and horse racing and polo remain an integral part of the scene. The city has a graceful Southern charm with historic mansions and tree-lined streets inviting shoppers to browse the many boutiques and stores.

Now also a retirement haven, the area offers a mixture of amenities to suit varying interests and needs. The University of South Carolina Aiken has an extensive continuing-education program, with enrichment courses and a variety of classes and programs for seniors in its Academy for Lifelong Learning. Its SeniorNet center focuses on building computer skills.

Aiken has a number of golf courses but also is only a short distance from Augusta, across the Savannah River in Georgia, home of the famed Masters Tournament at Augusta National Golf Club. It's also close to J. Strom Thurmond Lake, a major recreational area. Aiken Regional Medical Centers is a 230-bed, acute-care facility with services that include cardiovascular and cancer institutes.

Population: 28,829

Climate: High Low

	High	Low
January	58	33
July	94	70

Cost of living: Below average

Housing cost: The median price was $152,500 during the first half of 2007, according to the South Carolina Association of Realtors.

Information: Greater Aiken Chamber of Commerce, (803) 641-1111 or www.aikenchamber.net.

Beaufort

You saw Beaufort in the famous 1980s movie "The Big Chill," set in this coastal town with its large homes amid big oak trees dripping Spanish moss and a feeling life moved like molasses. This is the Lowcountry of legends, slow-paced but not lethargic, historic but full of good food and fun times.

Though not on the Atlantic Ocean, it's on an inlet with marshlands, perfect for those who enjoy boating, fishing, swimming or even watching wildlife that congregates here. It's about an hour north of Savannah, GA, and a little longer south of Charleston, SC, so you're near the multiple cultural advantages of both those larger cities.

African-American, Spanish, early American and West Indies influences meld here, contributing to colorful festivals and flavorful seasonings for the bounty of seafood.

If you're not the type to swing in a hammock, sip tea and read a book, you can kayak, explore museums and historic homes, enjoy a concert at the University of South Carolina Beaufort Performing Arts Center or play golf. There's not a shortage of activities.

You can easily hop over to take advantage of Hilton Head Island, with its shopping, multiple golf courses and faster pace — and return to enjoy the quieter lifestyle here. Boat people, water sports aficionados and wildlife enthusiasts take to this area.

Population: 12,029

Climate: High Low

January   58   39

July   91   74

Cost of living: Below average

Housing cost: The median sales price of a single-family home during the first eight months of 2007 was $236,000, according to the South Carolina Association of Realtors.

Information: Beaufort Regional Chamber of Commerce, (800) 638-3525 or www.beaufortsc.org.

Charleston

History is what makes Charleston. This is a city with a historical pedigree that predates the founding of our country. Its citizens were reading the South's first newspaper when George Washington was born. It operated the nation's first regularly scheduled passenger train, presented the first opera and organized the first chamber of commerce.

Most of all, the city has preserved thousands of buildings from earlier eras, giving it a charming patina of age. It is also a quintessential Southern city, where the first shot of the Civil War was fired and whose Catfish Row inspired George Gershwin's "Porgy and Bess." Yet it has kept up with the times so that newcomers enjoy its traditions together with a mild climate and all the advantages of modern life.

Charleston is close to excellent beaches and has a large arts component, theater, music and good restaurants. The famous Spoleto Festival brings superb performing and visual arts programs to the city annually. Continuing-education opportunities are available at the College of Charleston's Center for Creative Retirement, which offers weekly lectures and group outings.

"There's a sense of community here that surprised me," says Jane McMackin, 56, who moved in 2001 from St. Paul, MN, to the Isle of Palms, a Charleston suburb. "I never felt I wasn't welcome. There's a real mix on the Isle of Palms — some who moved in, some long-term residents." The mayor, she says, is a longtime resident; newcomer McMackin serves on the city council.

Population: 107,845

Climate: High Low

January   57   42

July   89   77

Cost of living: Slightly below average

Housing cost: The median sales price for single-family homes during the first half of 2007 was $302,644, according to the Charleston Trident Association of Realtors.

Information: Charleston Area Convention and Visitor Bureau, (843) 853-8000 or www.charlestoncvb.com.

Greenville

In the rolling foothills of northwestern South Carolina, historic Greenville was founded in the 1770s as a trading post along the Reedy River. It basks in a green sweep of oaks, pine and hickory graced with colorful sprays of peach and azalea blossoms in springtime.

Greenville is located in a region that boomed in recent years as industries ranging from BMW to Michelin opened North American branches here. With the companies came sophisticated urbanites, many of whom settled permanently and helped transform Greenville.

Today, Greenville's revitalized Main Street is a tree-shaded shopping district with scores of restaurants, renowned art collections and a drugstore with a soda fountain and a general store, both dating to the 1880s.

The Peace Center for the Performing Arts is the venue for a varied playbill ranging from opera, symphony and ballet to comedy, Broadway shows and live theater. The West End Historic District, a once-neglected warehouse area, now brims with activity as the arts and entertainment center. The Greenville County Museum of Art and the Bob Jones University Museum & Gallery house impressive collections ranging from Andrew Wyeth to the old masters.

There are numerous public and private golf courses and several national forests and state parks in the area in addition to walking trails along the Reedy River and waterfalls downtown.

Exceptional medical facilities are available in the Greenville Hospital System University Medical Center, a major teaching-and-research network with several campuses in the area, and the Bon Secours St. Francis Health System, with acclaimed care at two major facilities. Greenville is surrounded by a dozen colleges and universities that provide a wealth of culture, and a number have special programs for seniors.

Population: 57,428

Climate: High Low

January   50   31

July   89   69

Cost of living: Below average

Housing cost: The median sales price of homes for the first half of 2007 was $147,000, according to data from the South Carolina Association of Realtors.

Information: Greater Greenville Chamber of Commerce, (866) 485-5262 or www.greenvillechamber.org. The City of Greenville, www.greatergreenville.com., and Visitors Center, (800) 717-0023.

Hilton Head Island

In the South Carolina Lowcountry, Hilton Head Island is a popular retirement destination and romantic beach town that gets 2.5 million visitors a year. But its year-round population is only about 34,000.

Golfers are in heaven with more than 20 courses on the island and additional ones nearby on the mainland. All of the beaches are public, and the protected ecosystem includes thick stands of tall pines and live oaks and nature preserves with abundant wildlife. The climate is semitropical, and the waters are warm.

The Spanish arrived here in 1521, and sugar-cane farming was established by the late 1600s. The area, overrun by Union troops in 1861, is rich in Civil War history. After the 1860s, the island remained rather isolated and quiet until the 1940s and '50s, when a master-planned resort development began. The aesthetically pleasing locale works hard to balance nature with building. Development requires the use of earth tones and plenty of landscaping and green space, and signage is subdued.

The town boasts a strong cultural arts scene, with a symphony orchestra and a performing arts center with exhibitions and Broadway productions. The Hilton Head Regional Medical Center has campuses on the island and at neighboring Bluffton on the mainland. Savannah, GA, 35 miles south, offers additional advanced medical care. The University of South Carolina Beaufort's campus at Bluffton has an Osher Lifelong Learning Institute and other enrichment programs.

Retirees can select among a variety of housing options, such as gated communities, active-adult developments, apartments, farms and historic homes. Sun City Hilton Head, an amenity-filled, active-adult community with about 8,900 homes planned, is located at Bluffton.

Population: 33,838 year-round residents, 150,000 during the peak summer months.

Climate:

	High	Low
January	58	37
July	88	73

Cost of living: Above average

Housing cost: The median sales price of a single-family home during the first nine months of 2007 was $356,000, according to the South Carolina Association of Realtors.

Information: Hilton Head Island-Bluffton Chamber of Commerce and Visitor and Convention Bureau, (800) 523-3373 or www.hiltonheadisland.org.

Myrtle Beach

With 60 miles of clean white sand at its doorstep, the beach is what Myrtle Beach is all about. It is a busy, sometimes boisterous resort town, brimming with attractions, recreational opportunities, some 2,000 restaurants, megashopping and a host of clubs and theaters that make for a vibrant nightlife.

Swimming, surfing, sailboarding, parasailing, shell collecting and moonlight strolling are popular beach activities. Boating and fishing are big, both offshore and along the Intracoastal Waterway, which connects to backwater streams and marshes typical of Lowcountry South Carolina. Surfcasting is often lucrative here, and there are eight fishing piers.

At last count there were more than 100 golf courses in the area, many of them championship links, clearly making golf the No. 1 sport along the Grand Strand, as the area is known. But there are nearly 200 tennis courts as well.

The extent of Myrtle Beach's nightlife might come as a surprise. In recent years nine theaters — most of them elaborate country-music complexes similar to those in Branson, MO, — have sprung up within stomping distance of the sand. Among them: the Carolina Opry, Dolly Parton's Dixie Stampede and, hottest of all, the Alabama Theatre, created by country supergroup Alabama, who performs there regularly. The grandest showplace, however, is The Palace, filling its 2,700 seats with the long-running hit Le Grande Cirque, featuring a cast of 50 world-class acrobats.

As for shopping, go directly to Barefoot Landing, a megacomplex meant to appear as a rustic fishing village on the Intracoastal Waterway in North Myrtle Beach. It features more than 100 retail, entertainment and dining outlets. The Alabama Theatre is located there, as is a House of Blues.

Population: 28,597

Climate:

	High	Low
January	57	34
July	91	71

Cost of living: Below average

Housing cost: The median sales price of homes during the first half of 2007 was $213,250, according to the Coastal Carolinas Association of Realtors.

Information: Myrtle Beach Area Convention and Visitors Bureau/Chamber of Commerce, (800) 356-3016 or www.myrtlebeachinfo.com.

SOUTH DAKOTA

South Dakota has no state income tax but does have a state sales tax.

The state sales tax rate is 4%, but local governments can add to this amount.

Sioux Falls

Sioux Falls has no local income tax but does levy a sales tax.

Most purchases are taxed at a rate of 5.92%. Major consumer categories taxed at a different rate include: food away from home, which is taxed at a rate of 6.92%. Major consumer categories that are exempt from sales tax include: drugs and medical services.

Within the city limits of Sioux Falls the property tax rate is .016516. Homes are assessed at 100% of market value,

but the Department of Revenue sets ratios to adjust the assessment for each county. The value in Minnehaha County is .897. There is an assessment freeze for the elderly and disabled that reduces the assessed value of property subject to certain income limitations. Property tax does not cover garbage pickup.

There is no personal property tax in Sioux Falls.

Our couples relocating to Sioux Falls are subject to an automobile excise tax, which is 3% of the purchase price and is paid when the vehicle is initially reg-

istered in the state. If a vehicle owner paid a sales or excise tax in another state when the automobile was purchased, the previously paid amount is deducted from the South Dakota excise tax due. We've assumed our couples have paid a tax greater than or equal to the South Dakota excise tax. Our couples will pay a $55 registration fee for the Explorer and a $42 registration fee for the Camry. They will also pay a $5 title transfer fee per automobile, a $5 lien fee per automobile, a $1 solid waste fee per automobile and a $16 wheel tax per automobile at the time of registration. Thereafter, on an annual basis, our couples will pay a registration fee, wheel tax and solid waste fee, per automobile.

SOUTH DAKOTA TAX TABLE

Instructions

1. Find the Income in the far left column closest to your anticipated retirement income.
2. Find the Home Value closest to the value of the home where you will live in retirement.
3. Follow that row to your estimated Total Tax Burden at age 65 and beyond.

Income	Home Value	Property Tax & Other Fees	Personal Property Tax & Auto Fees	Sales Tax	Local Income Tax	State Income Tax	Total Tax Burden	Rank*
SIOUX FALLS								
$30,000	$125,000	$2,032	$131	$910	-	-	$3,073	126 of 173
	150,000	2,402	131	910	-	-	3,443	121 of 173
	175,000	2,773	131	910	-	-	3,814	118 of 173
$60,000	$150,000	$2,402	$131	$1,546	-	-	$4,079	87 of 203
	225,000	3,513	131	1,546	-	-	5,190	107 of 203
	300,000	4,624	131	1,546	-	-	6,301	117 of 203
$90,000	$225,000	$3,513	$131	$1,898	-	-	$5,542	38 of 203
	375,000	5,736	131	1,898	-	-	7,765	73 of 203
	525,000	7,958	131	1,898	-	-	9,987	90 of 203

*There are 203 cities in this book, 30 of which have higher than average home prices. We have estimated taxes for a tier of higher home values (and omitted the lowest tier) for these 30 cities. The city with the lowest tax burden for an income/home value combination is given the #1 rating; the higher the rating, the higher the total tax burden.

TENNESSEE

Tennessee has no state earned income tax but does levy an interest and dividends tax. Tennessee has a state sales tax.

The state interest and dividends tax rate is 6%, and it applies to income from stocks, bonds and notes receivable. In calculating the tax, there is no deduction for federal income tax paid. Interest from CDs, savings accounts, money market accounts and credit union accounts is exempt from tax. Interest from bonds issued by the federal, Tennessee or a local government in Tennessee is exempt from tax. Interest from commercial paper maturing in six months or less is exempt from tax. Dividends from Tennessee or national banks, from state or federal savings and loans doing business in Tennessee, from credit unions, and from insurance companies licensed to do business in Tennessee are exempt from tax. There is a $2,500 exemption for married couples filing jointly. Married couples filing jointly with gross income of less than $27,000 are exempt from tax. We've assumed our couples do not owe interest and dividends tax.

Major tax credits or rebates: none.

The state sales tax amount is 7% but local governments can add to this amount.

Since car registration and renewal fees differ within the state, see city information for details.

Crossville

Crossville has no local income tax but does levy a sales tax.

Most purchases are taxed at a rate of 9.75%. Major consumer categories taxed at a different rate include: groceries, which are taxed at a rate of 8.75%. Major consumer categories that are exempt from sales tax include: drugs and medical services.

Within the city limits of Crossville, the property tax rate is .0234. Homes are assessed at 25% of market value. There is a property tax relief credit for homeowners age 65 or older with combined gross income of $24,000 or less. Property tax includes garbage pickup.

Crossville has no personal property tax for individuals.

Our couples relocating to Crossville must pay a license fee of $35 per automobile. Thereafter, on an annual basis, our couples will pay a license fee per automobile.

Knoxville

Knoxville has no local income tax but does levy a sales tax.

Most purchases are taxed at a rate of 9.25%. Major consumer categories taxed at a different rate include: groceries, which are taxed at a rate of 8.25%. Major consumer categories that are exempt from sales tax include: drugs and medical services.

Within the city limits of Knoxville, the property tax rate is .055. Homes are assessed at 25% of market value. There is a property tax relief credit for homeowners age 65 or older with combined gross income of $24,000 or less. Property tax includes garbage pickup.

Knoxville has no personal property tax for individuals.

Our couples relocating to Knoxville must pay a county wheel tax of $36 per automobile, a plate fee of $22 per automobile, a title fee of $5 per automobile and an issuance fee of $9 per automobile. Thereafter, on an annual basis, our couples will pay a renewal fee and a county wheel tax, per automobile.

Maryville

Maryville has no local income tax but does levy a sales tax.

Most purchases are taxed at a rate of 9.25%. Major consumer categories taxed at a different rate include: groceries, which are taxed at a rate of 8.25%. Major consumer categories that are exempt from sales tax include: drugs and medical services.

Within the city limits of Maryville, the property tax rate is .0413. Homes are assessed at 25% of market value. There

is a property tax relief credit for homeowners age 65 or older with combined gross income of $20,000 or less. Property tax includes garbage pickup. There is a stormwater fee of $48 per year.

Maryville has no personal property tax for individuals.

Our couples relocating to Maryville must pay a license fee of $35 per automobile. Thereafter, on an annual basis, our couples will pay a license fee per automobile.

Memphis

Memphis has no local income tax but does levy a sales tax.

Most purchases are taxed at a rate of 9.25%. Major consumer categories taxed at a different rate include: groceries, which are taxed at a rate of 8.25%. Major consumer categories that are exempt from sales tax include: drugs and medical services.

Within the city limits of Memphis, the property tax rate is .074732. Homes are assessed at 25% of appraised value. There is a property tax relief credit for homeowners age 65 or older with combined gross income of $24,000 or less. Property tax does not cover garbage pickup.

Memphis has no personal property tax for individuals.

Our couples relocating to Memphis must pay a registration fee of $24 per automobile, a title fee of $13 per automobile, a city fee of $30 per automobile and a county wheel tax of $50 per automobile. Thereafter, on an annual basis, our couples will pay a renewal fee, a city fee, a county wheel tax and processing fee, per automobile.

Paris

Paris has no local income tax but does levy a sales tax.

Most purchases are taxed at a rate of 9.25%. Major consumer categories taxed at a different rate include: groceries, which are taxed at a rate of 8.25%. Major consumer categories that are exempt from sales tax include: drugs and medical services.

Within the city limits of Paris, the

property tax rate is .0366. Homes are assessed at 25% of appraised value. There is a property tax relief credit for homeowners age 65 or older with combined gross income of $24,000 or less. Property tax does not cover garbage pickup.

Paris has no personal property tax for individuals.

Our couples relocating to Paris must pay a licensing fee of $22 per automobile, a title fee of $11 per automobile, a county wheel tax of $34 per automobile and a clerk fee of $3 per automobile. Thereafter, on an annual basis, our couples will pay a licensing fee, a county wheel tax and a clerk fee, per automobile.

TENNESSEE TAX TABLE

Instructions

1. Find the Income in the far left column closest to your anticipated retirement income.
2. Find the Home Value closest to the value of the home where you will live in retirement.
3. Follow that row to your estimated Total Tax Burden at age 65 and beyond.

Income	Home Value	Property Tax & Other Fees	Personal Property Tax & Auto Fees	Sales Tax	Local Income Tax	State Income Tax	Total Tax Burden	Rank*
CROSSVILLE								
$30,000	$125,000	$732	$48	$1,450	-	-	$2,230	42 of 173
	150,000	878	48	1,450	-	-	2,376	38 of 173
	175,000	1,024	48	1,450	-	-	2,522	36 of 173
$60,000	$150,000	$878	$48	$2,469	-	-	$3,395	31 of 203
	225,000	1,317	48	2,469	-	-	3,834	20 of 203
	300,000	1,755	48	2,469	-	-	4,272	20 of 203
$90,000	$225,000	$1,317	$48	$3,034	-	-	$4,399	12 of 203
	375,000	2,194	48	3,034	-	-	5,276	7 of 203 ○
	525,000	3,072	48	3,034	-	-	6,154	8 of 203 ○
KNOXVILLE								
$30,000	$125,000	$1,719	$120	$1,374	-	-	$3,213	139 of 173
	150,000	2,063	120	1,374	-	-	3,557	129 of 173
	175,000	2,406	120	1,374	-	-	3,900	124 of 173
$60,000	$150,000	$2,063	$120	$2,340	-	-	$4,523	128 of 203
	225,000	3,094	120	2,340	-	-	5,554	123 of 203
	300,000	4,125	120	2,340	-	-	6,585	125 of 203
$90,000	$225,000	$3,094	$120	$2,876	-	-	$6,090	72 of 203
	375,000	5,156	120	2,876	-	-	8,152	87 of 203
	525,000	7,219	120	2,876	-	-	10,215	97 of 203
MARYVILLE								
$30,000	$125,000	$1,338	$48	$1,374	-	-	$2,760	96 of 173
	150,000	1,597	48	1,374	-	-	3,019	91 of 173
	175,000	1,855	48	1,374	-	-	3,277	84 of 173
$60,000	$150,000	$1,597	$48	$2,340	-	-	$3,985	80 of 203
	225,000	2,371	48	2,340	-	-	4,759	75 of 203
	300,000	3,146	48	2,340	-	-	5,534	77 of 203
$90,000	$225,000	$2,371	$48	$2,876	-	-	$5,295	30 of 203
	375,000	3,920	48	2,876	-	-	6,844	36 of 203
	525,000	5,468	48	2,876	-	-	8,392	47 of 203
MEMPHIS								
$30,000	$125,000	$2,515	$212	$1,374	-	-	$4,101	163 of 173
	150,000	2,982	212	1,374	-	-	4,568	161 of 173
	175,000	3,450	212	1,374	-	-	5,036	159 of 173
$60,000	$150,000	$2,982	$212	$2,340	-	-	$5,534	180 of 203
	225,000	4,384	212	2,340	-	-	6,936	175 of 203
	300,000	5,785	212	2,340	-	-	8,337	173 of 203

Income	Home Value	Property Tax & Other Fees	Personal Property Tax & Auto Fees	Sales Tax	Local Income Tax	State Income Tax	Total Tax Burden	Rank*
MEMPHIS continued								
$90,000	$225,000	$4,384	$212	$2,876	-	-	$7,472	141 of 203
	375,000	7,186	212	2,876	-	-	10,274	158 of 203
	525,000	9,989	212	2,876	-	-	13,077	159 of 203
PARIS								
$30,000	$125,000	$1,324	$116	$1,374	-	-	$2,814	102 of 173
	150,000	1,553	116	1,374	-	-	3,043	93 of 173
	175,000	1,781	116	1,374	-	-	3,271	83 of 173
$60,000	$150,000	$1,553	$116	$2,340	-	-	$4,009	82 of 203
	225,000	2,239	116	2,340	-	-	4,695	70 of 203
	300,000	2,925	116	2,340	-	-	5,381	70 of 203
$90,000	$225,000	$2,239	$116	$2,876	-	-	$5,231	28 of 203
	375,000	3,611	116	2,876	-	-	6,603	30 of 203
	525,000	4,984	116	2,876	-	-	7,976	33 of 203

*There are 203 cities in this book, 30 of which have higher than average home prices. We have estimated taxes for a tier of higher home values (and omitted the lowest tier) for these 30 cities. The city with the lowest tax burden for an income/home value combination is given the #1 rating; the higher the rating, the higher the total tax burden.

• Tennessee's Top Retirement Towns •

Crossville

Situated on the Cumberland Plateau an hour west of the Smoky Mountains, Crossville has an inviting landscape of rolling valleys and lush forests laced with streams. Autumn is a gift to the eye, and most of the year the greens of fairways rule.

Crossville calls itself the golf capital of Tennessee and rewards players with 11 courses (200 holes on the Cumberland Plateau) and weather mild enough to tee off most of the year. Most courses incorporate such natural features as rock formations and mountain streams. Residents also enjoy quick getaways, as Nashville is 90 minutes west, Knoxville an hour east and Chattanooga two hours south of Crossville.

The Cumberland County Playhouse, a top regional theater, typically hosts three different productions each week. Anglers enjoy fishing for largemouth bass, bluegill and catfish in the many nearby lakes, and hikers head for the scenic paths of the Cumberland Trail State Park. The jewel of Ozone Falls State Natural Area is the 110-foot waterfall, originally used to power the county's first gristmill and sawmill.

Since Crossville is the home of the U.S. Chess Federation, the Cumberland County Chess Club holds meetings every Thursday that are open to players of any ability or age.

"Crossville is a beautiful, progressive, well-maintained city with warm, friendly people, and the climate is ideal," says Ed Morrow, 75, a U.S. Marine Corps retiree.

Outside Crossville, Fairfield Glade, a residential-resort community, spreads across 12,000 acres with five golf courses, 11 lakes, two marinas and horseback riding trails along with residences targeted to retirees.

Population: 10,840
Climate: High Low
January 44 26
July 84 65
Cost of living: Below average
Housing cost: The average sales price of a single-family home during the first half of 2007 was $159,835, according to the Knoxville Area Association of Realtors.
Information: Crossville-Cumberland County Chamber of Commerce, (877) 465-3861 or www.crossville-chamber.com.

Knoxville

This rapidly growing city, located in the broad valley on the Tennessee River between the Cumberland and Great Smoky mountain ranges, has much to offer retirees. Sporting enthusiasts have a variety of options, from cheering on the home teams of the University of Tennessee to the fast action of Knoxville Ice Bear pro hockey. Six national parks are within 90 miles of the city, and the temperate four-season climate brings vivid fall color, a brief winter and a long spring filled with azalea and dogwood blooms.

The surrounding area is steeped in Appalachian tradition, characterized by communities with a strong work ethic and family-centered residents who are respectful of nature. Knoxville boasts plenty of museums commemorating early pioneers, modern arts and entertainment and offers a historic district and tours of Civil War sites and plantations. Residents also enjoy seeing the countryside on trips by riverboat and steam train.

In addition to sports, the 26,000-student UT Knoxville hosts plays, symphony concerts and esteemed lecturers from around the country. Their popular Seniors for Creative Learning program offers a full schedule of classes on a semester basis.

The UT Medical Center is east Tennessee's leading research hospital. It has the area's only "level one" trauma center and specializes in heart, lung, vascular and cancer care. Other facilities include Baptist Hospital and Parkwest Medical Center, and there are a handful of dedicated senior health centers in the area.

The cost of living is low, and there's a full range of housing choices — from ritzy estate living to log cabins, townhouses and city condos.

Population: 182,337
Climate: High Low
January   47   30
July   87   68
Cost of living: Below average
Housing cost: The median sales price of existing homes during the first half of 2007 was $155,100, according to the National Association of Realtors.
Information: Knoxville Chamber, (865) 637-4550 or www.knoxvillechamber. com.

Maryville

The college town of Maryville was established in 1795 on the site of a protective fort. During the Civil War, the city received considerable damage from artillery fire. However, most of the historic buildings downtown have been restored and now house restaurants, shops and government offices.

One of the notable restorations is the Palace Theater, built in the late 1860s. Today it hosts entertainment, often by nationally known artists, ranging from bluegrass and folk music to jazz, children's plays and vintage movies. Outdoor concerts are a regular feature at the town's Theatre in the Park. And, Maryville College, a noted four-year liberal arts school, hosts various cultural and sporting events throughout the year.

Besides entertainment in Maryville, residents can take advantage of the many dining and cultural choices in Knoxville, 15 miles away. It has one of the oldest and finest regional symphony orchestras in the country and is home to the University of Tennessee, which adds more cultural and sports events and has classes for seniors.

Additionally, Dolly Parton's Dollywood, a theme park and theater for musical performances, is 35 miles away in Pigeon Forge.

Maryville affords easy access to the Great Smoky Mountains National Park, 520,000 acres of wilderness laced with more than 800 miles of scenic trails for hiking and horseback riding, plus lakes and rivers for fishing, swimming and kayaking.

The Maryville-Alcoa-Blount County Parks and Recreation Commission also offers a wide range of activities, including special programs for residents over 50. The town has parks, pools, tennis courts, gyms and outdoor pavilions. Maryville's Greenway Trail is also the site for the annual Foothills Fall Festival, a popular event.

The county's medical needs are served by Blount Memorial Hospital, a 334-bed facility with general and surgical services.

Population: 26,433
Climate: High Low
January   47   30
July   87   68
Cost of living: Below average
Housing cost: The average price was $197,631 during the first half of 2007, according to the Knoxville Area Association of Realtors.
Information: Blount County Chamber of Commerce, (865) 983-2241 or www. blountchamber.com.

Paris

According to local lore, when commissioners in the 1820s wanted to name their town after the French hero of the American Revolution but didn't know how to spell "Lafayette," they settled on Paris, figuring he must have come from there.

Today about the only thing the two cities have in common is their names — and their Eiffel Towers (although at 60 feet, the Tennessee version is dwarfed by the original, which tops 1,000 feet).

Retirees looking for the good life for

less can forget about congestion, smog and state income tax in this affordable, laid-back Southern town. The only buzz here is likely to come from the mosquitoes — or the occasional sighting of country-western great Hank Williams Jr., who calls this area home part of the time.

Surrounded by pine forests, beautiful farms and the lakes of the Tennessee Valley, Paris offers a wealth of recreation and activities. Cast for crappie and bass among the catches in Kentucky Lake, one of the world's largest manmade lakes with more than 2,000 miles of shoreline. Or bring binoculars to spy ducks and Canada geese winging into the 51,000-acre Tennessee National Wildlife Refuge for the winter.

Paris' annual "World's Biggest Fish Fry" each April lures more than 100,000 parade watchers and catfish lovers for fun events. Other draws include the Paris-Henry County Heritage Center, a 1916 Italianate mansion displaying the county's history and visiting exhibits.

Golfers have a choice of a half-dozen courses in the area, including rugged terrain at The Tennessean Golf Club and lakeside play at Paris Landing State Park. Three colleges are nearby, and the city's performing arts center books productions and concerts. For big-city entertainment, it's 121 miles to Nashville and 141 miles to Memphis.

The Henry County Medical Center has a 142-bed hospital, 174-bed long-term care center, a cancer center and emergency services.

Population: 9,981
Climate: High Low
January   44   24
July   89   66
Cost of living: Below average
Housing cost: The median sales price for a single-family home during the first half of 2007 was $124,800, according to the Tennessee Valley Association of Realtors.
Information: Paris-Henry County Chamber of Commerce, (800) 345-1103 or www.paristnchamber.com.

TEXAS

Texas has no state income tax but does have a state sales tax.

The state sales tax rate is 6.25% but local governments can add to this amount.

Since car registration and renewal fees differ within the state, see city information for details.

Austin

Austin has no local income tax but does levy a sales tax.

Most purchases are taxed at 8.25%. Major consumer categories taxed at a different rate: none. Major consumer categories that are exempt from sales tax include: drugs, groceries and medical services.

Within the Enfield area of Austin, the property tax rate is .025254. Homes are assessed at 100% of market value. There are various exemptions off the city, community college, county and school district portions of the property tax. Property tax does not cover garbage pickup.

Austin has no personal property tax for individuals.

Our couples relocating to Austin must pay a registration fee of $59 per automobile, a title fee of $33 per automobile, a new resident fee of $90 per automobile, a road and bridge fee of $10 per automobile, an automation fee of $1 per automobile, a child safety fee of $2 per automobile and an insurance fee of $1 per automobile at the time of registration. Thereafter, on an annual basis, our couples will pay a registration fee, a county road and bridge fee, an automation fee, a child safety fee and an insurance fee, per automobile.

Boerne

Boerne has no local income tax but does levy a sales tax.

Most purchases are taxed at a rate of 8.25%. Major consumer categories taxed at a different rate: none. Major consumer categories that are exempt from sales tax include: drugs, groceries and medical services.

Within the city limits of Boerne, the property tax rate is .024372. Homes are assessed at 100% of market value. There are exemptions off the county and school portions of the property tax.

Property tax does not cover garbage pickup.

Boerne has no personal property tax for individuals.

Our couples relocating to Boerne must pay a registration fee of $59 per automobile, a title application fee of $28 per automobile, a new resident fee of $90 per automobile, a road and bridge fee of $11 per automobile and an insurance fee of $1 per automobile at the time of registration. Thereafter, on an annual basis, our couples will pay a registration fee, a road and bridge fee and an insurance fee, per automobile.

Brownsville

Brownsville has no local income tax but does levy a sales tax.

Most purchases are taxed at a rate of 8.25%. Major consumer categories taxed at a different rate: none. Major consumer categories that are exempt from sales tax include: drugs, groceries and medical services.

Within the city limits of Brownsville, the property tax rate is .02700527. Homes are assessed at 100% of market value. There are various exemptions off the city, county and school district portions of the property tax. Property tax does not cover garbage pickup.

Brownsville has no personal property tax for individuals.

Our couples relocating to Brownsville must pay a registration fee of $59 per automobile, a road and bridge fee of $10 per automobile, a title fee of $28 per automobile, a new resident fee of $90 per automobile, an automation fee of $1 per automobile and an insurance fee of $1 per automobile at the time of registration. Thereafter, on an annual basis, our couples will pay a registration fee, a county road and bridge fee, an automation fee and an insurance fee, per automobile.

Dallas

Dallas has no local income tax but does levy a sales tax.

Most purchases are taxed at a rate of 8.25%. Major consumer categories taxed at a different rate: none. Major consumer categories that are exempt from sales tax include: drugs, groceries and medical services.

In the Dallas Independent School District, the property tax rate is .02785774. Homes are assessed at 100% of market value. There are various exemptions off the city, community college, county, hospital and school district portions of the property tax. Property tax does not cover garbage pickup. Residents also pay approximately $48 per year for stormwater management fees.

Dallas has no personal property tax for individuals.

Our couples relocating to Dallas must pay a registration fee of $59 per automobile, a road and bridge fee of $10 per automobile, a title application fee of $33 per automobile, a new resident fee of $90 per automobile, an automation fee of $1 per automobile and an insurance fee of $1 per automobile at the time of registration. Thereafter, on an annual basis, our couples will pay a registration fee, a road and bridge fee, an automation fee and an insurance fee, per automobile.

Fredericksburg

Fredericksburg has no local income tax but does levy a sales tax.

Most purchases are taxed at a rate of 8.25%. Major consumer categories taxed at a different rate: none. Major consumer categories that are exempt from sales tax include: drugs, groceries and medical services.

Within the city limits of Fredericksburg, the property tax rate is .020005. Homes are assessed at 100% of market value. There is an exemption off the school district portion of the property tax. Property tax does not cover garbage pickup.

Fredericksburg has no personal property tax for individuals.

Our couples relocating to Fredericksburg must pay a registration fee of $59 per automobile, a title application fee of $28 per automobile, a new resident fee of $90 per automobile, a road and bridge fee of $12 per automobile and an insurance fee of $1 per automobile at the time of registration. Thereafter, on an annual basis, our couples will pay a registration fee, a road and bridge fee and an insurance fee, per automobile.

Georgetown

Georgetown has no local income tax but does levy a sales tax.

Most purchases are taxed at a rate of 8.25%. Major consumer categories taxed at a different rate: none. Major consumer categories that are exempt from sales tax include: drugs, groceries and medical services.

In the Sun City neighborhood of Georgetown, the property tax rate is .02491937. Homes are assessed at 100% of market value. There are exemptions off the school, farm and road, city and county portions of the property tax. Property tax does not cover garbage pickup. There is also a stormwater drainage fee of approximately $27 per year. Property tax does not include the homeowners association fee for Sun City. The additional fee is approximately $980 per year, and benefits to homeowners include landscaping, club memberships, residential activities and swimming and health facilities. We have not included the homeowners association fee in our calculations since it does not apply to all residents of Georgetown.

Georgetown has no personal property tax for individuals.

Our couples relocating to Georgetown must pay a registration fee of $59 per automobile, a road and bridge fee of $12 per automobile, a title application fee of $33 per automobile, a new resident fee of $90 per automobile, an automation fee of $1 per automobile at the time of registration. and an insurance fee of $1 per automobile at the time of registration. Thereafter, on an annual basis, our couples will pay a registration fee, a road and bridge fee and an insurance fee, per automobile.

Houston

Houston has no local income tax but does levy a sales tax.

Most purchases are taxed at a rate of 8.25%. Major consumer categories taxed at a different rate: none. Major consumer categories that are exempt from sales tax include: drugs, groceries and medical services.

In the Spring Branch Independent School District, the property tax rate is .0277407. Homes are assessed at 100% of market value. There are various exemptions off the city, county, community college and school district portions of the property tax. Property tax does not cover garbage pickup.

Houston has no personal property tax for individuals.

Our couples relocating to Houston must pay a registration fee of $59 per automobile, a road and bridge fee of $10 per automobile, a title application fee of $33 per automobile, a new resident fee of $90 per automobile, an automation fee of $1 per automobile, a child safety fee of $2 per automobile and an insurance fee of $1 per automobile at the time of registration. Thereafter, on an annual basis, our couples will pay a registration fee, a road and bridge fee, an automation fee, a child safety fee and an insurance fee, per automobile.

Kerrville

Kerrville has no local income tax but does levy a sales tax.

Most purchases are taxed at a rate of 8.25%. Major consumer categories taxed at a different rate: none. Major consumer categories that are exempt from sales tax include: drugs, groceries and medical services.

Within the city limits of Kerrville, the property tax rate is .024738. Homes are assessed at 100% of market value. There are various exemptions off the city, roads and school district portions of the property tax. Property tax does not cover garbage pickup.

Kerrville has no personal property tax for individuals.

Our couples relocating to Kerrville must pay a registration fee of $59 per automobile, a road and bridge fee of $10 per automobile, a title application fee of $28 per automobile, a new resident fee of $90 per automobile and an insurance fee of $1 per automobile at the time of registration. Thereafter, on an annual basis, our couples will pay a registration fee, a road and bridge fee, and an insurance fee, per automobile.

Marble Falls

Marble Falls has no local income tax but does levy a sales tax.

Most purchases are taxed at a rate of 8.25%. Major consumer categories taxed at a different rate: none. Major consumer categories that are exempt from sales tax include: drugs, groceries and medical services.

In the Marble Falls Independent School District, the property tax rate is .0226383. Homes are assessed at 100% of market value. There are exemptions off the county and school district portions of the property tax. Property tax does not cover garbage pickup.

Marble Falls has no personal property tax for individuals.

Our couples relocating to Marble Falls must pay a registration fee of $59 per automobile, a title application fee of $28 per automobile, a new resident fee of $90 per automobile, a road and bridge fee of $10 per automobile and an insurance fee of $1 per automobile at the time of registration. Thereafter, on an annual basis, our couples will pay a registration fee, a road and bridge fee and an insurance fee, per automobile.

McAllen

McAllen has no local income tax but does levy a sales tax.

Most purchases are taxed at a rate of 8.25%. Major consumer categories taxed at a different rate: none. Major consumer categories that are exempt from sales tax include: drugs, groceries and medical services.

In the McAllen Independent School District, the property tax rate is .026854. Homes are assessed at 100% of market value. There are exemptions off the county, city and school district portions of the property tax. Property tax does not cover garbage pickup.

McAllen has no personal property tax for individuals.

Our couples relocating to McAllen must pay a registration fee of $59 per automobile, a title application fee of $28 per automobile, a new resident fee of $90 per automobile, a road and bridge fee of $10 per automobile, an automation fee of $1 per automobile and an insurance fee of $1 per automobile at the time of registration. Thereafter, on an annual basis, our couples will pay a registration fee, a road and bridge fee, an automation fee and an insurance fee, per automobile.

San Antonio

San Antonio has no local income tax but does levy a sales tax.

Most purchases are taxed at a rate of 8.125%. Major consumer categories taxed at a different rate: none. Major consumer categories that are exempt from sales tax include: drugs, groceries and medical services.

In the Alamo Heights Independent School District, the property tax rate is .0278897. Homes are assessed at 100% of market value. There are exemptions off the various components of the property tax. Property tax does not cover garbage pickup. There is also a stormwater fee of approximately $47 per year.

San Antonio has no personal property tax for individuals.

Our couples relocating to San Antonio must pay a registration fee of $59 per automobile, a road and bridge

fee of $10 per automobile, a title application fee of $33 per automobile, a new resident fee of $90 per automobile, an automation fee of $1 per automobile, a child safety fee and a reflectorization fee which together are $2 per automobile and an insurance fee of $1 per automobile at the time of registration. Thereafter, on an annual basis, our couples will pay a registration fee, a road and bridge fee, an automation fee, a child safety fee, a reflectorization fee and an insurance fee, per automobile.

The Woodlands

The Woodlands has no local income tax but does levy a sales tax.

Most purchases are taxed at a rate of 8.25%. Major consumer categories taxed at a different rate: none. Major consumer categories that are exempt from sales tax include: drugs, groceries and medical services.

In the Alden Bridge neighborhood of The Woodlands, the property tax rate is .025561. Homes are assessed at 100% of

market value. There are exemptions off the various components of the property tax. There is a homeowners association fee (rate) of .00455 of assessed home valuation. Homeowner benefits due to this fee include landscaping and maintenance, fire and emergency medical response, special programs, residential activities and swimming and health facilities. The association fee also covers garbage pickup.

The Woodlands has no personal property tax for individuals.

Our couples relocating to The Woodlands must pay a registration fee of $59 per automobile, a road and bridge fee of $10 per automobile, a title application fee of $33 per automobile, a new resident fee of $90 per automobile, an automation fee of $1 per automobile and an insurance fee of $1 per automobile at the time of registration. Thereafter, on an annual basis, our couples will pay a registration fee, a road and bridge fee, an automation fee and an insurance fee, per automobile.

TEXAS TAX TABLE

Instructions

1. Find the Income in the far left column closest to your anticipated retirement income.
2. Find the Home Value closest to the value of the home where you will live in retirement.
3. Follow that row to your estimated Total Tax Burden at age 65 and beyond.

Income	Home Value	Property Tax & Other Fees	Personal Property Tax & Auto Fees	Sales Tax	Local Income Tax	State Income Tax	Total Tax Burden	Rank*
AUSTIN								
$30,000	$125,000	$2,056	$145	$1,038	-	-	$3,239	141 of 173
	150,000	2,661	145	1,038	-	-	3,844	146 of 173
	175,000	3,266	145	1,038	-	-	4,449	150 of 173
$60,000	$150,000	$2,661	$145	$1,825	-	-	$4,631	135 of 203
	225,000	4,476	145	1,825	-	-	6,446	163 of 203
	300,000	6,292	145	1,825	-	-	8,262	171 of 203
$90,000	$225,000	$4,476	$145	$2,268	-	-	$6,889	118 of 203
	375,000	8,107	145	2,268	-	-	10,520	164 of 203
	525,000	11,738	145	2,268	-	-	14,151	175 of 203
BOERNE								
$30,000	$125,000	$2,785	$142	$1,038	-	-	$3,965	160 of 173
	150,000	3,394	142	1,038	-	-	4,574	162 of 173
	175,000	4,003	142	1,038	-	-	5,183	162 of 173
$60,000	$150,000	$3,394	$142	$1,825	-	-	$5,361	171 of 203
	225,000	5,222	142	1,825	-	-	7,189	180 of 203
	300,000	7,050	142	1,825	-	-	9,017	182 of 203

There are 203 cities in this book, 30 of which have higher than average home prices. We have estimated taxes for a tier of higher home values (and omitted the lowest tier) for these 30 cities. The city with the lowest tax burden for an income/home value combination is given the #1 rating; the higher the rating, the higher the total tax burden.

Income	Home Value	Property Tax & Other Fees	Personal Property Tax & Auto Fees	Sales Tax	Local Income Tax	State Income Tax	Total Tax Burden	Rank*
BOERNE continued								
$90,000	$225,000	$5,222	$142	$2,268	-	-	$7,632	147 of 203
	375,000	8,878	142	2,268	-	-	11,288	174 of 203
	525,000	12,533	142	2,268	-	-	14,943	181 of 203
BROWNSVILLE								
$30,000	$125,000	$3,059	$142	$1,038	-	-	$4,239	167 of 173 Ψ
	150,000	3,734	142	1,038	-	-	4,914	167 of 173 Ψ
	175,000	4,690	142	1,038	-	-	5,870	168 of 173 Ψ
$60,000	$150,000	$3,734	$142	$1,825	-	-	$5,701	185 of 203
	225,000	5,759	142	1,825	-	-	7,726	190 of 203
	300,000	7,785	142	1,825	-	-	9,752	193 of 203
$90,000	$225,000	$5,759	$142	$2,268	-	-	$8,169	165 of 203
	375,000	9,810	142	2,268	-	-	12,220	185 of 203
	525,000	13,861	142	2,268	-	-	16,271	188 of 203
DALLAS								
$30,000	$125,000	$1,467	$142	$1,038	-	-	$2,647	85 of 173
	150,000	2,061	142	1,038	-	-	3,241	106 of 173
	175,000	2,656	142	1,038	-	-	3,836	119 of 173
$60,000	$150,000	$2,061	$142	$1,825	-	-	$4,028	83 of 203
	225,000	3,845	142	1,825	-	-	5,812	138 of 203
	300,000	5,630	142	1,825	-	-	7,597	158 of 203
$90,000	$225,000	$3,845	$142	$2,268	-	-	$6,255	87 of 203
	375,000	7,414	142	2,268	-	-	9,824	145 of 203
	525,000	10,982	142	2,268	-	-	13,392	164 of 203
FREDERICKSBURG								
$30,000	$125,000	$2,321	$143	$1,038	-	-	$3,502	150 of 173
	150,000	2,821	143	1,038	-	-	4,002	151 of 173
	175,000	3,321	143	1,038	-	-	4,502	152 of 173
$60,000	$150,000	$2,821	$143	$1,825	-	-	$4,789	147 of 203
	225,000	4,322	143	1,825	-	-	6,290	157 of 203
	300,000	5,822	143	1,825	-	-	7,790	161 of 203
$90,000	$225,000	$4,322	$143	$2,268	-	-	$6,733	108 of 203
	375,000	7,322	143	2,268	-	-	9,733	141 of 203
	525,000	10,323	143	2,268	-	-	12,734	154 of 203
GEORGETOWN								
$30,000	$125,000	$2,711	$145	$1,038	-	-	$3,894	158 of 173
	150,000	3,334	145	1,038	-	-	4,517	159 of 173
	175,000	3,957	145	1,038	-	-	5,140	161 of 173
$60,000	$150,000	$3,334	$145	$1,825	-	-	$5,304	167 of 203
	225,000	5,203	145	1,825	-	-	7,173	179 of 203
	300,000	7,072	145	1,825	-	-	9,042	183 of 203
$90,000	$225,000	$5,203	$145	$2,268	-	-	$7,616	146 of 203
	375,000	8,940	145	2,268	-	-	11,353	176 of 203
	525,000	12,678	145	2,268	-	-	15,091	183 of 203
HOUSTON								
$30,000	$125,000	$1,329	$145	$1,038	-	-	$2,512	69 of 173
	150,000	1,806	145	1,038	-	-	2,989	85 of 173
	175,000	2,283	145	1,038	-	-	3,466	99 of 173
$60,000	$150,000	$1,806	$145	$1,825	-	-	$3,776	61 of 203
	225,000	3,236	145	1,825	-	-	5,206	110 of 203
	300,000	4,666	145	1,825	-	-	6,636	130 of 203
$90,000	$225,000	$3,236	$145	$2,268	-	-	$5,649	48 of 203
	375,000	6,097	145	2,268	-	-	8,510	100 of 203
	525,000	8,957	145	2,268	-	-	11,370	127 of 203

Income	Home Value	Property Tax & Other Fees	Personal Property Tax & Auto Fees	Sales Tax	Local Income Tax	State Income Tax	Total Tax Burden	Rank*
KERRVILLE								
$30,000	$125,000	$2,880	$140	$1,038	-	-	$4,058	162 of 173
	150,000	3,498	140	1,038	-	-	4,676	164 of 173 Ψ
	175,000	4,117	140	1,038	-	-	5,295	163 of 173
$60,000	$150,000	$3,498	$140	$1,825	-	-	$5,463	176 of 203
	225,000	5,354	140	1,825	-	-	7,319	185 of 203
	300,000	7,209	140	1,825	-	-	9,174	187 of 203
$90,000	$225,000	$5,354	$140	$2,268	-	-	$7,762	151 of 203
	375,000	9,064	140	2,268	-	-	11,472	178 of 203
	525,000	12,775	140	2,268	-	-	15,183	184 of 203
MARBLE FALLS								
$30,000	$125,000	$2,597	$140	$1,038	-	-	$3,775	155 of 173
	150,000	3,163	140	1,038	-	-	4,341	156 of 173
	175,000	3,729	140	1,038	-	-	4,907	157 of 173
$60,000	$150,000	$3,163	$140	$1,825	-	-	$5,128	158 of 203
	225,000	4,861	140	1,825	-	-	6,826	174 of 203
	300,000	6,559	140	1,825	-	-	8,524	178 of 203
$90,000	$225,000	$4,861	$140	$2,268	-	-	$7,269	132 of 203
	375,000	8,257	140	2,268	-	-	10,665	168 of 203
	525,000	11,652	140	2,268	-	-	14,060	174 of 203
MCALLEN								
$30,000	$125,000	$3,037	$142	$1,038	-	-	$4,217	166 of 173 Ψ
	150,000	3,708	142	1,038	-	-	4,888	165 of 173 Ψ
	175,000	4,379	142	1,038	-	-	5,559	165 of 173 Ψ
$60,000	$150,000	$3,708	$142	$1,825	-	-	$5,675	182 of 203
	225,000	5,722	142	1,825	-	-	7,689	189 of 203
	300,000	7,736	142	1,825	-	-	9,703	192 of 203
$90,000	$225,000	$5,722	$142	$2,268	-	-	$8,132	162 of 203
	375,000	9,750	142	2,268	-	-	12,160	184 of 203
	525,000	13,778	142	2,268	-	-	16,188	187 of 203
SAN ANTONIO								
$30,000	$125,000	$2,765	$145	$1,023	-	-	$3,933	159 of 173
	150,000	3,463	145	1,023	-	-	4,631	163 of 173
	175,000	4,160	145	1,023	-	-	5,328	164 of 173 Ψ
$60,000	$150,000	$3,463	$145	$1,797	-	-	$5,405	173 of 203
	225,000	5,554	145	1,797	-	-	7,496	187 of 203
	300,000	7,646	145	1,797	-	-	9,588	190 of 203
$90,000	$225,000	$5,554	$145	$2,234	-	-	$7,933	157 of 203
	375,000	9,738	145	2,234	-	-	12,117	183 of 203
	525,000	13,921	145	2,234	-	-	16,300	189 of 203
THE WOODLANDS								
$30,000	$125,000	$2,974	$142	$1,038	-	-	$4,154	165 of 173 Ψ
	150,000	3,727	142	1,038	-	-	4,907	166 of 173 Ψ
	175,000	4,479	142	1,038	-	-	5,659	167 of 173 Ψ
$60,000	$150,000	$3,727	$142	$1,825	-	-	$5,694	184 of 203
	225,000	5,985	142	1,825	-	-	7,952	193 of 203
	300,000	8,243	142	1,825	-	-	10,210	195 of 203 Ψ
$90,000	$225,000	$5,985	$142	$2,268	-	-	$8,395	171 of 203
	375,000	10,502	142	2,268	-	-	12,912	190 of 203
	525,000	15,018	142	2,268	-	-	17,428	194 of 203 Ψ

*There are 203 cities in this book, 30 of which have higher than average home prices. We have estimated taxes for a tier of higher home values (and omitted the lowest tier) for these 30 cities. The city with the lowest tax burden for an income/home value combination is given the #1 rating; the higher the rating, the higher the total tax burden.

Austin

This state capital has beauty and brains, blending a hip, cosmopolitan atmosphere with gorgeous scenery, great recreational opportunities, affordable housing and seven area universities. Leading the educational scene is the University of Texas, which offers continuing-education courses attractive to retirees. But along with academics, UT has a year-round calendar of arts, cultural events, theater, musical performances, dance and more.

Explore UT's branch of the Osher Lifelong Learning Institute and you can enjoy small-group seminars covering everything from art, music, religion and literature to history, science and current events. It's a great way to explore new ideas and make new friends. The program also offers lectures by noted speakers and field trips and socials. Or join Elderhostel, an international non-profit organization providing educational adventures.

Downtown Austin has several historic districts chockablock with theaters, galleries, museums, shops and an entertainment complex featuring the best of live music and the arts. The city, in the rolling hills of central Texas, has a beautiful greenbelt with miles of recreational trails for walking, jogging and biking, plus 26 area golf courses.

The area is dotted with beautiful lakes where you can enjoy water sports, along with hiking, biking, hunting and fishing. A year-round mild climate provides more than 300 sunny days. Considered a gateway to the state's beautiful Hill Country, Austin also is the springboard to a variety of charming smaller communities that ring the city.

Population: 709,893, plus about 120,000 students

Climate:

	High	Low
January	59	39
July	95	74

Cost of living: Below average

Housing cost: The median sales price for a single-family home was $182,500 during the first half of 2007, according to the Austin Board of Realtors.

Information: Greater Austin Chamber of Commerce, (512) 478-9383 or www.austin-chamber.org.

Boerne

An old German settlement on the banks of Cibola Creek, Boerne quickly captures the hearts of many visitors with its scenic setting and favorable climate. It's a small town in the Texas Hill Country but within easy reach of San Antonio's many attractions. It has a charming downtown, distinguished with limestone buildings, and expansive views of the rocky hills speckled with green.

City slickers can get a taste of the ranching lifestyle not too far from a metropolitan scene. Grab your boots, partner, and scurry to the nearby San Antonio Rose Palace for equine events sponsored by country singer George Strait, a rope horse aficionado. The area around Boerne (pronounced Burney) still has working farms and ranches that influence the atmosphere of the town.

You also can catch a show of a different type at the Boerne Community Theatre or tour area caverns in the limestone bedrock. Retirees with a passion for the outdoors can enjoy golfing, birdwatching, hiking, biking and hunting.

Texas has no state income tax, and the cost of living here is measurably lower than in many other parts of the country. Historical attractions, museums, theme parks and shopping are within easy reach, and veterans are close to several military bases and hospitals in San Antonio.

"We were looking for a small-town community in the Texas Hill Country, and when we drove through Boerne, we knew this was it. It's just nice in all ways," says Tom Kobett, who moved from Houston.

Population: 8,707

Climate:

	High	Low
January	60	34
July	92	69

Cost of living: Average

Housing cost: The median sales price of single-family homes from Jan. 1, 2007, to Sept. 18, 2007, was $283,850, according to data from the local JVL Real Estate.

Information: Greater Boerne Chamber of Commerce, (830) 249-8000 or www.boerne.org. Boerne Convention and Visitors Bureau, (888) 842-8080 or www.visitboerne.org.

Georgetown

Georgetown may not be as well-known as the town of the same name outside Washington, DC, but it also boasts an exceptionally pretty, resident-friendly, restored downtown. Buildings dating from the late 1800s still serve shoppers as they stroll along Seventh Street, the city's quaint downtown drag.

The town is located on the edge of the Texas Hill Country, 25 miles north of Austin, the state capital. A major component of Georgetown is the 700-acre campus of Southwestern University, known as the first institution of higher learning in Texas. The school hosts a variety of cultural events, including concerts, plays and lectures by prominent speakers.

Historic Georgetown is complemented with modern amenities, including medical care through St. David's Georgetown Hospital, with cancer and cardiac care among its services. For those 50 and up, the Senior University Georgetown offers trips and noncredit classes and special guest lectures on topics ranging from literature and philosophy to the geoscience of the Texas Hill Country. There's a small annual fee for the program.

Nearby Austin adds more activities, with dining, shopping and a host of cultural and sports events at the University of Texas.

While the area has varied housing options, many retirees choose Sun City Texas, a large active-adult community west of town. It's developed by Del Webb, the leader in 55-plus communities.

Harold and Jean Steadman had retired to Buchanan Dam, TX. When they heard Sun City was coming to Georgetown, they immediately registered to buy one of the first homes. "Health care, planned programs and outings, clean air and a low crime rate get high marks," Harold says. "There are so many different things to do and opportunities to get involved. We'll never leave.

"This is my rest home," he adds.

Population: 42,467

Climate: High Low
January 59 35
July 96 72
Cost of living: Below average
Housing cost: For the first half of 2007, the median sales price of homes on the west side of town, including the Sun City Texas 55-plus community, was $225,000 and the median price on the east side of town was $135,000, according to the Williamson County Association of Realtors.
Information: Georgetown Chamber of Commerce, (512) 930-3535 or www. georgetownchamber.org.

Kerrville

Retirees who love culture, art and recreation are drawn to this Zane Grey-like town along the Guadalupe River in the beautiful Texas Hill Country. Set amid rolling hillsides dotted with sage wildflowers and oaks, Kerrville is the region's premier art community as well as the home of the noted Museum of Western Art, formerly called the Cowboy Artists of America Museum.

Since retirees make up nearly a third of the town's population, events and activities that are sponsored and operated by seniors are the norm here, rather than the exception. The multipurpose senior center offers square dancing, bridge, a special senior choir, adult hiking club and daily lunch program.

Fishing and boating are popular, along with swimming and floating in inner tubes in area rivers. Kerrville-Schreiner Park, a 517-acre facility along the Guadalupe River, has swimming, boating, fishing, camping and hiking trails with scenic views.

Downtown Kerrville, particularly along Water Street, boasts restored late 1800s buildings, some in stone, which now house art galleries, boutiques and restaurants. Kerrville hosts nonstop special events and festivals spring through fall. Among major attractions are the Kerrville Folk Festival, with live music, song-writing workshops, concerts, food and crafts; the Texas State Arts and Crafts Fair, which also has music; the Kerrville Wine and Music Festival, showcasing Texas wines; and the Texas Living Heritage Day, with a tribute to country-western singer Jimmie Rodgers. Apple orchards in the area sometimes have harvest celebrations.

Schreiner University adds a variety of programs and events. Kerrville is a medical hub, and its Sid Peterson Memorial Hospital is opening a new state-of-the-art regional medical center in 2008. Kerrville has a variety of affordable housing.

Population: 22,361
Climate: High Low
January 60 32
July 94 68
Cost of living: Below average
Housing cost: The median sales price for a single-family home was $174,000 for the first half of 2007, according to Coldwell Banker Heart of the Hills, Realtors in Kerrville.
Information: Kerrville Area Chamber of Commerce, (830) 896-1155 or www.kerr villetx.com. Kerrville Convention and Visitors Bureau, (800) 221-7958 or www. kerrvilletexascvb.com.

Marble Falls

This former ranching community outside the western reaches of the Austin metroplex and 85 miles north of San Antonio is a gem of a retirement haven for both boaters and golfers. Located on the Colorado River next to the largest chain of Texas lakes, known as the Highland Lakes, Marble Falls and nearby Horseshoe Bay offer the best of lakeside living amid one of the most attractive topographies in Texas — the Texas Hill Country.

"I absolutely love the water, and Brad loves the golfing," says Carol Hall, who retired with her husband to the area in 2000. "The sunrises and sunsets are so beautiful. We have Friday afternoon 'floats' on the water in the summer just so we can enjoy the company of friends while watching the sun go down." From their home on Horseshoe Bay, they enjoy expansive views of the lake lapping at their backyard foliage.

Aside from the splendid scenery and low cost of living in this hilly community, retirees enthuse about the friendliness and neighborly attitudes of Marble Falls residents. "It's about the quality of the friendship here," Brad says, "and it doesn't matter what income bracket you are in."

Golfers can choose from a number of championship courses, and equestrians have plenty of riding trails. Hikers and bikers can go somewhere different every day of the week, and boaters and fishermen can sample the chain of lakes. A quality hospital, Seton, is located in nearby Burnet, as well as the full range of medical care that Austin and San Antonio provide. Texas Tech University has a campus in Marble Falls for those seeking educational opportunities.

The town is enjoying an economic boom and offers a variety of housing. Many retirees also have selected the independent communities of nearby Horseshoe Bay and Meadow Lakes, and more communities are under development.

Population: 7,186 in Marble Falls, 42,896 in Burnet County
Climate: High Low
January 59 33
July 94 71
Cost of living: Below average
Housing cost: The average price of homes in Marble Falls is $195,000, but lakefront homes often start at $500,000, according to information from ERA Colonial Real Estate.
Information: Marble Falls-Lake LBJ Chamber of Commerce, (800) 759-8178 or www.marblefalls.org.

Rio Grande Valley (Brownsville, McAllen)

In the so-called South Texas tropics, where Texas and Mexico come together and the Rio Grande meets the Gulf of Mexico, you'll experience a zesty Tex-Mex blend of customs, language, music and cuisine. The Lower Valley, stretching from McAllen to Brownsville, welcomes snowbirds — or Winter Texans, as they're called here — with open arms and more than 50 retiree-oriented RV resorts.

Harlingen, with its pleasant palm-lined streets and convenient mid-valley location, is an ideal place to settle. Downtown is decorated with some 30 murals, and the revitalized Jackson Street District has dozens of antiques shops restored to their 1930s- and 1940s-era splendor. The Rio Grande Valley Museum, a five-building complex, helps visitors envision the history and culture of the valley. Harlingen also boasts the majestic Iwo Jima Monument, embodied in the original working model for the famous statue outside Washington, DC.

Day-trippers will find dozens of activities. Among them: the highly regarded Gladys Porter Zoo in Brownsville, famous for its collection of endangered species; the Texas Air Museum at Rio Hondo, featuring 50 historic aircraft; and, for beachgoers, the sands on South Padre Island. The shops, restaurants and clubs of Matamoros, Mexico, are only an hour away. Anglers rejoice in some of the best sportfishing anywhere, both offshore from Port Isabel or in the rich, brackish waters of South Padre's Laguna Madre Bay.

Because it's at the convergence of two major flyways, the Rio Grande Valley is known worldwide as a tropical birder's paradise. Fanciers of feathered wildlife should pick up a free birding guide at the Texas Travel Information Center in Harlingen and head to Bentsen-Rio Grande Valley State Park in Mission. The 760-acre park is home to the World Birding Center, a new complex where visitors can enjoy viewing stations and towers, an interpretive center and regular programs with park naturalists.

Population: 126,411 in McAllen; 172,437 in Brownsville; 64,202 in Harlingen; and 5,379 in Port Isabel.

Climate: High Low
January 70 50
July 96 76

Cost of living: Below average

Housing cost: The median sales price of homes in Harlingen during the first half of 2007 was $86,000, while the average price was $107,200, according to the Real Estate Center at Texas A&M University.

Information: Rio Grande Valley Chamber of Commerce, (956) 968-3141 or www.valleychamber.com.

San Antonio

San Antonio may be one of the 10 largest cities in the country, but it has the heart of a small town — and a low cost of living to match. Among major cities, San Antonio has one of the country's most affordable housing markets.

A longtime retirement haven for the military, the city lures seniors who want to live in a festive atmosphere that blends Native American, Mexican, Spanish and Old West cultures. The 2.5-mile-long River Walk winds through the heart of downtown, providing a parklike place below street level for strolling along the San Antonio River. Lined with trees, the River Walk has outdoor cafes, shops and entertainment, along with water taxis and tour boats.

The Alamo, fabulous art museums and Market Square, a festive Mexican-style plaza with arts and crafts shops, also draw culture-loving retirees and tourists. Whether you want to attend a street fair featuring Latin American cuisine and crafts or take in an opera, symphony or a Broadway production, it's here.

The city's many ethnic restaurants may expand more than your culinary horizon, but you can work off those hefty Tex-Mex calories at recreational venues ranging from 20-plus golf courses to bike paths and miles of trails for hiking and horseback riding. San Antonio is also on the edge of the Texas Hill Country, a recreational paradise with hiking, biking, camping as well as fishing and water sports in beautiful lakes.

San Antonio has world-class healthcare facilities, most notably the South Texas Medical Center, a complex with 12 hospitals among its 75 institutions. The city also is home to several military bases and a major military medical complex. It has a dozen colleges and universities in the area.

Population: 1.3 million

Climate: High Low
January 62 39
July 95 74

Cost of living: Below average

Housing cost: The median sales price of single-family homes was $150,400 for the first nine months of 2007, according to the San Antonio Board of Realtors.

Information: Greater San Antonio Chamber of Commerce, (210) 229-2100 or www.sachamber.org. San Antonio Convention and Visitors Bureau, (800) 447-3372 or www.sanantoniocvb.com.

UTAH

U tah has a state income tax and a state sales tax.

The state income tax rate is graduated from 2.3% to 6.98% depending upon income bracket. For married couples filing jointly, the rates are 2.3% on the first $2,000 of taxable income; 3.3% on the next $2,000 of taxable income; 4.2% on the next $2,000 of taxable income; 5.2% on the next $2,000 of taxable income; 6% on the next $3,000 of taxable income; and 6.98% on taxable income above $11,000.

In calculating the tax, there is a deduction for one-half of federal income tax paid. There is a retirement income exclusion of up to $7,500 for each person age 65 or older, subject to certain limitations. Social Security benefits subject to federal income tax are not exempt but may be included in the retirement income exclusion calculation. There is a standard deduction (equal to the standard federal deduction) of $12,300 for married couples filing jointly, both age 65 or older. The itemized federal deduction can be used instead if it was used on the federal calculation. There is a personal exemption of $2,475 per person from Utah adjusted gross income. There is a deduction for some health care insurance premiums and long-term care insurance premiums.

Major tax credits or rebates include: credit for taxes paid to other states. Our couples do not qualify for this program.

The state sales tax rate is 4.75%, but local governments can add to this amount.

Cedar City

Cedar City has no local income tax but does levy a sales tax.

Most purchases are taxed at a rate of 6.1%. Major consumer categories taxed at a different rate include: food away from home, which is taxed at a rate of 7.1%. Major consumer categories that are exempt from sales tax include: drugs, medical supplies and medical services.

Within the city limits of Cedar City, the property tax rate is .010562. Homes are assessed at 55% of market value. There is a state tax relief program that has four components: circuit breaker

property tax abatement available to residents 65 or older with a gross income below $26,157; indigent tax relief available to residents 65 or older with a gross income below $26,157; veteran's exemption; and blind exemption. Our couples do not qualify for these programs. Property tax does not cover garbage pickup. There is also a stormwater drainage fee of $36 per year.

Utah has a personal property tax, which is assessed by the Department of Motor Vehicles. The assessment is based on age for motor vehicles (uniform age-based fee). Other items are subject to a uniform fee-in-lieu of property tax. Medium and heavy duty trucks, commercial trailers and vessels 31 feet and longer are taxed at 1.5% of fair market value. Motor homes are taxed at 1.25% of fair market value.

Our couples relocating to Cedar City must pay a registration fee of $22 per automobile, an annual uniform fee, which is based on the age of the vehicle, of $150 per automobile, a new plate fee of $5 per automobile, a driver education fee of $3 per automobile, a title fee of $6 per automobile, a corridor fee of $10 per automobile and an uninsured motorist fee of $1 per automobile. Thereafter, on an annual basis, our couples will pay a registration fee, an annual uniform fee, a driver education fee, a corridor fee and an uninsured motorist fee, per automobile.

St. George

St. George has no local income tax but does levy a sales tax.

Most purchases are taxed at a rate of 6.25%. Major consumer categories taxed at a different rate include: food away from home, which is taxed at a rate of 7.25%. Major consumer categories that are exempt from sales tax include: drugs, medical supplies and medical services.

Within the city limits of St. George, the property tax rate is .008974.

Homes are assessed at 55% of market value. There is a state tax relief program that has four components: circuit breaker property tax abatement available to residents 65 or older with a gross income below $26,158; indigent tax relief available to residents 65 or older with a gross income below $26,158; veteran's exemption; and blind exemption. Our couples do not qualify for these programs. Property tax does not cover garbage pickup. There is also a stormwater drainage fee of $18 per year.

Utah has a personal property tax, which is assessed by the Department of Motor Vehicles. The assessment is based on age for motor vehicles (uniform age-based fee). Other items are subject to a uniform fee-in-lieu of property tax. Medium and heavy duty trucks, commercial trailers and vessels 31 feet and longer are taxed at 1.5% of fair market value. Motor homes are taxed at 1.25% of fair market value.

Our couples relocating to St. George must pay a registration fee of $22 per automobile, an annual uniform fee, which is based on the age of the vehicle, of $150 per automobile, a new plate fee of $5 per automobile, a driver education fee of $3 per automobile, a title fee of $6 per automobile and an uninsured motorist fee of $1 per automobile. Thereafter, on an annual basis, our couples will pay a registration fee, an annual uniform fee, a driver education fee and an uninsured motorist fee, per automobile.

Salt Lake City

Salt Lake City has no local income tax but does levy a sales tax.

Most purchases are taxed at a rate of 6.6%. Major consumer categories taxed at a different rate include: food away from home, which is taxed at a rate of 7.6%. Major consumer categories that are exempt from sales tax include: drugs, medical supplies and medical services.

In the Tax Area 013 of Salt Lake City, the property tax rate is .013918. Homes are assessed at 55% of market value. There is a state tax relief program that has four components: circuit breaker property tax abatement available to residents 65 or older with a gross income below $26,157; indigent tax relief available to residents 65 or older with a gross income below $26,157; veteran's exemption; and blind exemption. Our couples do not qualify for these programs. Property tax does not cover garbage pickup.

Utah has a personal property tax, which is assessed by the Department of Motor Vehicles. The assessment is based on age for motor vehicles (uniform age-based fee). Other items are subject to a uniform fee-in-lieu of property tax. Medium and heavy duty trucks, commercial trailers and vessels 31 feet and longer are taxed at 1.5% of fair market value. Motor homes are taxed at 1.25% of fair market value.

Our couples relocating to Salt Lake City must pay a registration fee of $22 per automobile, an annual uniform fee, which is based on the age of the vehicle, of $150 per automobile, a new plate fee of $5 per automobile, a driver education fee of $3 per automobile, a title fee of $6 per automobile, an air pollution control fee of $3 per automobile, a corridor fee of $10 per automobile and an uninsured motorist fee of $1 per automobile. Thereafter, on an annual basis, our couples will pay a registration fee, an annual uniform fee, a driver education fee, an air pollution control fee, a corridor fee and an uninsured motorist fee, per automobile.

UTAH TAX TABLE

Instructions

1. Find the Income in the far left column closest to your anticipated retirement income.
2. Find the Home Value closest to the value of the home where you will live in retirement.
3. Follow that row to your estimated Total Tax Burden at age 65 and beyond.

Income	Home Value	Property Tax & Other Fees	Personal Property Tax & Auto Fees	Sales Tax	Local Income Tax	State Income Tax	Total Tax Burden	Rank*
CEDAR CITY								
$30,000	$125,000	$942	$372	$927	-	-	$2,241	44 of 173
	150,000	1,087	372	927	-	-	2,386	41 of 173
	175,000	1,233	372	927	-	-	2,532	37 of 173
$60,000	$150,000	$1,087	$372	$1,575	-	$1,374	$4,408	120 of 203
	225,000	1,523	372	1,575	-	1,374	4,844	83 of 203
	300,000	1,959	372	1,575	-	1,374	5,280	63 of 203
$90,000	$225,000	$1,523	$372	$1,939	-	$4,162	$7,996	160 of 203
	375,000	2,394	372	1,939	-	4,162	8,867	114 of 203
	525,000	3,266	372	1,939	-	4,162	9,739	80 of 203
ST. GEORGE								
$30,000	$125,000	$815	$352	$950	-	-	$2,117	34 of 173
	150,000	938	352	950	-	-	2,240	30 of 173
	175,000	1,062	352	950	-	-	2,364	26 of 173
$60,000	$150,000	$938	$352	$1,613	-	$1,374	$4,277	109 of 203
	225,000	1,309	352	1,613	-	1,374	4,648	67 of 203
	300,000	1,679	352	1,613	-	1,374	5,018	51 of 203
$90,000	$225,000	$1,309	$352	$1,985	-	$4,162	$7,808	152 of 203
	375,000	2,049	352	1,985	-	4,162	8,548	102 of 203
	525,000	2,789	352	1,985	-	4,162	9,288	67 of 203
SALT LAKE CITY								
$30,000	$125,000	$1,137	$378	$1,002	-	-	$2,517	70 of 173
	150,000	1,328	378	1,002	-	-	2,708	67 of 173
	175,000	1,520	378	1,002	-	-	2,900	62 of 173
$60,000	$150,000	$1,328	$378	$1,702	-	$1,374	$4,782	146 of 203
	225,000	1,902	378	1,702	-	1,374	5,356	116 of 203
	300,000	2,476	378	1,702	-	1,374	5,930	95 of 203
$90,000	$225,000	$1,902	$378	$2,095	-	$4,162	$8,537	176 of 203
	375,000	3,051	378	2,095	-	4,162	9,686	139 of 203
	525,000	4,199	378	2,095	-	4,162	10,834	119 of 203

*There are 203 cities in this book, 30 of which have higher than average home prices. We have estimated taxes for a tier of higher home values (and omitted the lowest tier) for these 30 cities. The city with the lowest tax burden for an income/home value combination is given the #1 rating; the higher the rating, the higher the total tax burden.

Cedar City

Cedar City in southwestern Utah serves as the gateway to many of the state's spectacular national parks and monuments, including Zion, Bryce Canyon, Cedar Breaks, Grand Staircase and the north rim of the Grand Canyon. Hikes, from easy to difficult, and tour vehicles take you past fantastical sandstone pillars, spires and arches and to overlooks of canyons striated in hues of pink, coral and gray. At nearby Brian Head Ski Resort, known for its intermediate runs, skiers 65 and older receive discounted lift tickets.

If you're seeking cultural activities, the play's the thing in Cedar City. At Southern Utah University's noted Utah Shakespearean Festival, held each June through October, listen to the words of the Bard. From mid-July through August, laugh out loud at the comedy of a master chronicler of modern times at the Neil Simon Festival.

Judy Arnold, 72, retired from sales and management, enjoys the many amenities of Cedar City. "My husband had a heart problem, and we were very concerned about finding adequate facilities and highly trained doctors and nurses. Cedar City had what we needed," she says. "We were blown away by the variety of activities, both indoor and out, available in such a small community. There is so much going on here in terms of culture and entertainment. I also need to live in an area that has lots of sunshine. In Cedar City the sun shines over 300 days a year."

Cedar City is located along Interstate 15 and within an eight-hour drive of most major metro areas in the West. For glitz and big-name entertainment, Las Vegas is two and a half hours away.

Population: 25,665

Climate:

	High	Low
January	42	19
July	89	58

Cost of living: Below average

Housing cost: The median sales price of a single-family home during the first half of 2007 was $238,554, according to the Iron County Board of Realtors.

Information: Cedar City Area Chamber of Commerce, (435) 586-4484 or www.cedarcitychamber.com.

St. George

St. George sits in a stunning desert valley surrounded by red sandstone cliffs at an elevation of about 2,800 feet. It has an enviable location, 41 miles from Zion National Park and its towering sandstone walls and 125 miles from the red, pink and orange pinnacles and spires of Bryce Canyon National Park.

The desert climate is ideal for year-round recreation. Those who want more than hiking in Zion and Bryce can take hot-air balloon flights, go skydiving or join backcountry cycling tours and trail rides. More adventure awaits if you sign up for climbing instruction. Winter brings cross-country skiing and snowshoeing.

Annette and Les Taylor, who moved from Southern California to St. George in 1994, love to hike and enjoy the area's beauty, open spaces and clear blue skies. Annette cites another huge plus factor. "One of the best things about living here is the community spirit. In January 2005, a ravaging flood destroyed about 50 homes and damaged a considerable number of properties," she says, noting that numerous fundraisers collected about $500,000 to help those families.

The Taylors also enjoy the annual Huntsman World Senior Games, recognized as the premier sporting event for seniors. The games include a variety of sports, such as basketball, square dancing, triathlon, softball and cycling.

New developments are adding to the area's housing options. SunRiver St. George is an active-adult community built around an 18-hole golf course. Sunbrook, St. George's largest planned development, has nine communities around a golf course in the foothills.

St. George is in southwest Utah, six miles from the Arizona state line and 120 miles northeast of Las Vegas.

Population: 67,614

Climate:

	High	Low
January	54	27
July	102	68

Cost of living: Average

Housing cost: The median sales price of a single-family home for the first half of 2007 was $277,500, according to the Washington County Board of Realtors.

Information: St. George Area Chamber of Commerce, (435) 628-1658 or www.stgeorgechamber.com.

VERMONT

Vermont has a state income tax and a state sales tax.

The state income tax rate is graduated from 3.6% to 9.5% depending upon income bracket. For married couples filing jointly, the rates are 3.6% on the first $51,200 of taxable income; 7.2% on the next $72,500 of taxable income; 8.5% on the next $64,750 of taxable income; 9% on the next $148,100 of taxable income; and 9.5% on income above $336,550.

In calculating the tax, the income exemptions and deductions are the same as those allowed on the federal tax return.

Major tax credits or rebates include: credit for taxes paid to other states and renter rebate, which our couples do not qualify for; homeowner property tax rebate, which our couples qualify for; and additional property tax rebate if household income is less than $47,000, which some of our couples qualify for. In 2006, property tax rebates were issued as a reduction of income tax due or as a refund if the credit was greater than the tax liability. Beginning in 2007, these rebates will be deducted directly from property taxes.

The state sales tax rate is 6%.

Our couples relocating to the cities listed below may be subject to a use tax per automobile depending on the amount of tax paid in the state in which the vehicle was purchased. If sales tax of at least 6% was paid in another state that imposes a sales tax, at the time of purchase, no additional tax is due. If less than 6% was paid, the owner is required to pay the difference unless the vehicle was registered in the other state for three or more years. We've assumed our couples have paid tax greater than or equal to the use tax. Our couples must pay a registration fee of $60 per automobile, a title fee of $28 per automobile and a lien fee of $7 per automobile at the time of registration. Thereafter, on an annual basis, our couples will pay a registra-

VERMONT TAX TABLE

Instructions

1. Find the Income in the far left column closest to your anticipated retirement income.
2. Find the Home Value closest to the value of the home where you will live in retirement.
3. Follow that row to your estimated Total Tax Burden at age 65 and beyond.

Income	Home Value	Property Tax & Other Fees	Personal Property Tax & Auto Fees	Sales Tax	Local Income Tax	State Income Tax[†]	Total Tax Burden	Rank[*]
BURLINGTON								
$30,000	$125,000	$2,230	$120	$926	-	($628)	$2,648	86 of 173
	150,000	2,640	120	926	-	(876)	2,810	76 of 173
	175,000	3,050	120	926	-	(1,124)	2,972	70 of 173
$60,000	$150,000	$2,640	$120	$1,629	-	$803	$5,192	163 of 203
	225,000	3,870	120	1,629	-	59	5,678	131 of 203
	300,000	5,100	120	1,629	-	(686)	6,163	111 of 203
$90,000	$225,000	$3,870	$120	$2,032	-	$2,508	$8,530	175 of 203
	375,000	6,330	120	2,032	-	1,020	9,502	137 of 203
	525,000	8,790	120	2,032	-	(468)	10,474	108 of 203
WOODSTOCK								
$60,000	$150,000	$2,551	$120	$1,386	-	$80	$4,137	92 of 203
	225,000	3,737	120	1,386	-	(1,247)	3,996	28 of 203
	300,000	4,922	120	1,386	-	(2,573)	3,855	9 of 203 ○
$90,000	$225,000	$3,737	$120	$1,728	-	$1,411	$6,996	126 of 203
	375,000	6,108	120	1,728	-	(1,242)	6,714	33 of 203
	525,000	8,479	120	1,728	-	(3,895)	6,432	10 of 203 ○
	$600,000	$9,664	$120	$1,728	-	($5,221)	$6,291	2 of 30
	750,000	12,035	120	1,728	-	(7,016)	6,867	3 of 30
	900,000	14,406	120	1,728	-	(7,016)	9,238	4 of 30

[†]Property tax rebate is issued as a reduction of income tax due or as a refund if the credit is greater than the tax liability.
[*]There are 203 cities in this book, 30 of which have higher than average home prices. We have estimated taxes for a tier of higher home values (and omitted the lowest tier) for these 30 cities. The city with the lowest tax burden for an income/home value combination is given the #1 rating; the higher the rating, the higher the total tax burden.

tion fee per automobile.

Burlington

Burlington has no local income tax but does levy a sales tax.

Most purchases are taxed at a rate of 7%. Major consumer categories taxed at a different rate include: food away from home, which is taxed at a rate of 11%. Major consumer categories that are exempt from sales tax include: groceries, drugs, medical supplies and medical services.

Within the city limits of Burlington, the property tax rate is 1.64. Homes are assessed at 100% of market value. The assessed value is then divided by 100 to give the Property Grand List Value to which rates are applied. Property tax does not cover garbage pickup.

Burlington has no personal property tax for individuals.

Woodstock

Woodstock has no local income tax and does not levy an additional sales tax.

Most purchases are taxed at the state rate of 6%. Major consumer categories taxed at a different rate include: food away from home, which is taxed at a rate of 9%. Major consumer categories that are exempt from sales tax include: groceries, drugs, medical supplies and medical services.

Within the city limits of Woodstock, the property tax rate is 1.5807. Homes are assessed at 100% of market value. The assessed value is then divided by 100 to give the Property Grand List Value to which rates are applied. Property tax does not cover garbage pickup.

Woodstock has no personal property tax for individuals.

• Vermont's Top Retirement Town •

Woodstock

Horse trails lured retired English professor Margaret Edwards and husband David Green to Woodstock, some two and a half hours northwest of Boston and about five hours north of Manhattan.

After years of vacationing in the area, the couple, with retirement looming, wanted a serene place where they could ride their horses. They found what they wanted in a 30-acre compound with pastureland and a barn. The couple's new home plants them in a place of "cultural richness," according to Margaret, an Atlanta native. David, a New York City native, was a partner in a Boston accounting firm.

Describing the area as "so beautiful," she details ducks on a pond, trout in a lake and "dirt roads associated with the boonies."

"I like the drama of the weather," she says, explaining that it is necessary to "steel yourself for winter when the climate is harsh." Many residents migrate south during the cold months.

Despite that one negative, "this is a beautiful place, a great retirement community," she says of the area that was built as a shire town in 1799 and today has more than 200 homes on the National Register of Historic Places. Most of the village was constructed before 1830, leaving elegant Federal brick homes and Georgian clapboards around a classic oval village green in its center.

Those living in Woodstock (not to be confused with the upstate New York site that hosted a well-documented festival and concert in 1969) report that life is not hurried here. Golf, tennis, rowing on the Connecticut River and kayaking in nearby lakes, plus winter activities such as Nordic and alpine skiing, snowshoeing and ice skating, are possibilities.

While small, the town has some excellent restaurants and boutiques. It's only about 20 miles from Hanover, NH, home of Dartmouth College, which enhances the cultural scene. Besides a museum and arts center for performances and exhibitions, the college has the Institute for Lifelong Education at Dartmouth, offering courses, lectures and study trips.

Population: 3,182

Climate: High Low
January 27 2
July 81 54

Cost of living: Above average

Housing cost: The median sales price for a single-family home was $315,000 for the first eight months of 2007, according to Lang McLaughry Spera Real Estate in Woodstock.

Information: Woodstock Area Chamber of Commerce, (888) 496-6378 or www.woodstockvt.com.

VIRGINIA

Virginia has a state income tax and a state sales tax.

The state income tax is graduated from 2% to 5.75% depending upon income bracket. For married couples filing jointly, the rates are 2% on the first $3,000 of taxable income; 3% on the next $2,000 of taxable income; 5% on the next $12,000 of taxable income; and 5.75% on taxable income above $17,000.

In calculating the tax, there is no deduction for federal income tax paid. Federal, state and private pensions are not exempt. Social Security benefits are exempt. There is a $6,000 standard deduction from adjusted gross income for married couples filing jointly. There is a $900 personal exemption from adjusted gross income per person plus an $800 personal exemption from adjusted gross income per person for residents age 65 or older. There is an age deduction from income of up to $12,000 per person age 65 or older. The amount of this deduction depends on birth date, filing status and the combined federal adjusted gross income of both spouses.

Major tax credits or rebates include: credit for income taxes paid to other states and low-income tax credit, which our couples do not qualify for, and a spouse tax adjustment credit, which one of our couples qualifies for.

The state sales tax rate is 4%, but local governments can add to this amount.

Our couples relocating to the cities listed below must pay a title fee of $10 per automobile and a registration fee of $45 for the Explorer and $40 for the Camry at the time of registration. Thereafter, on an annual basis, our couples will pay a registration fee per automobile.

Abingdon

Abingdon has no local income tax but does levy a sales tax.

Most purchases are taxed at a rate of 5%. Major consumer categories taxed at a different rate include: groceries, which are taxed at a rate of 2.5%, and food away from home, which is taxed at a rate of 11%. Major consumer categories that are exempt from sales tax

include: drugs and medical services.

Within the town of Abingdon, the property tax rate is .0085. Homes are assessed at 100% of market value. There is a county senior citizen exemption for homeowners age 65 or older with gross income of $21,285 or less and net worth of $63,898 or less, excluding home value, and a town senior citizen exemption for homeowners age 65 or older with gross income of $17,000 or less and net worth of $40,000 or less, excluding home value. Property tax does not cover garbage pickup. There is also a vehicle decal fee of $20 per automobile.

Abingdon has a personal property tax rate of .021. Motor vehicles are assessed at 100% of loan value. All other items are assessed at 100% of market value. There is a personal property tax relief of 70% off the first $20,000 of assessed value for motor vehicles. Items subject to the tax include: motor vehicles, boats, airplanes and mobile homes.

Charlottesville

Charlottesville has no local income tax but does levy a sales tax.

Most purchases are taxed at a rate of 5%. Major consumer categories taxed at a different rate include: groceries, which are taxed at a rate of 2.5%, and food away from home, which is taxed at a rate of 9%. Major consumer categories that are exempt from sales tax include: drugs and medical services.

Within the city limits of Charlottesville, the property tax rate is .0099. Homes are assessed at 100% of market value. There is a senior citizen exemption for homeowners age 65 or older with gross income of $50,000 or less and net worth of $125,000 or less, excluding home value. There is also an exemption for homeowners with federal adjusted gross income of $50,000 or less with assessed property values of $238,000 or less. Property tax does not cover garbage

pickup. There is also a vehicle license fee of $29 for vehicles weighing 4,000 pounds or less and $34 for vehicles weighing over 4,000 pounds.

Charlottesville has a personal property tax rate of .042. Motor vehicles are assessed at at 100% of NADA trade-in value. Mobile homes, however, are taxed at the property tax rate of .0099 and assessed at 100% of market value. There is a personal property tax relief of 53% off the first $20,000 of assessed value for motor vehicles. Items subject to the tax include: motor vehicles, boats, trailers, motorcycles and mobile homes.

Richmond

Richmond has no local income tax but does levy a sales tax.

Most purchases are taxed at a rate of 5%. Major consumer categories taxed at a different rate include: groceries, which are taxed at a rate of 2.5%, and food away from home, which is taxed at a rate of 11%. Major consumer categories that are exempt from sales tax include: drugs and medical services.

Within the city limits of Richmond, the property tax rate is .0129. Homes are assessed at 100% of market value. There is a senior citizen exemption for homeowners age 65 or older with gross income of $50,000 or less and net worth of $200,000 or less, excluding home value. Property tax does not cover garbage pickup. There is also a city vehicle license fee of $23 for vehicles weighing 4,000 pounds or less and $28 for vehicles weighing over 4,000 pounds.

Richmond has a personal property tax rate of .0370. Motor vehicles are assessed at 100% of NADA trade-in value. There is a personal property tax relief of 60% off the first $20,000 of assessed value for motor vehicles. Items subject to the tax include: motor vehicles, boats, trailers, farm equipment and mobile homes.

Staunton

Staunton has no local income tax but does levy a sales tax.

Most purchases are taxed at a rate of 5%. Major consumer categories taxed at a different rate include: groceries, which are taxed at a rate of 2.5%, and food away from home, which was taxed at a rate of 10% in 2006. On July 1, 2007, the sales tax on food away from home increased to 11%. Major consumer categories that are exempt from sales tax include: drugs and medical services.

Within the city limits of Staunton, the property tax rate is .0096. Homes are assessed at 100% of market value. There is a senior citizen exemption for home-owners age 65 or older with gross income of $30,000 or less and net worth of $62,500 or less, excluding home value. Property tax does not cover garbage pickup. There is also a city vehicle license fee of $20 for vehicles weighing 4,000 pounds or less and $25 for vehicles weighing over 4,000 pounds.

Staunton has a personal property tax rate of .02. Motor vehicles are assessed at 100% of NADA retail value. Other items are assessed at 100% of market value. There is a personal property tax relief of 60% off the assessed value for motor vehicles. Items subject to the tax include motor vehicles, motor homes, motorcycles, trailers, campers, boats and mobile homes.

Williamsburg

Williamsburg has no local income tax but does levy a sales tax.

Most purchases are taxed at a rate of 5%. Major consumer categories taxed at a different rate include: groceries, which are taxed at a rate of 2.5%, and food away from home, which is taxed at a rate of 10%. Major consumer categories that are exempt from sales tax include: drugs and medical services.

Within the city limits of Williamsburg, the property tax rate is .0054. Homes are assessed at 100% of market value. Property tax includes garbage pickup.

Williamsburg has a personal property tax rate of .035. Motor vehicles are assessed at 100% of NADA loan value. Mobile homes, however, are taxed at the property tax rate of .0054 and assessed at 100% of market value. There is a personal property tax relief of 65% off the first $20,000 of assessed value for motor vehicles. Items subject to the tax include: motor vehicles, boats, trailers and motorcycles.

VIRGINIA TAX TABLE

Instructions

1. Find the Income in the far left column closest to your anticipated retirement income.
2. Find the Home Value closest to the value of the home where you will live in retirement.
3. Follow that row to your estimated Total Tax Burden at age 65 and beyond.

Income	Home Value	Property Tax & Other Fees	Personal Property Tax & Auto Fees	Sales Tax	Local Income Tax	State Income Tax	Total Tax Burden	Rank*
ABINGDON								
$30,000	$125,000	$1,283	$286	$778	-	-	$2,347	57 of 173
	150,000	1,495	286	778	-	-	2,559	57 of 173
	175,000	1,708	286	778	-	-	2,772	53 of 173
$60,000	$150,000	$1,495	$286	$1,346	-	$141	$3,268	23 of 203
	225,000	2,133	286	1,346	-	141	3,906	22 of 203
	300,000	2,770	286	1,346	-	141	4,543	31 of 203
$90,000	$225,000	$2,133	$286	$1,664	-	$1,493	$5,576	41 of 203
	375,000	3,408	286	1,664	-	1,493	6,851	37 of 203
	525,000	4,683	286	1,664	-	1,493	8,126	38 of 203
CHARLOTTESVILLE								
$30,000	$125,000	$980	$709	$749	-	-	$2,438	65 of 173
	150,000	1,227	709	749	-	-	2,685	65 of 173
	175,000	1,475	709	749	-	-	2,933	63 of 173
$60,000	$150,000	$1,377	$709	$1,296	-	$141	$3,523	40 of 203
	225,000	2,120	709	1,296	-	141	4,266	46 of 203
	300,000	2,862	709	1,296	-	141	5,008	50 of 203
$90,000	$225,000	$2,470	$709	$1,601	-	$1,493	$6,273	88 of 203
	375,000	3,955	709	1,601	-	1,493	7,758	72 of 203
	525,000	5,440	709	1,601	-	1,493	9,243	64 of 203
RICHMOND								
$30,000	$125,000	$1,844	$494	$778	-	-	$3,116	130 of 173
	150,000	2,166	494	778	-	-	3,438	119 of 173
	175,000	2,489	494	778	-	-	3,761	116 of 173

*There are 203 cities in this book, 30 of which have higher than average home prices. We have estimated taxes for a tier of higher home values (and omitted the lowest tier) for these 30 cities. The city with the lowest tax burden for an income/home value combination is given the #1 rating; the higher the rating, the higher the total tax burden.

Income	Home Value	Property Tax & Other Fees	Personal Property Tax & Auto Fees	Sales Tax	Local Income Tax	State Income Tax	Total Tax Burden	Rank*
RICHMOND continued								
$60,000	$150,000	$2,166	$494	$1,346	-	$141	$4,147	94 of 203
	225,000	3,134	494	1,346	-	141	5,115	101 of 203
	300,000	4,101	494	1,346	-	141	6,082	106 of 203
$90,000	$225,000	$3,134	$494	$1,664	-	$1,493	$6,785	110 of 203
	375,000	5,069	494	1,664	-	1,493	8,720	108 of 203
	525,000	7,004	494	1,664	-	1,493	10,655	114 of 203
STAUNTON								
$30,000	$125,000	$1,425	$380	$764	-	-	$2,569	74 of 173
	150,000	1,665	380	764	-	-	2,809	75 of 173
	175,000	1,905	380	764	-	-	3,049	76 of 173
$60,000	$150,000	$1,665	$380	$1,321	-	$141	$3,507	38 of 203
	225,000	2,385	380	1,321	-	141	4,227	44 of 203
	300,000	3,105	380	1,321	-	141	4,947	47 of 203
$90,000	$225,000	$2,385	$380	$1,633	-	$1,493	$5,891	56 of 203
	375,000	3,825	380	1,633	-	1,493	7,331	55 of 203
	525,000	5,265	380	1,633	-	1,493	8,771	57 of 203
WILLIAMSBURG								
$30,000	$125,000	$675	$433	$764	-	-	$1,872	19 of 173
	150,000	810	433	764	-	-	2,007	18 of 173
	175,000	945	433	764	-	-	2,142	16 of 173
$60,000	$150,000	$810	$433	$1,321	-	$141	$2,705	4 of 203 O
	225,000	1,215	433	1,321	-	141	3,110	4 of 203 O
	300,000	1,620	433	1,321	-	141	3,515	4 of 203 O
$90,000	$225,000	$1,215	$433	$1,633	-	$1,493	$4,774	20 of 203
	375,000	2,025	433	1,633	-	1,493	5,584	12 of 203
	525,000	2,835	433	1,633	-	1,493	6,394	9 of 203 O

*There are 203 cities in this book, 30 of which have higher than average home prices. We have estimated taxes for a tier of higher home values (and omitted the lowest tier) for these 30 cities. The city with the lowest tax burden for an income/home value combination is given the #1 rating; the higher the rating, the higher the total tax burden.

• Virginia's Top Retirement Towns •

Abingdon

In southwestern Virginia, retirees are flocking to this historic town and artists' colony in a mountain valley of well-tended farms and towns steeped in Southern charm. It has a comparatively moderate four-season climate.

Abingdon was chartered in 1778, and the town's 20-square-block historic district is lined with restored Victorian and Federal mansions and several beautiful inns and lodges. Its boasts cultural and educational amenities more typically found in much larger communities. Abingdon is noted for its live professional works at the world-famous Barter Theatre, where playwrights like Noel Coward, Tennessee Williams and Thornton Wilder accepted ham as roy-

alties. (George Bernard Shaw, a vegetarian, bartered for spinach.)

The William King Regional Arts Center houses several galleries. The Arts Depot is a gallery with working artists and hosts literary programs of the Appalachian Center for Poets and Writers. The Virginia Highlands Festival, a showcase of Appalachian culture, takes place over the first two weeks of August.

There are plenty of ways for retirees to stay physically fit. The Virginia Creeper National Recreation Trail is a 33-mile scenic rails-to-trails route popular with hikers, bikers, joggers, cross-country skiers and equestrians.

Southwest Virginia Higher Education Center offers continuing-education

courses on everything from the American Revolution to digital photography and hosts many outings, including spring wildflower field trips and tours of local vineyards.

Johnston Memorial Hospital offers extensive medical care, including a new cancer center. Roanoke, the commercial and major medical center of southwest Virginia, is about 134 miles northeast.

Population: 7,933
Climate: High Low
January   43   22
July   85   61
Cost of living: Below average
Housing cost: The median sales price of a single-family home during the first half of 2007 was $180,500, according to the

Information: *Abingdon Convention and Visitors Bureau, (800) 435-3440 or www. abingdon.com/cvb.html.*

Charlottesville

Charlottesville consistently rates high on lists of fine places to retire, but that doesn't mean the population scale is tilted toward the senior side. This is the home of the University of Virginia, whose 24,000 students keep the spring of youth a perpetual part of the community's character.

The university is also the source of Charlottesville's top-notch health care. The UVa Medical Center ranks among the best hospitals in the country. Also a teaching and research facility, its staff includes a geriatrics team of physicians and clinicians.

For many retirees, the university is a major draw to Charlottesville. The campus is noted for its beauty and classic architecture, and the school's sports teams and cultural events liven the scene. Its School of Continuing and Professional Studies has extensive programs open to the community, including enrichment classes, overnight symposiums and trips. The Institute on Aging at the university presents programs on current research.

Charlottesville itself is a gem. It owes much to Thomas Jefferson, who established the university and built his home, Monticello, outside town. Another presidential home, James Monroe's Ash Lawn-Highland, is virtually next door and James Madison's Montpelier is 27 miles away.

Besides having historical sites and numerous parks, the city is close to the Blue Ridge Mountains and Shenandoah National Park. A useful resource for seniors is the Jefferson Area Board for Aging, a nonprofit agency that provides information, programs and services, including matching people with volunteer opportunities.

Population: 40,315

Climate:

	High	Low
January	45	26
July	88	66

Cost of living: Above average

Housing cost: *The median sales price of a single-family home during the first nine months of 2007 was $280,000, according to the Charlottesville Area Association of Realtors.*

Information: *Charlottesville Regional Chamber of Commerce, (434) 295-3141 or www.cvillechamber.org.*

Williamsburg

Residents have a unique lifestyle here, mixing the modern 21st century with the Colonial 18th century. Nowhere else could you play golf, shop the outlets and chat with George Washington or Thomas Jefferson about prerevolutionary politics.

An integral part of this town is Colonial Williamsburg, a 301-acre restored capital of Colonial Virginia. It offers an authentic, interactive look at the lives and times of Williamsburg when it was a center of culture, commerce and government. Colonial Williamsburg adjoins the campus of the College of William and Mary, and nearby are the historic sites of Jamestown and Yorktown. Beyond enjoying the many programs at Colonial Williamsburg, retirees can volunteer or work part time at the settlement.

For modern fun, nearby Busch Gardens is popular with visiting grandchildren. Beaches and mountains also are within easy reach, and the many attractions of Washington, DC, are only about two and a half hours away.

Neal Robinson moved here from Kansas City in 1998 and now works as a part-time interpreter at Colonial Williamsburg. "My father and grandfather were both huge history buffs, and I guess that's where my interest started," he says. "I love American history, from the Revolution to the Civil War to World War II, and there are historic sites and lectures about all of these periods in the Williamsburg area." About a fourth of the paid "casual" interpreters are retirees, he says.

Population: 11,793

Climate:

	High	Low
January	49	28
July	89	67

Cost of living: Above average

Housing cost: *The median sales price of a single-family home during the first half of 2007 was $305,000, according to the Williamsburg Area Association of Realtors.*

Information: *Greater Williamsburg Chamber and Tourism Alliance, (757) 229-6511 or www.williamsburgcc.com.*

WASHINGTON

Washington has no state income tax but does have a state sales tax.

Major tax credits or rebates: none.

The state sales tax rate is 6.5%, but local governments can add to this amount.

Since car registration and renewal fees differ within the state, see city information for details.

Friday Harbor

Friday Harbor has no local income tax but does levy a sales tax.

Most purchases are taxed at a rate of 7.7%. Major consumer categories taxed at a different rate: none. Major consumer categories that are exempt from sales tax include: medical services, drugs and groceries.

Within the city limits of Friday Harbor, the property tax rate is .00779621. Homes are assessed at 100% of market value. There is a homeowner's exemption available to homeowners age 61 or older with household income of $35,000 or less. This exemption exempts the homeowner from excess levies, resulting in a property tax rate of .00612037; there are various other statewide exemptions that are available to homeowners age 61 or older with household income of $30,000 or less. Property tax does not cover garbage pickup.

Friday Harbor has no personal property tax for individuals.

Our couples relocating to Friday Harbor must pay a registration fee of $88 for the Explorer and $78 for the Camry. These include a license fee of $30 per automobile, an out of state fee of $15 per automobile, a weight fee of $20 for the Explorer and $10 for the Camry and other miscellaneous fees per automobile. Thereafter, on an annual basis, our couples will pay a license fee, a weight fee and other miscellaneous fees, per automobile.

Oak Harbor

Oak Harbor has no local income tax but does levy a sales tax.

Most purchases are taxed at a rate of 8.3%. Major consumer categories taxed at a different rate: none. Major con-

sumer categories that are exempt from sales tax include: medical services, drugs and groceries.

Within the city limits of Oak Harbor, the property tax rate is .00902622466. Homes are assessed at 100% of market value. There is a homeowner's exemption available to homeowners age 61 or older with household income of $35,000 or less. This exemption exempts the homeowner from excess levies, resulting in a property tax rate of .0069259608; there are various other statewide exemptions that are available to homeowners age 61 or older with household income of $30,000 or less. Property tax does not cover garbage pickup. There is also a storm drain fee of $66 per year.

Oak Harbor has no personal property tax for individuals.

Our couples relocating to Oak Harbor must pay a registration fee of $88 for the Explorer and $78 for the Camry. These include a license fee of $30 per automobile, an out of state fee of $15 per automobile, a weight fee of $20 for the Explorer and $10 for the Camry and other miscellaneous fees per automobile. Thereafter, on an annual basis, our couples will pay a license fee, a weight fee and other miscellaneous fees, per automobile.

Port Townsend

Port Townsend has no local income tax but does levy a sales tax.

Most purchases are taxed at a rate of 8.4%. Major consumer categories taxed at a different rate: none. Major consumer categories that are exempt from sales tax include: medical services, drugs and groceries.

Within the city limits of Port Townsend, the property tax rate is .00881417. Homes are assessed at 100% of market value. There is a homeowner's exemption available to homeown-

ers age 61 or older with household gross income of $35,000 or less. This exemption exempts the homeowner from excess levies, resulting in a property tax rate of .00630512; there are various other statewide exemptions that are available to homeowners age 61 or older with household income of $30,000 or less. Property tax does not cover garbage pickup. Homeowners also pay a stormwater fee, which averages $95 per year.

Port Townsend has no personal property tax for individuals.

Our couples relocating to Port Townsend must pay a registration fee of $88 for the Explorer and $78 for the Camry. These include a license fee of $30 per automobile, an out of state fee of $15 per automobile, a weight fee of $20 for the Explorer and $10 for the Camry and other miscellaneous fees per automobile. Thereafter, on an annual basis, our couples will pay a license fee, a weight fee and other miscellaneous fees, per automobile.

Seattle

Seattle has no local income tax but does levy a sales tax.

Most purchases are taxed at a rate of 8.8%. On April 1, 2007, the rate changes to 8.9%. Major consumer categories taxed at a different rate: food away from home, which is taxed at a rate of 9.3%. Major consumer categories that are exempt from sales tax include: medical services, drugs and groceries.

For residents of West Seattle, the property tax rate is .00962914. Homes are assessed at 100% of market value. There is a homeowner's exemption available to homeowners age 61 or older with household income of $35,000 or less. This exemption exempts the homeowner from excess levies, resulting in a property tax rate of .00698485; there are various other statewide exemptions that are available to homeowners age 61 or older with household income of $30,000 or less. Property tax does not cover garbage pickup.

Seattle has no personal property tax for individuals.

WASHINGTON TAX TABLE

Instructions

1. Find the Income in the far left column closest to your anticipated retirement income.
2. Find the Home Value closest to the value of the home where you will live in retirement.
3. Follow that row to your estimated Total Tax Burden at age 65 and beyond.

Income	Home Value	Property Tax & Other Fees	Personal Property Tax & Auto Fees	Sales Tax	Local Income Tax	State Income Tax	Total Tax Burden	Rank*
FRIDAY HARBOR								
$60,000	$150,000	$1,349	$100	$1,703	-	-	$3,152	19 of 203
	225,000	1,934	100	1,703	-	-	3,737	17 of 203
	300,000	2,519	100	1,703	-	-	4,322	22 of 203
$90,000	$225,000	$1,934	$100	$2,117	-	-	$4,151	7 of 203 O
	375,000	3,104	100	2,117	-	-	5,321	8 of 203 O
	525,000	4,273	100	2,117	-	-	6,490	11 of 203
	$600,000	$4,858	$100	$2,117	-	-	$7,075	4 of 30
	750,000	6,027	100	2,117	-	-	8,244	6 of 30
	900,000	7,197	100	2,117	-	-	9,414	6 of 30
OAK HARBOR								
$30,000	$125,000	$765	$100	$1,045	-	-	$1,910	24 of 173
	150,000	921	100	1,045	-	-	2,066	23 of 173
	175,000	1,034	100	1,045	-	-	2,179	20 of 173
$60,000	$150,000	$1,600	$100	$1,836	-	-	$3,536	41 of 203
	225,000	2,277	100	1,836	-	-	4,213	41 of 203
	300,000	2,954	100	1,836	-	-	4,890	43 of 203
$90,000	$225,000	$2,277	$100	$2,282	-	-	$4,659	17 of 203
	375,000	3,631	100	2,282	-	-	6,013	19 of 203
	525,000	4,985	100	2,282	-	-	7,367	26 of 203
PORT TOWNSEND								
$30,000	$125,000	$746	$100	$1,057	-	-	$1,903	22 of 173
	150,000	888	100	1,057	-	-	2,045	21 of 173
	175,000	990	100	1,057	-	-	2,147	18 of 173
$60,000	$150,000	$1,595	$100	$1,858	-	-	$3,553	43 of 203
	225,000	2,256	100	1,858	-	-	4,214	43 of 203
	300,000	2,917	100	1,858	-	-	4,875	42 of 203
$90,000	$225,000	$2,256	$100	$2,309	-	-	$4,665	18 of 203
	375,000	3,578	100	2,309	-	-	5,987	18 of 203
	525,000	4,900	100	2,309	-	-	7,309	24 of 203
SEATTLE								
$60,000	$150,000	$1,624	$234	$1,959	-	-	$3,817	63 of 203
	225,000	2,347	234	1,959	-	-	4,540	61 of 203
	300,000	3,069	234	1,959	-	-	5,262	60 of 203
$90,000	$225,000	$2,347	$234	$2,435	-	-	$5,016	22 of 203
	375,000	3,791	234	2,435	-	-	6,460	27 of 203
	525,000	5,235	234	2,435	-	-	7,904	30 of 203
	$600,000	$5,957	$234	$2,435	-	-	$8,626	9 of 30
	750,000	7,402	234	2,435	-	-	10,071	8 of 30
	900,000	8,846	234	2,435	-	-	11,515	8 of 30
SEQUIM								
$30,000	$125,000	$711	$100	$1,057	-	-	$1,868	18 of 173
	150,000	870	100	1,057	-	-	2,027	19 of 173
	175,000	986	100	1,057	-	-	2,143	17 of 173

*There are 203 cities in this book, 30 of which have higher than average home prices. We have estimated taxes for a tier of higher home values (and omitted the lowest tier) for these 30 cities. The city with the lowest tax burden for an income/home value combination is given the #1 rating; the higher the rating, the higher the total tax burden.

Income	Home Value	Property Tax & Other Fees	Personal Property Tax & Auto Fees	Sales Tax	Local Income Tax	State Income Tax	Total Tax Burden	Rank*
SEQUIM continued								
$60,000	$150,000	$1,435	$100	$1,858	-	-	$3,393	30 of 203
	225,000	2,063	100	1,858	-	-	4,021	32 of 203
	300,000	2,691	100	1,858	-	-	4,649	34 of 203
$90,000	$225,000	$2,063	$100	$2,309	-	-	$4,472	13 of 203
	375,000	3,318	100	2,309	-	-	5,727	13 of 203
	525,000	4,573	100	2,309	-	-	6,982	18 of 203
SPOKANE								
$30,000	$125,000	$789	$100	$1,082	-	-	$1,971	26 of 173
	150,000	972	100	1,082	-	-	2,154	25 of 173
	175,000	1,104	100	1,082	-	-	2,286	22 of 173
$60,000	$150,000	$2,404	$100	$1,902	-	-	$4,406	119 of 203
	225,000	3,517	100	1,902	-	-	5,519	121 of 203
	300,000	4,629	100	1,902	-	-	6,631	129 of 203
$90,000	$225,000	$3,517	$100	$2,364	-	-	$5,981	64 of 203
	375,000	5,741	100	2,364	-	-	8,205	88 of 203
	525,000	7,965	100	2,364	-	-	10,429	105 of 203
TACOMA								
$30,000	$125,000	$779	$234	$1,108	-	-	$2,121	35 of 173
	150,000	958	234	1,108	-	-	2,300	33 of 173
	175,000	1,088	234	1,108	-	-	2,430	31 of 173
$60,000	$150,000	$2,433	$234	$1,946	-	-	$4,613	134 of 203
	225,000	3,560	234	1,946	-	-	5,740	134 of 203
	300,000	4,687	234	1,946	-	-	6,867	135 of 203
$90,000	$225,000	$3,560	$234	$2,419	-	-	$6,213	84 of 203
	375,000	5,814	234	2,419	-	-	8,467	97 of 203
	525,000	8,067	234	2,419	-	-	10,720	116 of 203

*There are 203 cities in this book, 30 of which have higher than average home prices. We have estimated taxes for a tier of higher home values (and omitted the lowest tier) for these 30 cities. The city with the lowest tax burden for an income/home value combination is given the #1 rating; the higher the rating, the higher the total tax burden.

Our couples relocating to Seattle must pay a registration fee of $169 for the Explorer and $138 for the Camry at the time of registration. These include a license fee of $30 per automobile, an out of state fee of $15 per automobile, a Regional Transit Authority (RTA) excise tax based upon the year, make and model of the automobile of $81 for the Explorer and $60 for the Camry, a weight fee of $20 for the Explorer and $10 for the Camry and other miscellaneous fees per automobile. Thereafter, on an annual basis, our couples will pay a license fee, a weight fee, an RTA excise tax and other miscellaneous fees, per automobile.

Sequim

Sequim has no local income tax but does levy a sales tax.

Most purchases are taxed at a rate of 8.4%. Major consumer categories taxed at a different rate: none. Major consumer categories that are exempt from sales tax include: medical services, drugs and groceries.

Within the city limits of Sequim, the property tax rate is .00836854. Homes are assessed at 100% of market value. There is a homeowner's exemption available to homeowners age 61 or older with household income of $35,000 or less. This exemption exempts the homeowner from excess levies, resulting in a property tax rate of .0070818; there are various other statewide exemptions that are available to homeowners age 61 or older with household income of $30,000 or less. Property tax does not cover garbage pickup.

Sequim has no personal property tax for individuals.

Our couples relocating to Sequim must pay a registration fee of $88 for the Explorer and $78 for the Camry.

These include a license fee of $30 per automobile, an out of state fee of $15 per automobile, a weight fee of $20 for the Explorer and $10 for the Camry and other miscellaneous fees per automobile. Thereafter, on an annual basis, our couples will pay a license fee, a weight fee and other miscellaneous fees, per automobile.

Spokane

Spokane has no local income tax but does levy a sales tax.

Most purchases are taxed at a rate of 8.6%. Major consumer categories taxed at a different rate: none. Major consumer categories that are exempt from sales tax include: medical services, drugs and groceries.

In the Corbin Park area of Spokane, the property tax rate is .014828934573329. Homes are assessed at 100% of market value. There is a homeowner's exemption available to homeowners age 61 or older with household income of $35,000 or less. This exemption exempts the homeowner from excess levies, resulting in a property tax rate of .008126087654646; there are various other statewide exemptions that are available to homeowners age 61 or older with household income of $30,000 or less. Property tax does not cover garbage pickup.

Spokane has no personal property tax for individuals.

Our couples relocating to Spokane must pay a registration fee of $88 for the Explorer and $78 for the Camry. These include a license fee of $30 per automobile, an out of state fee of $15 per automobile, a weight fee of $20 for the Explorer and $10 for the Camry and other miscellaneous fees per automobile. Thereafter, on an annual basis, our couples will pay a license fee, a weight fee and other miscellaneous fees, per automobile.

Tacoma

Tacoma has no local income tax but does levy a sales tax.

Most purchases are taxed at a rate of 8.8%. Major consumer categories taxed at a different rate: none. Major consumer categories that are exempt from sales tax include: medical services, drugs and groceries.

In the tax code 005 area of Tacoma, the property tax rate is .01502305618. Homes are assessed at 100% of market value. There is a homeowner's exemption available to homeowners age 61 or older with household income of $35,000 or less. This exemption exempts the homeowner from excess levies, resulting in a property tax rate of .00798083422; there are various other statewide exemptions that are available to homeowners age 61 or older with household income of $30,000 or less. Property tax does not cover garbage pickup.

Tacoma has no personal property tax for individuals.

Our couples relocating to Tacoma must pay a registration fee of $169 for the Explorer and $138 for the Camry at the time of registration. These include a license fee of $30 per automobile, an out of state fee of $15 per automobile, a Regional Transit Authority (RTA) excise tax based upon the year, make and model of the automobile of $81 for the Explorer and $60 for the Camry, a weight fee of $20 for the Explorer and $10 for the Camry and other miscellaneous fees per automobile. Thereafter, on an annual basis, our couples will pay a license fee, a weight fee, an RTA excise tax and other miscellaneous fees, per automobile.

• Washington's Top Retirement Towns •

Port Townsend

People come to Port Townsend because of its small-town lifestyle. "It's a lovely little town with a lot of charm, old homes and a pretty downtown," says retiree Barbara Paul.

Yet the seaport is only one and a half hours away by ferry from Seattle and such big-city attractions as museums, professional sports teams and shopping. Once a haven for 1960s hippies and artists, Port Townsend is undergoing a renaissance. Its artistic heritage is still strong, and Port Townsend is one of only three Victorian seaports recognized on the National Register of Historic Places.

The town is ideal for those who enjoy an active, outdoor lifestyle. From the harbor, it's easy to take a day trip to the San Juan Islands and go kayaking, sailing, snorkeling or whale-watching. There are three golf courses within 20 minutes of downtown. Hiking in Olympic National Park is just 45 minutes away.

Among its many cultural activities, the town hosts jazz, country blues and chamber music events in the summer. Local stores provide unique shopping opportunities, augmented by major chain stores 35 to 45 minutes away.

"I love it. I can't imagine living anywhere else," says Barbara, who moved here from Delaware with her husband, Charlie, a few years ago. "We had been looking (for a retirement locale) for several years. Then we happened upon Port Townsend." The Pauls bought a Victorian home that needed work and stayed part time in Port Townsend while they renovated it and then moved permanently.

Population: 9,134

Climate: High Low
January 45 38
July 70 53

Cost of living: Above average

Housing cost: The median sales price for a single-family home during the first half of 2007 was $360,903, according to the Jefferson County Association of Realtors.

Information: Port Townsend Visitor Center, (888) 365-6978 or www.enjoypt.com.

Sequim

Washington's infamous rust doesn't have a fighting chance in this friendly, relaxed town in the state's "banana belt" between the majestic Olympic Mountains and the Strait of Juan de Fuca on the north coast of the Olympic Peninsula.

Mount Olympus, the crown jewel of the Olympics, blocks the frequent rains that soak the rest of the region, leaving Sequim in a rain shadow that enjoys 306 days of sunshine annually and receives just 16 inches of rain a year — about the same as Los Angeles. (By contrast, the rain forests just 60 miles west get a drenching 200-plus inches.) With mild temperatures year-round, Sequim is the ideal place for seniors who want to settle in the Northwest but aren't willing to settle for eight months of soggy weather.

Early homesteaders had to dig irrigation ditches by hand to bring in water from the nearby Dungeness River to water their crops — an effort that paved the way for the town's continued growth and is honored each year at the Irrigation Festival.

In recent years, sun-loving retirees make up an ever-increasing percentage of the population. Sequim is a magnet for those who enjoy boating, cycling, fishing, golfing and hiking. Or, you can go birding, beachcombing and crabbing at Dungeness Spit, whose bay is home to the famous (and delicious) Dungeness crab. At low tide, hikers can head out to the New Dungeness Lighthouse, at the end of the spit.

Seniors who flex their green thumbs are rewarded with flowers, vegetables and fruits of blue-ribbon proportions. The Sequim Open Aire Market features locally grown produce, and you can pick your own berries at several local raspberry and strawberry farms.

Housing in Sequim and the environs includes adult-only manufactured-home parks, condo and townhouse communities with clubhouses, single-family homes in established neighborhoods, custom homes in upscale golf estates and even mini-farms.

Population: 5,688

Climate: High Low
January 45 29
July 69 49

Cost of living: *Above average*

Housing cost: *The median sales price of a single-family home during the first half of 2007 was $295,000, according to a spokesman for the Sequim Board of Realtors.*

Information: *Sequim-Dungeness Chamber of Commerce, (800) 737-8462 or www.cityofsequim.com.*

Spokane

Called the Lilac City for the flowers that bloom here in the spring, Spokane sits at the east edge of the Columbia Plateau's wheat farms and steppe, where they meet the forested Selkirk Mountains. A series of dramatic falls from the Spokane River graces the center of town, and the city has developed an extensive skywalk system.

It has a semiarid climate, with cold winters and warm summers. The Cascade Range to the west somewhat protects the city from the influences of the Pacific Ocean air.

Although the largest city between Seattle and Minneapolis, it's noted for the surrounding great outdoors as well as urban amenities. There are 76 lakes, 33 golf courses, 11 wineries, five ski resorts, five national parks, the spectacular Columbia River Gorge and Grand Coulee Dam, all within an easy drive.

One of the area's finest attractions is the Spokane River Centennial Trail, a 67-mile-long path linking Spokane to Coeur d'Alene, ID, and paved for use by pedestrians, bicyclists and skaters.

In addition to museums, community festivals and a rich international culture, the city has several dozen organizations dedicated to music, theater, dance and the visual arts. The 1931, Art Deco-style Fox Theater is home to the Spokane Symphony, and the town is a regular stop for touring shows and concerts.

Founded in 1873, Spokane takes its name from that of an Indian tribe, meaning "Children of the Sun." The falls were a rich source of steelhead and salmon for early inhabitants. Silver deposits brought a boom in the late 1890s. Today, some housing choices in such areas as Browne's Addition, a national historic district west of downtown, include huge Queen Anne mansions.

Population: 198,081

Climate: High Low
January 33 22
July 82 55

Cost of living: Below average

Housing cost: *The median price was $189,750 during the first half of 2007, according to the National Association of Realtors.*

Information: *Greater Spokane Incorporated, (509) 624-1393 or www.move tospokane.com.*

Tacoma

Although Tacoma is a couple of hours from the Pacific by car, it has "anything you want to do with an ocean," according to Gary Brackett, business and trade development manager for the Tacoma-Pierce County Chamber. Tacoma is on Commencement Bay at the lower end of Puget Sound, which connects a huge metropolitan area and eventually leads, by way of the Strait of Juan de Fuca, to

the sea.

Significantly for military retirees, Tacoma also has McChord Air Force Base, neighboring Fort Lewis and Madigan Army Medical Center, as well as a VA hospital. About 45,000 military retirees live in the area and have access to their extensive facilities.

Although the area's cost of living is somewhat above average, there are compensations. The Pacific Northwest has wonderful scenery and a moderate climate. Average summer highs are 75 in July and August; average winter lows are in the 30s but above freezing. It rains (4.3 inches monthly on average), but that contributes to the area's scenic beauty.

The topography is varied. It's heavily forested with evergreens, and although Tacoma proper is low (sea level to 450 feet), the Olympic Mountains to the west and the Cascade Range to the east are spectacular. Mount Rainier's 14,411-foot summit is about 40 miles away as the crow flies.

As might be imagined, the sea and the mountains figure prominently in the area's recreational activities. Culturally, Tacoma has music, opera, theater and dance companies and some excellent museums, including the unusual Museum of Glass in the city's renovated waterfront district. The University of Puget Sound, Pacific Lutheran University and the University of Washington Tacoma add a lively educational scene.

Population: 196,532

Climate: High Low
January 46 36
July 75 55

Cost of living: Above average

Housing cost: *The median price of homes in the Tacoma metro area was $282,750 during the first half of 2007, according to the Washington Center for Real Estate Research.*

Information: *Tacoma-Pierce County Chamber, (253) 627-2175 or www.tacoma chamber.org.*

WEST VIRGINIA

West Virginia has a state income tax and does levy a state sales tax.

The state income tax rate is graduated from 3% to 6.5% depending upon income bracket. For married couples filing jointly, the rate is 3% on the first $10,000 of taxable income; 4% on the next $15,000 of taxable income; 4.5% on the next $15,000 of taxable income; 6% on the next $20,000 of taxable income; and 6.5% for taxable income above $60,000.

In calculating the tax, there is no deduction for federal income tax paid. Federal, state and private pensions are not exempt, although there is a deduction of up to $2,000 from certain federal and state pensions. Social Security

> ○ **Tax Heavens:** None
> Ψ **Tax Hells:** None
> **Top Retirement Towns:**
> Berkeley Springs, Charleston

benefits subject to federal tax are not exempt. There is an exemption allowance of $2,000 per person from adjusted gross income. There is a senior citizen deduction of up to $8,000 per person from adjusted gross income from any source. There is a low-income earned income exclusion for married couples filing jointly with adjusted gross income of $10,000 or less.

Major tax credits or rebates include: credit for income taxes paid to other

states, which our couples do not qualify for and senior citizen tax credit for property taxes paid, which one of our couples qualifies for.

The state sales tax rate is 6% and most purchases are taxed at this rate. There are no local sales taxes. Major consumer categories taxed at a different rate: groceries, which are taxed at 5%. The tax on groceries is decreasing to 4% as of July 7, 2007. Major consumer categories that are exempt from sales tax include: drugs and medical services.

Our couples relocating to Berkeley Springs and Charleston must pay a 5% privilege tax based on the NADA loan value of owned automobiles. The privilege tax is $539 for the Explorer and $638 for the Camry. As of July 1, 2007,

WEST VIRGINIA TAX TABLE

Instructions

1. Find the Income in the far left column closest to your anticipated retirement income.
2. Find the Home Value closest to the value of the home where you will live in retirement.
3. Follow that row to your estimated Total Tax Burden at age 65 and beyond.

Income	Home Value	Property Tax & Other Fees	Personal Property Tax & Auto Fees	Sales Tax	Local Income Tax	State Income Tax[†]	Total Tax Burden	Rank*
BERKELEY SPRINGS								
$30,000	$125,000	$948	$523	$882	-	($106)	$2,247	45 of 173
	150,000	1,135	523	882	-	(106)	2,434	44 of 173
	175,000	1,321	523	882	-	(106)	2,620	43 of 173
$60,000	$150,000	$1,135	$523	$1,505	-	$1,094	$4,257	106 of 203
	225,000	1,695	523	1,505	-	1,094	4,817	81 of 203
	300,000	2,254	523	1,505	-	1,094	5,376	68 of 203
$90,000	$225,000	$1,695	$523	$1,851	-	$3,161	$7,230	131 of 203
	375,000	2,814	523	1,851	-	3,161	8,349	92 of 203
	525,000	3,934	523	1,851	-	3,161	9,469	72 of 203
CHARLESTON								
$30,000	$125,000	$999	$594	$882	$52	($126)	$2,401	60 of 173
	150,000	1,214	594	882	52	(126)	2,616	60 of 173
	175,000	1,430	594	882	52	(126)	2,832	59 of 173
$60,000	$150,000	$1,214	$594	$1,505	$52	$1,094	$4,459	124 of 203
	225,000	1,861	594	1,505	52	1,094	5,106	100 of 203
	300,000	2,507	594	1,505	52	1,094	5,752	89 of 203
$90,000	$225,000	$1,861	$594	$1,851	$52	$3,161	$7,519	144 of 203
	375,000	3,153	594	1,851	52	3,161	8,811	111 of 203
	525,000	4,446	594	1,851	52	3,161	10,104	93 of 203

[†]Property tax credit is issued as a reduction of income tax due or as a refund if the credit is greater than the tax liability.
*There are 203 cities in this book, 30 of which have higher than average home prices. We have estimated taxes for a tier of higher home values (and omitted the lowest tier) for these 30 cities. The city with the lowest tax burden for an income/home value combination is given the #1 rating; the higher the rating, the higher the total tax burden.

the privilege tax has been eliminated for new residents moving into West Virginia with a vehicle already titled in their name in another state. Our couples must also pay a title fee of $10 per automobile, a lien fee of $5 per automobile and a registration fee of $30 per automobile at the time of registration. Thereafter, on an annual basis, our couples will pay a renewal fee per automobile.

Berkeley Springs

Berkeley Springs has no local income tax and does not levy an additional sales tax.

In the town of Bath, located in the Berkeley Springs area, the property tax rate is .01244 for Class II (owner-occupied, residential) property. Homes are assessed at 60% of market value. There is a homestead exemption of $20,000 off assessed value available to homeowners if at least one is age 65 or older. Property tax does not cover garbage pickup. There is also a public safety fee of $36 per year and a street fee of $48 per year.

Berkeley Springs has a personal property tax rate of .00622 for Class I items; a rate of .01244 for Class II items; and a rate of .02488 for Class IV items. Personal property is assessed at 60% of true and actual value. Items subject to the personal property tax include: Class I — notes, stocks, bonds, farm equipment and farm animals; Class II — owner-occupied residences and bona fide farms including mobile homes; Class IV — everything not in Class I and II inside of municipalities. If property is inside city limits, this would include vehicles, satellite dishes, pets, watercraft, aircraft, trailers, campers, motorcycles and other real estate. There is a homestead exemption of $20,000 off assessed value available to homeowners if at least one is age 65 or older for Class II items only. The Class I personal property tax is sometimes referred to as an intangibles tax in other states, and we do not include it in our calculations (see Intangibles Tax in Introduction). As of the 2008 tax year, there is no Class I property. We've assumed automobiles are the only items owned by our couples that are subject to personal property tax.

Charleston

Charleston has a local income tax but does not levy an additional sales tax.

The local income city service fee is $1 per week for employees based within the city of Charleston.

Within the city limits of Charleston, the property tax rate is .014363 for Class II (owner-occupied, residential) property. Homes are assessed at 60% of market value. There is a homestead exemption of $20,000 off assessed value available to homeowners if at least one is age 65 or older. Property tax does not cover garbage pickup. There is also a fire service fee of approximately $29 per year.

Charleston has a personal property tax rate of .0071815 for Class I items; a rate of .014363 for Class II items; and a rate of .028726 for Class IV items. Personal property is assessed at 60% of true and actual value.

Items subject to the personal property tax include: Class I — notes, stocks, bonds, farm equipment and farm animals; Class II — owner-occupied residences and bona fide farms including mobile homes; Class IV — everything not in classes I and II inside of municipalities. If property is inside city limits, this would include vehicles, satellite dishes, pets, watercraft, aircraft, trailers, campers, motorcycles and other real estate. There is a homestead exemption of $20,000 off assessed value available to homeowners if at least one is age 65 or older for Class II items only. The Class I personal property tax is sometimes referred to as an intangibles tax in other states, and we do not include it in our calculations. (See Intangibles Tax in Introduction.) As of the 2008 tax year, there is no class I property. We've assumed automobiles are the only items owned by our couples that are subject to personal property tax.

• West Virginia's Top Retirement Towns •

Berkeley Springs

In the state's eastern panhandle lies Berkeley Springs, a mountain town favored by retirees from the Baltimore-Washington, DC, metro area, 100 miles away. It's 25 miles northwest of Martinsburg, a town with a large regional hospital and several malls.

Long before settlers reached the Blue Ridge frontier, American Indians stopped at the warm mineral springs here in what would become the town of Bath. This is still the official name of the municipality, though it is known as Berkeley Springs.

It was one of the country's first spa towns by the mid-1700s, drawing summer visitors from the nation's capital who stayed in grand hotels, gambled and "took the waters" for their health.

Among the frequent visitors was George Washington, whose stone bathtub is still a point of interest.

The summer places were destroyed by fire, and today the historic structures date to the early 20th century. But the famous waters still flow from Warm Springs Ridge at a constant 74 degrees, and visitors still come to drink from the Lord Fairfax public tap, bathe in the old Roman Bath House or indulge in treatments at several modern spas.

The town's lively art and cultural scene includes festivals honoring food, wine, apple butter and, of course, water. During the annual Winter Festival of the Waters, drinking water is judged as seriously as for an international wine competition.

The town has whimsical touches, such

as the Depression-era Star Theatre, where the admission is still $3.75 and couches are 50 cents extra. The Ice House, a former 40,000-square-foot cold storage facility for apples, is now a community art center hosting concerts, art classes, theater productions and an artists' co-op.

Development has come slowly to Berkeley Springs and Morgan County, which is still 79 percent wooded. The highest point in the county is Cacapon Mountain, at 2,320 feet, and Cacapon Resort State Park has extensive recreational facilities including a golf course and miles of hiking trails.

Population: About 2,500 in town, 16,337 in the county

Climate:

	High	Low
January	44	23
July	88	60

Cost of living: Below average

Housing cost: The median price of homes the first half of 2007 was $200,275, according to Metropolitan Regional Information Systems.

Information: Berkeley Springs-Morgan County Chamber of Commerce, (304) 258-3738 or www.berkeleyspringscham ber.com. Travel Berkeley Springs, (800) 447-8797 or www.berkeleysprings.com.

Charleston

West Virginia is exceptionally scenic, centrally located and one of the most economical places to live, particularly among states in the more expensive eastern half of the country. Charleston, the capital, is in the southwestern part of the state, about halfway between Lexington, KY, and Roanoke, on the western edge of Virginia. North to south, Charleston is about halfway between Columbus, OH, and Winston-Salem, NC.

Now that you're oriented, think wild. The city is on the edge of a state forest and close to the New River Gorge National River. Both the New and nearby Gauley rivers are considered outstanding white-water rafting challenges. For hiking and biking enthusiasts, there are trails along the Kanawha River in the city and numerous outings beyond. The Appalachian Trail and all recreational venues of the Blue Ridge Parkway are within easy reach. In winter, there's skiing nearby.

Though not too large, the city has numerous amenities, as it's the governmental, cultural, economic, medical and shopping hub of the state. The downtown area has numerous landmarks, including Victorian-era buildings. The Charleston Civic Center hosts sports events and entertainment by top artists. The Clay Center for the Arts & Sciences of West Virginia has live productions and is home to the West Virginia Symphony Orchestra, a discovery museum and a giant-screen theater. There are several universities in the surrounding area, which add to the cultural scene as well as offering learning opportunities.

While it has enough attractions on its own, it's also not too far from Washington, DC, and Richmond and Charlottesville, VA.

Population: 50,846

Climate:

	High	Low
January	43	24
July	85	63

Cost of living: Below average

Housing cost: The average sales price of a single-family home during the first half of 2007 was $167,631, according to the Kanawha Valley Multiple Listing Service.

Information: Charleston Convention and Visitors Bureau, (800) 733-5469 or www. charlestonwv.com.

WISCONSIN

Wisconsin has a state income tax and a state sales tax.

The state income tax rate is graduated from 4.6% to 6.75% depending upon income bracket. For married couples filing jointly, the rates are 4.6% on the first $12,210 of taxable income; 6.15% on the next $12,220 of taxable income; 6.5% on the next $158,780 of taxable income; and 6.75% on taxable income above $183,210.

In calculating the tax, there is no deduction for federal income tax paid. Federal and state pensions are not generally exempt from tax, although Wisconsin does exempt pensions received by persons who were members of, or retired from, certain governmental retirement systems prior to

---

O Tax Heavens: None
Ψ Tax Hells: None
Top Retirement Towns:
Door County (Sturgeon Bay),
Madison

January 1, 1964. Private pensions are not exempt. Some Social Security benefits subject to federal tax are not exempt from tax. There is a sliding-scale standard deduction for married couples filing jointly that starts at $15,240 and decreases until it is completely phased out at Wisconsin adjusted gross income of $94,175. There is a personal exemption of $700 per person from Wisconsin adjusted gross income. There is also an

exemption of $250 per person for persons age 65 or older.

Major tax credits or rebates include: credit for income taxes paid to other states, working families credit and itemized deduction credit, which our couples do not qualify for; and school property tax credit and married couple credit, which some of our couples qualify for.

The state sales tax rate is 5%, but local governments can add to this amount.

Our couples relocating to the cities listed below must pay a plate registration fee of $55 per automobile, a title fee of $45 per automobile and a lien filing fee of $4 per automobile at the time of registration. Thereafter, on an annual basis, our couples will pay a plate registration fee per automobile.

WISCONSIN TAX TABLE

Instructions

1. Find the Income in the far left column closest to your anticipated retirement income.
2. Find the Home Value closest to the value of the home where you will live in retirement.
3. Follow that row to your estimated Total Tax Burden at age 65 and beyond.

Income	Home Value	Property Tax & Other Fees	Personal Property Tax & Auto Fees	Sales Tax	Local Income Tax	State Income Tax†	Total Tax Burden	Rank*
EAGLE RIVER								
$30,000	$125,000	$1,771	$110	$692	-	-	$2,573	75 of 173
	150,000	2,139	110	692	-	-	2,941	82 of 173
	175,000	2,507	110	692	-	-	3,309	88 of 173
$60,000	$150,000	$2,139	$110	$1,217	-	$1,738	$5,204	164 of 203
	225,000	3,242	110	1,217	-	1,687	6,256	156 of 203
	300,000	4,346	110	1,217	-	1,633	7,306	149 of 203
$90,000	$225,000	$3,242	$110	$1,512	-	$3,839	$8,703	180 of 203
	375,000	5,449	110	1,512	-	3,731	10,802	170 of 203
	525,000	7,656	110	1,512	-	3,697	12,975	157 of 203
MADISON								
$30,000	$125,000	$2,388	$110	$692	-	-	$3,190	137 of 173
	150,000	2,880	110	692	-	-	3,682	140 of 173
	175,000	3,373	110	692	-	-	4,175	136 of 173
$60,000	$150,000	$2,880	$110	$1,217	-	$1,663	$5,870	187 of 203
	225,000	4,358	110	1,217	-	1,573	7,258	182 of 203
	300,000	5,835	110	1,217	-	1,545	8,707	181 of 203
$90,000	$225,000	$4,358	$110	$1,512	-	$3,725	$9,705	189 of 203
	375,000	7,313	110	1,512	-	3,697	12,632	187 of 203
	525,000	10,268	110	1,512	-	3,697	15,587	185 of 203
MILWAUKEE								
$30,000	$125,000	$2,550	$110	$708	-	-	$3,368	146 of 173
	150,000	3,079	110	708	-	-	3,897	148 of 173
	175,000	3,608	110	708	-	-	4,426	149 of 173

Income	Home Value	Property Tax & Other Fees	Personal Property Tax & Auto Fees	Sales Tax	Local Income Tax	State Income Tax[†]	Total Tax Burden	Rank[*]
MILWAUKEE continued								
$60,000	$150,000	$3,079	$110	$1,245	-	$1,693	$6,127	191 of 203
	225,000	4,667	110	1,245	-	1,621	7,643	188 of 203
	300,000	6,255	110	1,245	-	1,546	9,156	186 of 203
$90,000	$225,000	$4,667	$110	$1,547	-	$3,773	$10,097	192 of 203
	375,000	7,842	110	1,547	-	3,697	13,196	192 of 203
	525,000	11,018	110	1,547	-	3,697	16,372	191 of 203
STURGEON BAY								
$30,000	$125,000	$2,368	$110	$692	-	-	$3,170	136 of 173
	150,000	2,824	110	692	-	-	3,626	134 of 173
	175,000	3,281	110	692	-	-	4,083	133 of 173
$60,000	$150,000	$2,824	$110	$1,217	-	$1,696	$5,847	186 of 203
	225,000	4,194	110	1,217	-	1,621	7,142	177 of 203
	300,000	5,563	110	1,217	-	1,549	8,439	176 of 203
$90,000	$225,000	$4,194	$110	$1,512	-	$3,773	$9,589	186 of 203
	375,000	6,933	110	1,512	-	3,697	12,252	186 of 203
	525,000	9,672	110	1,512	-	3,697	14,991	182 of 203

[†]School property tax credit is taken as a reduction of state income tax due.
[*]There are 203 cities in this book, 30 of which have higher than average home prices. We have estimated taxes for a tier of higher home values (and omitted the lowest tier) for these 30 cities. The city with the lowest tax burden for an income/home value combination is given the #1 rating; the higher the rating, the higher the total tax burden..

Eagle River

Eagle River has no local income tax but does levy a sales tax.

Most purchases are taxed at a rate of 5.5%. Major consumer categories taxed at a different rate: none. Major consumer categories that are exempt from sales tax include: drugs, groceries and medical services.

Within the city limits of Eagle River, the property tax rate is .01539. Homes are assessed at 95.6% of market value. There is a sliding-scale homestead property tax credit available for residents with household income of $24,500 or less. There is also a lottery and gaming tax credit. The amount of the credit is dependent upon the annual lottery revenue and the school district in which the homeowner resides. Property tax includes garbage pickup.

Eagle River has no personal property tax for individuals.

Madison

Madison has no local income tax but does levy a sales tax.

Most purchases are taxed at a rate of 5.5%. Major consumer categories taxed at a different rate: none. Major consumer categories that are exempt from sales tax include: drugs, groceries and medical services.

Within the Madison school district, the property tax rate is .019702. Homes are assessed at 100% of market value. There is a sliding-scale homestead property tax credit available for residents with household income of $24,500 or less. There is also a lottery and gaming tax credit. The amount of the credit is dependent upon the annual lottery revenue and the school district in which the homeowner resides. Property tax includes garbage pickup. There is also a stormwater fee. The amount of this fee depends on the size of the property.

Madison has no personal property tax for individuals.

Milwaukee

Milwaukee has no local income tax but does levy a sales tax.

Most purchases are taxed at a rate of 5.6%. Major consumer categories taxed at a different rate: food away from home, which is taxed at a rate of 5.85%. Major consumer categories that are exempt from sales tax include: drugs, groceries and medical services.

Within the Milwaukee school district, the property tax rate is .02241. Homes are assessed at 94.47% of market value. There is a sliding-scale homestead property tax credit available for residents with household income of $24,500 or less. There is also a lottery and gaming tax credit. The amount of the credit is dependent upon the annual lottery revenue and the school district in which the homeowner resides. Property tax does not cover garbage pickup.

Milwaukee has no personal property tax for individuals.

Sturgeon Bay

Sturgeon Bay has no local income tax but does levy a sales tax.

Most purchases are taxed at a rate of 5.5%. Major consumer categories taxed at a different rate: none. Major consumer categories that are exempt from sales tax include: drugs, groceries and medical services.

Within the Sturgeon Bay school district, the property tax rate is .01897. Homes are assessed at 96.27% of market value. There is a sliding-scale homestead property tax credit available for residents with household income of $24,500 or less. There is also a lottery and gaming tax credit. The amount of the credit is dependent upon the annual lottery revenue and the school district in which the homeowner resides. Property tax does not cover garbage pickup.

Sturgeon Bay has no personal property tax for individuals.

Door County (Sturgeon Bay)

Door County lures retirees looking for more of the good life, with more shoreline (estimated 300-plus miles), lighthouses (10) and state parks (five) than any other community in the United States. Add four moderate seasons and 11 picturesque New England-style villages with artsy and historic downtowns and you've got the Cape Cod of the Midwest.

Door County's climate is tempered by Lake Michigan. Winters are milder and summers cooler and less humid than inland destinations. On summer nights you'll probably need a sweat-shirt for strolls along the beach. Active seniors and those with creative leanings will feel at home in this year-round recreational playground with hiking, cycling and all types of water and snow sports.

Sturgeon Bay, the county seat, is the only city on the peninsula. A former lumber center, it has a quaint downtown, with unique shops, galleries, fine restaurants and B&Bs, and outdoor recreation at Potawatomi State Park. There's also a fully staffed hospital, two golf courses and a regional airport.

Fish Creek is the heart of Door County's art scene, with the Peninsula Players, a professional summer theater, and the American Folklore Theatre and Peninsula Art School. Ellison Bay is home to The Clearing, a famous school of the arts, literature and ecology, while Egg Harbor claims the Birch Creek Music Performance Center, a nationally acclaimed academy with evening concerts.

Ephraim's historic downtown is lined with elegant white buildings that reflect its Moravian heritage, and the town is a gateway to Peninsula State Park, Wisconsin's largest, with trails for year-round recreation. In winter, the lake freezes solid at Eagle Harbor and ice-fishing shanties spring up overnight. Sister Bay has a beautiful sand beach and waterfront park hosting weekly summer outdoor concerts and an acclaimed fall festival. Baileys Harbor is known for great birding and hiking, charter fishing tours and a wildflower preserve with a lighthouse and beach.

Housing in Door County ranges from moderately priced condos and single-family homes to pricey waterfront estates.

Population: 28,200 in the county

Climate:

	High	Low
January	24	9
July	74	58

Cost of living: Above average

Housing cost: The median sales price of a single-family detached home was $175,000 while the median sales price of a condo was $277,000 for the first half of 2007, according to the Door County Board of Realtors.

Information: Door County Visitor Bureau, (800) 527-3529 or www.doorcounty.com.

Madison

Students at the University of Wisconsin-Madison often refer to the state capital as "Madtown." The college dominates the city, enriching it immeasurably with both an academic and youthful feel.

But Madison is about a lot more than campus culture. It has a terrific location, just 80 miles west of Milwaukee and 140 miles northwest of Chicago, for those looking for a big-city fix. Set on an isthmus sandwiched by lakes Mendota and Monona, Madison offers sailing, paddling and windsurfing in the summer, and cross-country skiing, hiking and ice-skating in winter. As for those winters — they are very long and very cold.

Madison was picked as the best place to live in America as far back as 1948 in Life magazine, and it still ranks high. It has terrific bike paths and lots of locally grown organic food at the Dane County Farmers Market during much of the season.

It's also a sophisticated city, with Frank Lloyd Wright buildings, a thriving theater and arts community and a great dining scene. Coffee bars, record shops and thrift stores mix with upscale bars, restaurants and brewpubs. The university offers an endless array of learning opportunities for retirees.

Health care is another of Madison's strengths, with five general hospitals, more than 20 major medical clinics and UW-Madison's medical, nursing and pharmacy schools.

With performances by the Madison Repertory Theatre, opera and symphony orchestra, touring productions at the Overture Center for the Arts and a full schedule of performances at UW-Madison's many venues, there is world-class entertainment to be found on just about any night.

Population: 223,389

Climate:

	High	Low
January	28	6
July	82	58

Cost of living: Average

Housing cost: The median sales price of homes in the area during the first half of 2007 was $215,050, according to the Wisconsin Realtors Association.

Information: Greater Madison Convention and Visitors Bureau, (800) 373-6376 or www.visitmadison.com.

WYOMING

Wyoming has no state income tax but does have a state sales tax.

Major tax credits or rebates include: none.

The state sales tax rate is 4%, but local governments can add to this amount.

Our couples relocating to the cities listed below must pay a county fee per automobile based on the year and MSRP of the vehicle. The county fee is $417 for the Explorer and $315 for the Camry. Our couples must also pay a title fee of $9 per automobile, a Vehicle Identification Number (VIN) inspection fee of $5 per automobile, a lien fee of $10 per automobile and a state fee of $15 per automobile at the time of registration. Thereafter, on an annual basis, our couples will pay a county fee and a state fee, per automobile.

○ Tax Heavens: Cheyenne, Jackson
Ψ Tax Hells: None
Top Retirement Towns:
Cheyenne, Jackson

Cheyenne

Cheyenne has no local income tax but does levy a sales tax.

Most purchases are taxed at a rate of 6%. Major consumer categories taxed at a different rate: none. Major consumer categories that are exempt from sales tax include: groceries, drugs and medical services.

Within the city limits of Cheyenne, the property tax rate is .071. Homes are assessed at 9.5% of market value. There is a property tax relief program if qualified based on income and asset limitations. There is also an elderly and disabled tax rebate program subject to income limitations.

Property tax does not cover garbage pickup.

Cheyenne has no personal property tax for individuals.

Jackson

Jackson has no local income tax but does levy a sales tax.

Most purchases are taxed at a rate of 6%. Major consumer categories taxed at a different rate: none. Major consumer categories that are exempt from sales tax include: groceries, drugs and medical services.

Within the city limits of Jackson, the property tax rate is .058692. Homes are assessed at 9.5% of market value. There is a property tax relief program if qualified based on income and asset limitations. There is also an elderly and disabled tax rebate program subject to income limitations. Property tax does not cover garbage pickup.

WYOMING TAX TABLE

Instructions

1. Find the Income in the far left column closest to your anticipated retirement income.
2. Find the Home Value closest to the value of the home where you will live in retirement.
3. Follow that row to your estimated Total Tax Burden at age 65 and beyond.

Income	Home Value	Property Tax & Other Fees	Personal Property Tax & Auto Fees	Sales Tax	Local Income Tax	State Income Tax	Total Tax Burden	Rank*
CHEYENNE								
$30,000	$125,000	$1,023	$591	$755	-	-	$2,369	58 of 173
	150,000	1,192	591	755	-	-	2,538	55 of 173
	175,000	1,360	591	755	-	-	2,706	51 of 173
$60,000	$150,000	$1,192	$591	$1,327	-	-	$3,110	16 of 203
	225,000	1,698	591	1,327	-	-	3,616	14 of 203
	300,000	2,204	591	1,327	-	-	4,122	12 of 203
$90,000	$225,000	$1,698	$591	$1,649	-	-	$3,938	4 of 203 ○
	375,000	2,709	591	1,649	-	-	4,949	6 of 203 ○
	525,000	3,721	591	1,649	-	-	5,961	6 of 203 ○
JACKSON								
$60,000	$150,000	$1,016	$591	$1,327	-	-	$2,934	11 of 203
	225,000	1,435	591	1,327	-	-	3,353	8 of 203 ○
	300,000	1,853	591	1,327	-	-	3,771	7 of 203 ○
$90,000	$225,000	$1,435	$591	$1,649	-	-	$3,675	3 of 203 ○
	375,000	2,271	591	1,649	-	-	4,511	3 of 203 ○
	525,000	3,107	591	1,649	-	-	5,347	2 of 203 ○

*There are 203 cities in this book, 30 of which have higher than average home prices. We have estimated taxes for a tier of higher home values (and omitted the lowest tier) for these 30 cities. The city with the lowest tax burden for an income/home value combination is given the #1 rating; the higher the rating, the higher the total tax burden.

Income	Home Value	Property Tax & Other Fees	Personal Property Tax & Auto Fees	Sales Tax	Local Income Tax	State Income Tax[†]	Total Tax Burden	Rank[*]
JACKSON continued								
	$600,000	$3,525	$591	$1,649	-	-	$5,765	1 of 30
	750,000	4,362	591	1,649	-	-	6,602	1 of 30
	900,000	5,198	591	1,649	-	-	7,438	2 of 30

*There are 203 cities in this book, 30 of which have higher than average home prices. We have estimated taxes for a tier of higher home values (and omitted the lowest tier) for these 30 cities. The city with the lowest tax burden for an income/home value combination is given the #1 rating; the higher the rating, the higher the total tax burden.

• Wyoming's Top Retirement Towns •

Cheyenne

Situated at the north end of the Front Range, the Western city of Cheyenne provides residents with year-round activities and entertainment. Since the city is relatively close to Colorado's northern border and is only 90 miles from Denver, it benefits from Colorado's rapid growth but clings steadfastly to a slower pace of life. In addition, Cheyenne offers clean air, affordable housing, low taxes, little traffic congestion and good health care.

Pack your cowboy boots because Wyoming's capital kicks up a big celebration of its past. It boasts a colorful history as a railroad and military town started in the 1800s. Cheyenne Frontier Days, which dates to 1897, turns into the world's largest outdoor rodeo extravaganza with all kinds of entertainment each July.

Both the Cheyenne Depot Museum and the capitol, which date to the 1880s, are National Historic Landmarks. Formerly the Union Pacific Depot, the distinctive sandstone building now houses a visitor center and museum and hosts numerous city events in its lobby and plaza. Several other museums chronicle the pioneer history in art and artifacts. A symphony orchestra and little theater add to the cultural scene.

The capital has 600 acres of parks and a 15-mile greenbelt of walking paths. The Cheyenne Regional Medical Center offers comprehensive services, and the Laramie County Community College has a roster of enrichment courses. Fishing, hunting, hiking, boating and skiing are within easy reach. Medicine Bow National Forest and Medicine Bow Mountains are to the west, and Laramie, home of the University of Wyoming, is about 50 miles northwest.

Population: 55,314
Climate: High Low
January 37 15
July 82 53
Cost of living: Average
Housing cost: The average price for the first nine months of 2007 was $163,239 for existing single-family homes and $247,408 for new homes, according to data from the Cheyenne Board of Realtors and Multiple Listing Service.
Information: Greater Cheyenne Chamber of Commerce, (307) 638-3388 or www.cheyennechamber.org. Cheyenne Area Convention and Visitors Bureau, (800) 426-5009 and www.cheyenne.org.

Jackson

There's Jackson, and then there's Jackson Hole. Mountain men used the word "hole" to describe valleys surrounded by mountains. Thus, Jackson Hole is the valley, beginning south of Yellowstone National Park. The 48-mile-long valley sits at an elevation of about 6,200 feet at the base of the Teton Range. It's an area of wide, untouched open spaces and spectacular vistas. Jackson is the major town, located in the southern part of the valley.

Jackson serves as the gateway to two magnificent national parks: Grand Teton National Park, a mere five miles away, and Yellowstone, about an hour north. Grand Teton National Park's backcountry is accessible for hiking, horseback riding, rock climbing and wintertime snowshoeing and cross-country skiing. You can be very active in Yellowstone, camping in the backcountry, hiking, horseback riding and joining a ranger on a nature walk. Or, you can just enjoy watching Old Faithful and viewing the abundant wildlife — elk, deer, buffalo and grizzly bears.

Jackson is bordered by Bridger-Teton National Forest and has three ski resorts in the area. Snow King Resort is only six blocks from Jackson's town square. Jackson Hole Mountain Resort is at Teton Village, about 12 miles from town, and Grand Targhee Resort is on the western side of the Tetons on the Idaho border, about an hour northwest of Jackson. Alpine lakes and streams offer fly-fishing and rafting, and there are golf courses in the area.

Jackson's Western charm peaks during Old West Days every Memorial Day weekend with events such as a chuckwagon dinner, rodeos, a shootout and stagecoach rides.

But these surroundings and recreational opportunities come at a high price. With 97 percent of the land in the public domain, there's little room for expansion, raising the price of land for homes and boosting the cost of living.

Population: 9,215
Climate: High Low
January 37 20
July 81 61
Cost of living: Above average
Housing cost: The median sales price of a single-family home for the first half of 2007 was $806,287, according to the Teton County Assessors Office.
Information: Jackson Hole Chamber of Commerce, (307) 733-3316 or www.jacksonholechamber.com.

WASHINGTON, DC

Washington, DC, has an income tax and a sales tax.

The income tax rate is graduated from 4.5% to 8.7% depending upon income bracket. For married couples filing jointly, the rates are 4.5% on the first $10,000 of taxable income; 7% on the next $30,000 of taxable income; and 8.7% on taxable income above $40,000.

In calculating the tax, there is no deduction for federal income tax paid. Federal, District of Columbia and private pensions are not exempt, though there is a $3,000 exemption per person from federal and District of Columbia pensions. Social Security benefits are exempt. There is a $2,500 standard deduction from DC adjusted gross income for married couples filing jointly. There is a $1,500 personal exemption per person from DC adjusted gross income and there is an

additional personal exemption of $1,500 per person from DC adjusted gross income for persons age 65 or older.

Major tax credits or rebates include: credit for income taxes paid to other states and property tax credit if gross income is less than $20,000, which our couples do not qualify for; and low income credit, which one of our couples qualifies for.

Most purchases are taxed at a rate of 5.75%. Major consumer categories taxed at a different rate include: food away from home, which is taxed at a rate of 10%. Major consumer categories that are exempt from sales tax include: drugs and groceries.

Within the city limits of Washington,

DC, the property tax rate is .0088. Homes are assessed at 100% of market value. There is a homestead exemption of $60,000 off assessed value available to all homeowners. There is a reduction of 50% of property taxes due available to homeowners age 65 or older with federal adjusted gross income of less than $100,000. Property tax includes garbage pickup.

Washington, DC, has no personal property tax for individuals.

Our couples relocating to Washington, DC, must pay a registration fee per automobile based on the weight of the vehicle. The fee is $155 for the Explorer and $72 for the Camry. Our couples must also pay a title fee of $26 per automobile and a lien fee of $20 per automobile at the time of registration. Thereafter, on an annual basis, our couples will pay a registration fee per automobile.

WASHINGTON DC TAX TABLE

Instructions

1. Find the Income in the far left column closest to your anticipated retirement income.
2. Find the Home Value closest to the value of the home where you will live in retirement.
3. Follow that row to your estimated Total Tax Burden at age 65 and beyond.

Income	Home Value	Property Tax & Other Fees	Personal Property Tax & Auto Fees	Sales Tax	Local Income Tax	State Income Tax	Total Tax Burden	Rank*
WASHINGTON DC								
$30,000	$125,000	$286	$227	$825	-	-	$1,338	4 of 173 O
	150,000	396	227	825	-	-	1,448	4 of 173 O
	175,000	506	227	825	-	-	1,558	3 of 173 O
$60,000	$150,000	$396	$227	$1,433	$1,872	-	$3,928	73 of 203
	225,000	726	227	1,433	1,872	-	4,258	45 of 203
	300,000	1,056	227	1,433	1,872	-	4,588	33 of 203
$90,000	$225,000	$726	$227	$1,791	$4,128	-	$6,872	116 of 203
	375,000	1,386	227	1,791	4,128	-	7,532	63 of 203
	525,000	2,046	227	1,791	4,128	-	8,192	39 of 203

*There are 203 cities in this book, 30 of which have higher than average home prices. We have estimated taxes for a tier of higher home values (and omitted the lowest tier) for these 30 cities. The city with the lowest tax burden for an income/home value combination is given the #1 rating; the higher the rating, the higher the total tax burden.

Ranking of Total Tax Burdens for Retirees
Earning $30,000 and Owning a Home Valued at $125,000

Rank	City, State		Total Tax	Rank	City, State		Total Tax	Rank	City, State		Total Tax
1	WILMINGTON	DE	$111	59	DENVER	CO	$2,375	116	ORMOND BEACH	FL	$2,970
2	ANCHORAGE	AK	$182	60	CHARLESTON	WV	$2,401	117	FAYETTEVILLE	AR	$2,971
3	GRANTS PASS	OR	$1,273	61	VICKSBURG	MS	$2,405	118	BRADENTON	FL	$2,990
(TIE) 4	WASHINGTON	DC	$1,338	62	DANVILLE	KY	$2,413	119	OCALA	FL	$2,997
(TIE) 4	KALISPELL	MT	$1,338	63	LOUISVILLE	KY	$2,421	120	HATTIESBURG	MS	$3,014
6	MEDFORD	OR	$1,345	64	THOMASVILLE	GA	$2,437	121	DETROIT	MI	$3,029
7	BEND	OR	$1,433	65	CHARLOTTESVILLE	VA	$2,438	122	TUCSON	AZ	$3,031
(TIE) 8	COEUR d'ALENE	ID	$1,482	66	EUFAULA	AL	$2,440	123	LEESBURG	FL	$3,032
(TIE) 8	CAPE COD (BARNSTABLE)	MA	$1,482	67	GREEN VALLEY	AZ	$2,452	124	WILMINGTON	NC	$3,043
10	ASHLAND	OR	$1,522	68	CARSON CITY	NV	$2,470	125	FORT LAUDERDALE	FL	$3,065
11	OMAHA	NE	$1,550	69	HOUSTON	TX	$2,512	126	SIOUX FALLS	SD	$3,073
12	LINCOLN CITY	OR	$1,641	70	SALT LAKE CITY	UT	$2,517	127	MOUNT DORA	FL	$3,097
13	ATLANTA	GA	$1,727	71	NEW ORLEANS	LA	$2,519	128	HENDERSON	NV	$3,101
14	CAPE MAY	NJ	$1,771	72	JACKSONVILLE	FL	$2,539	129	PENSACOLA	FL	$3,102
15	CHARLESTON	SC	$1,784	73	HOT SPRINGS	AR	$2,556	130	RICHMOND	VA	$3,116
16	BATON ROUGE	LA	$1,831	74	STAUNTON	VA	$2,569	131	SYRACUSE	NY	$3,138
17	BILLINGS	MT	$1,843	75	EAGLE RIVER	WI	$2,573	132	WINTER HAVEN	FL	$3,155
18	SEQUIM	WA	$1,868	76	VERO BEACH	FL	$2,595	133	GAINESVILLE	FL	$3,157
19	WILLIAMSBURG	VA	$1,872	77	SIERRA VISTA	AZ	$2,596	134	COLUMBUS	OH	$3,162
20	BOISE	ID	$1,892	78	PRESCOTT	AZ	$2,612	135	TAMPA	FL	$3,163
21	SILVER CITY	NM	$1,901	79	LAKE HAVASU CITY	AZ	$2,613	136	STURGEON BAY	WI	$3,170
22	PORT TOWNSEND	WA	$1,903	80	ATHENS	GA	$2,624	137	MADISON	WI	$3,190
23	PORTLAND	OR	$1,907	81	GROVE	OK	$2,630	138	TRAVERSE CITY	MI	$3,212
24	OAK HARBOR	WA	$1,910	82	EDENTON	NC	$2,632	139	KNOXVILLE	TN	$3,213
25	PETOSKEY	MI	$1,923	83	BOULDER	CO	$2,645	140	MIAMI	FL	$3,222
26	SPOKANE	WA	$1,971	84	WAYNESVILLE	NC	$2,646	141	AUSTIN	TX	$3,239
27	SAVANNAH	GA	$1,987	85	DALLAS	TX	$2,647	142	CINCINNATI	OH	$3,244
28	EUGENE	OR	$1,998	86	BURLINGTON	VT	$2,648	143	LITTLE ROCK	AR	$3,252
29	CLEMSON	SC	$2,015	87	PALM COAST	FL	$2,654	144	RENO	NV	$3,260
30	SANTA FE	NM	$2,021	88	NORTH FORT MYERS	FL	$2,655	145	LAS VEGAS	NV	$3,270
31	MYRTLE BEACH	SC	$2,022	89	FLAGSTAFF	AZ	$2,660	146	MILWAUKEE	WI	$3,368
32	BILOXI	MS	$2,042	90	NEWARK	NJ	$2,669	147	CLEVELAND	OH	$3,390
33	NATCHITOCHES	LA	$2,096	(TIE) 91	FORT COLLINS	CO	$2,693	148	ST. PETERSBURG	FL	$3,433
34	ST. GEORGE	UT	$2,117	(TIE) 91	MURRAY	KY	$2,693	149	DADE CITY	FL	$3,460
35	TACOMA	WA	$2,121		**AVERAGE**		**$2,724**	150	FREDERICKSBURG	TX	$3,502
36	TOMS RIVER	NJ	$2,132	93	GREENVILLE	SC	$2,745	151	CASA GRANDE	AZ	$3,516
37	LEXINGTON	KY	$2,138	94	HENDERSONVILLE	NC	$2,749	152	CHAPEL HILL	NC	$3,583
38	FAIRHOPE	AL	$2,162	95	GAINESVILLE	GA	$2,753	153	WICHITA	KS	$3,650
39	DAHLONEGA	GA	$2,170	96	MARYVILLE	TN	$2,760	154	FARGO	ND	$3,764
40	BEAUFORT	SC	$2,174	97	ASHEVILLE	NC	$2,767	(TIE) 155	BALTIMORE	MD	$3,775
41	ST. SIMONS ISLAND	GA	$2,226	98	VENICE	FL	$2,773	(TIE) 155	MARBLE FALLS	TX	$3,775
42	CROSSVILLE	TN	$2,230	99	BLOOMINGTON	IN	$2,776	157	PROVIDENCE	RI	$3,778
43	COLORADO SPRINGS	CO	$2,240	100	ORLANDO	FL	$2,799	158	GEORGETOWN	TX	$3,894
44	CEDAR CITY	UT	$2,241	101	BREVARD	NC	$2,812	159	SAN ANTONIO	TX	$3,933
45	BERKELEY SPRINGS	WV	$2,247	102	PARIS	TN	$2,814	160	BOERNE	TX	$3,965
46	PORTSMOUTH	NH	$2,255	103	DELAND	FL	$2,867	161	DES MOINES	IA	$4,027
47	RUIDOSO	NM	$2,270	104	SARASOTA	FL	$2,877	162	KERRVILLE	TX	$4,058
48	PINEHURST	NC	$2,273	105	BRANSON	MO	$2,879	163	MEMPHIS	TN	$4,101
49	AIKEN	SC	$2,276	106	CAMDEN	ME	$2,901	164	KANSAS CITY	MO	$4,140
50	BUFFALO	NY	$2,282	107	ALBUQUERQUE	NM	$2,903	165	THE WOODLANDS	TX	$4,154
51	OXFORD	MS	$2,307	108	ST. AUGUSTINE	FL	$2,905	166	McALLEN	TX	$4,217
52	DOTHAN	AL	$2,316	109	OKLAHOMA CITY	OK	$2,916	167	BROWNSVILLE	TX	$4,239
53	MINNEAPOLIS	MN	$2,317	110	BRUNSWICK	ME	$2,922	168	CHICAGO	IL	$4,276
54	LAS CRUCES	NM	$2,322	111	NEW BERN	NC	$2,924	169	LANCASTER	PA	$4,713
55	MOUNTAIN HOME	AR	$2,323	112	PUNTA GORDA	FL	$2,925	170	PITTSBURGH	PA	$5,116
56	GRAND JUNCTION	CO	$2,325	113	PHOENIX	AZ	$2,931	171	HARTFORD	CT	$5,199
57	ABINGDON	VA	$2,347	114	LAKELAND	FL	$2,944	172	NEW HAVEN	CT	$5,200
58	CHEYENNE	WY	$2,369	115	JUPITER	FL	$2,969	173	EAST STROUDSBURG	PA	$5,759

Ranking of Total Tax Burdens for Retirees
Earning $30,000 and Owning a Home Valued at $150,000

Rank	City, State		Total Tax	Rank	City, State		Total Tax	Rank	City, State		Total Tax
1	WILMINGTON	DE	$116	59	PORTSMOUTH	NH	$2,608	116	DELAND	FL	$3,376
2	ANCHORAGE	AK	$182	60	CHARLESTON	WV	$2,616	117	TRAVERSE CITY	MI	$3,434
3	GRANTS PASS	OR	$1,437	61	BUFFALO	NY	$2,630	118	ST. AUGUSTINE	FL	$3,435
4	WASHINGTON	DC	$1,448	62	CARSON CITY	NV	$2,637	119	RICHMOND	VA	$3,438
5	MEDFORD	OR	$1,522	63	GREEN VALLEY	AZ	$2,650	120	HATTIESBURG	MS	$3,440
6	COEUR d'ALENE	ID	$1,585	64	DANVILLE	KY	$2,674	121	SIOUX FALLS	SD	$3,443
7	KALISPELL	MT	$1,596	65	CHARLOTTESVILLE	VA	$2,685	122	JUPITER	FL	$3,457
8	BEND	OR	$1,630	66	VICKSBURG	MS	$2,705	123	OCALA	FL	$3,461
9	CAPE COD (BARNSTABLE)	MA	$1,692	67	SALT LAKE CITY	UT	$2,708	124	LAKELAND	FL	$3,463
10	ASHLAND	OR	$1,700	68	LOUISVILLE	KY	$2,731	125	ORMOND BEACH	FL	$3,476
11	BILLINGS	MT	$1,843	69	THOMASVILLE	GA	$2,745	126	BRADENTON	FL	$3,505
12	LINCOLN CITY	OR	$1,880	70	HOT SPRINGS	AR	$2,763	127	LEESBURG	FL	$3,541
13	CHARLESTON	SC	$1,902	71	SIERRA VISTA	AZ	$2,767	128	COLUMBUS	OH	$3,544
14	OMAHA	NE	$1,905	72	PRESCOTT	AZ	$2,775	(TIE) 129	LAS VEGAS	NV	$3,557
15	CAPE MAY	NJ	$1,907	73	BOULDER	CO	$2,791	(TIE) 129	KNOXVILLE	TN	$3,557
16	PETOSKEY	MI	$1,923	74	LAKE HAVASU CITY	AZ	$2,796	131	RENO	NV	$3,579
17	ATLANTA	GA	$1,939	75	STAUNTON	VA	$2,809	132	LITTLE ROCK	AR	$3,597
18	WILLIAMSBURG	VA	$2,007	76	BURLINGTON	VT	$2,810	133	FORT LAUDERDALE	FL	$3,615
19	SEQUIM	WA	$2,027	77	EDENTON	NC	$2,841	134	STURGEON BAY	WI	$3,626
20	SILVER CITY	NM	$2,038	78	FLAGSTAFF	AZ	$2,842	135	MOUNT DORA	FL	$3,643
21	PORT TOWNSEND	WA	$2,045	79	GROVE	OK	$2,862	136	PENSACOLA	FL	$3,644
22	BOISE	ID	$2,065	(TIE) 80	FORT COLLINS	CO	$2,871	137	DETROIT	MI	$3,656
23	OAK HARBOR	WA	$2,066	(TIE) 80	WAYNESVILLE	NC	$2,871	138	SYRACUSE	NY	$3,669
24	BATON ROUGE	LA	$2,084	82	EAGLE RIVER	WI	$2,941	139	CINCINNATI	OH	$3,680
25	SPOKANE	WA	$2,154	83	ATHENS	GA	$2,955	140	MADISON	WI	$3,682
26	CLEMSON	SC	$2,164	84	VERO BEACH	FL	$2,976	141	WINTER HAVEN	FL	$3,746
27	SANTA FE	NM	$2,168	85	HOUSTON	TX	$2,989	142	TAMPA	FL	$3,748
28	MYRTLE BEACH	SC	$2,184	86	NEW ORLEANS	LA	$2,990	143	GAINESVILLE	FL	$3,771
29	PORTLAND	OR	$2,195	87	GREENVILLE	SC	$2,991	144	CLEVELAND	OH	$3,799
30	ST. GEORGE	UT	$2,240	88	JACKSONVILLE	FL	$2,994	145	MIAMI	FL	$3,838
31	FAIRHOPE	AL	$2,251	89	HENDERSONVILLE	NC	$2,998	146	AUSTIN	TX	$3,844
32	EUGENE	OR	$2,286	90	MURRAY	KY	$3,012	147	CASA GRANDE	AZ	$3,864
33	TACOMA	WA	$2,300	91	MARYVILLE	TN	$3,019	148	MILWAUKEE	WI	$3,897
34	BILOXI	MS	$2,304	92	NEWARK	NJ	$3,021	149	WICHITA	KS	$3,984
35	BEAUFORT	SC	$2,310	(TIE) 93	ASHEVILLE	NC	$3,043	150	CHAPEL HILL	NC	$3,986
36	COLORADO SPRINGS	CO	$2,353	(TIE) 93	PARIS	TN	$3,043	151	FREDERICKSBURG	TX	$4,002
37	NATCHITOCHES	LA	$2,363		AVERAGE		$3,059	152	ST. PETERSBURG	FL	$4,011
(TIE) 38	TOMS RIVER	NJ	$2,376	95	PALM COAST	FL	$3,064	153	DADE CITY	FL	$4,040
(TIE) 38	CROSSVILLE	TN	$2,376	96	NORTH FORT MYERS	FL	$3,065	154	PROVIDENCE	RI	$4,142
40	DOTHAN	AL	$2,378	97	BREVARD	NC	$3,071	155	FARGO	ND	$4,290
41	CEDAR CITY	UT	$2,386	98	BRANSON	MO	$3,078	156	MARBLE FALLS	TX	$4,341
42	SAVANNAH	GA	$2,391	99	GAINESVILLE	GA	$3,093	157	BALTIMORE	MD	$4,375
43	LEXINGTON	KY	$2,395	100	PHOENIX	AZ	$3,174	158	KANSAS CITY	MO	$4,515
44	BERKELEY SPRINGS	WV	$2,434	101	VENICE	FL	$3,186	159	GEORGETOWN	TX	$4,517
45	DAHLONEGA	GA	$2,452	102	NEW BERN	NC	$3,194	160	DES MOINES	IA	$4,550
46	GRAND JUNCTION	CO	$2,453	103	CAMDEN	ME	$3,209	161	MEMPHIS	TN	$4,568
47	RUIDOSO	NM	$2,466	104	OKLAHOMA CITY	OK	$3,218	162	BOERNE	TX	$4,574
48	MINNEAPOLIS	MN	$2,470	105	FAYETTEVILLE	AR	$3,234	163	SAN ANTONIO	TX	$4,631
49	PINEHURST	NC	$2,475	106	DALLAS	TX	$3,241	164	KERRVILLE	TX	$4,676
50	AIKEN	SC	$2,491	107	ALBUQUERQUE	NM	$3,256	165	McALLEN	TX	$4,888
51	DENVER	CO	$2,508	(TIE) 108	ORLANDO	FL	$3,271	166	THE WOODLANDS	TX	$4,907
52	MOUNTAIN HOME	AR	$2,511	(TIE) 108	PUNTA GORDA	FL	$3,271	167	BROWNSVILLE	TX	$4,914
53	ST. SIMONS ISLAND	GA	$2,518	110	BRUNSWICK	ME	$3,276	168	CHICAGO	IL	$4,929
54	EUFAULA	AL	$2,527	111	SARASOTA	FL	$3,281	169	LANCASTER	PA	$5,502
55	CHEYENNE	WY	$2,538	112	TUCSON	AZ	$3,295	170	NEW HAVEN	CT	$5,939
56	LAS CRUCES	NM	$2,547	113	BLOOMINGTON	IN	$3,296	171	HARTFORD	CT	$5,940
57	ABINGDON	VA	$2,559	114	WILMINGTON	NC	$3,330	172	PITTSBURGH	PA	$6,014
58	OXFORD	MS	$2,581	115	HENDERSON	NV	$3,354	173	EAST STROUDSBURG	PA	$6,759

Ranking of Total Tax Burdens for Retirees Earning $30,000 and Owning a Home Valued at $175,000

Rank	City, State		Total Tax	Rank	City, State		Total Tax	Rank	City, State		Total Tax
1	WILMINGTON	DE	$172	59	CHARLESTON	WV	$2,832	116	RICHMOND	VA	$3,761
2	ANCHORAGE	AK	$297	60	GREEN VALLEY	AZ	$2,848	117	ST. AUGUSTINE	FL	$3,783
3	WASHINGTON	DC	$1,558	61	OXFORD	MS	$2,856	118	SIOUX FALLS	SD	$3,814
4	GRANTS PASS	OR	$1,602	62	SALT LAKE CITY	UT	$2,900	119	DALLAS	TX	$3,836
5	KALISPELL	MT	$1,637	63	CHARLOTTESVILLE	VA	$2,933	120	LAS VEGAS	NV	$3,844
6	MEDFORD	OR	$1,699	64	DANVILLE	KY	$2,935	121	HATTIESBURG	MS	$3,865
7	COEUR d'ALENE	ID	$1,791	65	BOULDER	CO	$2,937	122	DELAND	FL	$3,885
8	BEND	OR	$1,827	(TIE) 66	PRESCOTT	AZ	$2,939	123	RENO	NV	$3,898
9	BILLINGS	MT	$1,843	(TIE) 66	SIERRA VISTA	AZ	$2,939	124	KNOXVILLE	TN	$3,900
10	ASHLAND	OR	$1,879	68	PORTSMOUTH	NH	$2,962	(TIE) 125	OCALA	FL	$3,926
11	CAPE COD (BARNSTABLE)	MA	$1,902	69	HOT SPRINGS	AR	$2,970	(TIE) 125	COLUMBUS	OH	$3,926
12	PETOSKEY	MI	$1,923	70	BURLINGTON	VT	$2,972	127	LITTLE ROCK	AR	$3,942
13	CAPE MAY	NJ	$2,044	71	BUFFALO	NY	$2,977	128	JUPITER	FL	$3,945
14	CHARLESTON	SC	$2,092	72	LAKE HAVASU CITY	AZ	$2,978	129	ORMOND BEACH	FL	$3,981
15	LINCOLN CITY	OR	$2,118	73	VICKSBURG	MS	$3,004	130	LAKELAND	FL	$3,982
16	WILLIAMSBURG	VA	$2,142	74	FLAGSTAFF	AZ	$3,024	131	BRADENTON	FL	$4,020
17	SEQUIM	WA	$2,143	75	LOUISVILLE	KY	$3,041	132	LEESBURG	FL	$4,049
18	PORT TOWNSEND	WA	$2,147	(TIE) 76	EDENTON	NC	$3,049	133	STURGEON BAY	WI	$4,083
19	SILVER CITY	NM	$2,174	(TIE) 76	STAUNTON	VA	$3,049	134	CINCINNATI	OH	$4,115
20	OAK HARBOR	WA	$2,179	78	FORT COLLINS	CO	$3,050	135	FORT LAUDERDALE	FL	$4,165
21	ATLANTA	GA	$2,264	79	THOMASVILLE	GA	$3,053	136	MADISON	WI	$4,175
22	SPOKANE	WA	$2,286	80	GROVE	OK	$3,093	137	PENSACOLA	FL	$4,185
23	SANTA FE	NM	$2,316	81	WAYNESVILLE	NC	$3,095	138	MOUNT DORA	FL	$4,188
24	BATON ROUGE	LA	$2,337	82	HENDERSONVILLE	NC	$3,246	139	SYRACUSE	NY	$4,201
25	FAIRHOPE	AL	$2,339	83	PARIS	TN	$3,271	140	CLEVELAND	OH	$4,208
26	ST. GEORGE	UT	$2,364	84	MARYVILLE	TN	$3,277	141	CASA GRANDE	AZ	$4,213
27	CLEMSON	SC	$2,383	85	BRANSON	MO	$3,278	142	PROVIDENCE	RI	$4,234
28	BOISE	ID	$2,412	86	ATHENS	GA	$3,285	143	DETROIT	MI	$4,283
29	OMAHA	NE	$2,424	87	GREENVILLE	SC	$3,303	144	WICHITA	KS	$4,318
30	MYRTLE BEACH	SC	$2,427	88	EAGLE RIVER	WI	$3,309	145	TAMPA	FL	$4,334
31	TACOMA	WA	$2,430	89	ASHEVILLE	NC	$3,319	146	WINTER HAVEN	FL	$4,336
32	DOTHAN	AL	$2,439	90	BREVARD	NC	$3,329	147	GAINESVILLE	FL	$4,386
33	COLORADO SPRINGS	CO	$2,466	91	MURRAY	KY	$3,330	148	CHAPEL HILL	NC	$4,390
34	PORTLAND	OR	$2,482	92	VERO BEACH	FL	$3,358	149	MILWAUKEE	WI	$4,426
35	BEAUFORT	SC	$2,520	93	NEWARK	NJ	$3,373	150	AUSTIN	TX	$4,449
36	CROSSVILLE	TN	$2,522		**AVERAGE**		**$3,396**	151	MIAMI	FL	$4,454
37	CEDAR CITY	UT	$2,532	94	PHOENIX	AZ	$3,418	152	FREDERICKSBURG	TX	$4,502
38	BILOXI	MS	$2,565	95	GAINESVILLE	GA	$3,433	153	ST. PETERSBURG	FL	$4,590
39	EUGENE	OR	$2,575	96	JACKSONVILLE	FL	$3,448	154	DADE CITY	FL	$4,620
40	GRAND JUNCTION	CO	$2,581	97	NEW ORLEANS	LA	$3,461	155	FARGO	ND	$4,816
41	MINNEAPOLIS	MN	$2,609	98	NEW BERN	NC	$3,464	156	KANSAS CITY	MO	$4,891
42	EUFAULA	AL	$2,615	99	HOUSTON	TX	$3,466	157	MARBLE FALLS	TX	$4,907
(TIE) 43	TOMS RIVER	NJ	$2,620	100	PALM COAST	FL	$3,474	158	BALTIMORE	MD	$4,975
(TIE) 43	BERKELEY SPRINGS	WV	$2,620	101	NORTH FORT MYERS	FL	$3,475	159	MEMPHIS	TN	$5,036
45	NATCHITOCHES	LA	$2,629	102	FAYETTEVILLE	AR	$3,498	160	DES MOINES	IA	$5,072
46	DENVER	CO	$2,642	103	CAMDEN	ME	$3,516	161	GEORGETOWN	TX	$5,140
47	LEXINGTON	KY	$2,653	104	OKLAHOMA CITY	OK	$3,520	162	BOERNE	TX	$5,183
48	RUIDOSO	NM	$2,662	105	TUCSON	AZ	$3,559	163	KERRVILLE	TX	$5,295
49	PINEHURST	NC	$2,676	106	VENICE	FL	$3,600	164	SAN ANTONIO	TX	$5,328
50	MOUNTAIN HOME	AR	$2,700	107	HENDERSON	NV	$3,608	165	McALLEN	TX	$5,559
51	CHEYENNE	WY	$2,706	108	ALBUQUERQUE	NM	$3,610	166	CHICAGO	IL	$5,583
52	DAHLONEGA	GA	$2,734	(TIE) 109	PUNTA GORDA	FL	$3,616	167	THE WOODLANDS	TX	$5,659
(TIE) 53	LAS CRUCES	NM	$2,772	(TIE) 109	WILMINGTON	NC	$3,616	168	BROWNSVILLE	TX	$5,870
(TIE) 53	ABINGDON	VA	$2,772	111	BRUNSWICK	ME	$3,629	169	LANCASTER	PA	$6,291
55	AIKEN	SC	$2,787	112	BLOOMINGTON	IN	$3,643	170	NEW HAVEN	CT	$6,678
56	SAVANNAH	GA	$2,796	113	TRAVERSE CITY	MI	$3,655	171	HARTFORD	CT	$6,680
57	CARSON CITY	NV	$2,804	114	SARASOTA	FL	$3,686	172	PITTSBURGH	PA	$6,912
58	ST. SIMONS ISLAND	GA	$2,810	115	ORLANDO	FL	$3,744	173	EAST STROUDSBURG	PA	$7,758

Ranking of Total Tax Burdens for Retirees
Earning $60,000 and Owning a Home Valued at $150,000

Rank	City, State		Total Tax	Rank	City, State		Total Tax	Rank	City, State		Total Tax
1	ANCHORAGE	AK	$182	69	JACKSONVILLE	FL	$3,902	136	MURRAY	KY	$4,638
2	WILMINGTON	DE	$1,205	70	NEWARK	NJ	$3,904	137	DANVILLE	KY	$4,649
3	CHARLESTON	SC	$2,525	71	PORTLAND	OR	$3,916	138	BRUNSWICK	ME	$4,665
4	WILLIAMSBURG	VA	$2,705	72	GAINESVILLE	GA	$3,924	139	PENSACOLA	FL	$4,701
5	HILTON HEAD	SC	$2,738	73	WASHINGTON	DC	$3,928	140	DADE CITY	FL	$4,707
6	CLEMSON	SC	$2,787	(TIE) 74	CARLSBAD	CA	$3,930	141	TUCSON	AZ	$4,711
7	CAPE MAY	NJ	$2,790	(TIE) 74	SAN JUAN CAPISTRANO	CA	$3,930	142	GAINESVILLE	FL	$4,716
8	MYRTLE BEACH	SC	$2,807	76	PALM COAST	FL	$3,931	143	TAMPA	FL	$4,739
9	PORTSMOUTH	NH	$2,913	77	PUNTA GORDA	FL	$3,938	144	LOUISVILLE	KY	$4,758
10	BEAUFORT	SC	$2,933	78	BILLINGS	MT	$3,947	145	ST. PETERSBURG	FL	$4,777
11	JACKSON	WY	$2,934	79	FORT COLLINS	CO	$3,969	146	SALT LAKE CITY	UT	$4,782
12	COEUR d'ALENE	ID	$2,966	80	MARYVILLE	TN	$3,985	147	FREDERICKSBURG	TX	$4,789
13	ATLANTA	GA	$2,974	81	EUGENE	OR	$4,007	148	WINTER HAVEN	FL	$4,794
14	NAPLES	FL	$3,062	82	PARIS	TN	$4,009	149	HOT SPRINGS	AR	$4,823
15	KEY WEST	FL	$3,067	83	DALLAS	TX	$4,028	150	GROVE	OK	$4,879
16	CHEYENNE	WY	$3,110	84	BOULDER	CO	$4,042	151	ALBUQUERQUE	NM	$4,883
17	AIKEN	SC	$3,114	85	ANNAPOLIS	MD	$4,043	152	MIAMI	FL	$4,890
18	BOSTON	MA	$3,149	86	SARASOTA	FL	$4,045	153	BLOOMINGTON	IN	$4,951
19	FRIDAY HARBOR	WA	$3,152	87	SIOUX FALLS	SD	$4,079	154	EDENTON	NC	$4,954
20	GRANTS PASS	OR	$3,158	(TIE) 88	PASO ROBLES	CA	$4,081	155	WAYNESVILLE	NC	$4,984
21	MEDFORD	OR	$3,243	(TIE) 88	OCALA	FL	$4,081	(TIE) 156	TRAVERSE CITY	MI	$5,111
22	TOMS RIVER	NJ	$3,259	90	HENDERSON	NV	$4,093	(TIE) 156	HENDERSONVILLE	NC	$5,111
23	ABINGDON	VA	$3,268	91	TEMECULA	CA	$4,124	158	MARBLE FALLS	TX	$5,128
24	KALISPELL	MT	$3,272	92	WOODSTOCK	VT	$4,137	159	COLUMBUS	OH	$5,148
25	WAILUKU	HI	$3,305	93	BOCA RATON	FL	$4,145	160	ASHEVILLE	NC	$5,156
26	CARSON CITY	NV	$3,316	94	RICHMOND	VA	$4,147	161	OKLAHOMA CITY	OK	$5,180
27	BILOXI	MS	$3,329	95	LOS ANGELES	CA	$4,160	162	BREVARD	NC	$5,184
28	BEND	OR	$3,351	96	ORLANDO	FL	$4,163	163	BURLINGTON	VT	$5,192
29	HONOLULU	HI	$3,374	97	DOTHAN	AL	$4,175	164	EAGLE RIVER	WI	$5,204
30	SEQUIM	WA	$3,393	(TIE) 98	SIERRA VISTA	AZ	$4,186	165	BRANSON	MO	$5,250
31	CROSSVILLE	TN	$3,395	(TIE) 98	RUIDOSO	NM	$4,186	166	CINCINNATI	OH	$5,280
32	ST. SIMONS ISLAND	GA	$3,422	100	LAKE HAVASU CITY	AZ	$4,188	167	GEORGETOWN	TX	$5,304
33	BATON ROUGE	LA	$3,432	101	JUPITER	FL	$4,189	168	NEW BERN	NC	$5,307
34	BOISE	ID	$3,446	102	LAS CRUCES	NM	$4,199	169	CASA GRANDE	AZ	$5,325
35	PETOSKEY	MI	$3,464	103	SAN FRANCISCO	CA	$4,206	170	FAYETTEVILLE	AR	$5,335
36	ASHLAND	OR	$3,476	104	PRESCOTT	AZ	$4,235	171	BOERNE	TX	$5,361
37	COLORADO SPRINGS	CO	$3,496	105	SCOTTSDALE	AZ	$4,249	172	DETROIT	MI	$5,390
38	STAUNTON	VA	$3,507	106	BERKELEY SPRINGS	WV	$4,257	173	SAN ANTONIO	TX	$5,405
39	GREENVILLE	SC	$3,518	107	DELAND	FL	$4,269	174	WILMINGTON	NC	$5,443
40	CHARLOTTESVILLE	VA	$3,523	108	BRADENTON	FL	$4,275	175	CELEBRATION	FL	$5,456
41	OAK HARBOR	WA	$3,536	109	ST. GEORGE	UT	$4,277	176	KERRVILLE	TX	$5,463
42	EASTON	MD	$3,541	110	RENO	NV	$4,282	177	CLEVELAND	OH	$5,475
43	PORT TOWNSEND	WA	$3,553	111	FLAGSTAFF	AZ	$4,286	178	MINNEAPOLIS	MN	$5,481
44	LONGBOAT KEY	FL	$3,578	112	LAS VEGAS	NV	$4,296	179	FARGO	ND	$5,501
45	CAPE COD (BARNSTABLE)	MA	$3,583	113	ST. AUGUSTINE	FL	$4,318	180	MEMPHIS	TN	$5,534
46	LINCOLN CITY	OR	$3,601	114	EUFAULA	AL	$4,324	181	LITTLE ROCK	AR	$5,540
47	DAHLONEGA	GA	$3,609	115	ORMOND BEACH	FL	$4,328	182	McALLEN	TX	$5,675
48	GRAND JUNCTION	CO	$3,619	(TIE) 116	PALM DESERT	CA	$4,351	183	BALTIMORE	MD	$5,682
49	THOMASVILLE	GA	$3,620	(TIE) 116	LEESBURG	FL	$4,351	184	THE WOODLANDS	TX	$5,694
50	OXFORD	MS	$3,627	118	NEW ORLEANS	LA	$4,356	185	BROWNSVILLE	TX	$5,701
51	NORTH FORT MYERS	FL	$3,637		**AVERAGE**		**$4,365**	186	STURGEON BAY	WI	$5,847
52	SANIBEL ISLAND	FL	$3,658	119	SPOKANE	WA	$4,406	187	MADISON	WI	$5,870
53	SIESTA KEY	FL	$3,671	120	CEDAR CITY	UT	$4,408	188	PROVIDENCE	RI	$6,028
54	DENVER	CO	$3,675	121	OJAI	CA	$4,425	189	BUFFALO	NY	$6,073
55	NEW YORK CITY	NY	$3,677	122	LAKELAND	FL	$4,427	190	CHAPEL HILL	NC	$6,099
56	NATCHITOCHES	LA	$3,681	123	LEXINGTON	KY	$4,429	191	MILWAUKEE	WI	$6,127
57	SILVER CITY	NM	$3,690	124	CHARLESTON	WV	$4,459	192	WICHITA	KS	$6,243
58	SAVANNAH	GA	$3,705	125	FORT LAUDERDALE	FL	$4,466	193	DES MOINES	IA	$6,281
59	VICKSBURG	MS	$3,740	126	MOUNTAIN HOME	AR	$4,485	194	CHICAGO	IL	$6,329
60	ATHENS	GA	$3,771	127	HATTIESBURG	MS	$4,486	195	OMAHA	NE	$6,569
61	HOUSTON	TX	$3,776	128	KNOXVILLE	TN	$4,523	196	NEW HAVEN	CT	$6,761
62	VERO BEACH	FL	$3,806	129	SEDONA	AZ	$4,549	197	KANSAS CITY	MO	$6,805
63	SEATTLE	WA	$3,817	130	PINEHURST	NC	$4,588	198	SYRACUSE	NY	$7,082
64	FAIRHOPE	AL	$3,836	131	PHOENIX	AZ	$4,590	199	HARTFORD	CT	$7,262
65	SANTA FE	NM	$3,868	132	CAMDEN	ME	$4,598	200	PHILADELPHIA	PA	$7,380
66	GREEN VALLEY	AZ	$3,875	133	MOUNT DORA	FL	$4,603	201	LANCASTER	PA	$7,391
67	VENICE	FL	$3,876	134	TACOMA	WA	$4,613	202	PITTSBURGH	PA	$8,023
68	SAN DIEGO	CA	$3,885	135	AUSTIN	TX	$4,631	203	EAST STROUDSBURG	PA	$8,631

Ranking of Total Tax Burdens for Retirees Earning $60,000 and Owning a Home Valued at $225,000

Rank	City, State		Total Tax	Rank	City, State		Total Tax	Rank	City, State		Total Tax
1	ANCHORAGE	AK	$1,022	69	CARLSBAD	CA	$4,694	136	NEW ORLEANS	LA	$5,769
2	WILMINGTON	DE	$1,460	70	PARIS	TN	$4,695	137	DELAND	FL	$5,797
3	CHARLESTON	SC	$3,097	71	SIERRA VISTA	AZ	$4,701	138	DALLAS	TX	$5,812
4	WILLIAMSBURG	VA	$3,110	72	SAN JUAN CAPISTRANO	CA	$4,714	139	BRADENTON	FL	$5,820
5	CAPE MAY	NJ	$3,199	73	PRESCOTT	AZ	$4,726	140	ORMOND BEACH	FL	$5,844
6	HILTON HEAD	SC	$3,279	74	LAKE HAVASU CITY	AZ	$4,735	141	BRANSON	MO	$5,852
7	WAILUKU	HI	$3,305	75	MARYVILLE	TN	$4,759	142	HENDERSONVILLE	NC	$5,857
8	JACKSON	WY	$3,353	76	ATHENS	GA	$4,763	143	LEESBURG	FL	$5,877
9	CLEMSON	SC	$3,444	77	RUIDOSO	NM	$4,774	144	ST. AUGUSTINE	FL	$5,908
10	MYRTLE BEACH	SC	$3,536	78	PORTLAND	OR	$4,777	145	ALBUQUERQUE	NM	$5,944
11	BEAUFORT	SC	$3,564	79	SCOTTSDALE	AZ	$4,797	146	BREVARD	NC	$5,960
12	COEUR d'ALENE	ID	$3,584	80	BILLINGS	MT	$4,803	(TIE) 147	LAKELAND	FL	$5,984
13	ATLANTA	GA	$3,609	81	BERKELEY SPRINGS	WV	$4,817	(TIE) 147	ASHEVILLE	NC	$5,984
14	CHEYENNE	WY	$3,616	82	FLAGSTAFF	AZ	$4,831	149	MINNEAPOLIS	MN	$5,993
15	HONOLULU	HI	$3,643	83	CEDAR CITY	UT	$4,844	150	BLOOMINGTON	IN	$5,997
16	GRANTS PASS	OR	$3,652	84	HENDERSON	NV	$4,853	151	OKLAHOMA CITY	OK	$6,086
17	FRIDAY HARBOR	WA	$3,737	85	NORTH FORT MYERS	FL	$4,867	152	FORT LAUDERDALE	FL	$6,115
18	KEY WEST	FL	$3,755	(TIE) 86	LAS CRUCES	NM	$4,874	153	NEW BERN	NC	$6,117
19	MEDFORD	OR	$3,774	(TIE) 86	EUGENE	OR	$4,874	154	FAYETTEVILLE	AR	$6,126
(TIE) 20	COLORADO SPRINGS	CO	$3,834	88	SANIBEL ISLAND	FL	$4,900	155	MOUNT DORA	FL	$6,239
(TIE) 20	CROSSVILLE	TN	$3,834	89	PASO ROBLES	CA	$4,904	156	EAGLE RIVER	WI	$6,256
22	ABINGDON	VA	$3,906	90	SAVANNAH	GA	$4,927	157	FREDERICKSBURG	TX	$6,290
23	NAPLES	FL	$3,918	91	ANNAPOLIS	MD	$4,936	158	COLUMBUS	OH	$6,294
24	BOSTON	MA	$3,932	92	GAINESVILLE	GA	$4,944	159	WILMINGTON	NC	$6,301
25	BEND	OR	$3,941	93	TEMECULA	CA	$4,947	160	PENSACOLA	FL	$6,325
26	PORTSMOUTH	NH	$3,974	94	VERO BEACH	FL	$4,951	161	CASA GRANDE	AZ	$6,371
27	TOMS RIVER	NJ	$3,992	95	NEWARK	NJ	$4,955	162	TRAVERSE CITY	MI	$6,397
28	WOODSTOCK	VT	$3,996	96	PUNTA GORDA	FL	$4,975	(TIE) 163	DADE CITY	FL	$6,446
29	AIKEN	SC	$4,002	97	MOUNTAIN HOME	AR	$5,051	(TIE) 163	AUSTIN	TX	$6,446
30	GRAND JUNCTION	CO	$4,003	98	SAN FRANCISCO	CA	$5,057	165	TAMPA	FL	$6,496
31	ASHLAND	OR	$4,012	99	LOS ANGELES	CA	$5,097	166	ST. PETERSBURG	FL	$6,514
32	SEQUIM	WA	$4,021	100	CHARLESTON	WV	$5,106	167	GAINESVILLE	FL	$6,560
33	KALISPELL	MT	$4,044	(TIE) 101	VENICE	FL	$5,115	168	WINTER HAVEN	FL	$6,565
34	DENVER	CO	$4,075	(TIE) 101	RICHMOND	VA	$5,115	169	LITTLE ROCK	AR	$6,575
35	PETOSKEY	MI	$4,084	103	SEDONA	AZ	$5,121	170	CINCINNATI	OH	$6,587
36	SILVER CITY	NM	$4,099	104	LAS VEGAS	NV	$5,157	171	CELEBRATION	FL	$6,647
37	FAIRHOPE	AL	$4,102	105	PALM COAST	FL	$5,161	172	CLEVELAND	OH	$6,702
38	BILOXI	MS	$4,113	106	PALM DESERT	CA	$5,189	173	MIAMI	FL	$6,738
39	CARSON CITY	NV	$4,123	107	SIOUX FALLS	SD	$5,190	174	MARBLE FALLS	TX	$6,826
40	BATON ROUGE	LA	$4,192	108	PINEHURST	NC	$5,191	175	MEMPHIS	TN	$6,936
(TIE) 41	CAPE COD (BARNSTABLE)	MA	$4,213	109	LEXINGTON	KY	$5,202	176	FARGO	ND	$7,078
(TIE) 41	OAK HARBOR	WA	$4,213	110	HOUSTON	TX	$5,206	177	STURGEON BAY	WI	$7,142
43	PORT TOWNSEND	WA	$4,214	111	OJAI	CA	$5,215	178	PROVIDENCE	RI	$7,161
44	STAUNTON	VA	$4,227	112	RENO	NV	$5,239	179	GEORGETOWN	TX	$7,173
45	WASHINGTON	DC	$4,258	113	SARASOTA	FL	$5,259	180	BOERNE	TX	$7,189
46	CHARLOTTESVILLE	VA	$4,266	114	JACKSONVILLE	FL	$5,266	181	WICHITA	KS	$7,244
47	EASTON	MD	$4,273	115	PHOENIX	AZ	$5,321	182	MADISON	WI	$7,258
48	ST. SIMONS ISLAND	GA	$4,298	116	SALT LAKE CITY	UT	$5,356	183	DETROIT	MI	$7,270
49	SANTA FE	NM	$4,310		AVERAGE		$5,382	184	CHAPEL HILL	NC	$7,309
50	LINCOLN CITY	OR	$4,316	117	DANVILLE	KY	$5,432	185	KERRVILLE	TX	$7,319
51	DOTHAN	AL	$4,358	118	HOT SPRINGS	AR	$5,444	186	BALTIMORE	MD	$7,482
52	NEW YORK CITY	NY	$4,402	119	OCALA	FL	$5,474	187	SAN ANTONIO	TX	$7,496
53	OXFORD	MS	$4,452	120	TUCSON	AZ	$5,502	188	MILWAUKEE	WI	$7,643
54	GREENVILLE	SC	$4,454	(TIE) 121	CAMDEN	ME	$5,519	189	McALLEN	TX	$7,689
55	DAHLONEGA	GA	$4,455	(TIE) 121	SPOKANE	WA	$5,519	190	BROWNSVILLE	TX	$7,726
56	GREEN VALLEY	AZ	$4,469	123	KNOXVILLE	TN	$5,554	191	DES MOINES	IA	$7,849
57	NATCHITOCHES	LA	$4,480	124	GROVE	OK	$5,574	192	KANSAS CITY	MO	$7,933
58	BOULDER	CO	$4,481	125	EDENTON	NC	$5,580	193	THE WOODLANDS	TX	$7,952
59	BOISE	ID	$4,486	126	ORLANDO	FL	$5,582	194	OMAHA	NE	$8,125
60	FORT COLLINS	CO	$4,505	127	MURRAY	KY	$5,594	195	BUFFALO	NY	$8,159
61	SEATTLE	WA	$4,540	128	BOCA RATON	FL	$5,600	196	CHICAGO	IL	$8,192
62	THOMASVILLE	GA	$4,544	129	JUPITER	FL	$5,653	197	NEW HAVEN	CT	$8,977
63	EUFAULA	AL	$4,587	130	WAYNESVILLE	NC	$5,656	198	PHILADELPHIA	PA	$9,363
64	SAN DIEGO	CA	$4,636	131	BURLINGTON	VT	$5,678	199	HARTFORD	CT	$9,482
65	VICKSBURG	MS	$4,638	132	LOUISVILLE	KY	$5,689	200	SYRACUSE	NY	$9,740
66	LONGBOAT KEY	FL	$4,640	133	BRUNSWICK	ME	$5,725	201	LANCASTER	PA	$9,759
67	ST. GEORGE	UT	$4,648	134	TACOMA	WA	$5,740	202	PITTSBURGH	PA	$10,717
68	SIESTA KEY	FL	$4,661	135	HATTIESBURG	MS	$5,762	203	EAST STROUDSBURG	PA	$11,630

Ranking of Total Tax Burdens for Retirees
Earning $60,000 and Owning a Home Valued at $300,000

Rank	City, State		Total Tax	Rank	City, State		Total Tax	Rank	City, State		Total Tax
1	WILMINGTON	DE	$1,624	69	FLAGSTAFF	AZ	$5,377	136	OCALA	FL	$6,868
2	ANCHORAGE	AK	$2,168	70	PARIS	TN	$5,381	137	FAYETTEVILLE	AR	$6,916
3	WAILUKU	HI	$3,305	71	SAN DIEGO	CA	$5,388	138	NEW BERN	NC	$6,927
4	WILLIAMSBURG	VA	$3,515	72	GREENVILLE	SC	$5,391	139	OKLAHOMA CITY	OK	$6,992
5	CAPE MAY	NJ	$3,609	73	CARLSBAD	CA	$5,458	140	ORLANDO	FL	$7,001
6	CHARLESTON	SC	$3,668	74	THOMASVILLE	GA	$5,468	141	ALBUQUERQUE	NM	$7,005
7	JACKSON	WY	$3,771	75	SAN JUAN CAPISTRANO	CA	$5,497	142	HATTIESBURG	MS	$7,039
8	HILTON HEAD	SC	$3,820	76	BOISE	ID	$5,525	143	BOCA RATON	FL	$7,056
9	WOODSTOCK	VT	$3,855	77	MARYVILLE	TN	$5,534	144	TRAVERSE CITY	MI	$7,061
10	HONOLULU	HI	$3,912	78	VICKSBURG	MS	$5,537	145	BLOOMINGTON	IN	$7,087
11	CLEMSON	SC	$4,101	79	LAS CRUCES	NM	$5,549	146	JUPITER	FL	$7,117
12	CHEYENNE	WY	$4,122	80	HENDERSON	NV	$5,613	147	WILMINGTON	NC	$7,160
13	GRANTS PASS	OR	$4,145	81	MOUNTAIN HOME	AR	$5,616	148	NEW ORLEANS	LA	$7,181
14	COLORADO SPRINGS	CO	$4,173	82	PORTLAND	OR	$5,639	149	EAGLE RIVER	WI	$7,306
15	BEAUFORT	SC	$4,196	83	SIESTA KEY	FL	$5,651	150	DELAND	FL	$7,324
16	COEUR d'ALENE	ID	$4,203	84	BILLINGS	MT	$5,660	151	ORMOND BEACH	FL	$7,360
17	PETOSKEY	MI	$4,220	85	SEDONA	AZ	$5,692	152	BRADENTON	FL	$7,366
18	ATLANTA	GA	$4,244	86	LONGBOAT KEY	FL	$5,701	153	LEESBURG	FL	$7,402
19	MYRTLE BEACH	SC	$4,265	87	PASO ROBLES	CA	$5,727	154	CASA GRANDE	AZ	$7,417
20	CROSSVILLE	TN	$4,272	88	EUGENE	OR	$5,740	155	COLUMBUS	OH	$7,440
21	MEDFORD	OR	$4,305	89	CHARLESTON	WV	$5,752	156	ST. AUGUSTINE	FL	$7,498
22	FRIDAY HARBOR	WA	$4,322	90	ATHENS	GA	$5,754	157	LAKELAND	FL	$7,540
23	FAIRHOPE	AL	$4,368	91	TEMECULA	CA	$5,769	158	DALLAS	TX	$7,597
24	GRAND JUNCTION	CO	$4,388	92	PINEHURST	NC	$5,795	159	LITTLE ROCK	AR	$7,610
25	CARSON CITY	NV	$4,433	93	ANNAPOLIS	MD	$5,828	160	FORT LAUDERDALE	FL	$7,765
26	KEY WEST	FL	$4,443	94	SAN FRANCISCO	CA	$5,909	161	FREDERICKSBURG	TX	$7,790
27	DENVER	CO	$4,475	95	SALT LAKE CITY	UT	$5,930	162	CELEBRATION	FL	$7,837
28	SILVER CITY	NM	$4,508	96	GAINESVILLE	GA	$5,965	163	MOUNT DORA	FL	$7,875
29	BEND	OR	$4,531	97	LEXINGTON	KY	$5,976	164	CINCINNATI	OH	$7,895
30	DOTHAN	AL	$4,542	98	NEWARK	NJ	$5,992	165	CLEVELAND	OH	$7,928
31	ABINGDON	VA	$4,543	99	OJAI	CA	$6,006	166	PENSACOLA	FL	$7,949
32	ASHLAND	OR	$4,548	100	PUNTA GORDA	FL	$6,012	167	DADE CITY	FL	$8,185
33	WASHINGTON	DC	$4,588	101	LAS VEGAS	NV	$6,018	168	WICHITA	KS	$8,245
34	SEQUIM	WA	$4,649	102	PALM DESERT	CA	$6,026	169	ST. PETERSBURG	FL	$8,251
35	TOMS RIVER	NJ	$4,726	103	LOS ANGELES	CA	$6,035	170	TAMPA	FL	$8,254
36	SANTA FE	NM	$4,753	104	PHOENIX	AZ	$6,051	171	AUSTIN	TX	$8,262
37	BOSTON	MA	$4,756	105	HOT SPRINGS	AR	$6,065	172	PROVIDENCE	RI	$8,295
38	NAPLES	FL	$4,774	106	RICHMOND	VA	$6,082	(TIE) 173	WINTER HAVEN	FL	$8,337
39	KALISPELL	MT	$4,815	107	VERO BEACH	FL	$6,095	(TIE) 173	MEMPHIS	TN	$8,337
40	CAPE COD (BARNSTABLE)	MA	$4,843	108	NORTH FORT MYERS	FL	$6,096	175	GAINESVILLE	FL	$8,404
41	EUFAULA	AL	$4,849	109	SAVANNAH	GA	$6,103	176	STURGEON BAY	WI	$8,439
42	PORT TOWNSEND	WA	$4,875	110	SANIBEL ISLAND	FL	$6,142	177	CHAPEL HILL	NC	$8,520
43	OAK HARBOR	WA	$4,890	111	BURLINGTON	VT	$6,163	178	MARBLE FALLS	TX	$8,524
44	AIKEN	SC	$4,891	112	RENO	NV	$6,197	179	MIAMI	FL	$8,586
45	BILOXI	MS	$4,898	113	EDENTON	NC	$6,206	180	FARGO	ND	$8,655
46	BOULDER	CO	$4,919	114	DANVILLE	KY	$6,215	181	MADISON	WI	$8,707
47	STAUNTON	VA	$4,947	115	GROVE	OK	$6,269	182	BOERNE	TX	$9,017
48	BATON ROUGE	LA	$4,952	116	TUCSON	AZ	$6,293	183	GEORGETOWN	TX	$9,042
49	EASTON	MD	$5,006	117	SIOUX FALLS	SD	$6,301	184	KANSAS CITY	MO	$9,060
50	CHARLOTTESVILLE	VA	$5,008	118	WAYNESVILLE	NC	$6,329	185	DETROIT	MI	$9,151
51	ST. GEORGE	UT	$5,018	119	VENICE	FL	$6,355	186	MILWAUKEE	WI	$9,156
52	LINCOLN CITY	OR	$5,030	120	PALM COAST	FL	$6,391	187	KERRVILLE	TX	$9,174
53	PORTSMOUTH	NH	$5,035		**AVERAGE**		**$6,393**	188	BALTIMORE	MD	$9,282
54	FORT COLLINS	CO	$5,041	121	CAMDEN	ME	$6,441	189	DES MOINES	IA	$9,417
55	GREEN VALLEY	AZ	$5,064	122	BRANSON	MO	$6,448	190	SAN ANTONIO	TX	$9,588
56	NEW YORK CITY	NY	$5,127	123	SARASOTA	FL	$6,473	191	OMAHA	NE	$9,681
57	ST. SIMONS ISLAND	GA	$5,174	124	MURRAY	KY	$6,549	192	McALLEN	TX	$9,703
58	SIERRA VISTA	AZ	$5,215	125	KNOXVILLE	TN	$6,585	193	BROWNSVILLE	TX	$9,752
59	PRESCOTT	AZ	$5,216	126	HENDERSONVILLE	NC	$6,603	194	CHICAGO	IL	$10,055
60	SEATTLE	WA	$5,262	127	LOUISVILLE	KY	$6,620	195	THE WOODLANDS	TX	$10,210
61	OXFORD	MS	$5,276	128	JACKSONVILLE	FL	$6,629	196	BUFFALO	NY	$10,245
62	NATCHITOCHES	LA	$5,278	129	SPOKANE	WA	$6,631	197	NEW HAVEN	CT	$11,193
63	CEDAR CITY	UT	$5,280	130	HOUSTON	TX	$6,636	198	PHILADELPHIA	PA	$11,346
64	LAKE HAVASU CITY	AZ	$5,282	131	BREVARD	NC	$6,736	199	HARTFORD	CT	$11,703
65	DAHLONEGA	GA	$5,301	132	MINNEAPOLIS	MN	$6,784	200	LANCASTER	PA	$12,127
66	SCOTTSDALE	AZ	$5,345	133	BRUNSWICK	ME	$6,785	201	SYRACUSE	NY	$12,397
67	RUIDOSO	NM	$5,362	134	ASHEVILLE	NC	$6,811	202	PITTSBURGH	PA	$13,410
68	BERKELEY SPRINGS	WV	$5,376	135	TACOMA	WA	$6,867	203	EAST STROUDSBURG	PA	$14,629

Ranking of Total Tax Burdens for Retirees
Earning $90,000 and Owning a Home Valued at $225,000

Rank	City, State		Total Tax	Rank	City, State		Total Tax	Rank	City, State		Total Tax
1	ANCHORAGE	AK	$1,022	69	PRESCOTT	AZ	$6,030	136	LAS CRUCES	NM	$7,346
2	WILMINGTON	DE	$3,280	70	GRANTS PASS	OR	$6,048	137	NEW YORK CITY	NY	$7,360
3	JACKSON	WY	$3,675	71	SCOTTSDALE	AZ	$6,078	138	BILLINGS	MT	$7,425
4	CHEYENNE	WY	$3,938	72	KNOXVILLE	TN	$6,090	139	HATTIESBURG	MS	$7,457
5	CAPE MAY	NJ	$4,029	73	DAHLONEGA	GA	$6,096	140	MURRAY	KY	$7,470
6	PORTSMOUTH	NH	$4,097	74	FLAGSTAFF	AZ	$6,116	141	MEMPHIS	TN	$7,472
7	FRIDAY HARBOR	WA	$4,151	75	THOMASVILLE	GA	$6,126	142	MOUNTAIN HOME	AR	$7,484
8	KEY WEST	FL	$4,158	76	FORT COLLINS	CO	$6,134	143	PINEHURST	NC	$7,511
9	CHARLESTON	SC	$4,210	77	DELAND	FL	$6,146	144	CHARLESTON	WV	$7,519
10	NAPLES	FL	$4,240	78	OXFORD	MS	$6,147	145	BLOOMINGTON	IN	$7,543
11	HILTON HEAD	SC	$4,398	79	EUFAULA	AL	$6,163	146	GEORGETOWN	TX	$7,616
12	CROSSVILLE	TN	$4,399	80	BRADENTON	FL	$6,169	147	BOERNE	TX	$7,632
13	SEQUIM	WA	$4,472	81	MEDFORD	OR	$6,170	148	LEXINGTON	KY	$7,641
14	CARSON CITY	NV	$4,506	82	ORMOND BEACH	FL	$6,193	149	CASA GRANDE	AZ	$7,678
15	CLEMSON	SC	$4,557	83	BOULDER	CO	$6,195	150	DANVILLE	KY	$7,737
16	MYRTLE BEACH	SC	$4,649	84	TACOMA	WA	$6,213	151	KERRVILLE	TX	$7,762
17	OAK HARBOR	WA	$4,659	85	ST. AUGUSTINE	FL	$6,230	152	ST. GEORGE	UT	$7,808
18	PORT TOWNSEND	WA	$4,665	86	LEESBURG	FL	$6,253	153	GROVE	OK	$7,833
19	BEAUFORT	SC	$4,677	87	DALLAS	TX	$6,255	154	TRAVERSE CITY	MI	$7,853
20	WILLIAMSBURG	VA	$4,774	88	CHARLOTTESVILLE	VA	$6,273	155	EDENTON	NC	$7,900
21	TOMS RIVER	NJ	$4,822	89	VICKSBURG	MS	$6,327	156	HOT SPRINGS	AR	$7,925
(TIE) 22	LONGBOAT KEY	FL	$5,016	90	BEND	OR	$6,337	157	SAN ANTONIO	TX	$7,933
(TIE) 22	SEATTLE	WA	$5,016	91	LAKELAND	FL	$6,360	158	CAMDEN	ME	$7,954
24	SIESTA KEY	FL	$5,037	92	SAN DIEGO	CA	$6,372	159	WAYNESVILLE	NC	$7,976
25	AIKEN	SC	$5,115	93	ATHENS	GA	$6,404	160	CEDAR CITY	UT	$7,996
26	NORTH FORT MYERS	FL	$5,189	94	CARLSBAD	CA	$6,430	161	LOUISVILLE	KY	$8,062
27	SANIBEL ISLAND	FL	$5,222	95	FORT LAUDERDALE	FL	$6,437	162	McALLEN	TX	$8,132
28	PARIS	TN	$5,231	96	ASHLAND	OR	$6,439	163	BRANSON	MO	$8,159
29	HENDERSON	NV	$5,270	97	SAN JUAN CAPISTRANO	CA	$6,450	164	BRUNSWICK	ME	$8,160
30	MARYVILLE	TN	$5,295	98	SEDONA	AZ	$6,469	165	BROWNSVILLE	TX	$8,169
31	VERO BEACH	FL	$5,327	99	SILVER CITY	NM	$6,571	166	HENDERSONVILLE	NC	$8,177
32	PUNTA GORDA	FL	$5,351	100	PHOENIX	AZ	$6,602	167	BREVARD	NC	$8,280
33	PETOSKEY	MI	$5,472	101	PASO ROBLES	CA	$6,612	168	ASHEVILLE	NC	$8,304
34	COLORADO SPRINGS	CO	$5,489	102	MOUNT DORA	FL	$6,615	169	OKLAHOMA CITY	OK	$8,315
35	VENICE	FL	$5,491	103	ANNAPOLIS	MD	$6,617	170	COLUMBUS	OH	$8,375
36	GREENVILLE	SC	$5,513	104	KALISPELL	MT	$6,666	171	THE WOODLANDS	TX	$8,395
37	PALM COAST	FL	$5,537	105	TEMECULA	CA	$6,683	172	ALBUQUERQUE	NM	$8,402
38	SIOUX FALLS	SD	$5,542	106	LINCOLN CITY	OR	$6,712	173	NEW BERN	NC	$8,437
39	FAIRHOPE	AL	$5,562	107	PENSACOLA	FL	$6,728	174	FARGO	ND	$8,457
40	LAS VEGAS	NV	$5,574	108	FREDERICKSBURG	TX	$6,733	175	BURLINGTON	VT	$8,530
41	ABINGDON	VA	$5,576	109	TUCSON	AZ	$6,783	176	SALT LAKE CITY	UT	$8,537
42	BOSTON	MA	$5,610	110	RICHMOND	VA	$6,785	177	WILMINGTON	NC	$8,621
(TIE) 43	SARASOTA	FL	$5,635	111	SANTA FE	NM	$6,811	178	FAYETTEVILLE	AR	$8,630
(TIE) 43	RENO	NV	$5,635	112	DADE CITY	FL	$6,822	179	CINCINNATI	OH	$8,676
45	WAILUKU	HI	$5,638	113	BOISE	ID	$6,823	180	EAGLE RIVER	WI	$8,703
46	JACKSONVILLE	FL	$5,642	114	SAN FRANCISCO	CA	$6,833	181	CLEVELAND	OH	$8,823
47	GREEN VALLEY	AZ	$5,643	115	LOS ANGELES	CA	$6,859	182	LITTLE ROCK	AR	$8,992
48	HOUSTON	TX	$5,649		AVERAGE		$6,865	183	BALTIMORE	MD	$9,170
49	GRAND JUNCTION	CO	$5,672	(TIE) 116	WASHINGTON	DC	$6,872	184	PROVIDENCE	RI	$9,483
50	BATON ROUGE	LA	$5,716	(TIE) 116	TAMPA	FL	$6,872	185	CHICAGO	IL	$9,528
51	DENVER	CO	$5,744	118	AUSTIN	TX	$6,889	186	STURGEON BAY	WI	$9,589
52	NEWARK	NJ	$5,771	119	ST. PETERSBURG	FL	$6,890	187	CHAPEL HILL	NC	$9,629
53	BILOXI	MS	$5,795	120	GAINESVILLE	FL	$6,896	188	MINNEAPOLIS	MN	$9,632
54	OCALA	FL	$5,823	121	GAINESVILLE	GA	$6,899	189	MADISON	WI	$9,705
55	ST. SIMONS ISLAND	GA	$5,880	122	SAVANNAH	GA	$6,918	190	DES MOINES	IA	$9,883
(TIE) 56	CAPE COD (BARNSTABLE)	MA	$5,891	123	OJAI	CA	$6,923	191	WICHITA	KS	$10,016
(TIE) 56	STAUNTON	VA	$5,891	124	PALM DESERT	CA	$6,925	192	MILWAUKEE	WI	$10,097
58	COEUR d'ALENE	ID	$5,921	125	WINTER HAVEN	FL	$6,941	193	KANSAS CITY	MO	$10,432
59	ORLANDO	FL	$5,931	126	WOODSTOCK	VT	$6,996	194	BUFFALO	NY	$10,435
60	DOTHAN	AL	$5,934	127	CELEBRATION	FL	$7,023	195	DETROIT	MI	$10,507
61	BOCA RATON	FL	$5,949	128	MIAMI	FL	$7,114	196	OMAHA	NE	$10,813
62	EASTON	MD	$5,950	129	PORTLAND	OR	$7,173	197	LANCASTER	PA	$11,202
63	HONOLULU	HI	$5,976	130	ATLANTA	GA	$7,212	198	PHILADELPHIA	PA	$11,539
64	SPOKANE	WA	$5,981	131	BERKELEY SPRINGS	WV	$7,230	199	NEW HAVEN	CT	$11,693
65	SIERRA VISTA	AZ	$5,982	132	MARBLE FALLS	TX	$7,269	200	SYRACUSE	NY	$12,004
66	NATCHITOCHES	LA	$5,986	133	EUGENE	OR	$7,270	201	PITTSBURGH	PA	$12,135
67	JUPITER	FL	$6,002	134	RUIDOSO	NM	$7,285	202	HARTFORD	CT	$12,198
68	LAKE HAVASU CITY	AZ	$6,003	135	NEW ORLEANS	LA	$7,301	203	EAST STROUDSBURG	PA	$13,049

Ranking of Total Tax Burdens for Retirees
Earning $90,000 and Owning a Home Valued at $375,000

Rank	City, State		Total Tax	Rank	City, State		Total Tax	Rank	City, State		Total Tax
1	ANCHORAGE	AK	$3,314	69	NORTH FORT MYERS	FL	$7,648	136	LAKELAND	FL	$9,473
2	WILMINGTON	DE	$4,182	70	SANTA FE	NM	$7,696	137	BURLINGTON	VT	$9,502
3	JACKSON	WY	$4,511	71	SANIBEL ISLAND	FL	$7,706	138	HENDERSONVILLE	NC	$9,669
4	CAPE MAY	NJ	$4,848	72	CHARLOTTESVILLE	VA	$7,758	139	SALT LAKE CITY	UT	$9,686
5	CARSON CITY	NV	$4,934	73	SIOUX FALLS	SD	$7,765	140	BLOOMINGTON	IN	$9,722
6	CHEYENNE	WY	$4,949	74	DAHLONEGA	GA	$7,788	141	FREDERICKSBURG	TX	$9,733
7	CROSSVILLE	TN	$5,276	75	OXFORD	MS	$7,796	142	FORT LAUDERDALE	FL	$9,736
8	FRIDAY HARBOR	WA	$5,321	76	NEWARK	NJ	$7,837	143	CASA GRANDE	AZ	$9,769
9	CHARLESTON	SC	$5,353	77	SAN DIEGO	CA	$7,876	144	CAMDEN	ME	$9,798
10	HILTON HEAD	SC	$5,480	78	CARLSBAD	CA	$7,958	145	DALLAS	TX	$9,824
11	KEY WEST	FL	$5,533	79	VENICE	FL	$7,970	146	BREVARD	NC	$9,832
12	WILLIAMSBURG	VA	$5,584	80	THOMASVILLE	GA	$7,974	147	ATLANTA	GA	$9,844
13	SEQUIM	WA	$5,727	81	PALM COAST	FL	$7,997	148	MOUNT DORA	FL	$9,887
14	WAILUKU	HI	$5,766	82	SAN JUAN CAPISTRANO	CA	$8,017	149	LOUISVILLE	KY	$9,924
15	CLEMSON	SC	$5,871	(TIE) 83	PHOENIX	AZ	$8,063	150	ASHEVILLE	NC	$9,959
16	BEAUFORT	SC	$5,941	(TIE) 83	SARASOTA	FL	$8,063	151	PENSACOLA	FL	$9,976
17	NAPLES	FL	$5,952	85	VICKSBURG	MS	$8,125	152	HATTIESBURG	MS	$10,010
18	PORT TOWNSEND	WA	$5,987	86	LINCOLN CITY	OR	$8,141	153	NEW BERN	NC	$10,057
19	OAK HARBOR	WA	$6,013	87	KNOXVILLE	TN	$8,152	154	NEW ORLEANS	LA	$10,126
20	FAIRHOPE	AL	$6,094	88	SPOKANE	WA	$8,205	155	OKLAHOMA CITY	OK	$10,127
21	MYRTLE BEACH	SC	$6,107	89	KALISPELL	MT	$8,209	156	FAYETTEVILLE	AR	$10,211
22	COLORADO SPRINGS	CO	$6,166	90	PASO ROBLES	CA	$8,258	157	ST. PETERSBURG	FL	$10,273
23	PORTSMOUTH	NH	$6,220	91	TEMECULA	CA	$8,327	158	MEMPHIS	TN	$10,274
24	TOMS RIVER	NJ	$6,259	92	BERKELEY SPRINGS	WV	$8,349	159	BRUNSWICK	ME	$10,281
25	DOTHAN	AL	$6,302	93	JACKSONVILLE	FL	$8,369	160	DADE CITY	FL	$10,299
26	GRAND JUNCTION	CO	$6,441	94	ATHENS	GA	$8,387	161	WILMINGTON	NC	$10,339
27	SEATTLE	WA	$6,460	95	ANNAPOLIS	MD	$8,402	162	TAMPA	FL	$10,388
28	HONOLULU	HI	$6,514	96	RUIDOSO	NM	$8,461	163	WINTER HAVEN	FL	$10,484
29	DENVER	CO	$6,543	97	TACOMA	WA	$8,467	164	AUSTIN	TX	$10,520
30	PARIS	TN	$6,603	98	TUCSON	AZ	$8,487	165	ALBUQUERQUE	NM	$10,524
31	EUFAULA	AL	$6,688	99	OJAI	CA	$8,505	166	TRAVERSE CITY	MI	$10,560
32	PETOSKEY	MI	$6,711	100	HOUSTON	TX	$8,510	167	GAINESVILLE	FL	$10,583
33	WOODSTOCK	VT	$6,714	101	SAN FRANCISCO	CA	$8,536	168	MARBLE FALLS	TX	$10,665
34	HENDERSON	NV	$6,790	102	ST. GEORGE	UT	$8,548	169	COLUMBUS	OH	$10,667
35	GREEN VALLEY	AZ	$6,832	103	PALM DESERT	CA	$8,600	170	EAGLE RIVER	WI	$10,802
36	MARYVILLE	TN	$6,844	104	OCALA	FL	$8,610	171	MIAMI	FL	$10,811
37	ABINGDON	VA	$6,851	105	MOUNTAIN HOME	AR	$8,615	172	LITTLE ROCK	AR	$11,062
38	AIKEN	SC	$6,892	106	LAS CRUCES	NM	$8,695	173	CLEVELAND	OH	$11,276
39	PRESCOTT	AZ	$7,010	107	PINEHURST	NC	$8,719	174	BOERNE	TX	$11,288
40	SIERRA VISTA	AZ	$7,011	108	RICHMOND	VA	$8,720	175	CINCINNATI	OH	$11,292
41	SIESTA KEY	FL	$7,016	109	LOS ANGELES	CA	$8,734	176	GEORGETOWN	TX	$11,353
42	GRANTS PASS	OR	$7,035	110	ORLANDO	FL	$8,769	177	MINNEAPOLIS	MN	$11,444
43	BOULDER	CO	$7,072	(TIE) 111	NEW YORK CITY	NY	$8,811	178	KERRVILLE	TX	$11,472
44	LAKE HAVASU CITY	AZ	$7,097	(TIE) 111	CHARLESTON	WV	$8,811	179	FARGO	ND	$11,611
45	LONGBOAT KEY	FL	$7,139	113	BOCA RATON	FL	$8,860	180	PROVIDENCE	RI	$11,751
46	CAPE COD (BARNSTABLE)	MA	$7,151	114	CEDAR CITY	UT	$8,867	181	WICHITA	KS	$12,018
47	COEUR d'ALENE	ID	$7,159	115	PORTLAND	OR	$8,897	182	CHAPEL HILL	NC	$12,050
48	SCOTTSDALE	AZ	$7,173	116	BOISE	ID	$8,901	183	SAN ANTONIO	TX	$12,117
49	FORT COLLINS	CO	$7,205		**AVERAGE**		**$8,911**	184	McALLEN	TX	$12,160
50	MEDFORD	OR	$7,232	117	JUPITER	FL	$8,931	185	BROWNSVILLE	TX	$12,220
51	BATON ROUGE	LA	$7,237	118	GAINESVILLE	GA	$8,940	186	STURGEON BAY	WI	$12,252
52	BOSTON	MA	$7,258	119	EUGENE	OR	$9,002	187	MADISON	WI	$12,632
53	FLAGSTAFF	AZ	$7,269	120	BILLINGS	MT	$9,138	188	KANSAS CITY	MO	$12,686
54	LAS VEGAS	NV	$7,296	121	EDENTON	NC	$9,152	189	BALTIMORE	MD	$12,770
55	STAUNTON	VA	$7,331	122	HOT SPRINGS	AR	$9,167	190	THE WOODLANDS	TX	$12,912
56	BILOXI	MS	$7,365	123	LEXINGTON	KY	$9,188	191	DES MOINES	IA	$13,019
57	GREENVILLE	SC	$7,387	124	DELAND	FL	$9,201	192	MILWAUKEE	WI	$13,196
58	SILVER CITY	NM	$7,390	125	GROVE	OK	$9,223	193	CHICAGO	IL	$13,254
59	EASTON	MD	$7,416	126	ORMOND BEACH	FL	$9,225	194	OMAHA	NE	$13,926
60	PUNTA GORDA	FL	$7,425	127	BRADENTON	FL	$9,260	195	DETROIT	MI	$14,268
61	ASHLAND	OR	$7,510	128	DANVILLE	KY	$9,303	196	BUFFALO	NY	$14,607
62	BEND	OR	$7,517	129	LEESBURG	FL	$9,304	197	PHILADELPHIA	PA	$15,506
63	WASHINGTON	DC	$7,532	130	WAYNESVILLE	NC	$9,322	198	LANCASTER	PA	$15,938
64	RENO	NV	$7,550	131	SAVANNAH	GA	$9,344	199	NEW HAVEN	CT	$16,125
65	NATCHITOCHES	LA	$7,583	132	BRANSON	MO	$9,356	200	HARTFORD	CT	$16,640
66	SEDONA	AZ	$7,612	133	MURRAY	KY	$9,381	201	SYRACUSE	NY	$17,319
67	VERO BEACH	FL	$7,616	134	CELEBRATION	FL	$9,404	202	PITTSBURGH	PA	$17,522
68	ST. SIMONS ISLAND	GA	$7,632	135	ST. AUGUSTINE	FL	$9,410	203	EAST STROUDSBURG	PA	$19,047

Ranking of Total Tax Burdens for Retirees
Earning $90,000 and Owning a Home Valued at $525,000

Rank	City, State		Total Tax	Rank	City, State		Total Tax	Rank	City, State		Total Tax
1	WILMINGTON	DE	$4,640	69	ST. SIMONS ISLAND	GA	$9,384	(TIE) 136	CELEBRATION	FL	$11,786
2	JACKSON	WY	$5,347	70	OXFORD	MS	$9,444	(TIE) 136	LOUISVILLE	KY	$11,786
3	ANCHORAGE	AK	$5,606	71	RENO	NV	$9,464	138	FAYETTEVILLE	AR	$11,792
4	CAPE MAY	NJ	$5,654	72	BERKELEY SPRINGS	WV	$9,469	139	JUPITER	FL	$11,860
5	CARSON CITY	NV	$5,674	73	DAHLONEGA	GA	$9,479	140	BLOOMINGTON	IN	$11,901
6	CHEYENNE	WY	$5,961	74	CARLSBAD	CA	$9,486	141	OKLAHOMA CITY	OK	$11,939
7	WAILUKU	HI	$6,141	75	PUNTA GORDA	FL	$9,500	142	CASA GRANDE	AZ	$11,995
8	CROSSVILLE	TN	$6,154	76	LINCOLN CITY	OR	$9,571	143	WILMINGTON	NC	$12,056
9	WILLIAMSBURG	VA	$6,394	77	SAN JUAN CAPISTRANO	CA	$9,584	144	DELAND	FL	$12,256
10	WOODSTOCK	VT	$6,432	78	RUIDOSO	NM	$9,636	145	ORMOND BEACH	FL	$12,257
11	FRIDAY HARBOR	WA	$6,490	79	PHOENIX	AZ	$9,700	146	BRADENTON	FL	$12,352
12	CHARLESTON	SC	$6,497	80	CEDAR CITY	UT	$9,739	147	LEESBURG	FL	$12,354
13	HILTON HEAD	SC	$6,562	81	MOUNTAIN HOME	AR	$9,746	148	BRUNSWICK	ME	$12,401
14	FAIRHOPE	AL	$6,627	82	KALISPELL	MT	$9,753	149	ATLANTA	GA	$12,476
15	DOTHAN	AL	$6,669	83	THOMASVILLE	GA	$9,821	150	HATTIESBURG	MS	$12,563
16	COLORADO SPRINGS	CO	$6,843	84	NEWARK	NJ	$9,903	151	LAKELAND	FL	$12,586
17	KEY WEST	FL	$6,909	(TIE) 85	PASO ROBLES	CA	$9,905	152	ST. AUGUSTINE	FL	$12,590
18	SEQUIM	WA	$6,982	(TIE) 85	VERO BEACH	FL	$9,905	153	ALBUQUERQUE	NM	$12,646
19	HONOLULU	HI	$7,053	87	VICKSBURG	MS	$9,922	154	FREDERICKSBURG	TX	$12,734
20	CLEMSON	SC	$7,185	88	PINEHURST	NC	$9,926	155	NEW ORLEANS	LA	$12,951
21	BEAUFORT	SC	$7,205	89	TEMECULA	CA	$9,972	156	COLUMBUS	OH	$12,959
22	GRAND JUNCTION	CO	$7,209	90	SIOUX FALLS	SD	$9,987	157	EAGLE RIVER	WI	$12,975
23	EUFAULA	AL	$7,213	91	LAS CRUCES	NM	$10,044	158	FORT LAUDERDALE	FL	$13,035
24	PORT TOWNSEND	WA	$7,309	92	OJAI	CA	$10,086	159	MEMPHIS	TN	$13,077
25	DENVER	CO	$7,343	93	CHARLESTON	WV	$10,104	160	LITTLE ROCK	AR	$13,132
26	OAK HARBOR	WA	$7,367	94	NORTH FORT MYERS	FL	$10,107	161	MOUNT DORA	FL	$13,159
27	MYRTLE BEACH	SC	$7,565	95	ANNAPOLIS	MD	$10,187	162	PENSACOLA	FL	$13,223
28	NAPLES	FL	$7,664	96	SANIBEL ISLAND	FL	$10,190	163	TRAVERSE CITY	MI	$13,267
29	TOMS RIVER	NJ	$7,694	97	KNOXVILLE	TN	$10,215	164	DALLAS	TX	$13,392
30	SEATTLE	WA	$7,904	98	SAN FRANCISCO	CA	$10,238	165	MINNEAPOLIS	MN	$13,697
31	BOULDER	CO	$7,949	99	NEW YORK CITY	NY	$10,261	166	CLEVELAND	OH	$13,729
32	PETOSKEY	MI	$7,951	100	PALM DESERT	CA	$10,275	167	DADE CITY	FL	$13,777
33	PARIS	TN	$7,976	101	TUCSON	AZ	$10,326	168	ST. PETERSBURG	FL	$13,837
34	GREEN VALLEY	AZ	$8,021	102	ATHENS	GA	$10,370	169	TAMPA	FL	$13,904
35	GRANTS PASS	OR	$8,022	103	EDENTON	NC	$10,405	170	CINCINNATI	OH	$13,907
36	SIERRA VISTA	AZ	$8,040	104	HOT SPRINGS	AR	$10,409	171	PROVIDENCE	RI	$14,018
37	PRESCOTT	AZ	$8,071	105	SPOKANE	WA	$10,429	172	WICHITA	KS	$14,020
38	ABINGDON	VA	$8,126	106	VENICE	FL	$10,450	173	WINTER HAVEN	FL	$14,027
39	WASHINGTON	DC	$8,192	107	PALM COAST	FL	$10,458	174	MARBLE FALLS	TX	$14,060
40	SILVER CITY	NM	$8,209	108	BURLINGTON	VT	$10,474	175	AUSTIN	TX	$14,151
41	FORT COLLINS	CO	$8,277	109	SARASOTA	FL	$10,491	176	GAINESVILLE	FL	$14,271
42	MEDFORD	OR	$8,293	110	BRANSON	MO	$10,554	177	CHAPEL HILL	NC	$14,470
43	LAKE HAVASU CITY	AZ	$8,297	111	LOS ANGELES	CA	$10,609	178	MIAMI	FL	$14,507
44	HENDERSON	NV	$8,309	112	GROVE	OK	$10,614	179	FARGO	ND	$14,765
45	PORTSMOUTH	NH	$8,342	113	PORTLAND	OR	$10,621	180	KANSAS CITY	MO	$14,940
46	SCOTTSDALE	AZ	$8,365	114	RICHMOND	VA	$10,655	181	BOERNE	TX	$14,943
47	MARYVILLE	TN	$8,392	115	WAYNESVILLE	NC	$10,667	182	STURGEON BAY	WI	$14,991
48	COEUR d'ALENE	ID	$8,396	116	TACOMA	WA	$10,720	183	GEORGETOWN	TX	$15,091
49	CAPE COD (BARNSTABLE)	MA	$8,411	(TIE) 117	LEXINGTON	KY	$10,734	184	KERRVILLE	TX	$15,183
50	SANTA FE	NM	$8,580	(TIE) 117	EUGENE	OR	$10,734	185	MADISON	WI	$15,587
51	ASHLAND	OR	$8,582	119	SALT LAKE CITY	UT	$10,834	186	DES MOINES	IA	$16,156
52	FLAGSTAFF	AZ	$8,592	120	BILLINGS	MT	$10,851	187	McALLEN	TX	$16,188
53	AIKEN	SC	$8,670	121	DANVILLE	KY	$10,869	188	BROWNSVILLE	TX	$16,271
54	BEND	OR	$8,697		**AVERAGE**		**$10,967**	189	SAN ANTONIO	TX	$16,300
55	SEDONA	AZ	$8,756	122	BOISE	ID	$10,980	190	BALTIMORE	MD	$16,370
56	BATON ROUGE	LA	$8,757	123	GAINESVILLE	GA	$10,982	191	MILWAUKEE	WI	$16,372
57	STAUNTON	VA	$8,771	124	JACKSONVILLE	FL	$11,096	192	CHICAGO	IL	$16,979
58	EASTON	MD	$8,881	125	HENDERSONVILLE	NC	$11,162	193	OMAHA	NE	$17,038
59	BOSTON	MA	$8,907	126	MURRAY	KY	$11,292	194	THE WOODLANDS	TX	$17,428
60	BILOXI	MS	$8,934	127	HOUSTON	TX	$11,370	195	DETROIT	MI	$18,029
61	SIESTA KEY	FL	$8,995	128	BREVARD	NC	$11,385	196	BUFFALO	NY	$18,780
62	LAS VEGAS	NV	$9,018	129	OCALA	FL	$11,397	197	PHILADELPHIA	PA	$19,473
63	NATCHITOCHES	LA	$9,181	130	ORLANDO	FL	$11,607	198	NEW HAVEN	CT	$20,557
64	CHARLOTTESVILLE	VA	$9,243	131	ASHEVILLE	NC	$11,615	199	LANCASTER	PA	$20,673
65	GREENVILLE	SC	$9,260	132	CAMDEN	ME	$11,641	200	HARTFORD	CT	$21,081
66	LONGBOAT KEY	FL	$9,262	133	NEW BERN	NC	$11,677	201	SYRACUSE	NY	$22,635
67	ST. GEORGE	UT	$9,288	134	SAVANNAH	GA	$11,769	202	PITTSBURGH	PA	$22,910
68	SAN DIEGO	CA	$9,380	135	BOCA RATON	FL	$11,771	203	EAST STROUDSBURG	PA	$25,046

Ranking of Total Tax Burdens for Retirees
Earning $90,000 and Owning a Home Valued at $600,000

Rank	City, State		Total Tax	Rank	City, State		Total Tax	Rank	City, State		Total Tax
1	JACKSON	WY	$5,765	11	SEDONA	AZ	$9,328	20	TEMECULA	CA	$10,794
2	WOODSTOCK	VT	$6,291	12	EASTON	MD	$9,614	21	OJAI	CA	$10,877
3	WAILUKU	HI	$6,328	13	BOSTON	MA	$9,731	22	NEW YORK CITY	NY	$10,986
4	FRIDAY HARBOR	WA	$7,075	14	SIESTA KEY	FL	$9,985	23	ANNAPOLIS	MD	$11,079
5	HILTON HEAD	SC	$7,103		AVERAGE		$10,022	24	SAN FRANCISCO	CA	$11,090
6	HONOLULU	HI	$7,322	15	SAN DIEGO	CA	$10,132	25	PALM DESERT	CA	$11,113
7	KEY WEST	FL	$7,597	16	CARLSBAD	CA	$10,249	26	SANIBEL ISLAND	FL	$11,432
8	NAPLES	FL	$8,520	17	LONGBOAT KEY	FL	$10,323	27	LOS ANGELES	CA	$11,547
9	SEATTLE	WA	$8,626	18	SAN JUAN CAPISTRANO	CA	$10,368	28	CELEBRATION	FL	$12,977
10	SCOTTSDALE	AZ	$9,001	19	PASO ROBLES	CA	$10,728	29	BOCA RATON	FL	$13,227
								30	PHILADELPHIA	PA	$21,456

Ranking of Total Tax Burdens for Retirees
Earning $90,000 and Owning a Home Valued at $750,000

Rank	City, State		Total Tax	Rank	City, State		Total Tax	Rank	City, State		Total Tax
1	JACKSON	WY	$6,602	11	SEDONA	AZ	$10,471	20	TEMECULA	CA	$12,439
2	WAILUKU	HI	$6,703	12	EASTON	MD	$11,080	21	LONGBOAT KEY	FL	$12,446
3	WOODSTOCK	VT	$6,867	13	BOSTON	MA	$11,379	22	OJAI	CA	$12,459
4	HONOLULU	HI	$7,861	14	SAN DIEGO	CA	$11,636	23	PALM DESERT	CA	$12,788
5	HILTON HEAD	SC	$8,185		AVERAGE		$11,637	24	SAN FRANCISCO	CA	$12,792
6	FRIDAY HARBOR	WA	$8,244	15	CARLSBAD	CA	$11,777	25	ANNAPOLIS	MD	$12,864
7	KEY WEST	FL	$8,973	16	SAN JUAN CAPISTRANO	CA	$11,935	26	LOS ANGELES	CA	$13,422
8	SEATTLE	WA	$10,071	17	SIESTA KEY	FL	$11,964	27	SANIBEL ISLAND	FL	$13,916
9	NAPLES	FL	$10,232	18	PASO ROBLES	CA	$12,374	28	CELEBRATION	FL	$15,358
10	SCOTTSDALE	AZ	$10,272	19	NEW YORK CITY	NY	$12,437	29	BOCA RATON	FL	$16,138
								30	PHILADELPHIA	PA	$25,423

Ranking of Total Tax Burdens for Retirees
Earning $90,000 and Owning a Home Valued at $900,000

Rank	City, State		Total Tax	Rank	City, State		Total Tax	Rank	City, State		Total Tax
1	WAILUKU	HI	$7,078	11	NAPLES	FL	$11,943	20	OJAI	CA	$14,040
2	JACKSON	WY	$7,438	12	EASTON	MD	$12,545	21	TEMECULA	CA	$14,084
3	HONOLULU	HI	$8,399	13	BOSTON	MA	$13,028	22	PALM DESERT	CA	$14,464
4	WOODSTOCK	VT	$9,238	14	SAN DIEGO	CA	$13,139	23	SAN FRANCISCO	CA	$14,495
5	HILTON HEAD	SC	$9,266	15	CARLSBAD	CA	$13,305	24	LONGBOAT KEY	FL	$14,569
6	FRIDAY HARBOR	WA	$9,414		AVERAGE		$13,314	25	ANNAPOLIS	MD	$14,649
7	KEY WEST	FL	$10,349	16	SAN JUAN CAPISTRANO	CA	$13,502	26	LOS ANGELES	CA	$15,297
8	SEATTLE	WA	$11,515	17	NEW YORK CITY	NY	$13,888	27	SANIBEL ISLAND	FL	$16,400
9	SCOTTSDALE	AZ	$11,544	18	SIESTA KEY	FL	$13,943	28	CELEBRATION	FL	$17,740
10	SEDONA	AZ	$11,680	19	PASO ROBLES	CA	$14,020	29	BOCA RATON	FL	$19,048
								30	PHILADELPHIA	PA	$29,389

TAX HEAVEN OR HELL

How do the cities we've profiled stack up against each other taxwise? The following charts show our 10 Tax Heavens and Hells for each of nine income/home value categories. Find the category that most closely matches the income and home value you anticipate for yourself in retirement.

If you don't see a city you're interested in, check the full ranking for each income/home value category — from Nos. 1 to 203 (Nos. 1 to 173 for the lowest income level and Nos.1 to 30 for the cities that include the three highest home values) — in the preceding pages.

Our charts do not take into account cost-of-living factors in the areas we examined. For instance, Jackson, WY, appears in several Tax Heaven charts, but residents there face very high real estate prices. Our charts rank cities solely by the tax burdens you will incur living there.

You may be surprised to see that not all of our Tax Heaven slots have been filled by cities from states with

Tax Heavens ○ ○ ○

$30,000 Income/$125,000 Home

			TAX
1	WILMINGTON	DE	$111
2	ANCHORAGE	AK	$182
3	GRANTS PASS	OR	$1,273
4	WASHINGTON	DC	$1,338
	KALISPELL	MT	$1,338
6	MEDFORD	OR	$1,345
7	BEND	OR	$1,433
8	COEUR d'ALENE	ID	$1,482
	CAPE COD (BARNSTABLE)	MA	$1,482
10	ASHLAND	OR	$1,522

$30,000 Income/$150,000 Home

			TAX
1	WILMINGTON	DE	$116
2	ANCHORAGE	AK	$182
3	GRANTS PASS	OR	$1,437
4	WASHINGTON	DC	$1,448
5	MEDFORD	OR	$1,522
6	COEUR d'ALENE	ID	$1,585
7	KALISPELL	MT	$1,596
8	BEND	OR	$1,630
9	CAPE COD (BARNSTABLE)	MA	$1,692
10	ASHLAND	OR	$1,700

$30,000 Income/$175,000 Home

			TAX
1	WILMINGTON	DE	$172
2	ANCHORAGE	AK	$297
3	WASHINGTON	DC	$1,558
4	GRANTS PASS	OR	$1,602
5	KALISPELL	MT	$1,637
6	MEDFORD	OR	$1,699
7	COEUR d'ALENE	ID	$1,791
8	BEND	OR	$1,827
9	BILLINGS	MT	$1,843
10	ASHLAND	OR	$1,879

$60,000 Income/$150,000 Home

			TAX
1	ANCHORAGE	AK	$182
2	WILMINGTON	DE	$1,205
3	CHARLESTON	SC	$2,525
4	WILLIAMSBURG	VA	$2,705
5	HILTON HEAD	SC	$2,738
6	CLEMSON	SC	$2,787
7	CAPE MAY	NJ	$2,790
8	MYRTLE BEACH	SC	$2,807
9	PORTSMOUTH	NH	$2,913
10	BEAUFORT	SC	$2,933

$60,000 Income/$225,000 Home

			TAX
1	ANCHORAGE	AK	$1,022
2	WILMINGTON	DE	$1,460
3	CHARLESTON	SC	$3,097
4	WILLIAMSBURG	VA	$3,110
5	CAPE MAY	NJ	$3,199
6	HILTON HEAD	SC	$3,279
7	WAILUKU	HI	$3,305
8	JACKSON	WY	$3,353
9	CLEMSON	SC	$3,444
10	MYRTLE BEACH	SC	$3,536

$60,000 Income/$300,000 Home

			TAX
1	WILMINGTON	DE	$1,624
2	ANCHORAGE	AK	$2,168
3	WAILUKU	HI	$3,305
4	WILLIAMSBURG	VA	$3,515
5	CAPE MAY	NJ	$3,609
6	CHARLESTON	SC	$3,668
7	JACKSON	WY	$3,771
8	HILTON HEAD	SC	$3,820
9	WOODSTOCK	VT	$3,855
10	HONOLULU	HI	$3,912

$90,000 Income/$225,000 Home

			TAX
1	ANCHORAGE	AK	$1,022
2	WILMINGTON	DE	$3,280
3	JACKSON	WY	$3,675
4	CHEYENNE	WY	$3,938
5	CAPE MAY	NJ	$4,029
6	PORTSMOUTH	NH	$4,097
7	FRIDAY HARBOR	WA	$4,151
8	KEY WEST	FL	$4,158
9	CHARLESTON	SC	$4,210
10	NAPLES	FL	$4,240

$90,000 Income/$375,000 Home

			TAX
1	ANCHORAGE	AK	$3,314
2	WILMINGTON	DE	$4,182
3	JACKSON	WY	$4,511
4	CAPE MAY	NJ	$4,848
5	CARSON CITY	NV	$4,934
6	CHEYENNE	WY	$4,949
7	CROSSVILLE	TN	$5,276
8	FRIDAY HARBOR	WA	$5,321
9	CHARLESTON	SC	$5,353
10	HILTON HEAD	SC	$5,480

$90,000 Income/$525,000 Home

			TAX
1	WILMINGTON	DE	$4,640
2	JACKSON	WY	$5,347
3	ANCHORAGE	AK	$5,606
4	CAPE MAY	NJ	$5,654
5	CARSON CITY	NV	$5,674
6	CHEYENNE	WY	$5,961
7	WAILUKU	HI	$6,141
8	CROSSVILLE	TN	$6,154
9	WILLIAMSBURG	VA	$6,394
10	WOODSTOCK	VT	$6,432

no state income tax. Florida, the top retirement state, has no state income tax, but only two of the 32 Florida cities we profile show up as a Tax Heaven (and for only one of our income/home value categories in each city). Why? Florida makes up for a lack of state income tax by collecting more revenue via sales and property taxes, although a number of Florida cities still surface in the tax-friendliest half of the rankings.

Our top-ranked Tax Heavens are Wilmington, DE, and Anchorage, AK, — although retirees may think twice about moving to Anchorage to save on their tax bills.

If you're looking for a warm-weather home, you will be pleased to know that many Sunbelt states are tax-kind to senior citizens. Among the best are cities in Alabama, Georgia, New Mexico, South Carolina, Tennessee and Virginia. Take care to note that there are sometimes sharp differences between cities in these states.

In general, taxes are highest in the Northeast and Midwest. Our Tax Hell charts include cities in Connecticut, Illinois, Michigan, Missouri, Nebraska, New York, Pennsylvania and Texas. Again, some cities in these states fare better than others.

Tax Hells ψ ψ ψ

$30,000 Income/$125,000 Home

			TAX
1	EAST STROUDSBURG	PA	$5,759
2	NEW HAVEN	CT	$5,200
3	HARTFORD	CT	$5,199
4	PITTSBURGH	PA	$5,116
5	LANCASTER	PA	$4,713
6	CHICAGO	IL	$4,276
7	BROWNSVILLE	TX	$4,239
8	McALLEN	TX	$4,217
9	THE WOODLANDS	TX	$4,154
10	KANSAS CITY	MO	$4,140

$30,000 Income/$150,000 Home

			TAX
1	EAST STROUDSBURG	PA	$6,759
2	PITTSBURGH	PA	$6,014
3	HARTFORD	CT	$5,940
4	NEW HAVEN	CT	$5,939
5	LANCASTER	PA	$5,502
6	CHICAGO	IL	$4,929
7	BROWNSVILLE	TX	$4,914
8	THE WOODLANDS	TX	$4,907
9	McALLEN	TX	$4,888
10	KERRVILLE	TX	$4,676

$30,000 Income/$175,000 Home

			TAX
1	EAST STROUDSBURG	PA	$7,758
2	PITTSBURGH	PA	$6,912
3	HARTFORD	CT	$6,680
4	NEW HAVEN	CT	$6,678
5	LANCASTER	PA	$6,291
6	BROWNSVILLE	TX	$5,870
7	THE WOODLANDS	TX	$5,659
8	CHICAGO	IL	$5,583
9	McALLEN	TX	$5,559
10	SAN ANTONIO	TX	$5,328

$60,000 Income/$150,000 Home

			TAX
1	EAST STROUDSBURG	PA	$8,631
2	PITTSBURGH	PA	$8,023
3	LANCASTER	PA	$7,391
4	PHILADELPHIA	PA	$7,380
5	HARTFORD	CT	$7,262
6	SYRACUSE	NY	$7,082
7	KANSAS CITY	MO	$6,805
8	NEW HAVEN	CT	$6,761
9	OMAHA	NE	$6,569
10	CHICAGO	IL	$6,329

$60,000 Income/$225,000 Home

			TAX
1	EAST STROUDSBURG	PA	$11,630
2	PITTSBURGH	PA	$10,717
3	LANCASTER	PA	$9,759
4	SYRACUSE	NY	$9,740
5	HARTFORD	CT	$9,482
6	PHILADELPHIA	PA	$9,363
7	NEW HAVEN	CT	$8,977
8	CHICAGO	IL	$8,192
9	BUFFALO	NY	$8,159
10	OMAHA	NE	$8,125

$60,000 Income/$300,000 Home

			TAX
1	EAST STROUDSBURG	PA	$14,629
2	PITTSBURGH	PA	$13,410
3	SYRACUSE	NY	$12,397
4	LANCASTER	PA	$12,127
5	HARTFORD	CT	$11,703
6	PHILADELPHIA	PA	$11,346
7	NEW HAVEN	CT	$11,193
8	BUFFALO	NY	$10,245
9	THE WOODLANDS	TX	$10,210
10	CHICAGO	IL	$10,055

$90,000 Income/$225,000 Home

			TAX
1	EAST STROUDSBURG	PA	$13,049
2	HARTFORD	CT	$12,198
3	PITTSBURGH	PA	$12,135
4	SYRACUSE	NY	$12,004
5	NEW HAVEN	CT	$11,693
6	PHILADELPHIA	PA	$11,539
7	LANCASTER	PA	$11,202
8	OMAHA	NE	$10,813
9	DETROIT	MI	$10,507
10	BUFFALO	NY	$10,435

$90,000 Income/$375,000 Home

			TAX
1	EAST STROUDSBURG	PA	$19,047
2	PITTSBURGH	PA	$17,522
3	SYRACUSE	NY	$17,319
4	HARTFORD	CT	$16,640
5	NEW HAVEN	CT	$16,125
6	LANCASTER	PA	$15,938
7	PHILADELPHIA	PA	$15,506
8	BUFFALO	NY	$14,607
9	DETROIT	MI	$14,268
10	OMAHA	NE	$13,926

$90,000 Income/$525,000 Home

			TAX
1	EAST STROUDSBURG	PA	$25,046
2	PITTSBURGH	PA	$22,910
3	SYRACUSE	NY	$22,635
4	HARTFORD	CT	$21,081
5	LANCASTER	PA	$20,673
6	NEW HAVEN	CT	$20,557
7	PHILADELPHIA	PA	$19,473
8	BUFFALO	NY	$18,780
9	DETROIT	MI	$18,029
10	THE WOODLANDS	TX	$17,428

To make the right retirement reloca
And now you can — with lin

You've got to have good information to make a good decision. And if you're wondering where to retire — one of the most important decisions you'll ever make — you need the best information available.

That's why the editors of *Where to Retire* magazine have commissioned this unique and informative series of *Special Reports*. They're practical, in-depth analyses of the most important issues involved in retirement relocation, in

SR1 How to Plan and Execute A Successful Retirement Relocation

See what 200 relocated retirees said when asked, "If you could move again, what would you do differently?" You'll save the small price of this report many times over with the first common mistake you avoid.

Our author has heard all the firsthand accounts of moves gone awry and will steer you away from the relocation potholes. We'll tell you how to find and negotiate with a moving company, what to expect to pay and how to avoid being gouged. We'll tell you when to move, what to take and what to leave behind. Step-by-step, we'll walk you through a careful and cost-efficient shutdown at your current address and get you up and running in your new home quickly and as inexpensively as possible. $4.95.

SR4 Should You Retire To a Manufactured Home?

Explore this popular but controversial lifestyle option if you're looking for top value for your housing dollar.

We'll tell you how manufactured homes have changed, how they compare to site-built homes and how safe they are from high winds and fire. We'll cover zoning restrictions, financing options and price appreciation over time.

We'll tell you who lives in manufactured homes and examine various options including land-lease and resident-owned communities, home-land packages and subdivisions. We'll tell you how to shop for a manufactured home, including how to be sure your home meets national standards. And we will advise you how to figure the total cost of ownership.

Finally, we'll cover the purchase, delivery, siting and inspection of your new home, including consumer protection laws and how to ensure you're getting what you paid for. Illustrated, $4.95.

SR5 Retiring Outside The United States

More than 350,000 retired Americans live outside the country, in places like Mexico, Uruguay, Costa Rica and Portugal. They go for three reasons: climate, a lower cost of living that translates into a higher standard of living, and the excitement of residing and traveling in a foreign country. Many go early in retirement, spend several years and then return home.

Sound interesting? Then you won't want to miss this informative primer on retiring abroad. We'll tell you how to determine if you'd be happy retiring abroad, how to find the country and town that best suit your lifestyle and how to adjust to everyday life in a new country. We'll discuss eight popular — and economical — foreign retirement spots and provide sources for additional information you might need. Finally, we'll tell you the most common (and costly) mistakes you could make in the process of moving abroad and how to avoid them. $4.95.

SR6 Discounts for Travelers 50 and Beyond

Good news for anyone who loves to travel! When you turn 50, you're automatically eligible for an impressive array of travel discounts. What's more, the older you get, the greater the number of airlines, hotels and others willing to offer you those savings. And when you hit 65, every age-related discount in the entire travel industry can be yours for the asking.

But you'll have to know where to look and whom to ask. That's why we produced this insider's guide to finding and getting discounts from airlines, hotels, rental car companies, theme parks, cruise lines and national parks. Also includes invaluable advice on when and how to use discount travel clubs, how to save 50% traveling off-season, how to get a rebate on every airline ticket and more. Whether traveling to check out retirement

tion, you've got to have all the facts.
ited-edition *Special Reports.*

an easy-to-read format.

Every *Special Report* is meticulously researched data, hard facts and unbiased reporting. No outside advertising is accepted.

Best of all, we've managed to keep the price for each *Special Report* to a very manageable $4.95, plus $2.25 total postage and handling no matter how many *Special Reports* you order.

---

sites, on business or strictly for pleasure, this guide can save you hundreds of dollars on your first trip. $4.95.

SR8 America's Most Affordable Retirement Towns

Would you like to pay less for everything from groceries and restaurants to movies and health care? Would you jump at the chance to trade your current house for one 50 percent larger, at no extra cost?

Many retirees succeed in slashing their cost of living when they relocate. They enjoy a higher standard of living in retirement because their dollar simply goes further in their new home town.

We considered nearly 200 retirement meccas in this country, from well-known to undiscovered, before compiling this list of 25 affordable towns that are also great for retirement. Each town profile includes interviews with relocated retirees and vital information on climate, housing cost, taxes, crime rate, overall cost of living, health care, educational opportunities and more. $4.95.

SR19 How to Get the Most Out of Social Security

Did you know that two people of identical age, earnings history, marital status and life expectancy can receive lifetime Social Security benefits that differ by $25,000 — or more — solely on the basis of when they asked for their retirement benefits to begin? It's true, which is why the date you pick to start Social Security is one of the most important decisions you will ever make. This report will help you make the correct decision and show you:

● How to get every dollar you deserve from Social Security ● How to avoid or reduce taxes you pay on Social Security ● Income that won't affect your benefits ● Who should start Social Security at age 62 and who should wait until age 70 ● Who can get disability benefits ● Techniques of thieves and

shysters who target Social Security recipients ● How to get an estimate of future benefits from the Social Security Administration — free ● How to know if you've started Social Security too early — and what to do about it ● Who is eligible for Supplemental Security Income ● How to apply for benefits for a loved one who can't handle his or her own finances ● How to get benefits based on your ex-spouse's earnings ● And much, much more.

Whether retirement is a distant dream, just around the corner or even if you're already receiving benefits, we'll show you how to maximize your benefits and avoid the mistakes that can cost you thousands of dollars. $4.95.

WHERE TO RET

If you missed any of our recent issues, it's not too late to order your personal copy, with the form below. Issues not shown are no longer available.

Special Issue 2000 (November): Fort Myers, FL; Whidbey Island, WA; Pinehurst, NC; Temecula, CA; Costa Rica; Tax Heavens; more.

Winter 2001 (January): Eugene, OR; Tallahassee, FL; Door County, WI; The Woodlands, TX; Kings Ridge in Clermont, FL; Budget Towns; Belize Retirement; Moving to an Academic Village; New Urbanism Neighborhoods; more.

Summer 2001 (May): America's 100 Best Master-Planned Communities; Top Towns for Singles; Low-Crime Havens; Touring the Pacific Northwest; more.

Winter 2002 (January): Grand Junction, CO; Ojai, CA; Chapel Hill, NC; Palm Coast, FL; Dataw Island, SC; Tax-Friendly Towns; The RV Life; The Changing Face of Active-Adult Communities; Stress-Free Moves; more.

March/April 2003: Portsmouth, NH; Henderson, NV; Greenville, NC; Vero Beach, FL; Lake Geneva, WI; Port Ludlow, WA; Towns for Art & Music Lovers; New Urbanism Neighborhoods; Eco-Friendly Communities; more.

September/October 2003: Myrtle Beach, SC; Roseville & Rocklin, CA; Pensacola, FL; Ocean County, NJ; Sequim, WA; Evergrene in Palm Beach Gardens, FL; Terrific Budget Towns; Retiring Solo; Condo Lifestyles; College-Linked Retirement Communities; more.

November/December 2003: Venice, FL; Waynesville, NC; Rockport, TX; Grants Pass, OR; Brunswick, ME; Penn National in Fayetteville, PA; Towns for a Fit Retirement; Mountain Locales; Walking Towns; Historic Towns; Cut Moving Costs; more.

January/February 2004: Healdsburg, CA; Mississippi Gulf Coast; Ruidoso, NM; Traverse City, MI; Kissimmee-St. Cloud, FL; Ford's Colony in Williamsburg, VA; Retirement Dream Homes; Low-Tax Towns; Places to Buy a Condo; Desert Towns; more.

March/April 2004: Easton, MD; Bend, OR; Siesta Key, FL; West St. Tammany Parish, LA; Blowing Rock, NC; The Woods in Hedgesville, WV; Places for Military Retirees; Island Living in the U.S.A.; Cooler Climes; Affordable Resort Areas; more.

May/June 2004: Shepherdstown, WV; Stowe, VT; Ferndale, CA; Tubac, AZ; Ormond Beach, FL; Heritage Hunt in Gainesville, VA; Retiring to the Bahamas; Great College Towns;

Colonial or Craftsman? Learning the Lingo of Home Styles

WHERE to RETIRE

MARCH/APRIL 2007

8 Dynamic Towns For New Careers

Southern Hospitality In Tallahassee, FL

Picturesque Villages On Cape Cod

Communities Gear Up for Fitness Craze

Low-Cost Haven: Murray, KY

Savory Places For Gourmets

Branson, MO: An Ozark Star

Linda and Roger LaRochelle of Murray, KY

Great Places to Start a Business in Retirement; more.

July/August 2004: Ashland, OR; Dothan, AL; Sarasota, FL; Grand Lake O' the Cherokees, OK; Chestertown, MD; Royal Harbor in Tavares, FL; Main Street Towns; Retiring to Border Towns in Mexico, Canada; more.

September/October 2004: Tucson, AZ; New Hope, PA; Chico & Paradise, CA; Cashiers, NC; Gainesville, FL; Four Seasons at Mirage in Ocean County, NJ; Budget Towns; Retirement at Sea and on the Road; Singles in Communities; more.

November/December 2004: Sierra Vista, AZ; Beaufort, SC; Wimberley, TX; DeFuniak Springs, FL; Poulsbo, WA; On Top of the World Communities in Ocala, FL; Beach Towns; Ski & Summer Towns; Checking Out a Master-Planned Community; more.

January/February 2005: Winter Garden, FL; Hot Springs, AR; Rancho Bernardo, CA; Connecticut River Valley; Natchez, MS; Villages of Rainbow Springs in Dunnellon, FL; Retiring to Hawaii; Low-Tax Towns; A House at Half the Cost (Manufactured Homes); Headache-Free Moves; Towns for Semiretirement; more.

March/April 2005: Redding, CA; Marble Falls, TX; Enterprise, AL; Bonita Springs, FL; Fort Collins, CO; Harmony, Osceola County, FL; Towns for Art & Music Lovers; New Urbanism Neighborhoods; Golf Communities; How States Tax Retirement Income; more.

May/June 2005: Anacortes, WA; Berkeley Springs, WV; Athens, GA; Ocala, FL; Tahlequah, OK; Jubilee at Hawks Prairie in Lacey, WA; New Home Designs; Places for a Second Home; Building Green: Environmentally Friendly Communities; more.

July/August 2005: America's 100 Best Master-Planned Communities; Towns for Outdoor Lifestyles; Retire to a Cruise Ship; What Singles Want in an Active-Adult Community; States Race to Attract Retirees; more.

September/October 2005: Grass Valley & Nevada City, CA; Annapolis, MD; Mountain Home, AR; Brevard, NC; St. Augustine, FL; Colonial Heritage in Williamsburg, VA; Wine Country Retirement; Budget Towns; Retiring to Panama; Four-Season Towns; CCRCs of the West; more.

November/December 2005: Abingdon, VA; Cape May, NJ; Bradenton, FL; Carlsbad, CA; Fredericksburg, TX; Fairfield Glade in Tennessee; Historic Towns; Sampling Lifestyles at Planned Communities; Beachfront Condo Living; more.

January/February 2006: Bellingham, WA; DeLand, FL; Cedar City, UT; Danville, KY; Gainesville, GA; Comanche Trace in Kerrville, TX; Low-Tax Towns; Post-Katrina Recovery in Retirement Areas; Manufactured Housing Trends; more.

March/April 2006: Dunedin, FL; Southern Delaware; Fayetteville, AR; Jackson Hole, WY; Medford, OR; GlenLakes in Weeki Wachee, FL; Military Towns; Lakeside Living; Towns With Political Traditions; Desert Oases; more.

May/June 2006: Boulder City, NV; Petoskey, MI; Cookeville, TN; Princess Anne, MD; Winter Haven, FL; Four Seasons at Metedeconk Lakes, Jackson, NJ; Places With Great Hospitals; Towns for Battlefield Buffs; Walking Towns; Making Friends in a New Community; more.

July/August 2006: Lake Havasu City, AZ; Boulder, CO; Stuart, FL; Lewisburg, WV; Franklin, NC; Sun City Shadow Hills, Indio, CA; Old West Towns; College Towns; Main Street Towns; Mars and Venus Circling Retirement; Homes That Cut Energy Costs; more.

September/October 2006: New Port Richey, FL; Granbury, TX; Clemson, SC; Lancaster, PA; Boise, ID; Bay Creek, Cape Charles, VA; Towns With Great Home Buys; Mountain Retreats; River Towns; Biggest City-to-City Retirement Migrations; CCRCs for Elderly Parents; Home Business Tax Implications; and more.

November/December 2006: Delray Beach, FL; Northern Neck, VA; El Dorado County, CA; Flathead Lake, MT; Boothbay Harbor, ME; Rarity Bay, Vonore, TN; The Condo Craze; Hot Condo Markets; Great Places Near Big Cities; Retiring to Southern Europe; Buying a Home Abroad; Grandchildproofing Your Home; more.

January/February 2007: The 100 Most Popular Places to Retire and the Best Choices in Coastal, 4-Season, Desert, Budget and Undiscovered towns; Caribbean Hot Spots; RV Havens; Cohousing Communities; CCRCs; more.

March/April 2007: Tallahassee, FL; Cape Cod, MA; Branson, MO; Vancouver, WA; Murray, KY; Glade Springs Village, Daniels, WV; A Guide to Home Styles; Towns for Post-Retirement Careers; Blue Ridge Mountain Havens; Savory Places for Gourmets; Communities Gear Up for Fitness Frenzy; more.

May/June 2007: Punta Gorda, FL; Durango, CO; Redmond, OR; New Hampshire Lakes Region; Low-Cost Haven: Florence/The Shoals, AL; Reynolds Plantation, Greensboro,

GA; Exciting Places to Retire Downtown; Finding Your Own Green Acres; Less-Costly California Destinations; University-Linked Commu-nities; Mississippi Coast Rebuilding; more.

July/August 2007: America's 100 Best Master-Planned Communities; The New Scene in Communities; Steps to Making a Stress-Free Move; Getting a Home That Suits You; Havens in the Heartland; Healthy Living — Places With Clean Air and Green Space; more.

September/October 2007: Clermont, FL; Carson City, NV; Pinehurst & Southern Pines, NC; Eagle River, WI; Yuma, AZ; Golden Isles & Brunswick, GA; Low-Cost Towns; Rocky Mountain Havens; Furnishing Your New Home; Towns With Great Heritages; more.

November/December 2007: Cape Coral, FL; Temecula, CA; Silver City, NM; The Poconos, PA; Oak Ridge, TN; Havens With Low-Cost Homes; Finding Your Retirement Eden; Relocating When You're Single; Checking Community Association Rules; more.

8 Great Books to Help You Make the Best Move of Your Life

■ **America's Best Low-Tax Retirement Towns**
Slash Your Taxes in Retirement!
Eve Evans & Elizabeth Niven
   This book ranks 203 metropolitan areas and retirement towns by the total tax burden on retirees. State and local taxes vary dramatically from state to state, and even between towns in the same state. It reveals the best and worst picks for folks in different income brackets and could help you save thousands a year in taxes. Includes Tax Heavens and Tax Hells. Also included: profiles of 102 Top Retirement Towns, as featured in Where to Retire.   **$18.95**

■ **America's 100 Best Places to Retire**
Undiscovered and Low-Cost Edens
Edited by Elizabeth Armstrong
   From the editors of Where to Retire magazine. Learn about climate, cost of living, home prices, taxes and health care in America's best retirement spots. Meet the retirees who've made the move and hear how they like their new hometown. Includes top picks in every region and highlights unknown and inexpensive retirement meccas.   **$18.95**

FOURTH EDITION

■ **Choose the Southwest**
Retirement Discoveries for Every Budget
John Howells
   Profiles 50 areas in Nevada, Utah, Colorado, Arizona, New Mexico and West Texas and includes all the basic data about costs of living, real estate, medical care, climate, recreation, culture, crime and safety. **$14.95**

■ **Choose Mexico**
Live Well on $600 a Month
John Howells & Don Merwin
   Mexico is a huge bargain for U.S. retirees. If you want to retire south of the border, you'll want the book recommended by Mexican consulates. It describes the best places to settle and covers housing,

finances, health care, legal requirements, shopping and recreation.   **$14.95**

■ **Choose Costa Rica**
Information for Retirement, Investment & Affordable Living
John Howells
   A vacation favorite, Costa Rica's low prices and liberal immigration laws attract an increasing number of Americans. Howells covers costs, medical care, housing, recreation, legal requirements and investment opportunities.   **$14.95**

■ **Choose the Pacific Northwest**
Includes Washington, Oregon and British Columbia
John Howells
   A close look at one of America's most desirable retirement areas, including housing, safety, climate, health care, transportation, entertainment, culture and recreation.   **$14.95**

■ **Where to Retire**
Best and Most Affordable Places
John Howells
   This book covers cities and towns in 22 states — from Virginia, the Carolinas and Florida to Texas, California and the Pacific Northwest. A wealth of information on climate, living costs, health care, taxes and lifestyle.   **$17.95**

■ **Retirement Migration in America**
Size, Trends and Economic Impact
Charles F. Longino Jr., Ph.D.
   420,000 Americans retire out of state every year, generating billions in sales for everything from real estate to health care and revitalizing rural America. Newly updated, this book quantifies the economic impact on every state and county in America for economic development agencies, developers, financial institutions and others who want to know where America's retirees are moving. **$39.95**

NEW EDITION

NOTES